BEYOND BERKELEY

A SOURCEBOOK IN STUDENT VALUES

EDITED BY

CHRISTOPHER G. KATOPE

AND

PAUL G. ZOLBROD

English Department

Allegheny College

The World Publishing Company

CLEVELAND AND NEW YORK

PUBLISHED BY The World Publishing Company
2231 West 110th Street, Cleveland, Ohio 44102

Published simultaneously in Canada by Nelson, Foster & Scott Ltd.

First Printing, 1966
Second Printing, November, 1966

Library of Congress Catalog Card Number: 66–13956

PRINTED IN THE UNITED STATES OF AMERICA

BEYOND BERKELEY
A Sourcebook in
Student Values

ACKNOWLEDGMENT

COMPILING an anthology of essays pertaining directly and indirectly to the student rebellion at Berkeley that took place late in 1964 turned out to be a far more complicated task than we had imagined. Had we not received a great deal of assistance and cooperation from many people, we scarcely could have assembled this collection. We appreciate the help we received from Miss Dorothy Jeanne Smith and Mrs. Julian L. Ross, both members of the Allegheny College Library staff, who made our research considerably easier than it would otherwise have been. And we wish to thank Dr. Lawrence Lee Pelletier, President of Allegheny College, who made it possible for us to obtain a grant which covered the expense of assembling our manuscript. Above all, we thank Mrs. Merle A. Mooney, who spent many hours conducting our correspondence, laboring over handwriting which was frequently illegible, and typing page after page of copy for us. Then too, we express our thanks to many of our colleagues at Allegheny for helping us gather the material from which we ultimately selected the readings we now include, and for their willingness to discuss freely the issues involved in the Berkeley affair. Other persons have also helped us in many ways, and while we may neglect to mention their names here we certainly do not withhold our appreciation. By no means the least of these unnamed individuals are scores of Allegheny College students and students at the University of California at Berkeley who offered candid and sincere comments about contemporary student problems and values. In a matchless way, they have made it possible for us to understand the issues considered in this volume better than we had understood them before.

The editors wish to thank the magazine and book publishers who have given permission to reprint the following.

James Cass, "What Happened at Berkeley," *Saturday Review*, January 16, 1965. Reprinted by permission of *Saturday Review* and the author.

C. B. Cox, "Berkeley's Angry Young Men," *Manchester Guardian*, December 7, 1964. Reprinted by permission of the *Manchester Guardian* and the author.

A. H. Raskin, "The Berkeley Affair: Mr. Kerr vs. Mr. Savio and Company," *The New York Times Magazine*, February 14, 1965. © 1965, by the New York Times Company. Reprinted by permission, and by permission of the author.

Nathan Glazer, "What Happened at Berkeley," *Commentary*, February, 1965. Reprinted from *Commentary* by permission; copyright © 1965 by the American Jewish Committee.

Sidney Hock, "Academic Freedom and the Rights of Students," *The New York Times Magazine*, January 3, 1965. (Formerly, "Freedom to Learn but Not to Riot") © 1965, by the New York Times Company. Reprinted by permission, and by permission of the author.

Paul Goodman, "Thoughts on Berkeley," *The New York Review of Books*, January 14, 1965, reprinted by permission of the author and *The New York Review of Books*. Copyright © 1965, New York Review Incorporated.

Mario Savio, "The Berkeley Student Rebellion of 1964," *The Free Speech Movement and the Negro Revolution*, published by News & Letters, 1965, 8751 Grand River, Detroit, Michigan 48204.

Samuel Kaplan, "The Revolt of an Elite: Sources of the FSM Victory," *Graduate Student Journal*, Spring, 1965. Reprinted by permission of the author. Slightly revised from its first appearance in the *Graduate Student Journal*.

Henry F. May, "The Student Movement: Some Impressions at Berkeley," Reprinted from *The American Scholar*, Volume 34, Number 3, Summer, 1965. Copyright © 1965 by the United Chapters of Phi Beta Kappa. By permission of the publishers.

Irving Howe, "Berkeley and Beyond," *The New Republic*, May 1, 1965. Reprinted from *The New Republic*, © 1965, Harrison-Blaine of New Jersey, Inc.

Paul Woodring, "Who Makes University Policy?" *Saturday Review*, April 17, 1965. Reprinted by permission of *Saturday Review* and the author.

Clark Kerr, "The Idea of a Multiversity." Reprinted by permission of the publishers from Clark Kerr *The Uses of the University*. Cambridge, Mass.: Harvard University Press, Copyright, 1963, by the President and Fellows of Harvard College.

Alfred North Whitehead, "Universities and Their Function," from *The Aims of Education*. Reprinted with permission of the Macmillan Company from *The Aims of Education* by Alfred North Whitehead. Copyright 1929 by the Macmillan Company, Copyright Renewed 1957 by Evelyn Whitehead.

Carl Lotus Becker, "Freedom of Learning and Teaching." Reprinted by permission of Alfred A. Knopf, Inc. from *Freedom and Responsibility in the American Way of Life* by Carl Becker. Copyright, 1945 by Alfred A. Knopf, Inc. & The University of Michigan.

Andrew Hacker, "The College Grad Has Been Short-Changed," *The New York Times Magazine*, June 6, 1965. © by the New York Times Company. Reprinted by permission, and by permission of the author.

Harold Taylor, "American Idealism, 1965," *Saturday Review*, June 26, 1965. Reprinted by permission of the *Saturday Review* and the author.

William Sloane Coffin, Jr., "Don't Tell Them to Play It Safe," *Life* Magazine, May 30, 1965. Copyright © 1965 Time Inc. All Rights Reserved.

"Students Speak," from "The Thing for Us Right Now Is the Movement," *Life* Magazine, May 30, 1965. Copyright © 1965 Time Inc. All Rights Reserved.

Bill Ward, "Why the Students Revolt," *The Nation*, January 25, 1965. Reprinted by permission of *The Nation* and the author.

Mervin B. Freedman, "Roots of Student Discontent," *The Nation*, January 14, 1965. Reprinted by permission of *The Nation* and the author.

Louis E. Reik, "War of the Generations," *The Nation*, May 16, 1959. Reprinted by permission of *The Nation* and the author.

J. Glenn Gray, "Salvation on the Campus," *Harper's Magazine*, May, 1965. Reprinted from *Harper's Magazine* by permission of the author, J. Glenn Gray.

Hastings Rashdall, "Student Life in the Middle Ages," from *The Universities of Europe in the Middle Ages*, by permission of the Clarendon Press, Oxford.

Immanuel Kant, "What Is Enlightenment?" From Immanuel Kant: *On History*, edited by Lewis White Beck, copyright © 1957 by The Liberal Arts Press, Inc., © 1963 by The Bobbs-Merrill Company, Inc., reprinted by permission of the Liberal Arts Press Division of The Bobbs-Merrill Company, Inc.

John Stuart Mill, from *On Liberty*. This selection is reprinted from *English Prose of the Victorian Period*, edited by C. F. Harrold and W. D. Templeman, by permission of Oxford University Press, Inc.

Thomas Carlyle, from "Democracy," Chapter XIII of *Past and Present*, reprinted from *British Poetry and Prose* (Lieder, Root and Lovell, Volume 2), Houghton Mifflin Company.

Henry David Thoreau, "Civil Disobedience." Reprinted from *The American Tradition in Literature*, Revised, Volume I. Edited by Sculley Bradley, Richmond Croom Beatty and E. Hudson Long. By permission of W. W. Norton & Company, Inc. Copyright © 1956, 1957, 1961 by W. W. Norton & Company, Inc.

Ralph Waldo Emerson, "Self-Reliance." Reprinted from *The American Tradition in Literature*, Revised, Volume I. Edited by Sculley Bradley, Richmond Croom Beatty and E. Hudson Long. By permission of W. W. Norton & Company, Inc. Copyright © 1956, 1957, 1961 by W. W. Norton & Company, Inc.

Clinton Rossiter, "The Conservative View of Man and Society." Reprinted by permission of Alfred A. Knopf, Inc. from *Conservatism in America*, 2nd Rev. Edit. by Clinton Rossiter. Copyright © 1962, by Clinton Rossiter.

Learned Hand, "Freedom of Dissent." *The New York Times Magazine*, February 16, 1955, © 1955 by the New York Times Company. Reprinted by permission.

Congress shall make no law respecting an establishment of religion, or prohibiting the free exercise thereof; or abridging the freedom of speech, or of the press; or the right of the people peaceably to assemble, and to petition the Government for a redress of grievances.

The First Amendment,
United States Constitution

We believe it is right to have a great respect for the labors, the vigils, the drudgery, the deprivations, the pains and the perils encountered by the students in order to acquire the precious pearl of science. . . .

Philip the Fair, King of France.
Spoken in 1312 and quoted in Gabriel
Compayre, *Abelard and the Origin
and Early History of Universities*
(New York, 1893), p. 101.

CONTENTS

Part Three: THE TRADITION OF LIBERTY AND RESPONSIBILITY

INTRODUCTION

SHORTLY after the end of 1964 the now famous Berkeley rebellion finally subsided. And sure enough, in the quiet but tense aftermath of that hectic controversy a large number of news analysts and commentators, social critics, students, professors and campus administrators began to study the Berkeley affair in retrospect for a variety of publications. By now it is impossible to estimate the number of printed pages devoted to the Free Speech Movement and to its implications and consequences. We may safely assume that people will not cease writing about that series of events for many years to come. Yet for all that has been said concerning the Berkeley affair, it remains a confusing and enigmatic issue. Were the California students actually angry because their freedom of speech and advocacy had been denied, or does their discontent spring from certain more nebulous or reactionary motives? Is the modern multiversity as impersonal and stultifying as the dissident students claim, or have they merely attributed to the multiversity what is actually true of our entire society? And what right do these young people have to depart from legal processes in expressing their displeasure? The answers to these questions do not come easily, nor would any answers to such questions necessarily be absolute. The more one reads about Berkeley, the less certain he becomes that absolute answers exist at all. And the proliferation of essays, books and articles on Berkeley has failed by far to explain everything.

As for ourselves, even after reading a large number of items about Berkeley, many written by knowledgeable writers who had actually been on the scene, we failed to understand all the issues involved. As closely as we tried to observe the Free

Speech Movement from our distant eastern vantage point, we felt that our comprehension of it was far from complete. But we felt that if the trouble in Berkeley was important enough to warrant all the attention it received, it was certainly momentous enough to deserve a more thorough understanding than we were then capable of giving it. So we decided in August, 1965, that one of us should visit Berkeley, if only to become acquainted with the environment of so much unrest.

Although for a number of reasons the visit to Berkeley was disappointing, one could not but respect the Berkeley students very highly. It is gratifying to see young people so active, so idealistic and so politically aware. These students are far more admirable than students were during the McCarthy era and the Eisenhower years. In the fifties students were cool and blasé, looking ahead to next Saturday's football game with Notre Dame or Wisconsin and forward to the training programs into which they would hire themselves with Proctor and Gamble or Westinghouse. At that time there was as yet no civil rights movement to become involved in. Nuclear warfare was a vague reality, but no concrete threat. The Peace Corps was not even a concept then, and nobody seemed inclined to fight a War on Poverty. There was an absence of liberalism on campuses, but then there were no campus conservative groups either. College students huddled safely in the middle, either satisfied with Eisenhower or indifferent to Stevenson, concerned only with their own placid lives. For those who had gone straight from high school to college it was a time of peace; for those who were Korean veterans the war was now over. Even then, however, class cards were processed by computers which were not to be folded, spindled or mutilated; but nobody objected.

What a contrast today's students offer, especially students at a place like Berkeley. Many of them object so strongly to the war in Vietnam that they will throw themselves in front of troop trains to oppose it. Many others are so adamantly in favor of fighting an unlimited war against the Communists that they wear buttons on their lapels bearing the image of a supersonic bomber and the words, "Drop it!" Some had risked harassment and embarrassment to campaign against Goldwater at the Cow Palace during the 1964 Republican National Convention; others had spent that same summer in Mississippi, risking nothing less than their lives in behalf of Southern Negroes. They want more control in society than they have, and they certainly think they are entitled to more control over their own lives. Their grievances against the multiversity are real enough to them, and, in our opinion, many of these grievances are justifiable. They complain about classrooms filled with three hundred students and about professors they heard but never spoke with. Their university had deteriorated into a kind of "knowledge factory," they grumbled, dedicated only to the proliferation of weapons, advertising and flaccid middle-class propaganda. They spoke passionately about the Bancroft Strip, that sacred patch of land outside the main campus gate where they could at least conduct an open forum on the issues they found so important. And in attempting to deny them the right to use that strip for their own political purposes, the University administration had gone too far, depriving them of what they insisted was theirs by virtue of campus tradition and the First Amendment to the Constitution.

But while the students' problems were real and their complaints frequently sound, their solutions were naive or abstract. Repeatedly, when asked what they might require of the ideal university, none could give a tenable answer. Some said that they didn't know what kind of place they wanted the Berkeley Campus to be; they only knew that they didn't like the place it was. Others insisted that the Board of Regents should be disbanded so that the University could make its own policy and run itself. Still others suggested simply that the entire University administration should be done away with. One student, an extremely intelligent, sophisticated junior who was kind enough to conduct a tour of the campus and patient enough to answer an endless series of questions, demonstrated the oversimplified and abjectly unsympathetic attitude which many students have toward the administration. Walking through the library, she spoke with some pride of the efficiency of the place. She described in great detail the process by which undergraduates requested books and received them. She was asked if she had any sympathy or respect for the people who administered the library and who were responsible for the machinery by which three million volumes were catalogued, shelved and distributed among a community of more than twenty-five thousand readers. "No," she replied. "These people are administrators, and regardless of what they do for us their only real concern is with themselves."

This co-ed exemplifies what sometimes seems too true of dissatisfied young people, especially the dissatisfied Berkeley students. Quick to criticize what seems wrong, and grudging in their praise of what suits them, they have no idea how they would replace what they would eliminate. In the fall of 1964 this girl was arrested and faced a jail term for defending a cause she believed in. Hundreds of other students likewise paid the price of prison sentences to preserve their right to advocate their views along the Bancroft Strip, and it is pleasant to know that students are again willing to pay such a price for such an ideal. But if we must acknowledge their ability to discover what is wrong with a campus or a government or a society, can we trust their ability to recognize what is right? Assuming that we know what the Berkeley students dislike, how are we to know what they want if they do not know themselves? The Bancroft Strip is theirs again, but they are still dissatisfied with their campus and their society. They have asked the right questions and hurled the right challenges at the adult world; but they have no solutions to offer, no real answers to give. That realization became a disappointment. Many of us hoped that the California students might fill the vacuum they seemed to want to create. Until someone knows how to fill that vacuum, the Free Speech Movement remains an enigma.

Suppose that the students are right; suppose the University has become a part of that grossly mechanical power structure that manufactures the components of automation, national defense, material goods and packaged masscult, even while it burns up individual human beings as fuel. Furthermore, suppose that the multiversity, impersonal and bureaucratic monolith that it now is, has become an undesirable institution which should be eliminated. What *are* we to replace it with? And even supposing that the students themselves should undertake to eliminate the multiversity or at least to sweeten it some and to enlighten it, are they to undertake that task irresponsibly and at the expense of an at least tolerably efficient legal order? The students themselves do not seem to be able to answer such questions, and as long as the answers are lacking the Berkeley uprising remains a disappointingly incomprehensible puzzle.

But one must be careful not to overstate this disappointment. For some clarification was achieved during the trip to California, and in making that particular clarification we discovered an additional justification for compiling this volume of essays.

As nebulous and as unclear as the Berkeley controversy remains, even in the wake of the publication of thousands of pages of writings on Berkeley, a principle now appears paramount. Whatever the Free Speech Movement is finally to come to mean, and whatever its real causes, it must be placed in perspective. The events that occurred in California during the autumn of 1964 cannot be sealed in a glass case and viewed in isolation. They did not take place in a carefully controlled laboratory and should not be written about as in a lab report. The Berkeley issue is not the real issue here, but only an alarmingly dramatic manifestation of an issue which is larger and more sobering than anything that happened on the main campus of the University of California. The Berkeley events fit somewhere in that endless stream of ideas and events which we call history, and they mingle freely and invisibly among all the other elements that somehow compound themselves into what we call our society. Another student at Berkeley drove that point home, perhaps inadvertently, and by what he said placed the whole Berkeley Movement in two broad contexts, both of which are indispensable to a final, necessary understanding.

This young man, a sophomore during the explosive Berkeley autumn, looked nothing like the public's somewhat hackneyed and prejudiced image of a dissident student. He wore no beard, was not at all unscrubbed and had no spectacularly long haircut. He would have looked inconspicuous on any small, peaceful campus or in any fraternity house. He wore khaki trousers, a clean sport shirt, sneakers. Under his arm were tucked several texts and a spiral notebook, familiar tools of the student trade. "I'm no extremist," he said when asked about his commitment to the Free Speech Movement. "Politically, I'm a mugwump, I guess. I just didn't like seeing my friends go to jail." One cannot say that he was a typical Berkeley rebel, but only because not one of them is typical.

They are all individuals who have in common a gnawing dissatisfaction. Otherwise they differ strikingly from each other. "It has occurred to me," this student said, "that during the course of my education I have become aware of a world I find I do not approve of." He said that his home was in Los Angeles. "Have you ever been there?" he asked. "It's an awful place, a sprawling, smoggy city with no center, full of people who scramble in all that foul, polluted air to make money." And he described freeways, neon jungles, vast parking lots and poorly built homes that resembled one another and looked as though they had been built to last no more than twenty years. "I wonder why adults can't see these things for themselves," he added. "Everybody's running around trying to understand us 'beatniks.' Hell, if they want to figure out what's wrong, they should try to understand our society. That's where the trouble is. And universities are a part of that society. And if grown-ups want to know what's wrong, it's the absurd society they've got to study, not us."

"This fight of yours against society and against the multiversity," he was then asked, "do you think it's really your fight? Do you think you're waging a battle that your professors should be waging instead?"

"Maybe," he answered. "But who are they? Who are these professors? Maybe when I'm an upperclassman I'll get to know a few, if I'm lucky and turn out to be a good student. But right now I don't know who they are. They're all pretty busy, doing research and going after defense contracts. There isn't a Socrates among them that I can see, and they're scarcely interested in teaching let alone setting an example. I'm not getting much education from them. I'm getting my education here, right here!" And with that, he thrust his finger down on the table he was manning on the Bancroft Strip. "I got my education last fall during the strike," he repeated, still poking that table with his index finger.

"What do you mean?" he was asked.

"Simple," he answered. "Everybody was talking about civil disobedience so I read Thoreau. There was a lot of talk about the Bill of Rights and I got to understand that pretty thoroughly. Then there's the business of how we organized, how we managed to swipe a mimeograph and how we moved it from place to place, cellar to cellar, stopping only long enough to cut a stencil and to print up ten thousand pamphlets. Know what I learned then? I learned what it must have been like to belong to the French Resistance or the Norwegian Underground during the Second World War. I learned what it meant to fight for something you believe in, even if you have to fight on the run. But you don't learn that in the classroom. The people who run this university seem to have forgotten about it all. About the Bill of Rights, I mean, and about Thoreau. They're only interested in running this place as smoothly as possible. All they want to teach us is how to run a corporation like this one or how to get into graduate school and stay there. They're not interested in the past or in any tradition. Not at all. If they really want to understand us, they should understand this tradition I'm talking about. I learned last fall that we have a tradition to maintain, a tradition of liberty and responsibility, as corny as it may sound. That's what they've got to understand. Understand that and they'll understand us."

Thus he plotted the locus of the Berkeley controversy, and perhaps he is correct in saying that if we want to understand rebellious students today, we must understand the society they have suddenly noticed and the tradition they have rediscovered. Perhaps Berkeley is a reaction against the former and an attempt to clarify and resurrect the latter. If so, we would do well to become aware of both as we attempt to understand student rebellions wherever they occur.

We think that the suggestion is a valid one, and in assembling this book we have tried to carry it out. In the first part we include a number of essays that concentrate more or less exclusively on Berkeley itself and on what happened there during the fall of 1964. In the second part, we include essays that deal with other campuses or with colleges and college students in general. And we have been careful to select items which, although they deal explicitly with campus problems and student values, reflect the state of our society and allude frequently to the interplay between society and education. The college campus, after all, is a reflection of the society in which it exists; from that society it draws its personnel and adopts values and methods, and by repudiating their schools, students are rejecting certain elements in their total environment. Finally, in the third part, we include items by writers who have contributed to our entire tradition and who have established, defined and clarified some of the issues that were invoked by the Berkeley students and their opponents alike, issues, moreover, that will certainly be invoked again and again in the future, away from the campus as well as on it.

Since we are English teachers and conduct courses in composition and essay writing, we wanted at first to compile a book that would serve as a useful writing text, one that would provide examples of various kinds of essays and illustrate many of the methods of rhetoric and some of the devices of effective style. But as the Berkeley controversy continued and as student unrest spread across the country to other campuses, we began to realize that a book such as the one we wanted to prepare might be useful in other courses also, and might even be of general interest to the reader who wishes to know more about contemporary higher education and about timeless ideals. The issues that arose at Berkeley ought to be faced by educated people everywhere and certainly should be aired in and out of the classroom on our campuses. What happened at the University of California applies to what has happened to men everywhere and at all times, and to what will undoubtedly happen to them again and again in society after society, whenever they suspect that their freedom to speak, to act or to learn is jeopardized. Relationships exist between the unrest at Berkeley and our entire heritage, and students especially would do well to discover these relationships, to think about them, to write about them clearly and alertly, even to argue about them among themselves or with their elders. And we hope that this volume will serve to provide such stimulation.

P.G.Z.
C.G.K.

1

What
Happened
at
Berkeley?

A Chronology of the Berkeley Rebellion

September 14, 1964: In the aftermath of student activity during the Republican National Convention, Katherine Towle, Dean of Students at the University of California at Berkeley, notified all off-campus organizations that the Bancroft entrance to the Berkeley Campus would be closed to all student political action. Traditionally a place for impromptu public meetings and open discussion, the Bancroft Strip had been known as a Hyde Park-type safety valve.

September 21–28, 1964: Leaders of the various student organizations formed a United Front. They met with Dean Towle, who clarified University rules without modifying them and gave the students concrete restrictions. On September 28, 1,000 students picketed Chancellor Edward W. Strong at a University meeting. At this meeting, Mr. Strong offered new clarifications of rules, apparently changing the reasons for their fresh application to the Bancroft Strip.

September 30–October 2, 1964: The administration singled out a few students for sanctions. But all students involved in the controversy insisted on being punished equally. Five

3

students called on the deans on September 30. Four hundred others waited outside the deans' offices until early morning, when Chancellor Strong announced that eight students were indefinitely suspended without a hearing. Many Berkeley students contended that the penalties against these eight and the procedures used against them were contrary to University regulations. As a result, a protest rally was scheduled for noon, October 1. At 11:45, police arrested Jack Weinberg, a recent graduate manning a table on the Bancroft Strip, for trespassing. Students spontaneously surrounded the police car in which Weinberg was placed and where he remained for thirty-three hours. Meanwhile, California President Clark Kerr declared that negotiations between student leaders and University officials were impossible and called in five hundred Oakland police.[1]

October 3–5, 1964: The United Front, joined by representatives of conservative and religious groups as well as independent students, became the Free Speech Movement. At the same time, the University administration established a Political Study Committee and referred the cases of the eight suspended students to a committee appointed by Chancellor Strong. Students of the Free Speech Movement claimed that Strong's action was a violation of an agreement made on October 2 to have this committee appointed by the Academic Senate. Despite their resentment, however, the students continued to observe their moratorium on demonstrations.

October 13–28, 1964: Before a large audience, the administration's Political Study Committee heard fifty students voice their opinions. Forty-nine of the students requested the Committee's dissolution. A Graduate Coordinating Committee was then formed, contributing seven delegates to the Free Speech Movement's executive committee. On October 28, students prompted the formation of what they considered

---

1. In a letter to the Editor of the *Saturday Review* (March 6, 1965), Clark Kerr stated that "It is a matter of public record that the Governor, not the university administration, was responsible for the involvement of off-campus police."

a more equitable Political Study Committee and a new committee on discipline appointed by the Academic Senate. But a subsequent dispute over the agenda of the new Political Study Committee emphasized that a major source of agitation among the students was freedom of advocacy.

November 7–10, 1964: According to members of the Free Speech Movement, the administration's final stand on the Political Study Committee issue restricted free speech. The students insisted that their freedom of speech was protected by nothing less than the First Amendment to the Constitution. On November 9, they resumed manning tables on the Bancroft Strip. On November 10, the Dean notified seventy students that they had been cited for violation of University regulations. In defiance of the regulations which prohibited political activity on Bancroft, two hundred teaching assistants manned tables there. And other members of the Free Speech Movement demanded that they too be cited by the Dean, insisting again upon being punished along with reprimanded students.

November 20–23, 1964: Four thousand Berkeley students held a public rally on the campus, moving to hold silent vigil while the Regents accepted President Kerr's solution to the growing crisis. The Regents agreed to modify their policy regarding student political activity. But they also agreed that organizations and individuals should be severely punished for illegal advocacy, and that new disciplinary measures should be established. Stunned and angered, students of the Free Speech Movement voted to stage a sit-in in Sproul Hall.

November 24–December 4, 1964: During Thanksgiving vacation, the Free Speech Movement demanded full freedom of advocacy and prepared to occupy Sproul Hall unless their demands were met. Along with the teaching assistants, members of the Graduate Coordinating Committee voted overwhelmingly in favor of a strike. After a rally on December 2, 800 students began an orderly occupation of

Sproul Hall as a last resort to petition for grievance and to protest continued arbitrary treatment and punishment by the University administration. During the sit-in, the students maintained strict discipline. Early the following morning, Berkeley police began moving in and arresting the students. The students then began their strike and few classes were held. Meanwhile, 900 faculty members met and requested that amnesty, freedom and advocacy be granted to the students. But by now great confusion prevailed on the Berkeley Campus.

December 7–8, 1964: Meeting over the weekend, a group of department chairmen presented President Kerr with a proposed compromise solution. At 11 A.M., Kerr addressed an assembly of faculty members and students in the Greek Theatre. But there the Free Speech Movement condemned Kerr's proposals as being inadequate, even while graduate students agreed to suspend their strike until after a meeting of the Academic Senate. At this meeting, the Senate voted 824 to 115 against control of student speech and political advocacy. The Free Speech Movement expressed its support of the Academic Senate resolution, and an uneasy peace was restored.

December 15, 1964–January 3, 1965: The Board of Regents refused to accept the proposal made by the Academic Senate. But they did consent to appoint a committee to examine the various issues and meet with students, faculty members and others involved in the controversy. On January 2, Martin Meyerson was appointed Acting Chancellor as a replacement for Edward W. Strong. On January 3, the new Chancellor announced that open discussion and political activity would again be permitted on the Berkeley Campus during certain hours.

What Happened at Berkeley

JAMES CASS

James Cass, Associate Education Editor of the Saturday Review Education Supplement, *was Director of Research and Development for the National Citizens Council for Better Schools from 1956 to 1960. He has also served as a consultant to the Governor's Committee on Higher Education in New York. He is the co-author of the* Comparative Guide to American Colleges *(with Max Birnbaum).*

THE University of California at Berkeley, where a series of student demonstrations erupted last fall, is, paradoxically, reaping the fruits of success. For many years Berkeley, most prestigious of the university's eight campuses, has sought to build a faculty whose eminence would be second to none, and to attract a student body that would rival the nation's best. To a very large degree it has succeeded—but it has not yet learned to cope effectively with its success.

For reasons of size, circumstance, and personality, pressures within the student body have long been building. In a year when the issue of human equality and its twin supports— freedom of speech and of political action—have been posed so dramatically for the whole nation by the civil rights movement, it is not surprising that Berkeley's politically aware students should be especially sensitive. When, therefore, the ad-

7

ministration abruptly closed a campus safety valve shortly before the fall term opened, the result, predictably, was an explosion of massive proportions that has rocked this great institution to its foundations. And the end is not yet in sight. Given the most sensitive administration handling of the situation—which it certainly has not received to date—it will be many months before the scars of recent events are healed. Meanwhile, it remains to be seen whether the university can survive without serious, permanent damage.

There is general agreement on the chronology of events; there is far less agreement on why they occurred and what they mean for higher education generally. Briefly, these are the facts:

The university has for many years had regulations "prohibiting the collection of funds and the use of university facilities for the planning and implementing of off-campus political and social action." However, a small, brick-paved area about twenty-six by sixty feet immediately outside Sather Gate on the south side of the campus—the main entrance for pedestrians—provided an outlet for the social and political conscience of the campus community. Here students with a "cause" have, for many years, set up their card tables, easels, and placards, passed out handbills and flyers, solicited funds and recruited converts.

It was in this area, at the corner of Telegraph and Bancroft, that student volunteers for William Scranton were recruited during the Republican National Convention. It was here that students were recruited by the Ad Hoc Committee to End Discrimination to picket the Oakland *Tribune* on September 4, for alleged discrimination in hiring—a charge that has been strongly denied by former Senator William F. Knowland, editor of the paper and a leading supporter of Senator Goldwater in California. It was here, too, that students were sought for picketing and sit-ins at other business establishments in neighboring San Francisco.

This was the situation when, on September 14, Dean of Students Katherine A. Towle pulled the string. In a letter to all student organizations and their advisors, she reminded them of university regulations and announced that beginning September 21 solicitation of funds and recruitment of members for social and political causes were henceforth banned from the formerly exempt area outside Sather Gate as well as from the campus proper. The safety valve was closed.

Within a matter of days after September 14 some twenty student organizations had formed a United Front coalition to oppose the university's action. These groups were notable primarily for the remarkable diversity of viewpoints they represented. They included Slate (a vociferously liberal student political organization), Campus CORE, California Council of Republicans, University Society of Individualists. W.E.B. DuBois Club, Young Peoples Socialist League, University Young Democrats, University Young Republicans, Young Socialist Alliance, Campus Women for Peace, Youth for Goldwater, Student Committee for Travel to Cuba, Student Committee for "No on Proposition 14," University Friends of SNCC, Students for a Democratic Society, College Young Republicans, Students for Independent Political Action, Youth Committee Against Proposition 14, Independent Socialist Club, and the Inter-Faith Council.

The administration responded to formation of the United Front by liberalizing the rules to permit distribution of information, but denied the right to advocate or organize social or political action. The students rejected the proposal and, on September 21, the United Front held its first rally on the steps of Sproul Hall, the university administration building, hard by Sather Gate.

A week later, on September 28, the administration reinterpreted its rules to allow distribution of campaign literature and similar materials, and designated eight "Hyde Park" areas on campus where discussion and debate of social and political issues could take place, but it announced also that those engaging in "illegal politics" might be expelled. Since there had for many years been serious questions about the constitutionality of the university's restrictions on student activity, a number of United Front organizations, in an effort to make a test case, deliberately defied the university regulations by manning tables to organize political and social action. On September 30 the university "indefinitely suspended" eight students involved in the test case, and 400 other students promptly signed statements that they were equally guilty and demanded disciplinary hearings. The stage was set for the fantastic events that followed.

The next day a protest rally was held on the steps of Sproul Hall. A former graduate student in mathematics, Jack Weinberg, who was manning a CORE table on Sproul steps, was arrested for trespassing and placed in a police car that had been driven onto the campus sidewalk. A crowd of some 3,000 students promptly enveloped the police car and held it captive, with Weinberg inside, for more than thirty hours—from approximately noon of October 1 to early evening of the following day. Meanwhile, students had entered Sproul Hall and initiated a sit-in to demand discussion of the eight students who had been suspended, but they left voluntarily after a brief clash with the police.

On October 2, university officials, members of the faculty, and student leaders met to discuss their differences. In the course of the meeting, students agreed to a moratorium on illegal protests, the administration agreed to submit the cases of the eight suspended students to the Academic Senate, powerful official organization of the whole Berkeley faculty, and a ten-man committee of faculty, administration representatives and students was appointed to investigate campus problems and recommend solutions. As a result, the 450 police who had assembled to force removal of the police car departed, the demonstrators dispersed, and Weinberg was booked, but released, since the university had agreed not to press charges.

At about this same time, the United Front coalition was reorganized as the Free Speech Movement (FSM) under the leadership of Mario Savio, a senior philosophy major, a frequent speaker at student rallies, and one of the eight students who had been suspended. The new organization proved to be a highly organized but loosely structured organization that attracted and used effectively a wide range of student talent, and that displayed a sure sense of political strategy in dealing with the administration.

The new name of the organization was psychologically effective, but hardly accurate since the question at issue was whether students had the right on campus to solicit funds, seek recruits, and make plans for off-campus political and social action, mainly in the field of civil rights, aimed at the surrounding community. The Hyde Park areas on campus offered ample opportunity for traditional freedom of speech.

In the days that followed, the Academic Senate passed a resolution favoring "maximum freedom for student political activity," and President Clark Kerr (chief administrative officer of the state-wide university—each campus is administered by its own chancellor) asked the Academic Senate to set up an *ad hoc* committee to advise on disciplining the eight suspended students. On October 21 the committee requested that the chancellor reinstate the suspended students temporarily, pending their hearing and a report, but the request was denied.

On November 5, impatient with a deadlock within the faculty-student-administration committee, FSM resumed picketing of Sproul Hall. This action was followed four days later by a rally, and tables were again manned on Sproul steps in defiance of university regulations. Some sixty to seventy students were ordered to appear before the dean and 800 other students promptly signed statements declaring that they were equally guilty. The administration then disbanded the faculty-student-administration committee, charging that FSM had violated the truce agreement.

On November 12 the *ad hoc* committee of the Academic Senate considering disciplinary action against the eight suspended students criticized the administration as "harsh and arbitrary" in its handling of these cases and recommended censure for six of the students and suspension for six weeks for the other two, Savio and Art Goldberg.

When the Regents, governing body of the university, on November 20 held their regular monthly meeting on the Berkeley campus, they accepted the recommendation of President Kerr and Chancellor Strong for suspension of all eight students for the period from September 30 to November 20, and for placing Savio and Goldberg on probation. At the same time, the Regents took a long step toward meeting student demands by modifying previous policy to allow, in certain designated areas, "planning, implementing, raising funds or recruiting participants for lawful off-campus action." Advocacy of action that might prove unlawful, however, remained subject to university discipline.

Students reacted to this modification of the regulations by holding another rally on Sproul steps and marching to University Hall where the Regents were meeting. Two days later they again demonstrated their displeasure over the university's insistence on retaining the right to discipline students for off-campus activities by staging a three-hour sit-in in Sproul Hall. And on November 25, the university sent letters of reprimand to some sixty students who had manned illegal tables at the rally on November 9.

Five days later, on November 30, FSM called another rally, but it was poorly attended—about 200 students gathered. It appeared that the Free Speech Movement, in the face of the liberalized regulations adopted by the Regents on November 20, was running out of steam—until it was announced that the administration had notified four of its leaders, Savio, Art Goldberg, Jackie Goldberg, and Brian Turner, that they again faced disciplinary action for the demonstrations of October 1 and 2, two months before. Before nightfall students were again rallying to the FSM standard and events were fast moving toward a violent climax.

On December 1, FSM repeated its assertion that only the courts have the right to regulate political activity, on or off campus, and demanded that the university drop charges against its leaders within twenty-four hours or face a demonstration. Savio threatened that if the demands were not met, "the university machine will come to a grinding halt." He also warned his followers: "Be prepared to risk going to jail." The university ignored the FSM ultimatum.

The following day FSM called a rally at noon in front of Sproul Hall. Before a crowd of some 6,000 students, Mario Savio gave an impassioned justification for civil disobedience:

"There's a time when the operation of the machine becomes so odious, makes your heart so sick, that you can't take part . . . you've got to put your bodies upon the gears, and upon the wheels, upon the levers, tie up all the apparatus and make it stop, and you've got to indicate to the people who run the machine . . . that unless you're free, the machine will be prevented from working at all." Then he led nearly 1,000 cheering students into Sproul Hall where they staged a massive sit-in.

Early in the morning of December 3, after administration efforts to prevail upon the students to leave had failed, Governor Edmund G. Brown ordered that the demonstrators be arrested and removed by force from the hall. Asserting that state laws must be enforced and state institutions allowed to function, the governor characterized the action of the demonstrators as "anarchy." Arrest records are reported to show that of 814 arrested, 590 were students, 89 were teaching and research assistants or university employees, and 135 were wives or husbands of students or other non-student FSM sympathizers. Removal of the demonstrators took approximately twelve hours; it was completed shortly after three o'clock on the afternoon of December 3.

The university community was profoundly shocked by the police action on campus. A campus-wide strike was called and large numbers of graduate students picketed university buildings in protest. Faculty members, barred by the police from entering the administration building of their own university, spontaneously arranged an informal meeting to consider the crisis. At their meeting the faculty passed resolutions calling for amnesty for students against whom disciplinary action was pending, and for a change in regulations so that students would not be subject to university discipline for off-campus political activities. Members of the faculty also met with the judge before whom the arrested students were brought to help in setting and posting bail, and raised $8,500 bail among their own members.

The following day student picketing of university buildings

continued and many classes did not meet. Estimates of the strike's effectiveness vary, but it appears that substantially more than half of the university's classrooms were closed. During the weekend of December 5 and 6, behind-the-scenes activity was intense. The chairmen of all the departments on campus constituted themselves a Council of Chairmen and worked out with President Kerr an agreement designed to ease the tense situation.

On Monday, December 7, departmental meetings were held to discuss the agreement reached with President Kerr. The proposals were approved and the agreement was presented to the student body at a special convocation that morning by Professor R. A. Scalapino, chairman of the Council of Chairmen, and President Kerr. It included amnesty for all students against whom university charges were pending—both the four leaders who faced disciplinary action for the October 1 and 2 demonstrations and the 800 students arrested at Sproul Hall days before. But the substantive issue of off-campus political and social activity was deferred, awaiting the report of the Academic Senate's Committee on Academic Freedom.

It appeared that the presentation of the agreement had made a positive impression on the many thousands of students present. But as President Kerr turned away from the podium and walked toward a dressing room at the back of the stage, where a press conference was to follow immediately, Mario Savio appeared at the left side of the stage and walked to the microphone. Before he could speak, two campus policemen came up behind him and dragged him bodily to the back of the stage. He was later allowed to speak and contented himself with a ninety-second announcement of a noon rally to be held on Sproul steps.

FSM promptly branded the agreement of the Council of Chairmen and President Kerr inadequate, but picketing was suspended until after the scheduled meeting of the Academic Senate.

The following day, December 8, the Academic Senate met and approved the recommendations of its Committee on Academic Freedom for resolving the "free speech" controversy. The vote was 824 to 115—a 7 to 1 majority. The proposed solution to the controversy included: 1) amnesty for all student activities prior to December 8th, 2) "reasonable regulation" of student political activity on campus "to prevent interference with the normal functions of the university," 3) the university shall not restrict the content of speech or advocacy, or seek to regulate off-campus student political activity, and 4) future disciplinary measures for political activity shall be determined by a committee of the Academic Senate.

The recommendations of the Academic Senate were immediately embraced by FSM as proposing "what we have been after for months." The university administration, on the other hand, noted that they involved "such basic changes in the policies affecting all campuses of the university" that action on them would have to wait until the Regents could make a decision.

Thus the matter stood when the Regents convened at the administration building of the university's Los Angeles campus on December 17–18. Action taken was designed primarily to buy more time in which to reach a decision and meanwhile, to avoid a direct confrontation of opposing points of view from which each side would find it difficult to retreat at a later date. Specifically, the Regents 1) declined to divest themselves of authority for disciplining students and to hand this authority over to the faculty—a responsibility that rested with the Berkeley faculty until 1938, 2) appointed a committee of Regents to undertake a comprehensive review of university policies and develop recommendations for the Board that would provide "maximum freedom on campus consistent with individual and group responsibility," and 3) stated that until the committee reported, existing rules would be enforced, but that the Regents "do not contemplate that advocacy or content of speech shall be restricted beyond the purview of the First and Fourteenth Amendments to the Constitution."

Word of the Regents' action was received in Berkeley in near-record time and FSM leaders promptly rejected it as "horrendous" and a "repudiation of FSM." Members of an emergency faculty committee of the Academic Senate, which met with the Regents as they were reaching their decision, were far more reserved in their comments. They characterized the action as "a great step forward," but noted that it was "not a full and satisfactory settlement."

The effort of the Regents to put off a final decision had much to recommend it. Christmas vacation at Berkeley began as they were meeting in Los Angeles on December 18. When students returned January 4, just two weeks remained before end-of-semester examinations and it appeared that many students—especially graduate students—who were willing to devote time and energy to FSM demonstrations at mid-semester might prove reluctant to prejudice their academic careers at exam time. FSM promised to determine during the holidays what action the organization would take after January 4. Indications were that it would depend, at least in part, on how sympathetically the Academic Senate received the report of its emergency committee, and the degree of unanimity with which the faculty urged students to forego further demonstrations until the special committee of the Regents reported. But as *SR* went to press the future remained obscure.

The events at Berkeley have unfolded with the inexorability of a classical tragedy—and the final act remains to be played. Yet the question remains: Why Berkeley? Why didn't it happen at UCLA, or Wisconsin, or Michigan? There are many answers, and they concern all those elements that make Berkeley so uniquely itself—its students and faculty, its location and traditions, its role as the leading campus of the nation's greatest state university, and the bureaucratic problems that grow out of sheer size and phenomenally rapid growth.

Because of its size (about 27,500 students are enrolled, roughly 18,000 of them undergraduates) and its standards (students who rank in the top 12 per cent of their high school class are eligible to apply to any one of the university's campuses, but Berkeley gets more than its share of the very best students), the Berkeley student body includes the largest number of very bright, well-prepared students of any university campus in the world.

The status that Berkeley enjoys within the University of California, as well as among the universities of the world, is solidly based on the eminence of its faculty. A number of Nobel laureates are counted among its members as well as leading scholars in many disciplines. It would seem that all should be idyllic in this academic Garden of Eden. But so prestigious a faculty and so capable a student body do not make for administrative ease—and there are other factors.

Students who are attracted to Berkeley by famous teachers find that too often they are met only in lecture courses, along with several hundred other undergraduates. Many of the famous names are far too busy with the research and writing commitments to have much time for undergraduate classes—to say nothing of individual students. Much of the teaching is done by Teaching Assistants (TAs), themselves only a year or two out of undergraduate school and more intent on their graduate studies than their undergraduate students. Some of the TAs, to be sure, are good teachers who take their classroom responsibilities very seriously, but some do not.

At other points, too, the undergraduate feels pressure from the size of the institution and the impersonality of its bureaucratic operation. If his professors are distant figures whom he does not know, the administration is even more remote and the Regents function in another universe. Unlike many other universities where undergraduate life is organized in units of manageable size—around individual dormitories, or separate colleges, or fraternities and sororities—at Berkeley there are few institutions of this kind within the university. Fewer than half the students live in university housing and only about one-fifth of them live in fraternities and sororities. For mature, highly motivated, self-directed students who are prepared to benefit from the superb academic facilities offered by the university, few problems may exist. For others the problems may be severe.

As a result of size and circumstance, then, communication within the university has broken down—communication between student and teacher, between student and administration, and even between faculty and administration. Students feel alienated from the university, mere numbers on an IBM card, figures in a line at the library desk. They refer to the university as "the factory" and claim that the administration views them as the raw material for the university's educational production line. Intelligent, informed, and sensitive to the world around them, they seek a place in which they can achieve a sense of identity that the university denies them.

Because of the breakdown in communication, the administration apparently miscalculated the depth and the breadth of the feeling engendered among students by the Free Speech Movement. Growing, in large part, out of the civil rights movement, and tied closely in leadership and objectives to the local drive for civil rights, it aroused a flood of youthful militance for which the administration was not prepared.

As the Free Speech Movement developed, it was obvious that it attracted ardent adherents from the full spectrum of political allegiance. Yet the charge was repeatedly made in newspapers and elsewhere that the movement was Communist-inspired—or Communist-dominated—or at least strongly influenced by Communists. It is a charge worth examining, for there are a number of inter-related factors that bear on it.

First, for many years there has been a strong tradition of political and social activism within the Berkeley student body. Although always a relatively small percentage of the student body, the activists have been vocal and visible, and have influenced student culture.

Second, San Francisco and the Bay area have a strong surviving tradition of native American radicalism dating back to the San Francisco general strike, and before that to Jack London's waterfront days. And it remains today an area in which adherents of the radical left can enjoy a surprising degree of respectability and status.

Third, the campus is surrounded by modest homes and apartment houses where many students live, as well as substantial numbers of ex-students, non-students, and sometime-students who find at Berkeley a focus for their intellectual and cultural interests. Many of these individuals have become a part of the campus community. The result is a bohemian environment that more nearly approximates the Left Bank than it does that of other American universities.

Fourth, a very visible minority of bona fide students are

given to long hair, beards, and the officiously picturesque raiment of the bohemian or beatnik.

In such a setting it is easy to visualize massive Communist influences at work, but it is harder to document them. There are, to be sure, members of the radical left who are eager to make their influence felt in any movement of this kind. One well known Communist appeared on campus during the demonstrations and made sure that his picture was taken by a local newspaper. And given the varied membership of FSM, it would be impossible to avoid some "influence." But the issue, if there is one, is how important that influence was in competition with the many pulling in other directions.

Both the FSM executive committee of fifty members and the eleven-man steering committee include individuals affiliated with Communist and radical socialist organizations, although they represent a small minority of each group. A number of observers, however, have noted that it was the civil rights organizations (CORE and SNCC) that provided the impetus for radical action, while the far-left groups often held out for more moderate approaches. Mario Savio, the acknowledged leader of FSM, is a member of SNCC, has no political affiliation, and appears to represent others in the group in his essentially anti-political attitude toward social action. The rhythm and melody of his impassioned rhetoric seem more reminiscent of the syndicalists or I.W.W. of a generation or two ago than they do of the contemporary class struggle. And, in relation to adult influence in the movement, another one of the leaders is reported to have said, "We have a saying in the movement that you can't trust anybody over thirty."

Perhaps most significant, however, is the unanimity of thought and action that the disparate groups that make up FSM have been able to reach. The organizations representing the far left, usually divided among themselves by profound ideological differences, have demonstrated an unprecedented solidarity. And their capacity for finding a common meeting ground with the more conservative organizations is only slightly less notable. It seems clear that the limited issues with which FSM concerned itself provided a basis for agreement that had little to do with political affiliation or revolutionary commitments.

But what of the students who were not leaders? Were they responsible young adults, typical of the student body generally, or were they representative of fringe groups and hangers-on? Noon rallies on Sproul Hall steps, at various times, drew groups ranging from a few hundred to 6,000 or more. The strike on December 3–4 was observed by an estimated 12,000 students. But most significant is an analysis of the students arrested during the Sproul Hall sit-in on December 3. Prepared by "A Fact-Finding Committee of Graduate Political Scientists," the analysis is contained in a Preliminary Report on "The Berkeley Free Speech Controversy."

According to the report, of the undergraduates arrested, 47 per cent had better than B averages; 71 per cent of the graduate students had averages between B and A; twenty were Phi Beta Kappa; eight were Woodrow Wilson Fellows; twenty had published articles in scholarly journals; 53 were National Merit Scholarship winners or finalists; and 260 received other academic awards.

"Not only are these students among the brightest in the university," the report continues, "but they are also among the most advanced in their academic careers. Nearly two-thirds are upper-division or graduate students."

As to the political affiliations of the students arrested on December 3, the report states that 4.5 per cent belonged to "radical groups" (DuBois Club, Young Socialist Alliance, Young People's Socialist League, Independent Socialist Club); 18.2 per cent belonged to liberal groups such as the Young Democrats; 25.6 per cent were members of civil rights organizations such as NAACP and CORE; 1.2 per cent were affiliated with conservative groups; 7.3 per cent belonged to religious organizations; and 57 per cent had no political affiliation.

The Free Speech Movement has been described in many ways: as a revolutionary plot and as a kind of socially conscious panty raid; as an inter-generational rebellion of son against father, and as an expression of pure youthful idealism. It is doubtless all of these and more. But whatever the multiplicity of forces at work, there seems little doubt that the central appeal to students who never before involved themselves in social or political action is found in the civil rights movement that has dramatized for an entire generation the issues of free speech and action. And the response to that appeal came from a student body of exceptional competence and sensitivity, whose members had few other places to give their allegiance.

The problems facing the university administration and Regents in handling so complex a matter are enormous. All state universities must constantly combat community and legislative pressures, and the problem is especially acute in the nation's most politically volatile state. In addition, in California the Governor sits as president of the Regents, and the Lieutenant Governor, the speaker of the Assembly, and the State Superintendent of Public Instruction (an elective office) are all *ex officio* members.

Within the university, competing demands are equally strong. Berkeley's pre-eminent faculty was assembled, in large part, by "raiding" other campuses, and the loyalty of individual members is primarily to their discipline rather than to the institution. Therefore, if the environment at Berkeley should cease to be conducive to scholarly work, not only would the university have difficulty in enticing new men, but many already on campus could, and almost certainly would, listen to the blandishments of other leading institutions.

The situation is further complicated by the complex administrative structure of the university in which the lines of responsibility and authority are not always clear between the administration of the Berkeley campus (the chancellor's office) and the state-wide university administration (the president's office), which is located on the Berkeley campus. To operate effectively, the two administrations must speak with a single voice, but in the present controversy this has not always been the case—and both the image and the substance of the university have suffered.

As president of the state-wide university, Clark Kerr has

emerged as principal spokesman for the administration in the current controversy. A number of commentators have pointed out the supreme irony of a situation in which he should become the focus of FSM invective. An industrial relations expert and labor mediator of national repute, he became chancellor of the Berkeley campus in 1952 and moved to the president's office in 1958. His administration during these twelve years has been one of the most liberal in the university's history. He was, for instance, instrumental in resolving the bitter loyalty oath controversy of a dozen years ago, and in 1963 was a leader in the move to liberalize university regulations to allow Communist speakers on campus. Just last spring he received the American Association of University Professors' Alexander Meiklejohn Award in recognition of his "outstanding contributions to the cause of academic freedom."

In addition, he has analyzed more completely than anyone else the nature of the huge modern university—the multiversity—and clearly foreseen its consequences, both human and institutional. In the 1963 Godkin Lectures at Harvard (later published as *The Uses of the University*) he forecast the student revolt against a "faculty in absentia," institutional impersonality, and "a blanket" of rules that smother the individual.

Finally, he has sought, unsuccessfully, to find a means to provide small, more manageable groupings of students on Berkeley's campus. And in planning new campuses of the university—at Santa Cruz, for example—he has insisted that undergraduates be grouped in clusters of small colleges, with access to common facilities, so that they may enjoy the advantages of the multiversity without becoming lost in its mass.

Yet for all his understanding of the problem and the respect of his colleagues, President Kerr is sharply criticized for his handling of the current controversy. He is accused of understanding the problem but not the people involved. He is remote and inaccessible even to the faculty, and has virtually no contact with students.

President Kerr is criticized, too, for his concept of the role of the leader in the multiversity as essentially the mediator who seeks effective compromise among competing forces. Un-

der ordinary circumstances the mediator-leader may successfully avoid destructive conflict and forward the welfare of
the university. Under extraordinary circumstances, such as
those that developed at Berkeley, it appears that a firmer,
more positive role might prove more effective. But the over-
lapping authority of campus administration and the state-wide
university administration, also based at Berkeley, may have
inhibited firm, consistent action by either.

The events at Berkeley have a significance far beyond the
confines of the San Francisco Bay area. What has happened
there is an advanced example of the ferment on many campuses. Therefore, we should try to understand the sources of
student unrest before it grows to crisis proportions.

Ten years ago there was widespread concern with the political and social apathy of the nation's college students. It
was possible, then, to wish that more of them would take to
heart Oliver Wendell Holmes' admonition that, "It is required
of a man that he should share the passion and action of his
time—at peril of being judged not to have lived." Today,
when it seems that many students have heard Justice Holmes'
message, we need not shrink from the result. A passion for
social justice among the nation's youth is a prize that should
be eagerly sought. But we must understand clearly that this
is not the only source of ferment.

The modern university has left its cloister and entered the
market place. Far from concerning itself solely with the
search for ultimate truth and time-tested perspectives it has
come to serve the immediate needs of contemporary society.
The scholar's skills are no longer applied solely to man's past,
but in very large part to humanity's future. Notable advantages have been gained by the university from its new role,
but there are dangers, too, in making higher education so
responsive to the importunate community. And the students,
perceiving the role of the university in serving government,
business, industry, and others, wonder why it should not serve
their immediate needs equally.

Almost inevitably students will have a greater voice in the

affairs of the university in the future. Certainly today's better prepared and more knowledgeable students should have a larger voice in determining the rules that govern them, and in other campus matters. But demands are also being made by some of the more advanced student groups for a voice in determining policy on the curriculum, in selecting faculty, and related matters. Surely these are of vital concern to students, and almost certainly their demands to be heard in relation to them will increase. Yet, just as the demands of society for research projects and other services cannot always be met without distorting the basic role and function of the university, so the immediate interests of students, which seem so urgent, may be better served by a long view of ultimate objectives. Experience in other countries—notably in South America—demonstrates clearly that a policy of allowing students a major voice in some sensitive areas of university policy can lead to academic chaos.

Therefore, university administrators, increasingly, must be careful not to confuse the demands of students that can lead to anarchy on the campus with the desire for freedom to participate freely in the great social movements of our time, and the request to contribute a responsible voice in university matters that concern them directly. These will not always be easy to distinguish—not least because the distinctions will sometimes be confused in the minds of the students themselves.

And there will be other barriers to understanding. However lofty their morals, student manners are often atrocious. The etiquette of social protest is changing; new standards of speech and action are being widely accepted. Therefore, it is doubly necessary to listen carefully to what students say, rather than to how they say it. Also, students who are passionately devoted to attacking injustice in our society are often impatient with the slow process of orderly procedure. Having learned the techniques of civil disobedience, they will sometimes employ them to seek goals for which their use is not appropriate. The objective of the university must be not only to provide an environment of freedom, but, both within the classroom and without, to instill a surer sense of responsibility.

The administrator's lot has never been an easy one, and

certainly it will be even more difficult in the years ahead. To meet the future successfully will take a large measure of firmness, sensitivity, and above all, human understanding.

Berkeley's Angry Young Men
C. B. COX

This article on the clash between students and administration on the Berkeley campus of the University of California is by a Visiting Professor in the department of English who is senior lecturer in English at the University of Hull.

O N Thursday, December 3, 768 student demonstrators at Berkeley, University of California, were arrested and carted off to prison. During the arrests many students refused to co-operate, and made themselves limp. Some were kicked and pulled down a flight of stairs by the ankles, their heads banging on each step. The anger felt by the police towards the students reflects the general reaction of the people of California. A janitor at the university called the demonstrators "scum." The California Alumni Council, representing more than 50,000 Berkeley graduates, demanded stern disciplinary measures. A Republican State assemblyman accused the demonstrators of being Communists, a word Americans use for anyone they dislike. The dispute goes back to the Republican National Convention in the Cow Palace, San Francisco in June, during which Berkeley students took part in a demonstration in favour of Scranton. As a result supporters of Goldwater put pressure on the university administration to enforce existing laws that prohibited political recruiting and fund raising on campus.

When I arrived at Berkeley in late August, I was delighted to find the entrance crowded with students soliciting for all kinds of political and religious groups. Some Negroes were chanting evangelical hymns; Left-wing and Right-wing groups pressed their literature into my hands. In California, of course, outdoor activity of this kind is possible even in winter. For some years a wide space of pavement just outside the university had become a Hyde Park area, where tables could be set up for the distribution of literature and soliciting of funds. In the past there had been a tacit agreement that this area was outside the university's jurisdiction. In September the university administrators made their first move by declaring the use of this area by political groups illegal. Their action affected all groups, from "Youth for Goldwater" to the organisations recruiting for civil rights.

Immediately the first of a series of student protests took place on the steps of Sproul Hall, the university administrative building. Eventually a sit-in demonstration was organised; students crowded into Sproul Hall, disrupting the work of the administration. As with CND in Britain, the use of civil disobedience alienated the conservatives, and the so-called Free Speech Movement was taken over by liberals and civil rights campaigners.

The administrators alternated weakly between admissions of error, suspension of student leaders, and major concessions. A protracted series of negotiations ended two or three weeks ago with most of the student demands accepted, and with new political liberties for the campus. Moderates on the Academic Senate had worked hard to effect a compromise between the intransigent Chancellor Strong and the militant, idealistic students. The Free Speech Movement seemed to be dying down, and mass demonstrations no longer blocked the main exit each noon. At this moment the administration announced that it was taking disciplinary action against the student leaders and liberal organisations for minor offences during the earlier demonstrations.

This sudden decision shocked the campus. Either the administrators were incredibly stupid, or they were deliberately trying to bring about a new conflict with the students. The situation moved inevitably towards tragedy. The Free Speech Movement organised a major sit-in at Sproul Hall. About a thousand students filed up the steps in an orderly manner, with Joan Baez, the American folk-singer, singing the civil rights song "We Shall Overcome" over a megaphone, and the Stars and Stripes waving at their head. The next day at 4 a.m. the police moved in, and began their arrests. Now the academic staff have organised a huge fund to bail out the 768 demonstrators, while at the time of writing large numbers of other students are on strike.

At a faculty meeting to discuss the arrests, a professor of history admitted that with the rapid growth of the university he had been happy to hand over the administration to professionals, and to devote himself to his research. Another professor said simply, "We teach the students liberal values. They fight for them on campus, and the administration puts them in gaol." In the Berkeley dispute the Academic Senate has had little power, and some of its most important resolutions have been ignored. The Senate, of course, is split in its attitude towards civil disobedience, but largely agreed that much of the present mess is due to administrative blunders.

A University community has very special characteristics, and power over its affairs should always be kept in the hands of academics. The professional administrator is often unsympathetic to the arrogance and idealism, stupidity and generosity of the usual student groups. The student leader, Mario Savio, has repeatedly accused the administration of treating the university as a factory, training the students in the techniques necessary for material success. This situation is not so impossible in Britain. With the expansion of universities it is going to be less easy to maintain liberal traditions. British university teachers who wish to be rid of all administrative chores might consider the plight of their colleagues at Berkeley, desperately struggling to gain power to rule their own campus.

In the San Francisco Bay area there are no quality newspapers and there is no BBC. Without such means of communication it is almost impossible for the average citizen to hear rational discussion of the issues involved.

This dispute over a small area of pavement might seem trivial compared with the violence of the disputants. A professor of English pointed out to me that the conflict is symbolic. Many of the students in the FSM had spent their vacation assisting the civil rights campaign in the South.

Among intelligent young people in America there is a new spirit, energetic, idealistic, non-conformist, politically alive, which is fighting the evils of a degenerate capitalism. The instinctive American conservatism is receiving a fundamental challenge, and it is reacting with angry violence. The new students are making a major reappraisal of the American way of life, and putting their beliefs into practice. It is often said that the Berkeley campus is the most politically alive in America, and that what happens here today will be repeated all over America in five years' time.

In Berkeley the dispute continues. When the President announced a compromise solution to 13,000 students and staff gathered in the open-air Greek Theatre, Mario Savio grabbed the microphone, and was carried off stage, struggling and shouting in the arms of six brawny policemen. As the academics filed out, their sad, worried faces reflected the damage this dispute is causing to one of the greatest universities in the world.

The Berkeley Affair:
Mr. Kerr vs. Mr. Savio & Co.
A. H. RASKIN

A staff member of The New York Times *for more than thirty years, A. H. Raskin specializes in the labor-management field. His interest goes beyond his specialization, however, as this selection demonstrates. As a professional journalist, he has won a number of awards and distinctions, including the Sidney Hillman Memorial Award, the George Polk Award and the Page One Award of the New York Newspaper Guild.*

WHAT turned the University of California's world-renowned campus here into a snake pit of unrepressed animosities? As my helicopter rattled across the moondappled water of San Francisco Bay on its way toward this strangely

riven academic center, it seemed to me two men were probably best equipped to supply the answer. In the process, they
could go far toward explaining a simmering unrest on other
campuses across the nation, and in every corner of our corporate society.

One man was Dr. Clark Kerr, 53, the quiet-spoken Quaker
whose duties as president of the university make him Big
Daddy to 72,000 students on nine California campuses. The
other was Mario Savio, the charismatic 22-year-old undergraduate who had emerged as the archangel of student revolt
at Berkeley.

My effort to get the answer from Savio got off to a rocky
start. We had arranged to meet at the headquarters of the
Graduate Coordinating Committee. This is a key unit in the
Free Speech Movement (F.S.M.), the coalition of undergraduates, graduate students and teaching assistants that grew out
of an ill-timed, worse-explained and now-rescinded administration order that barred all on-campus solicitation for political
or civil-rights demonstrations mounted off the campus.

The committee office is a garret over the university's drama
workshop, not far from the main gate to the huge, hillside
campus. The visitor climbs a flight of wooden outside stairs
and finds himself in a barren room that is dark despite the
dazzling sunlight outside. The nearest thing to a real piece of
furniture is a battered green sofa, with sags where the springs
should be. A square table with a telephone fills one corner,
and there are a half-dozen camp chairs. Under the table is a
mound of picket signs. The mood is "Waiting for Lefty" done
off-Broadway.

Savio, a slim six-footer with frizzy pale hair, peeled off the
short, fleece-lined coat that has become a sort of personal trade-
mark. His first words were a flat refusal to participate in any
interview if I intended to focus on him as *the* communicator
for the F.S.M. "Anything like that will just perpetuate a
misrepresentation that the press has already done too much to
build up," he said. "This is not a cult of one personality or of
two personalities; it is a broadly based movement and I will
not say anything unless it is made clear that the F.S.M. is
not any single individual."

A way around that roadblock was ready at hand—a joint

discussion with the six other members of the collective leadership who had accompanied Savio to the conference. It started with everybody sounding off against Sidney Hook's view in The Times Magazine (Jan. 3) that academic freedom was primarily for teachers and that the only imperative right for students was freedom to learn. Savio said they wanted equal space to reply; also they wanted to sue. I told them to go ahead if they thought they had a case. Finally, we got to what I wanted to talk about—namely, what they thought the issue at Berkeley had been and whether there was still any real issue left.

It was a somewhat formless encounter, a blend of a graduate seminar in political science and "Catch-22." People wandered out and others filled their chairs; getting in questions was harder than getting back answers. Yet, it was an engaging group—lucid in exposition, quick in rebuttal, manifesting no unease at differences of interpretation or emphasis within their own circle.

The Berkeley mutineers did not seem political in the sense of those student rebels in the turbulent Thirties; they are too suspicious of all adult institutions to embrace wholeheartedly even those ideologies with a stake in smashing the system. An anarchist or I.W.W. strain seems as pronounced as any Marxist doctrine. "Theirs is a sort of political existentialism," says Paul Jacobs, a research associate at the university's Center for the Study of Law and Society, who is one of the F.S.M.'s applauders. "All the old labels are out; if there were any orthodox Communists here, they would be a moderating influence."

The proudly immoderate zealots of the F.S.M. pursue an activist creed—that only commitment can strip life of its emptiness, its absence of meaning in a great "knowledge factory" like Berkeley. That is the explanation for their conviction that the methods of civil disobedience, in violation of law, are as appropriate in the civilized atmosphere of the campus as they are in the primordial jungle of Mississippi. It was an imaginative strategy that led to an unimaginable chain of events.

Trouble began on Sept. 14, a week before the opening of

classes, when the dean of students suddenly shut off the only area on campus where students had been free to collect funds and enlist adherents for off-campus political or social action. This island for activists was a 26-by-60-foot patch of bricked-over ground, called the Bancroft Strip, just outside the principal pedestrian entrance.

The decision to embargo the Strip, made in the climactic days of an election campaign that would settle both the Presidency and the fate of California's controversial fair housing law, forged a united front of protest extending from campus Goldwaterites to Maoist members of the Progressive Labor party.

With the memory of the mutiny thick in the gloomy garret, the collective leadership of the F.S.M. spent the next three hours telling me what they thought the rebellion was *really* about.

They are convinced that the abrupt decision to close the Bancroft Strip represented a university capitulation to right-wing forces angered by student picketing and sit-ins to compel the hiring of more Negroes in Bay area businesses. Specifically, they blame former Senator William F. Knowland, editor of The Oakland Tribune, whose paper was a special target. (Knowland says he didn't do it.)

The cutoff in political recruitment confirmed a conviction already held by some of the students that bankers, industrialists, publishers and other leaders of the Establishment in the Board of Regents were making a concentration camp out of the "multiversity"—a term coined by Kerr in a series of lectures at Harvard nearly two years ago to describe the transformation of a modern university, like Cal, into a vast techno-educational complex.

This conviction was not diminished by the extreme freedom the university has long allowed students to express their own political views, however unorthodox, at "Hyde Park" areas inside the campus. Even during the ban on the use of campus property for organizing off-campus political action, students retained their liberty to invite Communists, Nazis or Black Muslims to address meetings at the university. They also could—and often did—agitate for the right to smoke marijuana, to be able to buy contraceptives at the University Bookstore or for other far-out objectives.

All this has been going on for years in an atmosphere particularly congenial to the flowering of undergraduate rebellion. The whole Bay area has a long Left Bank tradition of hospitality to radical movements and off-beat behavior. Czeslav Milosz, a Polish poet and defector, who served on the faculty, left convinced that Berkeley and Greenwich Village were "the only two places in America you can be free." The mild year-round climate also helps. "There is no place in the world where uncomfortable people can feel so comfortable," said a visiting British professor.

Taken aback by the vehement student reaction to the recruitment taboo, the Regents in November restored the right to mount political action—not only in the Bancroft Strip but in several areas where it had never been allowed before. However, the F.S.M. is still unhappy because the new ruling specifies that only "lawful" off-campus activities can be planned on campus.

The rebels argue that students should have the same right as other citizens to participate in the political and social affairs of the outside community. What is "unlawful" ought to be determined solely by civil and criminal courts, not by a university administration or faculty. The university's only area of proper regulation over political activity should be the establishment of minimal time-place-manner rules to guarantee that anything the students do on campus does not interfere with classes or the orderly conduct of university business. Such is the current focus of what is left of the "free speech" issue.

Remembering centuries of "town vs. gown" controversies all over the world, in which universities had always fought to keep their campuses from coming under police rule, I asked the F.S.M. leaders whether their insistence on leaving disciplinary authority to the municipal law-enforcement agencies might not destroy the whole concept of academic sanctuary and expose them to much harsher treatment.

Savio, a philosophy major who graduated at the top of his class from New York City's Martin Van Buren High School, had a blunt answer: "That is a specious argument. The campus is already crawling with cops of the most insidious kind from the 'Red squad' and every other kind of undercover agency." Myra Jehlen, a comely, solemn Phi Beta Kappa from C.C.N.Y. and a Woodrow Wilson graduate scholar in English, added a postscript: "Immunity from police prosecution only applies to panty raids and fraternity guys. We're not interested in that."

She was the only coed in the group. Across the room was her husband, Carl Riskin, who had gone to Cambridge in England on a fellowship after graduating *magna cum laude* from Harvard and was now completing his Ph.D. thesis at Berkeley. He spoke seldom, but with force and precision.

Next to him sat Martin Roysher, a sophomore from Arcadia, Calif., whose casually correct clothes reflected the freshman year he spent at Princeton. He looked so young it was hard to believe he was out of high school, yet he, too, spoke crisply about everything from alienation to the importance of erasing any differentiation between the freedom of students and citizens to act upon their political beliefs.

Here, too, was Jack Weinberg, a former graduate student in math and now a civil-rights activist in CORE, who gained fame overnight as "the man in the police car" in the first of the mass upheavals last Oct. 1. Stephan Weissman, the red-bearded chairman of the Graduate Coordinating Committee, pulled a few picket signs from under the table and squatted on the floor. Robert Starobin, a Cornell B.A., who has been a teaching assistant in history at Berkeley for three years, is writing his Ph.D. dissertation on industrial slavery before the Civil War. Stocky and assertive, his talk bristled with complaints about the "power structure" and its determination to stifle civil-rights activity at Berkeley.

The one whose views evoked least challenge was the youth group's senior citizen, Hal Draper, a part-time librarian at the university who graduated from Brooklyn College in the Great Depression and is now fiftyish. A leader of the old American Student Union, he drifted through various wings of the Trotskyite movement and is currently an editor of New Politics, a journal intended to offer an outlet for all shades of Socialist thought. A Draper pamphlet called "The Mind of Clark Kerr" has become the F.S.M.'s bible in its fight against "the university factory." Dedicated to the students who immobilized the police car, the leaflet depicts Kerr as the preacher of docile submission to a technocratic juggernaut that will stamp out all individuality and all liberty.

The longer my conversation with the students went on, the clearer it became that the political battle was only a symptom of a larger revolt against the bigness and impersonality of the "multiversity" itself. If Clark Kerr is the high priest of the multiversity, social critic Paul Goodman is its Antichrist and thus beloved of the F.S.M. The opening theme of an F.S.M. pamphlet is a declaration by Goodman that in the United States today, "students—middle-class youth—are the major exploited class. . . . They have no choice but to go to college." Rejecting their role as factory workers on an academic assembly line, the F.S.M. demands a humanized campus, a "loving community" based on comradeship and purpose.

"We must now begin the demand of the right to know; to know the realities of the present world-in-revolution, and to have an opportunity to think clearly in an extended manner about the world," says the F.S.M. credo. "It is ours to demand meaning; we must insist upon meaning!"

What is behind this manifestese? Does it betoken a desire to dismantle the University of California, or to establish a student soviet that would make all educational policy? The F.S.M. leaders disclaim such grandiose ideas.

"This is not a matter of rolling back the multiversity," says Myra Jehlen. "But it is our view that this university does neglect its students. We have no contact with the community of scholars, except to see a professor across 500 feet of lecture hall. Teaching assistants have to serve as parents for the students."

Savio deplores the extent to which the university's professors and facilities are involved in research for the Government and giant corporations. "It is a distortion, and too bad, that the university does not stand apart from the society as it is. It would be good to return to an almost totally autonomous body of scholars and students. But what we have now is that the Pentagon, the oil and aircraft companies, the farm interests and their representatives in the Regents consider the university as a public utility, one of the resources they can look on as part of their business."

And who should run things? Says Starobin: "Our idea is that the university is composed of faculty, students, books and ideas. In a literal sense, the administration is merely there to make sure the sidewalks are kept clean. It should be the servant of the faculty and the students. We want a redemocratizing of the university. Courses are clearly up to the faculty, but students should be able to convey their ideas. Dormitory regulations should be up to the students who live in the dorms. A bipartite or tripartite committee should have the final say in promulgating minimal rules on the time, place and manner of political activity."

There was much, much more before I asked whether they felt that the turmoil had accomplished anything. Myra Jehlen answered first: "Of course, you never win finally. New problems will always arise. But there has been a great strengthening of democratic institutions on the campus. The kind of actions we've taken, the important function of students in society—these have been vindicated. Yes, we have won, though how much is not clear."

Savio was more succinct: "We committed the unpardonable sin of being moral and being successful."

The setting was very different that evening when I visited Kerr at his home in El Cerrito, five miles from the campus. It is a glass-walled ranch house on a lofty bluff overlooking the Bay. Velvety lawns roll down to an old quarry in the canyon far below. There is a swimming pool, and flowers, shrubs and vines grow in junglelike profusion in a great glass-roofed patio.

But Kerr is not a man for rich living, even though his salary of $45,000 a year puts him $900 ahead of Governor Edmund Brown as the state's highest-paid official. He is frugal even of time. If Kerr gets to an airport and discovers the plane will be 15 minutes late, he is furious at the lost time. But if it will be an hour late, he is contented; he will sit quietly in a corner of the airport, begin writing memos, speeches, articles or even a chapter for a book.

Kerr works with the same intensity at home. Each afternoon a squad of eight secretaries at his office in University Hall pack a great sheaf of papers into a cardboard box. A driver returns them before noon the next day. Each carries a notation in green ink written in an incredibly pinched, yet distinct, hand—the marching orders by which the biggest of big universities is run.

The commander's invariable uniform is a navy blue suit and white shirt. His mind has extraordinary range and a rare capacity for turning discord into consensus. Kerr ranks among the country's half-dozen most effective peacemakers in the volatile realm of labor-management warfare—a skill that has prompted every President since Harry S Truman to enlist his help. In the middle of the disturbances at Berkeley, President Johnson asked him to accept appointment as Secretary of Health, Education and Welfare. All Kerr will say about that or any other post is that he still expects to be president of Cal on its centenary in 1968.

Among the many ironies of the Berkeley explosions is that Kerr now finds himself under savage attack from the left after more than a decade of demands for his ouster by right-wing critics. Leading the fight against a loyalty oath, he became so popular with the rest of the Berkeley faculty that in 1952, when the Regents decided to restore the goodwill they had lost in two bitter years, they named Kerr as chancellor. In 1959, a year after the Regents moved him up to president, Kerr again aroused right-wing ire by granting an honorary degree to Prof. Edward C. Tolman, who had been forced to resign for refusing to sign the oath. A year later he induced the Regents to name a new building in Tolman's honor.

When Berkeley students were arrested in 1960 for disrupting a hearing of the House Un-American Activities Committee in San Francisco, Kerr resisted demands to suspend or expel the demonstrators. He ignored similar conservative outcries last summer when undergraduates were arrested for a civil-rights sit-in at the Sheraton-Palace Hotel.

The liberalization of faculty and student rights during the Kerr administration earned for him and the Regents the American Association of University Professors' 1964 Alexander Meiklejohn award for conspicuous contributions to academic freedom. Less than six months later he was being denounced as an enemy of free expression by many on his own campus.

Kerr was not consulted on the fateful order shutting the Bancroft Strip. He was in Tokyo on his way home from a seven-week economic mission to the Iron Curtain countries on the day it was issued.

"It was perfectly apparent," Kerr says, "that the decision was a mistake, both in the action itself and in the way it was done. There was no advance consultation with the students, the over-all university administration or anyone else. When a privilege had been extended as long as that had been, there should have been consultation—and especially against the background of an impending national election and intense student involvement in civil rights."

(A Dostoevskian bit of background, still unknown to the students: Kerr foresaw in September, 1959, that the Strip would eventually be a source of trouble because there was no logical basis for exempting it from the no-politics rule that applied everywhere else on campus. He got the Regents to agree that it ought to be turned over to the city for use as a public plaza. But, for reasons still unexplained, the university's treasurer never carried out the instructions to deed over the Strip. If he had, the whole melancholy chain of events might never have begun.)

Kerr agrees with the F.S.M. thesis that students should have as much political freedom as anyone else in the community. The only difference is that he thinks they already have it. In his judgment, the rules governing political expression on campus, including the right to invite heretics of all political persuasions to speak at student meetings, give Berkeley undergraduates more freedom than bank clerks, factory workers or 99 per cent of the general citizenry.

He ridicules the notion that the university has been succumbing to the "power structure" in the dispute over civil-rights activity. "I had to fight some extremely tough battles against some very powerful legislators who felt we should kick out students who were arrested for sit-ins in the Bay area, but we never yielded an inch," Kerr says. "It just would not have been in character for us to say that the only place the students could fight for Negro rights was in Mississippi."

As for the Bancroft Strip, Kerr says that "whatever pressure preceded the order involved the loading of the galleries at the Republican convention with Berkeley students whooping it up for Scranton against Goldwater."

The F.S.M. indictment of the "multiversity" brings a special twinge to Kerr because every charge the insurgents now raise he foresaw with greater incisiveness as long ago as April, 1963, when he gave the Godkin lectures at Harvard.

Those talks described, with apparent fatalism but decided unenthusiasm, the evolution of a "mechanism held together by administrative rules and powered by money." Kerr predicted that undergraduates would feel so neglected and depersonalized that the revolt they once engaged in against the faculty *in loco parentis* would turn into an even more destructive uprising against the faculty *in absentia*. Everything Kerr warned of then is embodied now in the F.S.M. lament that the student is being down-graded to the status of an I.B.M. punch card in a computerized multiversity.

Kerr concedes that the multiversity is a disturbing place for many students, but he disputes that it is devoid of meaning. "One of the advantages of a big city or a big university— as against a smaller and more monolithic closed community— is that people can find those things which may mean something to them," he says. "They are given a choice.

"It would be terribly stultifying to find yourself in a place which has a single meaning, and that meaning is the same for everyone. The only kind of society that has only a single meaning is an authoritarian one. It seems to me that is a place where you would really expect rebellion. Essentially, what the

F.S.M. are saying is that they are rebelling against freedom of choice."

When I noted that the students objected not to too many meanings, but to the absence of any, Kerr replied:

"In fact, there is a lot of opportunity to participate, only it takes a little longer and requires more initiative to find it. Many tend to be overwhelmed by their opportunities; there are so many lectures to choose from, so many things to do, that they tend to become lost. They are torn too many ways and wind up condemning the whole structure."

The notion that the university, for all the magnitude of its Federal and industrial involvement (it is receiving $246 million this year for operating three giant atomic installations, plus $175 million in research grants and contracts), has become an arm of the Pentagon or big business also draws a rebuttal from Kerr. "The university," he says, "is intertwined with all society. And if it is overbalanced in any direction as compared with the surrounding society, it is in the fact that it is a source of dissent and social criticism. You could say it is a tool of the critics, and that is one of the things that make it so dynamic."

All this brought us back to the students' overriding complaint—the enormous size of Berkeley, with 27,500 students on a single campus, and the obliteration of the individual's relationship to faculty and administration. Kerr's answer dwelt more on society's inescapable needs than confidence that alienation could be overcome.

"Every day makes it clearer that the university's invisible product, knowledge, is likely to be the most powerful single element in our culture," he says. "With so many young people pounding at our gates, we're up against a tremendous assignment. To take the position that we won't grow would be a terribly irresponsible thing."

Kerr is a philosopher-pragmatist of the technocratic society, probably the ablest and most creative in the educational field. His guiding principle is individual disengagement. He preaches the idea that each person can best protect his own happiness in a society of bigness by developing pluralistic attachments.

"If you invest all of yourself in an institution," he says, "you become a slave. It becomes a prison, not an agency of liberation." This road to the independent spirit is just the opposite of that traveled by the F.S.M. and its leaders. Their goal is commitment, but there is a good deal of confusion about precisely what it is they are committed to.

And who is listening, now that the clear-cut issue created by the closing of the Bancroft Strip and the blackout of political recruiting has been resolved? The signs are that the overwhelming support for F.S.M. aims among students of all political hues and of no hues has evaporated along with the issue.

Moreover, there are strong indications of strain inside the F.S.M. steering committee, now a much more ingrown group than in the initial days of across-the-board coalition. Many would like to disband the movement. Hal Draper said frankly that it might go into "an inactive phase." Ed Rosenfeld, the F.S.M.'s press officer, says that one thought under consideration is to establish a cooperative coffeehouse, on a nonprofit basis, near the campus. "It would be a civilized gathering place in the best European manner," he says, "a suitable forum for debates and discussion."

Back at the heliport for the return flight, I tried to evaluate the Berkeley uprising against the memories of my own days of rebellion as president of the C.C.N.Y. class of '31. It was a time when one worker in four was jobless and the misery of the Great Depression was beginning to grip the land. We had been ready to picket our own commencement in cap and gown, but we chickened out at the last minute for fear of losing our degrees.

These students, for all their talk of setting up an espresso joint as a monument to their mutiny, were a tougher, smarter breed, more ready to go for broke.

But what did they accomplish, besides effecting the cancellation of an order the university admits never should have been issued?

They have done one important thing that may prove of considerable help to Berkeley and all other big universities.

They have cut through the multifarious concerns of an administration that must deal with every agency of government, including those in 50 countries abroad, and forced it to recognize that it is sitting on a volcano of neglected, seething students.

Kerr, who has always recognized the need for diversity in multiversity, already is hard at work on measures to improve the quality and the immediacy of instruction. He aims to break down the idea that research, not teaching, is the mission of the good professor. Both roles are vital, Kerr believes, and so does the man he has brought in as acting chancellor, Dean Martin Meyerson of the College of Environmental Design.

Last fall's earthquake also has shaken the administration and faculty into a heightened awareness of the need for teamwork to lessen the students' belief that no one cares whether they go or stay, that undergraduate needs are passed over in favor of lucrative research contracts, book-writing projects and traveling lectureships all over the world. Prof. Arthur M. Ross, the enterprising chairman of an emergency executive committee elected by the faculty in the blackest period last December, expresses confidence that a genuine educational overhaul is in prospect. Most of his colleagues agree.

What goes into the curriculum and who teaches what courses will be a matter for the faculty to determine, but both Kerr and Ross feel students can have a useful advisory role. A larger area of authority for students in disciplinary committees and in other forms of self-government also is in prospect. All these developments should help still the discord at Berkeley, but—much more important—they will help make it a better institution of learning.

One of the imponderables in trying to guess whether peace has really come to the campus is that some F.S.M. activists obviously have developed a vested interest in finding things to fight about. They seem to operate on the theory that, in a system they believe is basically corrupt, the worse things get, the easier it will be to generate mass resistance.

This is not a novel theory in radical movements, but it is

not one that makes for stability. When the police dragged Savio and the 800 others out of Sproul Hall, he exulted, "This is wonderful—wonderful. We'll bring the university to our terms." When Paul Jacobs told an F.S.M. leader that he had advised Kerr to enter Sproul on the night of the sit-in and talk to the students (advice Kerr did not take), the insurgent asked sourly, "What side are you on?"

The reckless prodigality with which the F.S.M. uses the weapon of civil disobedience raises problems no university can deal with adequately. Mass discipline carried the danger of martyrdom and a spread of sympathetic disorders to other campuses.

Garrisoning the grounds with police runs so counter to the essential concept of the university as a redoubt of tolerance and reason that it is perhaps the worst solution of all. At Berkeley it brought the faculty into open alliance with the students against the administration. Yet, the alternative of giving students total immunity could engender a situation akin to that in the University of Caracas, where student revolutionaries use the campus as a fortress from which to sally forth to attack the general society.

"We fumbled, we floundered, and the worst thing is I still don't know how we should have handled it," Kerr acknowledges. "At any other university the administrators wouldn't have known how to handle it any better."

Menacing as is this new disruptive device, one even graver danger sign outranks all others raised by the mess at Berkeley. That is the degree to which it evidences a sense of lost identity, a revulsion against bigness, that is affecting all of our society. On the campus it takes the form of antagonism against the multiversity. In the mass production unions this same feeling of impending obliteration recently spurred rank-and-file strikes against General Motors and Ford, and may erupt again in the basic steel industry this spring. The longshoremen, fearing the shiny face of automation, voted down contracts that gave them lifetime job security and a generous wage guarantee—principally because they felt the machine was grinding them and their jobs into nothingness.

A similar mood of irrationality, of vaporous but paralyzing

apprehension, stalks all our institutions in a time of unmatched material prosperity and individual well-being. Young people, in particular, study the unemployment statistics and decide that society is in a conspiracy to provide security for the older generation at the expense of the youngsters outside waiting to get in. Education is the magic carpet over the hurdles that make the dropout the shutout in our society. But, even at this most distinguished of universities, bigness robs many students of individual dignity or purpose. This feeling helps explain the spread of drug addiction and senseless crime among many well-to-do youngsters. All are part of an alienation that turns even affluence and security into worthless prizes.

This may prove to be the nation's critical challenge, potentially more damaging than the international crises that monopolize so much of our concern and our budget. If Berkeley cannot imbue life with a sense of fulfillment and content, where will we find it? Kerr, the mediator-innovator, must become a gladiator—pioneering new paths in intergroup relations and giving new vitality to democratic standards that rest on knowledge.

What Happened at Berkeley

NATHAN GLAZER

Nathan Glazer is Professor of Sociology at Berkeley. He is the author of The Social Basis of American Communism *and* American Judaism, *and co-author of* The Lonely Crowd (*with David Riesman and Reuel Denney*) *and* Beyond the Melting Pot (*with Daniel P. Moynihan*).

As I write this, in late December, we in Berkeley are in the Christmas lull. The university's 18,000 undergraduates are for the most part at home, many of the faculty and even some of the graduate students are away. But despite the quiet, the campus is full. The American Physical Society is meeting, which probably explains why it is still difficult to find a parking space even with a faculty sticker ($72 a year). For the first time in weeks, the steps of Sproul Hall, the administration building, are bare of demonstrators and loudspeakers, the entries to the campus are empty of tables collecting money, students handing out literature, or posters announcing meetings. But faculty studies, teaching-assistant rooms, and libraries are busy and show no signs that this a holiday.

The Regents of the University of California met the day before the Christmas recess began, declared that they "do not contemplate that advocacy or content of speech [on the Berkeley campus] shall be restricted beyond the purview of the First and Fourteenth Amendments to the Constitution," and set up a committee to review university policies in consultation with faculty and students "with the intent of providing maximum freedom consistent with individual and group responsibility." (After an earlier meeting, on November 20, during which thousands of students were sitting outside being led by Joan Baez in singing, the Regents had said that their policy was to make campus facilities available for "planning, implementing or raising funds or recruiting participants for lawful off-campus action, not for unlawful. . . .") The Emergency Executive Committee of the Berkeley Division of the Academic Senate (the faculty) issued an optimistic statement after the Regents' meeting, asserting that substantial progress had been made.

Despite all this, I—and many other faculty members—are filled with foreboding. We see neither a clear nor a near end to the crisis. And I am afraid it will not be easy for our friends in other places to understand what is going on here; it is hardly possible for those of us closest to it to agree on an interpretation.

To begin with, we must dispose of the ingeniously simple slogan of "free speech" which has made it possible for so many who are far from the events at Berkeley to send in forthright statements in support of the Free Speech Movement or the position adopted by the Faculty on December

8 (that political advocacy or organization should be limited only by minimum regulations designed to permit the university to function normally). Those of us who watched the Free Speech Movement (FSM) daily set up its loud-speakers on the steps of the administration building to denounce the President, the Chancellor, the newspapers, the Regents, the faculty, and the structure and organization of society in general and universities in particular, could only admire the public-relations skill exhibited in the choice of a name for the student movement. Life, however, is not so simple as to present us with a classic free speech issue on the shores of San Francisco Bay.

During 1963–64, my first year as a teacher at Berkeley, student political activity was vigorous beyond anything I had recently seen at any other American college. In front of the concrete posts that mark the main pedestrian entrance to the campus from the busy intersection of Telegraph Avenue and Bancroft Way, one could find, on an ordinary school day, students handing out leaflets advertising many different kinds of political meetings and actions, to be held on the campus itself and off it as well. Various student groups would set up tables stacked with literature, both free and for sale, and members of the group would be available at the tables for discussion, information, and argument. The chief groups represented were socialists—evolutionary, revolutionary, and ambiguous; civil rights organizations such as CORE, or Friends of SNCC; Young Democrats; Young Republicans; and Conservatives. One could expect to come upon supporters of Khrushchev or Mao, Castro or Ho Chi-Minh, marijuana or LSD, not to mention the more garden-variety political and social positions. (We smiled then at the backwardness of Eastern campuses where straight sex was still an issue; only homosexuality or perversion, it seemed, could make an issue at Berkeley.) Outdoor meetings were also held at this same location, often as preludes to expeditions to San Francisco, Oakland, and downtown Berkeley to picket business establishments which had failed to negotiate or sign an agreement with CORE or some other civil-rights organization. On the campus itself, large posters were always in evidence announcing a great variety of events, many of them political. Berkeley was one of the few places in the country, I imagine, where in 1964 one could hear a public debate between the supporters of Khrushchev and Mao on the Sino-Soviet dispute— there were organized student groups behind both positions.

Of course regulations existed, administered by deans of students, which these groups had to observe in conducting their activities on campus. For example, the university required 72 hours' notice for visiting speakers. If a speaker was controversial, the university would demand that a tenured member of the faculty chair the meeting. On occasion, disputes broke out between the university and a student group over who should pay for putting out the chairs on Dwinelle Plaza (the open-air area in the center of campus where particularly large meetings are held), or whether a student group sponsoring a speaker who was expected to draw a large crowd (for example, Malcolm X) should be required to pay for police protection. These disputes were perhaps portents of what was to come, but the regulations did not seem to inhibit a degree of political activity that was perhaps unique on American campuses.

Nor did they inhibit a number of actions that can only be considered questionable political stunts. Thus, Slate, a student political party, decided that it would be a good idea to bring the West Coast leader of the American Nazi party to the university. He spoke in the largest enclosed space on campus, the men's gym. I do not recall any objections from the administration. The morning of his talk, young men and women wearing Nazi uniforms were posted at the chief entrances to the campus, handing out leaflets announcing the meeting. Later I heard an intense argument between two students at one of the entrances; it transpired that the young Nazi-clad figures were not really Nazis, but adherents of the liberal-progressive Slate, who had hit upon this as a clever way to publicize the meeting.

On another occasion, Slate invited the chief western organizer for the John Birch Society—I chaired that meeting. One could only conclude that inviting Communists to the Berkeley campus had become pretty tame, and an aspiring progressive organization had to invite John Birchers and Nazis to get an audience or to assert its absolute belief in free speech. But whatever one thought of this particular tack adopted by Slate, it was clear that free speech prevailed on the Berkeley campus.

It turned out, at the beginning of the fall semester of 1964, that this grand chaos—as it appeared—of oratory, advocacy, and action, was based on a tangle of distinctions that only the administrative staff that dealt with regulations affecting student organizations, and the leaders of the organizations they regulated, understood—and perhaps not even they. The regulations go back to a time when no political activity of any kind was allowed on campus. Under this earlier situation, even candidates for the Presidency were not allowed to speak at Berkeley: to have permitted such a thing would presumably have involved the university in "politics," and as a state university it was not supposed to be involved in politics. But gradually these rules were qualified and changed to the point where the Berkeley campus, like all other campuses that are proud of their devotion to the principle of free speech, was allowed to have Communist speakers. Largely as a result of such changes, last spring President Clark Kerr was given the Alexander Meiklejohn award by the American Association of University Professors for having made a major contribution to academic freedom.

But through all these modifications of earlier restrictions, a distinction was maintained. The campus was a place for "free speech." It was not, however, a place for advocacy,[1] for organization, or for collecting money. Thus an "off-campus" political organization (like CORE) could run a meeting "on-campus" but would have to explain to those present that certain kinds of discussion (for example, on implementing a demonstration) must be held off-campus. This was not as great a hardship as it might have been in other colleges or universities, where the campus is separated physically from the town (as is Stanford) or where the community possesses few meeting places suitable for student groups. Further, just as

Berkeley is required to be free of "politics," it is also required to be free of religion in all forms—proselytization, worship, or even the organizational activities of student religious groups. The city of Berkeley, however, surrounds the university. And across the street which marks off campus from city, there is a row of institutions—YMCA, Methodist, Jewish, Episcopalian, etc.—which have often been available for political meetings banned on campus.

But to return to the distinction that underlay the regulations (or that some people in the administration believed underlay them)—that is, between "speech" on the one hand, and "advocacy and organization" on the other: traditionally, the chief area for advocacy was the sidewalk in front of the concrete posts which mark the boundary of the university. This was also the area where impromptu meetings would precede the march to the picket lines and the demonstration sites. But at the beginning of the fall semester of 1964, the university administration decided to enforce the distinction between "speech" and "advocacy and organization" on the strip of sidewalk in front of the posts (which is also the property of the Regents of the University of California).

Various reasons for this decision have been given. The administration at first asserted that the number of tables and meetings had become so great as to interfere with traffic. The students argued that there were more forceful reasons. During the preceding summer, while the Republican Convention met at the Cow Palace, students were recruited here not only for the usual civil rights activities (which included in this case blocking the entrances to the Cow Palace for a while) but to pack the galleries for Scranton. During that summer, in addition, civil rights demonstrators decided to move against the Oakland *Tribune*, owned by the family of former Senator Knowland, and the students charged that it was his complaint that led the administration to ban "advocacy and organization" on the strip of sidewalk in question.

There now began a conflict between two very unevenly matched opponents: the student political organizations and the administration of the Berkeley campus of the University of California. Berkeley has a long history of student agitation for the widening of freedom of political action on campus. This history has involved petition, picketing, demonstrating, research and argument, and the like. Many alumni of these efforts are still on and around the campus. A number of lawyers, in and outside the law school, have been involved in such past disputes and know them in detail. But the present student constellation differs markedly from that of only a few years ago, and thus a radically new style was adopted for this newest conflict with the administration over political activity.

The great new factor has, of course, been the civil rights movement, and particularly the development of the new techniques of civil disobedience, which opened up the lunch counters of the South and then spread to the North. Nowhere have these techniques been adopted with more enthusiasm and success than in the Bay Area. Last year hundreds of Berkeley students—along with students from San Francisco State College and elsewhere, and non-students as well—"sat-in" at a chain of lunch counters, "shopped-in" at a chain of supermarkets (they would fill a cart with groceries, let the clerk reckon the total on his machine, and then leave the mess of groceries on the counter, insouciantly declaring they did not have the money to pay for them), "slept-in" at the Sheraton Palace Hotel, lay down in the automobile showrooms of Van Ness Avenue. This activity led in each case to an agreement to hire a certain number of Negro workers. It also led in some cases to mass arrests and mass trials, which seriously strained the court system of San Francisco. The fact that the state of California has a law banning discrimination in employment and a commission devoted to ending discrimination in employment seemed to leave the demonstrators unmoved. Indeed, they often insisted that they themselves rather than the state agency should police the agreements they had won from the employers.

The civil rights movement created a situation among the student political groups on campus quite different from the one which had prevailed when such groups were fighting for the loosening of the strict regulations which once governed their political activity. Besides introducing new tactics, the civil rights movement developed a large body of students committed to these tactics, and a substantial body of public opinion—in the faculty and among the liberal population of the area—sympathetic to them. Admittedly, Berkeley was ideally suited to serve the expansion of the radical civil rights movement in the North. It had never been affected to the extent other colleges were by the mood of the "silent generation" of the 50's. (In 1960, remember, when the House Un-American Activities Committee met in San Francisco City Hall, hundreds of Berkeley students were willing to attempt to disrupt its hearings.) Indeed, in 1957, when I visited Berkeley for the first time, a number of socialist youth leaders from the East had just migrated here, because they found the political climate peculiarly congenial to their work. (In addition, it was my impression that Communism too retained more life and relevance in the Bay Area than in the East.) Some of these socialist youth leaders became students; some worked at the university; others worked in the community, becoming part of the penumbra of campus life which at Berkeley involves many people who are neither students, faculty, nor staff, but who may have been part of the university at one time in the past and who possibly will again be part of it in the future.

The strains produced by the application of the new tactics in the mild racial climate of San Francisco had already been intense. Was the Bay Area Mississippi, it was asked, that actions had to be taken which destroyed private businesses when there was legal redress for the wrongs that the students believed existed? Few people in public life thought so. Even many liberals were troubled, and during 1963–64, some state legislators and others demanded that the university move against the students who had been arrested in civil-rights actions. President Kerr refused, asserting that what students did off-campus was their business, so long as they did not use campus facilities for it. Here again was the distinction between speech on the one hand and advocacy and organization on the other. On this distinction the President, the Regents, and Chancellor Strong of the Berkeley campus apparently hoped to ride out the hard year ahead, while student leaders were attempting to produce the degree of chaos in the surrounding community that they calculated was necessary to achieve fair treatment for Negroes.

When the Chancellor's office passed on to the lesser members of the administrative hierarchy the decision that the strip of land on Bancroft Way outside the concrete posts was now to become subject *de facto* (as it had been *de jure*) to the university ban on advocacy, collection, and organization, the student leaders and their constituencies were already attuned to and experienced in the use of the new tactics. The first rank of the administrative hierarchy to deal with the new regulations, on the other hand, were deans who up till now, one assumes, had been concerned principally with such matters as lock-out rules in female dormitories. Initially the student groups protested the new regulations to these deans. They were immediately able to show that the distinction between "speech" and "advocacy" was difficult or impossible to maintain and ridiculous in an election year; they also showed that traffic could easily flow despite the tables. The administration withdrew somewhat; tables were permitted and advocacy was allowed, but collection and organization were still prohibited. This was unsatisfactory to the students, who resorted to a direct test of whether the administration would enforce the new regulations: they set up their tables and collected money. A number were then directed to appear before a dean on September 29 to discuss these violations. The official account of the Chancellor to the faculty, presented a few weeks later, will suggest something of the quality of the ensuing confrontation:

> At 3 o'clock that afternoon some 300–400 students moved into the second floor of Sproul Hall and Mario Savio announced that all of them acknowledged violating University regulations in the same manner as those students who had been instructed to make appointments with the Dean of Students, and they all wanted similar appointments. The Dean of Men declared that he was then concerned only with observed violations, and if students wanted appointments they could leave their names and he would determine

if and when such could be made. He also asked [the students who had been observed in violations] to go in and see a dean because each was involved in a matter of personal discipline, and requested that the crowd disperse, since he had scheduled a meeting of the leaders of the student organizations and their advisers to discuss the problem at 4 o'clock. Savio responded that the group would not leave unless they were guaranteed that the same disciplinary action would be meted out to all there. Unable to make such guarantees, the Dean of Men again asked the group to leave, and later announced that since, in the opinion of the administration and some of the advisers of the student groups who had come to attend the 4:00 meeting, the environment was not conducive to reasonable discussion, the meeting was cancelled. . . . The group remained in Sproul Hall until 2:40 in the morning.

In this way, what had originally been a protest by all the student political groups—from revolutionary socialist to extreme conservative—was transformed very early into a movement run by the civil rights leaders. For as soon as the tactics of the protest "escalated" into questionably legal activities (like sitting-in at Sproul Hall, which was done for the first time on September 29) the right-wingers could not go along. They were still part of the protest movement for a few more days. But they stood aside from further escalations—the surrounding of the campus police car containing an arrested prisoner on October 1, the loose and then the tight sit-in at Sproul Hall that day which prevented the deans from leaving or anyone from entering, the decision to maintain the sit-in around the police car throughout October 2. By that time, it was clear that the leadership of the movement was now coming exclusively from the civil rights and left-wing political groups. But there were too few students directly committed to the left-wing groups to provide the necessary "bodies"—to use the term popular with the civil rights leaders. Only the civil rights groups, and only with the good issues handed to them by administration action, could raise hundreds ready to sit-in.

On October 2, the movement won its first great victory—
the withdrawal of the menacing array of police that had been
concentrated on the campus, and a meeting with Clark Kerr
in which a pact was signed calling for an administration-
faculty-student committee to deal with the issue of political
activity. At this meeting with President Kerr, the right-wing
and religious student groups were still represented. Then the
Free Speech Movement, at a marathon two-day meeting, organized itself officially, and from that meeting neither the
right-wing nor the religious groups emerged with any positions
of leadership. More than that, the Young Democrats and even
the right-wing Socialists, who had played an important role
in the demonstration around the police car, were excluded.
In a pattern similar to other and grander revolutions, the student uprising had moved to the left—into the control of the
civil rights leaders identified with direct action, and of the
leaders of groups in a direct or indirect line of descent from
the Communist and Trotskyist student political groups of the
past. As for the followers, they mainly came from students
involved in or touched by the civil rights movement.

If the leadership of the student movement was rapidly concentrated into a coherent and tightly knit cadre, sharing very
much the same philosophy and outlook, the other elements
of the university community were split and in disarray. Let
us look first at the "administration." Where in the history of
American higher education has the administration of a university loomed so large as at Berkeley? In the past, presidents,
faculties, and boards of trustees have been important—but
administrations? This is another sense in which Berkeley may
be unique; and yet one fears that the future of American
higher education may be foreshadowed here. Everyone—arriving faculty members, arriving deans, visiting authorities—
is astonished by the size of the administration at Berkeley,
and in the statewide University of California. One large building near the campus is completely devoted to the statewide
administration, another on the campus to the Berkeley administration. The title "dean," which at other universities carries
dignity, is used at Berkeley to cover a wide variety of jobs,
only some of them academic (where the traditional dignity

still attaches to the title), but many deans have not come up through the faculty and have little to do with it. They deal with student affairs. For presumably 27,000 students provide a good number of non-academic problems which neither the faculty nor the academic deans would want to be bothered with.

Academic matters are handled by the academic deans and their assistants. The size of these staffs is impressive, and unfortunately—given certain conditions—necessary. Many students move to Berkeley from other campuses of the state university, from state colleges, from junior colleges, from other institutions outside the state. Each institution has its own requirements—for entrance, for graduation, for majors—and the work done elsewhere therefore has to be evaluated and harmonized to the Berkeley requirements. The evaluations are often argued and fought over, and the student is often frustrated in his fight. In the end a bureaucracy is probably the only system by which a vast number of cases can be managed equitably. Yet while the rules may be just, the sense of justice done is rarely communicated by a clerk or an assistant dean's determination. Could we operate with a smaller administration? Very likely. Yet one thinks of such matters as vast numbers of migrating undergraduates to be fitted into the university, and thousands of graduate students, a large proportion of whom are also employees receiving regular checks for research assistantships, teaching assistantships, fellowships. There are also hundreds of new faculty members every year, each of whom has had to be passed on by various committees. There are scores of research institutes, hundreds of research contracts, each involving separate budgets, all to be coordinated. It is difficult to communicate any sense of the scale of the administration at Berkeley. Let me give a personal report: when I arrived in Berkeley after working for the Federal Government, my feeling was that the quality of the two settings—organization piled upon organization, reaching to a mysterious empyrean height—was remarkably similar. I understood from other faculty members that this was rather new, that it was only in recent years that the administration had become so huge.

Ironically, President Kerr, in his Godkin lectures,[2] has offered the best general text—perhaps the only existing one—on what is happening. The students have been among its most avid readers, and have not shared the admiration of some reviewers of the book who see in the University of California, as described by its President, the democratic university of the future, combining high standards and mass education. President Kerr describes the shift from the liberal arts college offering a humane education, to the early university which trained men in the traditional professions and for scholarship and college teaching, to the modern "federal grant" university, half of whose budget may come from federal research grants.

It would be an error to think of these grants as being devoted only to warmaking and to statecraft. Vast sums flow for social and psychological and policy research, research as useful to a benign welfare state—or, for that matter, a modern authoritarian state—as to a cold-war America. Obviously, however, the federal grant university is not entirely dependent on federal grants. All undergraduate and graduate teaching is covered by state funds, and in many departments—languages, philosophy, history, English, art, and music—little if any part of faculty salaries comes from research grants. Nevertheless, the effect of the federal millions is larger than one would suspect from a direct accounting of where the money goes. The research funds strengthen the university's capacity to compete for faculty, for they allow members to be relieved from teaching and to supplement their regular nine-month salary from a research budget during the summer. These funds also permit the recruitment of greater numbers of graduate students, who normally expect to be supported out of research and teaching assistantships—and even if the latter are covered by state funds, the students are there because federal money will eventually support their own research.

It is easy to conclude that everyone benefits from this except the undergraduate, whose instruction is largely in the hands of teaching assistants. And yet a year ago, when I was spending my first term on the Berkeley campus, I could not find much restiveness or resentment among the undergraduates. Indeed, several told me they preferred Berkeley to the junior colleges and state colleges from which they had come, despite the fact that a layer of graduate students was interposed between them and the professional staff. And they said that the lectures at Berkeley were more stimulating despite the size of the classes. Of course, such undergraduates had moved to Berkeley from schools with smaller classes for other reasons besides the quality of the education, whatever that might be: the life of the campus and the college town around it was undoubtedly a great attraction.

But resentment ran higher, I would judge, among graduate students, many of whom discovered that their professors were just as busy when it came to bothering with them as they were where undergraduates were concerned. Once again the pleasurable environment of learning had escaped them; they were working hard as research assistants and teaching assistants, on other men's research and courses, but they were denied the satisfaction of an intellectual community which brought students and teachers together. Their relations with faculty were too often quite businesslike, the exchanges of services for money. And how could it be otherwise when the professors were burdened with so many governmental, teaching, administrative, and research duties?

Resentment also ran high among the faculty. Many remembered an easier life as junior faculty, on the Berkeley campus or elsewhere. They could not understand why they were always so busy, and found that scholarly labors could best proceed away from the campus. Thus many protected themselves from their students and their colleagues by working at home. But there was another source of resentment for them—the incorporation of Berkeley, which had previously enjoyed a good deal of independence, into the structure of the statewide university, with its eight or nine campuses and its statewide administration, trying to coordinate the varied institutions that had been brought together or were coming into existence as parts of the University of California. Berkeley's incorporation meant that in one matter after another which affected faculty —the shift from semesters to quarters, the setting of standards of admission, the distribution of students among campuses—decisions could be and were taken that were not the decisions the faculty, or individual members of it, wanted.

As a result of these changes, and as a result of the administration's insensitivity to the problems involved, a degree of distance developed between statewide and campus administration, between administration and faculty, between faculty and students, that may well have been unique in American education. The question we must ask, however, before distributing blame is this: given the need or the desire to create an enormous system of statewide university education, how could such a situation have been avoided?

Certainly the faculty, while complaining of the inaccessibility of the administration and its insensitivity to faculty needs, was not very responsive on its own part to student needs. A public meeting some of us ran on the problems of education at Berkeley last year was attended by only a handful of faculty (and not much more than a handful of undergraduates and graduate students). The faculty does not respond enthusiastically to occasional efforts by the administration to get it to consider ways of improving undergraduate education. But at the same time it must be said that faculty members generally censor their impulses to educational reform because they are aware of the many barriers that would have to be vaulted to get the change through. The new faculty member learns rapidly enough that if he devotes himself to his research, his courses, and his pro forma service on committees, he is doing all that is expected of him—and all that any reasonable man, in the prevailing system, would want to undertake.

The university administration, then, was both rigid—as we all knew from experience—and fragile—as we discovered in the crisis raised by its attempt to change the *de facto* rules governing student political activity. For in the situation created first by reasonable student demands and secondly by new and radical student tactics, the administration showed itself incapable of consistent, decisive, or effective action.

Again and again it was forced to withdraw from positions either because they were poor ones, or poorly argued and defended, or because the higher levels (the President) moved in and changed the positions taken lower down (the Chancellor).

The confusion above, a confusion veiled by silence and inaccessibility, could only increase by geometric progression down below. Asked to enforce policies about whose rationale and stability they were uncertain, the deans could only put up a very poor show, and in the course of the crisis the student leaders—having discovered very early how to break through to the top—treated them with greater and greater insolence and arrogance. Rapidly becoming more expert in the techniques of organization and publicity, these leaders soon added a powerful wing to their original movement—the graduate students. They soon discovered too that there was little to fear in breaking the rules, for the faculty was so unsympathetic to the administration and its rigid and mechanical handling of the problem that, while it would not at first directly support the students and their tactics, it was always ready to attack the administration.

The next casualties were the Chancellor and the Vice-Chancellors. As early as October 2 the President, ignoring the advice and actions of the Chancellor's office, had intervened to make a direct pact with the students—which the Chancellor was expected to carry out. More important than the structure of authority which permitted the Chancellor to be overridden was the fact that neither he nor his staff could come up with a leader to handle a political crisis for which a close study of the French and Russian revolutions might well have provided the only suitable training. Certainly there was no one at this level who could influence the students or deal effectively with them. Nor, as it turned out, was there anyone at this level who could deal effectively with the faculty and convince them that the matter was being handled intelligently or morally. On at least two important occasions faculty members— including myself—who did not support the tactics of the students felt that the administration had acted against the spirit or the letter of an agreement in trying to discipline student leaders. In both cases it was unclear whether it was the Chancellor,

the President, or the Board of Regents—the highest authority
—who had ordered the action. But whatever the facts, the
Chancellor's authority was weakened by these incidents.

We must now speak in more detail about the role of the
faculty. At the start, the faculty for the most part looked upon
the conflict between the administration and the students as
detached and neutral outsiders. From the beginning, however,
groups of faculty members thrust themselves into the situation
as mediators. They (or some of them) were distinguished
from the great majority of their colleagues by the fact that
they had been involved in student politics in the past and remained interested in them in the present. The first such group
of mediators (of which I was one) helped to draw up the
pact of October 2. But we eventually joined the administration as casualties of the developing crisis. We became casualties, I believe, owing to the critical change in the issues of
the conflict that occurred around the beginning of November.
This change became apparent in the discussions of the faculty-
student-administration committee that had been set up by the
October 2 pact. For the first month there had been two fairly
straightforward issues: the attempt of the administration to
change the status quo, which all the student political groups,
left and right, and all interested faculty opposed; and secondly, the student tactics, which some of the student groups
and most of the interested faculty opposed, but which everyone agreed should not lead to disciplinary action (on the
ground that the original issue which had occasioned the tactics had been a just one). To my mind, these two problems
were settled when the administration's representatives on the
committee provisionally accepted a much wider range of political advocacy and organization on campus than had been
permitted before, and when a second committee (faculty)
set up under the October 2 pact called for the lifting of the
suspensions that had been pronounced against the students
who had violated the old regulations.

Until this point, the interested faculty members and the
student FSM leaders had stood together. But now the student
leaders and the administration raised a new issue, created by
the prospective liberalization of the rules. If the campus was
to be opened up for advocacy and organization, what of ad-

vocacy and organization that led to illegal actions or was designed to produce illegal actions? This was no abstract question. The administration's insistence on a line between the legal and illegal—a line it had not drawn when no advocacy or organization was permitted on campus—was immediately seen by the students as a threat to actions they were already planning (against the Oakland *Tribune,* various local merchants, etc.) and which in their minds were being held up by the involvement of their forces in the campus dispute. (They were, of course, aware of the large number of potential recruits they had attracted on the basis of the free-speech issue.) The student leaders fully expected further mass arrests as a result of these actions, and they hoped to protect their rear against university discipline.

On this issue of illegal action the faculty-student-administration committee split in November. The student representatives insisted on a specific guarantee that nothing they advocated or organized on campus would lead to any measures by the university against them or their organizations. The administration members insisted on the right to discipline individuals or organizations who advocated or organized illegal action. The faculty group proposed a formula which neither gave the students a specific guarantee of immunity nor the administration a specific ban against illegal action on campus. Under this formula the students would have conducted their demonstrations and sit-ins in all likelihood safe from university interference, for the university's policy of the year before had been not to discipline those arrested for civil rights activities and it seemed improbable that this policy would be changed. If, however, the university decided on a change, the students could have tested in the courts its right to punish them for illegal action advocated or organized on campus—a contingency which, they asserted, would be "against the 1st and 14th amendments" and would constitute "double jeopardy."

This course, which would have permitted the students to turn their attention to what they felt to be such critical substantive problems as discrimination on the Oakland *Tribune,* they rejected. Their movement would not give up the issue provided them by the split on the question of illegal action. Those faculty members like myself who had been sympathetic until this time, but now withdrew their support, were denounced orally and in print as "finks" and stooges of President Kerr (who had become the *bête noir* of the students, his hand seen in every move).

On this issue the students decided to abrogate the pact of October 2 (in which they had agreed to stick to legal action), pronounced (on their own authority) new rules to govern political activity on campus, and began to operate under them. The students now hoped that the Regents would give them what the committee set up under the pact of October 2 had not, but on November 20, the Regents insisted on maintaining the distinction between lawful and unlawful actions. At this point the student leaders split, some arguing for further drastic measures, others urging *de facto* acceptance of the new rules under which they had full freedom of action, but were threatened by the possibility of university punishment for illegal action. A new sit-in was staged at Sproul Hall, which involved only 300 students; the administration did not act against it, and it was called off after a few hours.

Then, on November 30, it was learned that the administration (Strong? Kerr? the Regents?) had summoned four student leaders to appear before the Faculty Committee on Student Conduct (advisory to the Chancellor) to hear charges against them stemming from their tussles with the police on October 1 and 2. As a result of this blunder, an issue that was capable of arousing the students—the disciplining of their leaders—was fortuitously tied to one that could not—immunity for advocacy or organization of illegal action. The rest of the story has been covered by the national news media. Once again, on December 2, Joan Baez—no other figure in the United States could better symbolize the tangle of protests, amorphous and specific, that moved the students—sang with them as they occupied Sproul Hall. In the early morning of December 3, a small army of police began carrying out students—about 800 of them. That afternoon, yet another impromptu group of mediating faculty, the department chairmen, met to formulate a compromise which offered full amnesty to the students for the actions of the past two months; they hoped to sell this to the President and the Regents. On December 4, a long threatened strike of teaching assistants was launched, and on Sunday, December 6, the President and the Regents accepted the department chairmen's compromise.

By this time, however, the student leaders had glimpsed the possibility of complete success. For some days a substantial number of liberal faculty members had been preparing a resolution which asserted that political activity on campus should be regulated only as to "time, place, and manner" in order not to interfere with the functioning of the university, and they were rounding up support for its adoption. The great majority of this group had little sympathy for FSM tactics, but they believed its position on the rules was right. In any case, the larger part of the faculty had now become involved, because they had been forced to confront and take a stand on the strike of their teaching assistants. Many were also shocked by the December 3 police action. The FSM hoped that the faculty resolution supporting their position would pass and they joined its drafters in campaigning for it.

On December 7 the compromise negotiated by the department chairmen was presented by Professor Robert Scalopino and President Kerr to the student body and faculty at a large open-air meeting at the Greek Theater. The radicalization of the students—thousands of whom had now participated in sit-ins, strikes, and picketing—had proceeded at a frightening pace over the weekend; full victory was now seen as possible, and the compromise was denounced by the student leaders as a "sell-out." It was at this meeting that Mario Savio, head of the FSM, attempted to seize the microphone, and the campus police dragged him away.

Because of their desperate desire to settle things, because of their experience of one administration failure after another, I believe most of the faculty was by now ready to accept any agreement that might lead to peace. The administration—President Kerr and Chancellor Strong—was absent and silent when a thousand members of the Academic Senate met on

December 8 and by a huge vote endorsed the resolution of the liberal faculty members mentioned above. This resolution —in addition to backing the view that political activity should be unrestricted except for time, place, and manner—demanded that responsibility for disciplinary measures in the area of political activitity should be placed in the hands of the faculty. Having lived through months of non-existent or ineffective leadership and increasing disruption and disorder, the faculty also voted for the election of a strong Emergency Executive Committee to represent it. A few days later, however, as if in recoil from the resolution, the faculty elected a moderate executive committee, the majority of whom had not been identified with the preparation and propagation of the resolution that had been adopted so overwhelmingly.

But what of the issue of illegal political activity itself? Did the seven-to-one vote of the faculty resolve that? I do not believe so. At the December 8 meeting Professor Lewis Feuer proposed an amendment to the main resolution which would have excepted speech or advocacy "directed to immediate acts of force and violence" from the general immunity. In support of this amendment, he spoke not of the civil rights movement, which was uppermost in the minds of all the protagonists, but of Mississippi, which such a resolution as had been endorsed by the faculty would deny a university administration the right to move against a chapter of the Ku Klux Klan, and of pre-Nazi Germany, where a similar position in effect prevented university administrations from moving against Nazi students engaged in the destruction of the ground-rules of democratic society. The discussion was intense. Many of those who opposed Feuer were convinced that his amendment raised serious constitutional issues. On the whole it was obvious to those of us who supported his amendment—and had other amendments in mind as well—that the temper of the faculty did not favor any extended consideration of the issues at that time. The students were barred from the meeting, but thousands were outside, and we could hear their roars of approval or disapproval as the debate went on. It was scarcely necessary to be reminded of the terrible power of the student movement, though two professors, both of whom supported the majority resolution, did remind us that chaos was at the door. I think there was a good deal of hysteria mixed in with the action of the Berkeley Division of the Academic Senate that day. Afterward men who had been friends for years but had taken opposite sides approached each other with hesitation, and felt it necessary to reaffirm their friendship, so deeply had their emotions become involved.

I hope it is now clear why the issue on the Berkeley campus is not simply one of "free speech." The immediate issue is the student demand that the university allow them facilities for full political action and give up its right to discipline them for what it considers improper use of these facilities. If the university is to be equated with the administration, the students have a point. For the administration has the least claim to the power to determine the standards which govern the university. But what of the Regents, who represent the people of the state? What of the faculty? What of the students? Are all incapable of determining what is proper on a university campus? The constitution of the university—the distribution of powers among its various elements—may well be out of joint. At one time the faculty exercised student discipline at Berkeley; on some campuses it is the faculty and students together. Constitutions can be changed. But should the constitution of a university include a grant of immunity to any and all forms of action that go by the name of politics? If it did, the university would abdicate its responsibility to set standards for its students, its faculty, and its staff in one critical area of their life on the campus. We are now in the following ridiculously inconsistent posture at Berkeley: no religious activity of any kind is allowed on the campus and no one challenges that; students can be penalized for infractions of rules involving the consumption of liquor and the like, and no one challenges that; but it is asserted that any political action whatever should be permitted without any step being taken by the university against any person or organization as a result.

It is possible that this huge and on the whole practically

oriented university has no basis on which to set any standards. I am not sure we have come to this yet. The students—now backed by most of the faculty—view any assertions of power by the university as designed only to reduce the scope of their self-evidently good and just activity. They do not see that the power to regulate on the basis of standards appropriate to a university also increases the potential scope of their activity and protects them from the civil arm. It is easier to run meetings on the Berkeley campus than on the city streets— even the streets of enlightened cities. The students and their faculty supporters do not agree that this higher degree of freedom, established under the protection of the university's authority, may be organically connected to the university's power to regulate this freedom and prevent its abuse.

How then is the dispute to be finally resolved? One can envisage circumstances that would give us a temporary peace, but it would be a very fragile one. Many of the FSM leaders are also deeply concerned with the academic conduct of the university, the curriculum, the courses, the character of the faculty, the nature of student-faculty relations. It is a concern which many faculty members applaud. But if strikes and sit-ins should be held on the campus to impose student views of how the university should be run academically—and nothing in FSM ideology prevents this—there would be an end to peace once again.

Secondly, one must see these events in the context of the students' desire to protect their university status and privileges while conducting their operations in the community. Will the community in turn, however, respect these rights and privileges if the actions of the Berkeley students maintain their intensity of 1963–64, or if, as the students hope, they increase in intensity? A number of supermarkets against which they directed some of their most powerful efforts, I notice, have closed down. Will the community, which votes hundreds of millions of dollars for the university through the state legislature, remain docile in the face of what they may consider a one-sided bargain?

At a press conference called by a group of faculty members after the mass arrests on December 3, Professor Henry May, chairman of the history department, was asked by newsmen what lay at the bottom of the crisis. He answered thoughtfully that he saw two major issues. One was the inevitable strains and pressure stemming from the attempt to create at Berkeley a mass university that would at the same time be great; the second was the rise of new forms of political action which aroused deep emotions and whose legal status was in doubt. I believe these are the two chief underlying causes of what is happening at Berkeley. We have the answer to neither problem; this is why we must be concerned and disturbed, and why what is happening at Berkeley is more than a local story.

Epilogue, January 6.—On January 1, the Regents suddenly appointed a new Acting Chancellor for the Berkeley campus, Martin Meyerson. He took office at a time when the Emergency Executive Committee of the Academic Senate was performing prodigies in negotiating with and mollifying all parties. With the advice of the Emergency Executive Committee, the new Chancellor issued temporary and minimal "fail-safe" rules (the language of nuclear warfare in common in the controversy) with which to greet the students returning from vacation, and FSM is abiding by them. Meyerson has brought a new atmosphere to the campus, and every day we congratulate each other on an unaccustomed peace.

NOTES

1. "Advocacy" was used throughout the ensuing dispute to mean advocacy of *action,* not of ideas.
2. *The Uses of the University,* 1963.

Academic Freedom and the Rights of Students

SIDNEY HOOK

Sidney Hook, a distinguished American philosopher, writer and editor, was educated at the City College of New York and Columbia University. He studied also in Berlin, Munich and Moscow. A disciple of John Dewey, he frequently applies the concepts of pragmatism and logical analysis to clarify and evaluate social and political problems. He is the author of such works as Towards the Understanding of Karl Marx, From Hegel to Marx, The Hero in History *and* Education for the Modern Man.

A MERICANS are accustomed to reading about universities as storm centers of political disturbance in Latin and Asiatic countries. In a country like the United States, however, most criticism of student bodies in the past has been directed against their political apathy. The fact, therefore, that a building was seized by students at the Berkeley campus of the University of California, bringing all administrative activities to a halt, that a strike was declared, paralyzing teaching, and that the Governor of the most populous state in the Union, after the arrest of some 800 students, felt it necessary to appeal for problems to be solved "by evolution not revolution," should give not only educators but all reflective citizens pause.

It has focused attention upon a question of considerable complexity—the rights, and the responsibilities, of students.

Since so much of the controversy and agitation swirls around the slogans of freedom, the first question to be asked is: Do students enjoy the right of academic freedom? This depends on what is meant by academic freedom. Perhaps the best short definition was offered by Arthur O. Lovejoy, founder, together with John Dewey, of the American Association of University Professors.

"Academic freedom," he wrote, "is the freedom of the teacher or research worker in higher institutions of learning to investigate and discuss the problems of his science and to express his conclusions, whether through publications or the instruction of students, without interference from political or ecclesiastical authority, or from the administrative officials of the institution in which he is employed, unless his methods are found by qualified bodies of his own profession to be clearly incompetent or contrary to professional ethics."

A number of interesting implications may be drawn from this definition. First, academic freedom exists primarily for "teachers"—in the most comprehensive sense of that term. Strictly speaking, it makes no sense to talk of "academic freedom" for students. Students have a right to freedom to learn. The best guarantee of freedom to learn is academic freedom for those who teach them. Where teachers are deprived of academic freedom, students are *ipso facto* deprived of the freedom to learn.

The converse, however, is not true. It is simply false both in logic and in fact to assert that freedom to teach and freedom to learn are indivisible. Many things may interfere with the student's freedom to learn—poverty, racial discrimination, inadequate transportation—which have no direct relevance to academic freedom. The latter may flourish in institutions to which students are unjustly denied the opportunity to enter. The movement to abolish poverty, discrimination and other social evils in order to give students access to education and to effective freedom to learn flows from their *moral* rights as persons and from their *civil* rights as citizens. They are not corollaries of academic freedom. To deny this would make the university responsible for the entire state of society and its reform.

Second, academic freedom is not a civil right like freedom of speech. A teacher who is dropped or refused a post on grounds of incompetence, because, say, he indoctrinates his students with the belief that the earth is flat, or that the Elders of Zion are engaged in a conspiracy to destroy America, or that Communists are 20th-century Jeffersonian democrats, is not being deprived of freedom of speech. He can still proclaim his discovery from the house tops. As a citizen he can talk nonsense without let or hindrance. But in order to talk "nonsense" in the academy with impunity—and strange things *can* be heard within it!—a teacher must win the right to do so by certification from his peers that he is competent and by having acquired tenure. What may sound like nonsense to the plain citizen may be the birth of a revolutionary discovery.

The same consideration applies to the student.

There is no direct connection between the student's freedom to learn and his freedom of speech. The controlling consideration must be his freedom to learn. If restrictions are placed on freedom of speech—aside from those which exist on the freedom of *all* citizens—they must be justified by the educational needs of the student and reasonable institutional provisions for its expression. It is one thing to set up a miniature Hyde Park on some corner of the campus and encourage students to use it; it is another to allow them to call a mass meeting on Prexy's lawn at dawn.

Third, responsibility for the certification of a teacher's competence, and for interpreting and applying the rules of tenure, must ultimately lie in the hands of the faculty. The faculty should also set the educational standards which students are required to measure up to. Students may be free to learn but sometimes they don't learn enough. Students too, therefore, must earn the right to continue as students. Higher education is not a civil right like the right to a fair trial or other Bill of Rights freedoms that do not have to be earned.

Fourth, an important aspect of the faculty's responsibility

for the entire educational enterprise is ultimate control over the classrooms, meeting halls and other educational facilities of the campus and over the conditions of their use. This has a bearing, as we shall see, on some crucial questions.

The extent to which these principles are applied is affected by the fact that legal authority in American higher institutions of learning is vested either in Boards of Regents or in corporate boards of laymen. While there is no practicable way of reversing this historical trend, immense progress has been made in winning over those with legal authority to the acceptance of enlightened principles of academic freedom which in effect entrust educational policy to the faculties. This has been a gradual and sometimes painful development, but today academic freedom is in a more flourishing state than ever before in its history. It is only when one remembers how many and onerous were the religious, political and social restrictions upon the teacher's freedom in the past that one can grasp the remarkable progress that has been made.

What is true of the teacher's academic freedom is also true of the student's freedom to learn. My own lifetime spans a period from relative tyranny in the classroom to open inquiry. During my freshman year in college, I gave two reports in a class in political science. In the first, I defended Charles A. Beard's approach to the Constitution—to the manifest disapproval of the teacher. In the second, I argued that Calhoun's logic was superior to Webster's in their famous debates. This was too much for the instructor who ejected me from the class with the indignant observation: "When you aren't preaching sedition you are preaching secession!" That could hardly happen today. Although conditions are not uniform, almost everywhere the climate of opinion and practice is healthier than it used to be.

The issues that agitate campuses today are more likely to arise from the behavior of students than from actions of the faculty. Of these, some stem from rules governing the students' personal and social behavior, and some from efforts to regulate their extracurricular political activities both on and off campus.

Confusion, and sometimes needless controversy, arise from a failure to distinguish between the area of conduct in which students may justifiably exercise their rights as individual citizens and that which is related to the specific function of the college and to the business which presumably brings the student to school. To indicate the relevance of this distinction, let us examine some of the concrete issues that have provoked controversy in recent years.

The first concerns the personal morality of students. Unfortunately, personal morality for many people refers exclusively to sexual behavior, but, properly understood, it embraces every form of individual conduct whose consequences have some bearing on the welfare of others. On the assumption that in institutions of higher learning we are not dealing with children, standards of personal deportment should initially be left to the students themselves. In the interests of safety, however, it is necessary to establish rules and regulations governing the use of cars, liquor, smoking and visits to dormitories, but, wherever possible, these rules should be administered by the students themselves. Anything students can properly do for themselves as adults should be left to them. To student self-government, broad-based and representative, can be entrusted many of the functions incidental to organized student life in the college community—although the faculty cannot forgo exercising some oversight as a kind of appeals body to see that fair play is done.

Should students be permitted to organize political groups on campus or invite speakers of extremist political views to address them? This kind of problem has occasioned far more bitter controversy than problems of purely personal behavior. And failure to define the issue properly has prevented the right kind of questions from being asked and the relevant considerations brought to bear.

A student request which may have considerable educational

validity may be wrongfully denied because it is mistakenly put forward as a political demand. This is particularly true with respect to who should be allowed to speak on a university campus. This has nothing to do with questions of free speech or academic freedom. Political speakers can reach students in many ways. If the faculties do not permit the use of college facilities to individuals outside of the academic community, they are not denying the civil right of freedom of speech to speakers, who can easily address students off-campus, or the civil right of freedom to listen to students, who can attend their meetings off-campus. This is a false issue.

The genuine issue is the *educational* one. It is on educational, not political, grounds that a valid case can be made for permitting recognized student organizations to invite speakers of their choice to the campus to discuss any topic, no matter how controversial. The educational process cannot and should not be confined merely to the classroom. Students should be encouraged to pursue their educational interests on their own initiative, and contemporary issues which convulse society are legitimate subjects of inquiry.

Faculties and administrations often suffer from educational timidity. They are unduly fearful when a speaker of extremist views is invited to the campus. If a college is doing its job properly, it doesn't require Fascists or Communists to instruct its students about Fascism or Communism. But so long as students want to hear such speakers—often to see them in the flesh and to find out how they tick mentally—there can be no reasonable educational objection to their appearance— particularly if it is made clear that such speakers do not represent the views of the student body or faculty.

If students and faculty cannot cope with the "arguments" of the Lincoln Rockwells and Gus Halls, then the college is failing badly in its educational task. In an open and honest forum, the cause of freedom and democracy can triumph over all challengers. And as for the vaunted "public image" (horrid phrase!) of the college, the prolonged controversy and newspaper publicity attendant upon banning a speaker is usually far more damaging than the one-day sensation provided by his appearance. For one thing seems assured by experience. A prolonged controversy over an invitation to an extremist almost always guarantees him an overflow audience when he does finally appear.

In the rare cases in which the need for control of student activities does arise, failure on the part of the faculty to draw the line means that it has abdicated from its educational responsibilities. For example, students, sometimes unfortunately abetted by junior faculty personnel, will occasionally try to break up meetings with speakers with whom they disagree. A self-respecting faculty cannot tolerate such activities. Similarly, if outside groups send professional organizers onto the campuses of large metropolitan universities to recruit students or to provoke incidents with the administration or faculties, they should be barred from access.

Then, too, small groups of students, zealots in some cause, will occasionally violate the rules of fair discussion and honest advocacy. I could fill a volume describing stratagems of this kind I have observed over a lifetime. A few students, for example, will organize a "Free Speech Forum" or something else with a libertarian flavor. Their first speaker will be Lincoln Rockwell or someone of his kidney. Thereafter, featured as "a reply" to Fascism, will come a succession of Communist speakers, sometimes paid from general student or school funds. The "educational" point of the forum is to build up Communism in its various disguises as the only real answer to Fascism.

Complaints about the absense of liberal speakers are met with the statement that liberals have been invited but refused to come. The evidence? A carbon copy of a letter to a liberal figure 2,000 miles or more distant, the original of which he may never have received. Where representatives of the student body are unable to prevent dishonest practices of this kind, the faculty is justified in stepping in.

The same general principles should govern student publications. On educational grounds, students should be encouraged to publish their own newspapers, periodicals and pamphlets, exchanging ideas, commenting on great issues, testing and challenging their teachers' views. But it would be ridiculous to say that this freedom is absolute and exempts them from restraints against slander and libel. Particularly obnoxious is the circulation of anonymous literature on campus defaming members of the student body or faculty.

Only those who believe it is possible to be liberal without being intelligent will affirm that the content of speech is always privileged, irrespective of its effects.

The very fact that speech can be used not only for advocacy—which is permissible—but for incitement, defamation and slander—which is not—shows how absurd it is to hold that speech should never be restricted. There should be no prior censorship, of course, unless there is convincing evidence that a speaker plans to incite to violence. We do not have to wait for a mob actually to move to lynch someone before we stop the agitator inciting it.

The irony of the situation is that students in our mass institutions of learning suffer today far more from the failure of faculties to attend to the students' individual educational needs than from alleged suppressions of their freedom of speech. The students' freedom to learn is frustrated by crowding, inferior staffing and by the indifference of many faculties to the best methods of classroom teaching. Colleges still operate on the absurd assumption that anyone who knows anything can teach it properly. It is an open scandal that the worst teaching in the American system of education takes place at the college level.

In some universities, large introductory courses where skillful teaching is of critical importance in arousing student interest are turned over to young, inexperienced graduate assistants at the outset of their careers who stumble along by trial and error and groping imitation of the models of teaching they vaguely remember. No wonder they sometimes play up to students, joining them in their vague resentments against the educational establishment in a kind of compensatory camaraderie. Some observers believe that unless conditions change the real revolt on campus will some day be directed against the shoddy educational treatment to which students have been subjected. As the numbers of students grow the situation deteriorates.

A sense of proportion, a pinch of humor and a draft of common sense are wonderful specifics against friction, but they vanish when either students or faculty resort to ultimatums. Both sides have a mutual interest in keeping the educational enterprise going. When problems and difficulties arise they must be routed through recognized channels of petition, complaint and protest. The officially elected representatives of the student body should meet periodically with representatives of the faculty which, when grave issues are at stake, should sit as a committee of the whole.

Attempts by any group, even when it feels it has a legitimate grievance, to short-circuit official channels, to appeal over the heads of the representative student body for mass demonstrations or strikes, to threaten force and violence or to resort to so-called passive resistance should be condemned by both students and faculty. Such tactics are not only destructive of the atmosphere in which teaching and learning can take place, they prejudice the chances for reaching mutually satisfactory settlements.

The student "Free Speech Movement" at the University of California had every right to press for a modification of university rules governing campus and off-campus activities. What was shocking, however, was its deliberate boycott and by-passing of the Associated Students, the elected representative organization of the student body. It neither used the existing channels of protest nor sought to avail itself of the remedies open to it.

Even more shocking was the demagogic and odious comparison drawn by some students between the situation at the university, which, despite its restrictions, is still far more liberal than most, and the situation in Mississippi. And worst of all was the resort to tactics of mass civil disobedience which could only be justified in extreme situations in behalf of basic principles of freedom. Except in such situations, changes in the laws of a democratic community must be urged by practices within the law.

Almost as shocking as the action of the students in seizing

university property was the failure of the faculty of the university to condemn the action. Indeed, by failing to couple their call for an amnesty for students with a sharp rebuke for their actions, the faculty seemed to condone indirectly the students' behavior. Apparently those who wanted to be heroes were to be spared the consequences of their heroism.

The administration of the university also seems at fault in not anticipating developments on campus. Signs of student unrest and dissatisfaction were apparent many months ago. The faculty, therefore, should have been brought into the picture much earlier and entrusted with the formulation of rules of conduct, in consultation with official representatives of the student body, and with their subsequent enforcement.

The really disquieting aspect of the situation at the University of California, however, was the extremism of the student leaders, the lengths to which they were willing to go—at one point, bloodshed and possible loss of life seemed imminent— and the contemptuous and disingenuous account they gave of their behavior. One of them described their activities as "controversial measures to begin a dialogue." Student concern with the content and method of their education is sure to grow and should be encouraged. But if they are going to lie down, seize buildings and call strikes whenever their demands are not granted by faculty and administration, it bodes ill for the future.

Even before the events at Berkeley, I read literature distributed by a strong student group at the University of California calling for "the total elimination of course, grade and unit system of undergraduate learning" and urging other proposals—not all of them as silly. But what was definitely not silly or funny in the light of what has happened was the injunction to students to resort ultimately to "civil disobedience" to get their way! It is a safe bet to anyone who knows the psychology of students that once they get away with the tactic of civil disobedience in protesting a minor rule, their demands —and their conduct—will grow wilder and more unreasonable.

No service is done to students by flattering them or by giving them the impression they can acquire an education in any other way than by hard intellectual discipline—by accepting the logic of ideas and events. They cannot be encouraged too much to broaden their intellectual interests, and they certainly must not be discouraged from giving expression to their generous enthusiasms for civil rights, for human welfare, for peace with freedom. But good works off campus cannot be a substitute for good work on campus. Ultimately, the good causes our society always needs have a better chance of triumphing if their servitors equip themselves with the best education our colleges and universities can give them.

Thoughts on Berkeley
PAUL GOODMAN

A noted and outspoken social critic, Paul Goodman is a Fellow at the Institute for Policy Studies in Washington, D.C. His most recent book is Compulsory Mis-Education; *others include* Making Do *and* Growing Up Absurd.

1

THE function of administration is to expedite the essential academic business of teaching and learning, e.g., as secretary and janitor; and protectively to represent the academic community in its external relations, e.g., in court or as fund-raiser. When administration becomes the dominant force in tne community, however, it is a sign that extra-mural powers are in control—State, Church, or Economy—and the administration is their agent. Notoriously, Image-burnishing and fund-raising disregard or even prevent teaching and learning.

At Berkeley, the students griped that the University of California has become a "factory, disregarding faculty and students," a factory to process professional licences and apprentices for technological corporations, and to do extra-mural contracted research. The particular bone of contention, the Free Speech ban, seems also to have been extra-murally instigated, by backlash elements, persons like Senator Knowland, etc. The administration certainly acted with panic, under outside pressure and out of touch with its own community.

At present in the United States, students—middle-class youth—are the major exploited class. (Negroes, small farmers, the aged are rather out-caste groups; their labor is not needed and they are not wanted.) The labor of intelligent youth *is* needed and they are accordingly subjected to tight scheduling, speedup, and other factory methods. Then it is not surprising if they organize their CIO. It is frivolous to tell them to go elsewhere if they don't like the rules, for they have no choice but to go to college, and one factory is like another.

2

Thus far in the Berkeley revolt, two new factors have emerged: 1) The students want to extend the concept of Academic Freedom from *Lehrfreiheit* (freedom of professors to teach according to their lights) to include *Lernfreiheit* (freedom of students to ask for what they need to be taught, and if necessary to invite teachers, including advocates of causes.) I shall return to this later. 2) The Faculty energized by the students, wants to resume prerogatives that it had given up to the administration, e.g., discipline. This is probably the more important issue; but in my opinion the administration cannot agree (and the Regents have so voted) to the Faculty resumption of prerogatives, because this could go very far and entirely unmake the academic-factory; e.g., the Faculty might hire or teach in disregard of Image, Endowments, or Research grants; they might resist huge classes or abolish grading. The question, then, will be whether there are enough professors who are concerned for the academic community to fight it out, rather than pursuing their grants and independent research.

It is useful to recall the important student strike, a few years ago, at New York State University at Oyster Bay (now Stony Brook). Here the State tried to impose a new President, to turn the Liberal Arts school into an engineering institute. The students were angered by disregard of their physical and social needs; the Faculty was indignant at the attempt to fragment the divisional system into departments that could be administratively subjugated. Backed by the Faculty, very many students struck and the new President had to go.

Generally speaking, student efforts to get an education befitting free men rather than slaves can succeed only with strong Faculty backing, for the students are transient, they do not *definitely* know what they want, they do not know the score behind the scenes and thus they can be abashed by administrative double-talk. On the other hand, given the supine history of American faculties in our sectarian and trustee-ridden colleges, and given the present extra-mural careerism of the important professors, the students must lead if there is to be any change.

3

The extension of Academic Freedom to the claim to Freedom-to-Learn implies a revolutionary change in the status of American college-going. Up to now, American collegians have been regarded, and have regarded themselves, as late-adolescents; but the claim to *Lernfreiheit* means that they are young adults who are capable of knowing what they ought to get.

This is, of course, the (non-English) European and Latin tradition. It goes with early sexual maturity, with economic independence (often in bohemian poverty), and with active involvement in politics. Classically, in Europe, it has also involved drawn-out education, many moratoria, much changing of schools and career plans, and "being a student" as itself a kind of profession of young adults, especially of the upper class.

Some of these changes are evident in this country. Whatever parents and administrators may say about extended sexual tutelage and *in loco parentis*, the young are practicing earlier sexual maturity without apologies. The past ten years have witnessed a remarkable resurgence of youthful political engagement. And since the selective service, it becomes far-fetched to deny the eighteen-year-old vote. It is hard to see how the university can welcome recruiters for Peace Corps or Army and disallow CORE or SNCC. (Incidentally, since the Supreme Court's "abatement" decision the illegal activity has turned out to be legal after all!) Administration itself has dealt a mortal blow to the notion of late-adolescence by its persistent attempts to abolish the fraternity system, which was a bulwark of Youth House and Social Life ideology (leading, for instance, to trivial student governments). I do not think the aim of Administration has been to treat the students as young adults; rather, the abolition of fraternities seems to be an attempt to tighten control, increase academic performance, and to gouge rent (since dormitories are built with Federal funds). Nevertheless, the effect of abolition must be student maturation, demands to live off-campus or to liberalize dormitory rules, to lower rents and improve food, and to be represented by a government that is not otiose.

On the other hand, there are strong American influences to prevent student maturation and independence. First, the frantic career-drive, spurred by the anxiety of middle-class parents, leading to conformism, and willingness to submit to scheduled mis-education, credits, and grading, in order to get a diploma quick. Secondly, the students are not financially independent; tuition is exceedingly high, so that it is impossible to opt for independent poverty; scholarships and loans put the student under administration control. Probably most important, the universal compulsory school-going without alternative choices, is infantile. In 1900, only 6 per cent graduated from high school. We thus have conflict: the direct and evident need for the students as a working class of the economy would tend to make the students more mature; but the conditions of their collegiate exploitation tend to make them insecure and immature.

The evolution of both Faculty and Student organizations in the United States has been different from the communities of scholars in Europe. We do not have community guilds but rather national unions. The Faculty unions—e.g., The American Association of University Professors or the Teachers Union—were first formed as defensive leagues; my guess is that they will now begin to take the offensive. I can conceive of them declining to take graduate students from Ole Miss; or defending the principles of the original Mobilization for Youth, as a committee of the American Sociological Association has done; or attacking the entrenched Boards of Education with new ideas for the public schools. On the other hand, the Student unions—e.g., the Student Peace Union, the Students for a Democratic Society—started largely for extra-mural political reasons; but my guess is that they will now, as at Berkeley, look to improve the academic community. In this the National Students Association could be a leader. Hopefully, as I have said, the student activity will revive the dormant community of the faculty.

In my opinion, the chief *political* action of students would, at present, be intra-mural—humanizing the making cultural the academic community—for the colleges and universities have become so tightly interlocked with the dominant tightly interlocked system of society that any *intra-mural* improvement will be a profound shock to the system. Also, in these matters the students can really know what they are talking about.

4

What is the role of a student government? In our contemporary conditions, it is interesting to hark back to the "Nations," the powerful student government of medieval universities.

The medieval student government was a band to bargain collectively on rent with the townspeople, on food prices with the tavern-keepers. Our present governments could bargain this way with both the town and the administration, the bookstores, the Co-op.

In medieval conditions, the Nations bargained with the Faculty on tuition. With us this is wholly an administrative matter. One thinks of the students of City College in New York going to Albany on the tuition fight. A related issue is class size and immature section men. The tuition mounts, but the student gets less and less for his money. A few years ago there was a strike on this issue (I think successful) at Rochester.

A purpose of the Nations was to regulate morals and keep the peace, in order to prevent outside sanctions; and if need be to get the Faculty to rescue students in trouble with the secular arm. They were also a *conjuratio*, a sworn league for mutual aid in sickness and other troubles, a kind of lodge.

Besides these medieval functions, our modern situation requires some new student government powers. In the frantic expansion, there is a vast amount of building. On visits to eighty colleges around the country, however, I have seen scarcely a single new dormitory that shows any thought (or concern) for the student users. And there are fancy facades but lousy food. The students certainly ought to have an advisory role from the beginning in any plans for new physical plant. (The Faculty, let me say, should have more than an advisory role, instead of being routinely consulted and disregarded.) Further, in the present lockstep grading and scheduling, students should have a say in rules of Moratoria and Transfer, so that they can shape their educations to their own current powers and concerns, and not be short-changed on "credits." Ultimately, Faculty must and will control what it teaches and how it teaches, but the students must come to their studies voluntarily, when they are ready; they cannot be force-fed.

I submit that all these matters could be better dealt with by concerted self-interest than by paternalistic administrators and guidance counselors. Further, I think that professors would be delighted to be teaching mature young persons who can take care of themselves. The GI-bill without shell-shock.

The Berkeley Student Rebellion of 1964

MARIO SAVIO

Perhaps the most articulate of the student leaders of the Free Speech Movement, Mario Savio is a native New Yorker now in his early twenties. He is a former philosophy student at the Berkeley Campus who sees the American educational system as "totally dehumanized, totally impersonalized, created by a society which is wholly acquisitive."

THERE are quite a few students who have attended school at Berkeley who went South to work with the Student Non-violent Co-ordinating Committee, and who have been active in the civil rights movement in the Bay Area. At the end of last summer, some of these students returned from Mississippi, having taken part in the COFO Summer Project. I was one of these returning students. We were greeted by an order from the Dean of Students' Office that the kind of on-campus political activity which had resulted in our taking part in the Summer Project was to be permitted no longer.

It is a lot easier to become angry at injustices done to other people than at injustices done to oneself. The former requires a lower degree of political consciousness, is compatible with a higher political boiling point. You become slowly, painfully aware of those things which disturb you in the ways society oppresses you by taking part in activities aimed at freeing and helping others. There is less guilt to suffer in oppressing the arbitrary power exercised over yourself. Thus, the order banning student politics on campus was an ideal locus of fierce protest. It combined an act of bureaucratic violence against the students themselves with open attack on student participation in the Bay Area civil rights movement. The seemingly inexhaustible energy which the Berkeley students had so long devoted to the struggle for Negro rights was now turned squarely on the vast, faceless University administration. This is what gave the Free Speech Movement its initial impetus.

But the new restrictions were not aimed so much at curtailing activity which would result in civil rights work in the South as at halting the very active participation of students in the civil rights movement in the Bay Area. The University was apparently under considerable pressure to "crackdown" on the student activists from the right-wing in California business and politics. William Knowland, who has become symbolic of this pressure, managed Goldwater's statewide campaign; the reactionary Oakland *Tribune,* which Knowland publishes, has played a major role in creating the myth of Berkeley, the "little red school house." Last March when about 160 demonstrators, including many University students, were arrested at the Sheraton-Palace Hotel while protesting a discriminatory hiring policy, Don Mulford, conservative Republican State Assemblyman from the University district, was severely critical of the Berkeley administration for not expelling the then arrested students. Student pressure on Bay Area business resulted in business pressure on the University; the University responded by trying to restrict student political activity.

The liberal University of California administration would have relished the opportunity to show off in the national academic community a public university enjoying complete political and academic freedom *and* academic excellence. And if student politics had been restricted either to precinct work for the Democrats and Republicans, or to advocacy (by public meetings and distribution of literature) of various forms of wholesale societal change, than I don't believe there would have been the crisis there was. In any case an accommodation between the bureaucrats and the students could more easily have been achieved. The corporations represented on the Board of Regents welcome Young Democrats and Young Republicans as eager apprentices, and sectarian "revolutionary" *talk* can be tolerated because it is harmless. The radical student activists, however, are a mean threat to privilege. Because the students were advocating consequential actions (because their advocacy was consequential): the changing of hiring practices of particular establishments, the ending of certain forms of discrimination by certain concrete acts— because of these radical *acts,* the administration's restrictive ruling was necessary.

Which is easy to understand. The First Amendment exists to protect consequential speech; First Amendment rights to advocacy come into question only when actions advocated are sufficiently limited in scope, and sufficiently threatening to the established powers. The action must be radical *and* possible: picket lines, boycotts, sit-ins, rent strikes. The Free Speech Movement demanded no more—nor less—than full First Amendment rights of advocacy on campus as well as off: that, therefore, only the courts have power to determine and punish abuses of freedom of speech. The Berkeley Division of the Academic Senate endorsed this position on December 8, 1964 by declaring against *all* University regulation of the content of speech or advocacy—by a vote of 824 to 115.

Probably the most meaningful opportunity for political involvement for students with any political awareness is in the civil rights movement. Indeed, there appears to be little else in American life today which can claim the allegiance of men. Therefore, the action of the administration, which seemed to the students to be directed at the civil rights movement, was felt as a form of emasculation, or attempted emasculation. The only part of the world which people could taste, that wasn't as flat and stale as the middleclass wasteland from which most of the University people have come, that part of the world was being cleanly eliminated by one relatively hygienic administrative act. The student response to this "routine directive" was outraged protest.

Student civil rights action in the Bay Area has been significant and will become increasingly so. I am sure we haven't seen the last of the administration's attempts either to limit, or, if possible, to eliminate activity of this kind. On the other side, I think last semester has shown that such attempts, if drastic enough to be effective, are bound to end in disaster. So, what we have to fear is not some extreme act, such as was attempted last September, but rather petty harassments of various sorts, and the not-so-pretty exclusion of "non-students" from the campus, toward which legislation recently passed by the State Legislature is directed. I believe it unlikely for the students to rally in opposition to such harassment; probably we shall have to be content with opposing decisively only gross provocation, which probably now the administration has learned not to attempt.

But the civil rights movement is only one aspect of the dual motivation of FSM support. And this is so because people do find it easier to protest injustices done to *others:* even adverting to injustice done oneself is often too painful to be sustained for very long. When you oppose injustice done others, very often—symbolically sometimes, sometimes not so symbolically—you are really protesting injustice done to yourself. In the course of the events of the fall, students became aware, ever more clearly, of the monstrous injustices that were being done to them as students.

We found we were being denied the very possibility of "being a student"—unquestionably a *right*. We found we were severed from our proper roles: students denied the meaningful work one must do in order to be a student. Instead we were faced with a situation in which the pseudo-student role we were playing was tailor-made to further the interests of those who own the University, those vast corporations in whose interest the University is managed. Time past when the skills required of laborers were nowhere near so great as the ones required now, bosses built schools for their own children. Now the bosses build schools for the children of their workers. They build schools to further their own interests.

Accordingly, the schools have become training camps—and providing grounds—rather than places where people acquire education. They become factories to produce technicians rather than places to live student lives. And this perversion develops great resentment on the part of the students. Resentment against being subjected to standard production techniques of speedup and regimentation; against a tendency to qualify education—virtually a contradiction in terms. Education is measured in units, in numbers of lectures attended, in numbers of pages devoted to papers, number of pages read. This mirrors the gross and vulgar quantification in the society at large—the *real* world—where everything must be reduced to a lowest common denominator, the dollar bill. In our campus play-world we use play money, course units.

It is understandable that resentment should develop among the students. However, it was not always so easy for the students to understand the causes of their own resentment. It is not as easy to see what is oppressing the subject as to see what is oppressing the others. Nevertheless, we students did become more and more aware of the factory education which we were being provided.

It is significant that the President of the University of California should be the foremost ideologist of this "Brave New World" conception of education. President Clark Kerr dreamed up the frightening metaphors: "the knowledge industry," "the multiversity," which has as many faces as it has publics, be they industries of various kinds, or the Federal Government, especially the Pentagon and the AEC. He also invented the title "the captain of bureaucracy," which he is, by anthology with earlier captains of industry. He is the person directly charged with steering the mighty ship along the often perilous course of service to its many publics in government and industry. Not to *the* public, but to its many publics, the Kerrian whore is unlawfully joined.

Those disciplines with a ready market in industry and government are favored and fostered: the natural sciences, engineering, mathematics, and the social sciences when these serve the braintrusting propaganda purposes of "liberal" government. The humanities naturally suffer, so that what should be the substance of undergraduate education suffers. The emphasis is given to research instead of to teaching undergraduates. Teaching graduate students is less affected by this prostitution since such teaching is intimately bound to research. But the undergraduate has become the new dispossessed; the heart has been taken from his education—no less so for science students—for the humanities are no longer accorded the central role they deserve in the university.

And of course there are whole areas which never see the light in undergraduate instruction. Who takes undergraduate courses in the history of the labor movement, for example? Certainly no one at the University of California. Likewise, American Negro history is a rarity and is still more rarely taken seriously. To be taken at all seriously it would have to be seen as central to all American history.

In a healthy university an undergraduate would have time to do "nothing." To read what he wants to read, maybe to sit on a hill behind the campus all alone or with a friend, to "waste time" alone, dreaming in the Eucalyptus Grove. But the university, after the manner of a pesky social director, sees to it the student's time is kept filled with anti-intellectual harassment: those three credits in each three unit course, those meaningless units themselves. The notion that one can somehow reduce Introductory Quantum Mechanics and Philosophy of Kant to some kind of lowest common denominator (three units a piece) is totally irrational, and reflects the irrationality of a society which tries to girdle the natural rhythms of growth and learning by reduction to quantitative terms, much as it attempts to market the natural impulses of sex.

From my experience, I should say the result is at best a kind of intellectual cacaphony. There are little attractions in various places, philosophy in one corner, physics in another, maybe a bit of mathematics every now and again, some political science—nothing bearing any relationship to anything else. Everything requires too many papers, too much attendance at lectures, two-thirds of which should never have been given, and very few of which resulted from any serious thought later than several years or earlier than several minutes before the lecture period. It is easy to see that there should be real resentment on the part of the students. But it is resentment whose causes are, as we have seen, very difficult for the student to perceive readily. That is why what occurred last semester gained its initial impetus from the very different involvements of what are mostly middle-class students in the struggles of the Negro people. Thus, it was both the irrationality of society, that denies to Negroes the life of men, and the irrationality of the University, that denies to youth the life of students, which caused last semester's rebellion.

The Revolt of an Elite: Sources of the FSM Victory
SAMUL KAPLAN

A graduate student in sociology at Berkeley, Samuel Kaplan received his B.A. in Springfield, Massachusetts. Between 1955 and 1959 he was editor and reporter for the Springfield (Mass.) Union.

THE Free Speech Movement (FSM) at the Berkeley campus of the University of California surprised nearly all who observed it during its few months of rebellion in the autumn of 1964. Most of those who were surprised also found cause for outrage, not only in the methods and goals of the students, but also, and perhaps most of all, in their victory. The FSM not only called a strike of at least ten thousand students to "bring the campus to a grinding halt" (to recall the Luddite rhetoric that occasionally seized the student leadership), but even obtained what it was seeking and what the university administration denied it could grant: free speech and assembly for students on campus, as protected under the First and Fourteenth Amendments.

The rebellion began when the administration tried to extend to a brick sidewalk at the major entrance to campus rules prohibiting political activity, particularly the use of card tables and signs. The FSM forced the administration to retract this extension of the rules and then virtually to abolish the rules altogether for most of the other open areas on campus. As a result, the card tables have been moved from the brick walk to the central campus plaza before the administration building. There student activists have established a vivid political bazaar to advocate political positions of many kinds, solicit donations, and recruit new workers—all activities that before the rebellion had been wholly or partly forbidden on campus.

To be sure, these reforms could all be limited or lost at some time. Nonetheless, the immediate victory of the FSM during the rebellion itself was unmistakable. Though opposed by the governor, the state legislature, the press, and the public, and of course the university administration, which twice called out and once used a sizable corps of policemen, the Free Speech Movement eventually forced the officials of the university to surrender to its demands.

At least two major questions need to be considered to understand how the FSM triumphed against this considerable array of power. First, when the usual course of American campus protests is to begin feebly and die almost at the outset, why was the FSM hardy at its birth and militant thereafter? And second, how did it attract so many students to its support? The answers to these questions will help to explain the sources of the movement's success, for without unusual militancy at the beginning, the protest would not have survived; and without winning the support of at least a substantial minority of the student body, FSM could not have achieved victory.

I

University administrations often enough impose restrictive rules on student political activity. For most students, the usual response is apt to be little more than a slight restiveness, if anything at all. Even for those students who care about their politics, the reaction is likely to lack force, amounting to not much more than a few dormitory bull sessions about the tyranny of petty deans and a somewhat more discreetly phrased resolution in the student legislature.

FSM was a striking exception. When the Berkeley administration moved at the start of the fall semester of 1964 to outlaw student politicking on the brick sidewalk at the Telegraph-Bancroft entrance to campus, students promptly initiated a stubborn, uncompromising protest that led finally through massive civil disobedience to greatly liberalized rules. Far from offering the usual empty flourish, the students opposed to the sidewalk restrictions organized militantly,[1]—the protest's first surprise.[2]

The major sources of this surprising militancy appear to be four in number. To begin with, the recent social and political activity of Berkeley students has made available a relatively large number of militant activists. Since the late 'fifties, students at Berkeley, perhaps more so than students elsewhere, have become increasingly active and aggressive in political and social matters, notably civil rights.[3] For a number of reasons, Berkeley has attracted many student militants, especially those on the left,[4] and simultaneously has served as a sort of training ground in militancy for others. One explanation of the early militancy of the protest, then, is that when the September restrictions were imposed, the militants, who were among those most affected, simply responded in character.[5]

The mere availability of militant students, however, cannot account for the nature of the first protests. The protesting students first had to join together and make themselves and their opposition to the rules visible. Considering the size of the Berkeley student body (about 27,000), a few dozen, even a few hundred, politically aggressive students, could have disappeared into the swamp of campus activities. And not just because of the size of the student body. It is at least a plausible thesis that students are—in the well-worn term of the day—"fragmented." For a protest to begin, it must somehow overcome the many centrifugal forces that make for the assumed fractionation of campus life.

But despite all the complaints of isolation, the lack of cohesion, the excessive separateness forced on students by the impersonal immensity of the place, the militants in fact knew one another and were well organized, for some purposes at any rate. About half of the eighteen groups which originally banded together to oppose the extension of the rules to the brick walk had been active in civil rights work the previous year and before. A few other groups in this alliance, which was first called the United Front but soon became known as the FSM, drew their membership from students concerned with civil rights. The leadership and the rank-and-file of both kinds of groups, consequently, had often worked together, especially under the auspices of SNCC and CORE, which possess both the public stature and singleness of purpose to make them suitable meeting grounds for even the most fractious members of the divided and sub-divided left. Even in the sit-in of December 2–3, when the protest had spilled beyond the militants, the proportion of participants who belonged to SNCC and CORE was about 25 per cent and another 18 per cent belonged to groups which formally took part in civil rights activity.[6] To a lesser but still significant extent, there were also some social connections between the militants on the left and those on the right. At a minimum, both had shared the pleasures and difficulties of politicking from the brick walkway, as well as a commitment to activism. The sudden interdict made them immediate partners in deprivation, even if in politics they were hostile competitors. As a result, an intricate web of social relations existed to sustain a new apparatus of protest.

Third, continuing participation in public action, especially in civil rights demonstrations, provided the militants an education in the skills of protest. From its beginnings, the free speech protest bore the brand of experts, not because outsiders had infiltrated or had been imported into the leadership, but on the contrary because the weekends in San Francisco against the Sheraton-Palace and Auto Row, the resistance of Slate against the intermittent efforts to banish it from campus,[7] and summers in the south had made experts of the insiders.

Thus, even before the September regulations were issued, the militants were organized into groups which had already achieved a largely unplanned and even unacknowledged cohesion. In their activities they had forged the tools of protest.

But again, the simple availability of such resources, of an accessible pool of militant students, possessing a plenitude of organizational skills, cannot lead directly to a protest movement—else the Berkeley campus would have been in perpetual ferment. In addition to these resources, there must also be something to oppose, a wrong that seems threatening or objectionable enough to justify the extensive commitment demanded by an attempt to resist a powerful administration.

There is no doubt that the September restrictions were seen almost immediately as worthy of such commitment by the leaders of the United Front. Their extravagant denunciations of the regulations bear witness that they saw them as intolerable deprivations of their rights to free speech on campus. A former chairman of Slate declared that the regulations were "another in a long series of acts to curtail either right or left wing political action on campus" and added that they were part of an attempt "to prevent all exposure of political action being taken."[8] Similarly, another student leader has recently offered the retrospective opinion that it "was immediately evident to the bulk of concerned students that the new regulations would cripple the [local civil rights] movement *entirely.*"[9]

The reasons the students felt so threatened by the new regulations are somewhat opaque, however. Among other things, for instance, the September restrictions were not the harshest ever put into force in recent years on the Berkeley campus. In 1961, for example, Slate lost official campus recognition, ostensibly because it identified itself as a "campus political party" in a letter it sent to the paper at Ohio State University. The same year, President Kerr ruled that political and social action groups could no longer establish themselves on campus or use the university's name to describe themselves—a regulation that weighed on Slate but had much broader restrictive application. The student legislature was prohibited by fiat from making any statement on "off-campus" issues; and at least twice was explicitly forced to abandon consideration of proposals to extend financial aid to various civil rights activities in the south. Many students objected to these restraints, and sometimes sought to overturn them, often through shrewd and persistent campaigns; but they managed to live calmly under them. No one, certainly, ever took the militant position that the United Front adopted almost at once in September.

Furthermore, the September restrictions probably would not

have had the crippling effects imputed to them, although they would have hampered some activities and forced organizations to employ alternative means to raise money and supporters. The civil rights groups, which supplied the bulk of the original leadership of the United Front, were in fact the ones best emplaced to survive hardily without use of the brick walk, since their large membership, their considerable visibility, and their connections in the wider community gave them many resources to fall back on.

Moreover, the September restrictions were quickly whittled away by compromise—but the protest remained militant nonetheless. The compromises would have permitted the use of the brick walk for attempts to influence voting on both candidates and propositions in the forthcoming state and national election. Indeed, one of the administration's two proffered compromises during the first 14 days of the semester extended such electioneering to eight other places on campus. The compromises also would have allowed tables and posters on the brick walk in behalf of organizational activities. After compromise, the residue of the September restrictions would have been three limitations on off-campus activity not directly connected with some project authorized by the university: no advocacy of direct action, no solicitation of funds, no recruitment of participants.

To be sure, the relative mildness of restrictions does not justify them—only the justice of them can do that. Still, measured against their earlier acquiescence in other, harsher restrictions, the students' refusal to live with the September regulations, especially after the compromises, is surprising. And in fact, far from compromising, the students insisted that it was "their duty to society" to disobey the rules by persisting at their tables on the walk. So firm was their commitment that five days after the rules were issued, and on the same day (September 21) that the first compromise was offered, some 75 students began an overnight protest vigil on the steps of the administration building. Thereafter the United Front moved to gather to itself wider support while extending its demands; and when the second compromise was offered a week later a leader of the protest warned: "We won't stop now until we've made the entire campus a bastion of free speech."[10]

The intensity of this reaction cannot be explained, as I have indicated, solely by the existence of a number of militant, skillful, and well-organized students, nor by the objective hazards in the September restrictions. Something had to produce in the militants a sense that they were being harshly repressed by those restrictions, even if they were not as severe as earlier regulations. In both the recent and past history of political life on campus and the efforts of the university to regulate it can be found a cluster of factors which encouraged the students to judge the September regulations against standards which made those regulations seem unusually oppressive. Some of these factors stimulated the students to feel a greater need than in the past for political freedom on campus; while others stimulated them to expect that at a minimum the university would maintain previous freedoms and perhaps would even enlarge them. But the September restrictions, however mild they might have been objectively, frustrated both need and expectation.

Both the robust campus commitment to civil rights work and the campaign for the state and national elections made the use of the brick walk seem especially important. Civil rights work, indeed, carried over into the campaign, especially into the struggle over Proposition 14, which sought (successfully, as it turned out) to strike down open housing laws enacted by the legislature. Both liberals and conservatives were exercised over the proposition, just as they both saw the Presidential election as pregnant with both especial danger and especial opportunity. The September restrictions would have swept both liberals and conservatives from the field of campus activity at a crucial time.

In a number of ways, the restrictions also frustrated the students' expectations about the kind of regulations on political activity that the university would impose. For one thing, the September restrictions in effect reversed the "Sather Gate tradition." [11] Since at least the 'twenties, Berkeley students have used the area just to the south of Sather Gate, which served as a boundary and main entry way to campus, as a forum for meetings and other demonstrations which were not allowed on campus. Even after 1958, when Sather Gate ceased to be a campus boundary because the land south of it was acquired for construction of the Student Union and other buildings, the tradition endured: the free speech area was transferred to the site at Telegraph and Bancroft.[12] Even the name of the tradition was kept, though the move made it anachronistic. The September restrictions would have brought the Sather Gate tradition virtually to an end.

But traditions are resistant to destruction when they continue to have lively supporters, as this one clearly did, not so much because people venerate tradition, but more because they come to see the actions permitted by particular traditions as part of their rights. Consequently, whatever the merits of the university's position about political action on campus, and whatever the merits of its assertion that it had to administer the brick walk as it did the rest of the campus, the students took the September restrictions to be an effort to abrogate rights that the administration itself had recognized for many years.[13]

The students' widespread civil rights activity in the broader community also served to raise their expectations of political freedom on campus. Regulated by civic institutions, the students came to think of themselves primarily as citizens, rather than as members of the university. When they continued their civil rights and other political work on campus, they expected to operate under the same civic standards, not under the special discipline a private organization reserves for its members.

Finally, the recent trend toward greater student freedom at Berkeley has disposed students to expect the maintenance of newly achieved freedoms and perhaps even further modifications of existing restrictions on campus political activity. Since 1958, when Clark Kerr became president, rules governing student politics have been gradually liberalized to allow, for example, communists to speak on campus, the distribution of political and other non-commercial literature on campus, the establishment of free speech areas on campus, speeches by political figures,[14] and so on. For these and other contributions to academic freedom, the American Association of University Professors bestowed its Alexander Meiklejohn award on Kerr and the university in the spring of 1964. But another result was the encouragement of student optimism about political rules, especially since the students themselves had worked effectively to win more liberal regulations. With such expectations, students would be sure to see additional restrictions, no matter how temperate, as outrageous deprivations, deserving of their most unrelenting resistance. To put the paradox in its sharpest form, the greater the students' freedom, the more restricted they felt by even the mildest regulations.

This interpretation makes sense out of the contrary, and apparently contradictory, insistence by the administration that the University of California is freer than it has been for many years. From their differing perspectives, the administration and the students could come to polar views, without either engaging in hypocrisy.

These last three factors suggest the thesis that the militant students, and perhaps others as well, suffered "relative deprivation." That is, their social and historical positions encouraged them to compare themselves with themselves or others who operated in more favorable conditions. The sociologist Samuel Stouffer and his associates found in their studies of the adjustment of men to army life during World War II that "relative deprivation" helped to account for many apparent paradoxes—for instance, that Northern Negroes appeared to make a better adjustment to army life in southern camps, even though they said they wanted to be stationed in the north and that they resented the discrimination they encountered. "When, eventually, it was suggested that the Northern Negro soldier in the South had very great advantages over Negro civilians in the South and that the advantages over Negro civilians in the North were much less, a clue to the paradox appeared." [15] Other perplexing findings by Stouffer were clarified in a similar way.

The concept of "relative deprivation," of course, is not new, though its systematic use is. Tocqueville clearly had something of the same idea in mind in his analysis of the French Revolution: "For the mere fact that certain abuses have been remedied draws attention to the others and they now appear more galling; people may suffer less, but their sensibility is exacerbated. . . . In the reign of Louis XVI the most trivial pinpricks of arbitrary power caused more resentment than the thoroughgoing despotism of Louis XIV." [16] Other commentators on the French,[17] Russian,[18] Nazi,[19] and American Revolutions [20] have exploited the concept.

While the FSM revolt was hardly of such revolutionary dimensions, we can, I think, extend the concept of relative deprivation to the students' situation at Berkeley with little difficulty to understand why at least some students saw the September restrictions as harshly restrictive as soon as they were promulgated and therefore worthy of militant opposition.

II

Even the militancy of the early protest could not have triumphed, however, without much broader support than it had in the first two or three weeks of the semester. The number of students who supported the United Front and then the FSM, no matter what the aims and tactics of those organizations, is difficult to judge. A rough approximation, based on the number of students who took part in two sit-ins that appeared to lack general support, would be about 500 and certainly no more than 800. On September 30, from 300 to 500 students, who had gone into Sproul Hall to harass efforts to bring disciplinary action against eight leaders of the United Front, elected to sit-in (and stayed until 2:30 a.m. of October 1). A similar number, about 300, took part in a sit-in at Sproul on November 23, just after the Regents, meeting in Berkeley, compromised by clarification and apparently quelled the fiercer sentiments of revolt in most of the students. Since some 3000 students had marched across campus to a protest rally during that meeting of the Regents, FSM found itself embarrassed by what must have seemed an abrupt disappearance of support and abandoned the sit-in within three hours.

Of course, the early strength of FSM did not rest solely on its most militant members. Even in September there were many students who, while unwilling to participate in sit-ins, were prepared to join in other kinds of illegal or risky activities. During the first weeks of the semester, about 500 students signed a declaration of guilt saying they had manned unauthorized tables and realized they were hence subject to expulsion from the university. On October 1, perhaps 1500 students took part in the capture of a police car which came onto the Sproul Hall plaza to arrest a former student working at an unauthorized table. It is unlikely, however, that even this many students could have won the broad reforms that the movement finally achieved.

By December, however, a great many more students had actively joined the rebellion. A measure of the spread of militance is the number of students who joined the sit-in at Sproul Hall on December 2. Between 1000 and 1500, or at least twice as many as had merely signed the declaration of guilt, entered the building; and nearly 800 of them stayed to be arrested. After the arrests, rallies collected crowds sometimes numbering 10,000 or 12,000.

Some differences of opinion have emerged over the extent of support for the subsequent strike. President Kerr has claimed, for example, that the strike was not an overwhelming success and "hardly touched any school or college except Letters and Science."[21] Even this claim, however, testifies to widespread support for the strike, since Letters and Science includes slightly more than three-quarters, or about 13,000, of the undergraduates. The president's assessment also neglects the graduate students, who were probably most affected by the strike. Several other, and quite separate, efforts to estimate the extent of support for FSM and the strike itself suggest that about half of the 27,000 students sympathized with the movement.[22]

A revolution may not require a majority for success against the opposition of a stable institution or society endowed with formal, coercive powers, but it cannot hope to win its aims without at least a significant minority. Even the militancy of the early free speech protest could not have triumphed without some of the broader support it eventually did acquire when, sporadically, more and more students abandoned for a time their loyalties to the official university and, so to speak, defected to the rebellion. In the remainder of this paper I would like to speculate on how the character of campus life and the processes of the free speech protest, together with the unwitting cooperation of the administration, finally brought about half the student body into opposition to the formal government of the university.

As many have observed, our parents not the least, the adolescent years are difficult in America.[23] Whether as juvenile delinquents, teen-agers, or college kids, adolescents are widely portrayed in colors of violence, rebellion, and casual hedonism. Not wholly, of course: there is also the image of adolescents as Boy Scouts, Youths for Christ, 4-H Club members [24]—and as National Merit Scholars and student body presidents. The great majority of American youth do seem to behave in a conventional manner or in "conventional versions of subterranean traditions"—reasonable facsimiles of such traditions as delinquency, radicalism, and Bohemianism with their most offensive features eliminated or moderated.[25]

A number of social scientists have tried to account for the origin of these subterranean traditions. They generally agree that adolescents are peculiarly vulnerable to rebellion because the demands imposed on them by adults are often ambiguous and contradictory.[26] Adolescents are often evaluated by adult standards, even while they are not allowed the activities which are the necessary emblems for acceptance as full adults. They are too old to play, yet not old enough to hold an adult's job; but in American culture it is difficult for a man to have self-respect without a job, and almost impossible to have the respect of others.[27] The catalog of similar contradictions is familiar: teen-agers are expected to comport themselves with adult dignity, but are punished for the vices adults freely enjoy; they may be drafted into military service, but are not allowed to vote; they are encouraged to sexual play, but are condemned for intercourse (when, for many, they are at the height of their sexual powers); and so on.[28]

Subterranean modes of behavior serve to answer these and other contradictions in the position of youth in several ways: they offer compensatory pleasures for those which are forbidden; they provide a mask from the obligations of adulthood;

they allow participation in prohibited behavior; they permit the expression of hostility toward the adult world. Conventionalized versions of radicalism, Bohemianism, and delinquency serve in the same ways, presumably catering to the great majority of youth whose experience of strain is relatively mild.[29]

The strains encountered by youth in the passage from childhood to adulthood are both prolonged and exacerbated by collegiate life. Of course, it is true that campus life bestows certain immediate advantages which reduce the strains: for instance, it screens adolescents from parental supervision, it makes legitimate some activities otherwise restricted to adults, it confers some prestige. At the same time, however, it intensifies the discrepancies between the student's actual life and the expectations he and others hold for him.

The discrepancies are emphasized partly by the aging process. To be a high school senior at 17 without a job is not the same as to be a college senior at 21 without a job—or a graduate student at 30. Students in patently vocational training may be consoled by some sense of occupational identity; but many students, especially those who are vocationally uncertain, continue to prefer the spacious pleasures of the liberal arts. College also delays the attainment of other signs of adulthood. Despite the growing prevalence of marrying while in school, the marriage rate for collegiate youth is much lower than for those of the same age outside of college. Even the recreation of college youth bears more resemblance to the recreation of teen-agers than of adults. For such reasons, it is difficult for their elders, and perhaps even themselves, to see college youth as grown up. So around adults, undergraduates often say they are "just students," rather than full members of the society, just as women, likewise conscious of the central importance of occupation, describe themselves as "just housewives."

The inconsistencies between what is expected of college students and what they do are, in a broad sense, "status discrepancies."[30] That is, students experience simultaneously both high and low rank in the various social positions they occupy. By virtue of chronological age they hold the high status of adults, while by virtue of studenthood they hold the low status of children. But there is another and stricter sense in which the notion of status discrepancy applies to them.

Most students come from families with relatively high social rank: their fathers are usually professionals, corporate executives, or owners of middle-sized businesses. In the schools they attended before entering college (or graduate school), the students attained high rank through scholastic success. To be in college denotes high rank. And they can look forward, not without reason, to the continued enjoyment of high rank after graduation; indeed, graduate students can well expect to become the new national elite.[31] Thus college students experience high status coming, staying, and going. But within college they are virtually at the bottom of the campus hierarchy. They may be treated disdainfully even by secretaries—especially by secretaries, one might say, since secretaries are able to borrow the prestige of their bosses without acquiring the concommitant obligations. In their classes, where they are more likely to place academically in the middle, college students are apt to be unnoticed by their professors for at least a year or two, and often for their full stay.

What is true of college in general is even truer of the larger and more eminent schools. Berkeley, of course, is among the very largest and the most eminent.[32] Hence, the usual student at Berkeley is likely to come from a family of even higher social rank than the students at most colleges; he is apt to have done even better in high school, or in college if he is in graduate school; and he is likely to expect even greater occupational success. But the eminence and size of Berkeley make the competition tougher, not only competition for grades but competition for notice, notice of any kind, from professors or teaching assistants or fellow students. In his previous schooling the student led his classes and won shows of concern and even deference from his teachers; and when things went badly —poor grades, misbehavior, emotional confusion—teachers were apt to be attentive and guidance counselors available. At Berkeley and schools like it, the student is not reduced to a number—though campus hyperbole would have it so—but he is likely to find himself in relative obscurity. He is suddenly déclassé.

Meanwhile, the very eminence of the school convinces the students who are admitted, even the dullest, that they are members of an elite. Freshmen tend to assume that anyone who finished in the top eighth of his high school class—a requirement for matriculation at Berkeley—must be very bright: "No one dumb gets in this school," they say of one another.[33] Such certainties of superior intelligence, however, make the discrepancy between statuses even greater, and discouraging as well: "Whatever you say, this is no university; this is just a big, big highschool; the biggest ever."[34]

These unsettling discrepancies of status are emphasized further when the college has a well-developed bureaucracy. In Max Weber's words, bureaucracies level social differences,[35] so that students find themselves being treated as of uniformly inferior status. To an elite, accustomed to shows of concerns from their teachers and other school officials, the dispassionate disregard of social distinctions may be a bureaucracy's great sin.[36]

Observers and members of the free speech protest at Berkeley have made much of the claim that "bureaucratic alienation" was widespread on campus and contributed significantly to the support for the FSM. Hostility toward the bureaucratic mode of campus administration was a recurrent theme in the propaganda directed largely to the movement's followers. Perhaps the most eloquent of the FSM's rhetoric was Mario Savio's speech to the sit-ins at Sproul Hall on December 2: "There is a time when the operation of the machine becomes so odious, makes you so sick at heart, that you can't take part. . . ." [37]

For all this, the roots of support for the protest would seem to be elsewhere, in the more general inconsistencies of student status. Large-scale academic bureaucracies, like large-scale schools themselves, are of relatively recent origin. Rebellious student outbursts, however, have occurred on many college campuses during almost every era of American life. Commentators have recognized the prevalence of such outbursts by analyzing or dismissing the free speech protest as though it were no different from the panty raids and other non-political outbursts of earlier periods. This casual fusion obscures much of what is valuable about the FSM but it does recognize that both the FSM (and other political movements) and panty raids (and other non-political outbursts) serve as campus facsimiles or equivalents of the subterranean traditions.[38]

Thus, with or without a bureaucracy, a college campus contains a population with a strong predisposition to rebellious behavior. Such rebellious behavior may involve only a few people at a time and be relatively private, as, of course, do many of the activities of the subterranean traditions and their conventionalized counterparts among people unconnected with colleges. Once a public outburst begins on a college campus, however, many students are apt to join in, not only because most of them experience the tension that results from their inconsistencies of status, but also because the social and physical character of campus life encourages their participation in several ways.

For one thing, students have natural groups on and around campus. These groups, whether formal or informal, foster considerable linkage among the students.[39] Further, the widespread existence of such groups puts many students in touch with natural leaders. Hence, if the leaders are drawn into a public activity, they are likely to carry some of their followers along. In addition, since students share a common status, and make themselves highly identifiable to one another as students,[40] they tend to be natural allies.[41] The irregularity of academic work, which promotes a looseness of regimen quite unlike the routine of much of daily life, also encourages students to take part in collective activities by making them free to wander about campus, or, when something is brewing, to go quickly to the action.[42] Finally, the campus itself offers such a diversity of attractions—including classes—that it focuses the attentions of a high proportion of the student body on it. It usually includes a complex of buildings to provide special non-academic services: student union, dining halls, theater, bookstore, and so on. Entryways and walkways are not scattered randomly, but rather occupy or become strategic positions at and on which students congregate. The auxiliary campus of beer parlors, movie houses, record shops, street corners, and the like also operate to bring the students together in large groups.[43] When, therefore, circumstances provide an opportunity for crowd behavior, the social situation of students makes it likely that they will learn of it, have associates in it, and have time to join themselves; while the physical organization of campus offers emergent rebellions a chance to reach a large audience of potential supporters with little trouble. From this point of view, especially considering the students' latent tendencies toward rebelliousness, the infrequency of student outbursts is the main thing to explain.[44]

At any rate, once the free speech protest managed to begin and persist (for the reasons suggested in Section I of this paper), it found itself the beneficiary of both the proclivity of students to participate in rebellious activities and the channeling effects of the social and physical character of campus life. The very growth of FSM in these unintended ways led to further growth, since new supporters were apt to encourage their own unaffiliated friends to join. The expansion of FSM support along a network of already existing social relations continued until the links of friendship reached out so far that only a rare student could have been entirely isolated from encouragement by a friend or respected associate to join the movement. It may even be that some students took the very size of the FSM as evidence that it was worthy of their support.

The multiple character of the activities of FSM also served to make the movement appealing to a diversity of students. Just as most youths outside of college participate in blander versions of the subterranean traditions, so on campus most students join only in conventionalized outbursts, in which real violence or thoroughgoing defiance of the law is tempered.[45] One reason that the FSM attracted and held broad support was that it offered opportunities for participation in either manifestly aggressive or conventionalized versions: one could help capture a police car, or one could merely sign a petition; one could sit in and be arrested, or one could simply stay away from classes during a strike.

At the same time, the FSM moved toward formal legitimacy. Over the course of the semester, more and more faculty openly or covertly shifted their loyalties to the movement, even if often with certain reservations. Despite their reservations, professors saw a number of appealing features in the FSM: its ideology of academic freedom was consonant with their professional code; its identification with the civil rights movement coincided with their own political liberalism;[46] its hostility to the formal administration concurred with their resentment over a number of recent and less recent administrative actions, including the imposition of a loyalty oath, supported by the administration, in the early 1950s; and its anger about the intrusion into campus affairs by external, especially police, forces agreed with their historic sense of the secular autonomy of the campus. For at least some students, the defection of faculty to the rebellion made it seem legitimate. The similar defection of teaching assistants, who carry some prestige and probably know more undergraduates than the regular faculty, had the same effect.[47]

Of course, these same moral themes of the FSM ideology served to justify the protest to the student body as well as to the faculty. But the act of rebellion itself, including civil disobedience, also needed justification. Part of the justification came simply from the moral weight—and the effectiveness—of such disobedience in the civil rights movement. More fundamentally, however, the moral tradition of the West is in many respects the classroom of rebellion; and from that point of view it is perhaps only reasonable that "On the Duty of Civil Disobedience" is required reading for many freshmen at Berkeley, as elsewhere.[48]

One final set of factors must be examined for an understanding of the FSM victory. To a certain extent, a rebellion is a contest whose outcome rests on the relative ability of the competing forces to marshal their resources effectively. The campus and university administrations hold in such a contest considerable powers which are usually sufficient to maintain social order against efforts to disrupt it. Yet it seems clear that the FSM gained tactical superiority early and maintained it; while the powers of the administration were so misused that on some occasions the administration appeared to resuscitate a dying movement.

Certainly, for instance, the administration rescued the FSM from what was at best a partial victory and apparent dissolution when it elected in late November to re-open disciplinary proceedings against four of the movement's leaders. At the time, FSM appeared to be practically destroyed, as its inability to recruit more than 300 pickets for the sit-in of November 23 testifies. The rule modifications accepted by the Regents at their meeting of November 20 seemed to have satisfied most of the student body. But as soon as the four leaders received notices that they were to be subject to discipline for their part in the protest which had brought about the Regents' and the administration's compromises, FSM was able to recruit more than 1000 students for a sit-in on December 2.[49] Apparently the administration either did not know or did not care that its disciplinary attempts would quell the peace and touch off a toughened continuation of the protest. Either way, the action smacks of ineptitude.[50]

Actually, this failure to comprehend the temper of the student body appears to have been an enduring difficulty for administration leaders throughout the controversy. For example, President Kerr suggested over and over, almost from the start, that only a few "hard-core" students supported the movement. Similarly, he seemed to believe that the movement included enough Communists of one sort and another for him to remark it on several occasions. Some observers have proposed that President Kerr and other administrators did not really believe what they were saying. The tactics they employed against the movement, however, make it seem plausible that they were convinced of the accuracy of what they said.

The assumption that they believed what they said would account, for instance, for their efforts to eliminate a supposedly small hard-core that was the heart of the protest: destroy the core, and the movement would die. President Kerr has acknowledged himself that the university "counted" on the discussions between the administration and the FSM leadership during October and November "to separate the well-intentioned students from the hard-core recalcitrants."[51] The same assumption would explain the decisions to summon police to campus on October 2 and again on December 3. Similarly, the frequent attempts to identify the FSM as Communist or Communist infiltrated[52] could have been based on the assumption that since only a few students really cared about what FSM stood for, most would drop out once they learned the movement was Red.[53] Or, again, the futile convocation assembled by President Kerr in the Greek Theater on December 7 makes no sense if he knew that at least half the student body was actively hostile to his policies. On the other hand, if he believed that a widespread consensus still existed on campus against the FSM, then the convocation was the proper stroke to bring that consensus to bear.

What may have happened—let us speculate—is that the layers of officials between the student body and the upper administration [54] actually did put the president and his chief assistants out of touch with the student body. Certainly the president must not have comprehended the depth and spread of consternation and resentment the students felt toward the claims he made about them. The "breakdown of communication" is the cant problem of our day, invoked at every juncture, but it does appear that within the bureaucracy at Berkeley the flow of information was slow and muddy.[55] It also appears that the administration made little effort to call in students and others for purely informational purposes, even when information was needed to substantiate the most serious charges.[56]

A more serious source of the administration's difficulty seems to have been the division, and finally the conflict, between the chief officials of the Berkeley campus administration and the president of the university. While at some times the local officers were allowed to deal with the rebellion, at other times President Kerr intervened in their stead. On occasion he plainly repudiated the decisions of his subordinates. Thus the administration subverted its own authority. Indecisive, ambiguous, appearing sometimes to concede its guilt in some matters, the administration simultaneously encouraged the FSM to greater boldness and persuaded the faculty that it, rather than the administration, was the effective seat of campus authority.

Beyond the loss of opportunities to bring the protest to a stop, or to keep the peace once it was established, the administration's errors conferred on the FSM great moral advantage. Whatever the legal merits, the use of police on campus unquestionably turned almost the entire faculty against the administration. The arrests of December 3 certified the moral respectability of the movement; and, indeed, made the defense of the FSM and the defense of the civil sanctity of the campus nearly equivalent, at least for the time.[57] Not that the administration had been unwarned: after some 500 policemen had been called to campus on October 2 (presumably to assist, if necessary, in freeing the captured police car), a group of professors placed a black-bordered advertisement in the student newspaper, declaring that "This threat of force was wrong, and . . . must never be repeated."[58] But even this unusual repudiation was not heard.

The administration's inability to obtain adequate information about the mood of the student body or the faculty was a symptom of a more general ailment that sometimes affects bureaucracies: a certain incapacity to deal effectively with anything that is not routine. Such rigidity endangers a bureaucracy that is in the midst of rapid change; it makes necessary risk-taking practically impossible.[59] The FSM, even though it developed an emergent bureaucracy of its own, had very few routines to which it was bound and so was forced to improvise: a special sense in which it held the initiative. In part, the FSM had to improvise because of the novelty of the situation and the recency of its own beginnings. It may also be that it attracted to itself, for a number of reasons, essentially entrepreneurial persons, students whose own parents hold entrepreneurial rather than bureaucratic jobs and hence are likely to employ entrepreneurial styles in their public conduct.[60] In unstable contexts, the entrepreneurial mode may be better fitted than the bureaucratic for successful short-run adaptation.

The FSM held another advantage in personnel over the administration. As everyone has said, the movement had leaders and followers who were trained in the techniques of protest, while the administration lacked experience in dealing with sit-ins and other kinds of civil disobedience; but what has been much less commonly remarked is that the FSM simply had more talent than the administration. And why not? At an eminent university, especially one with a vast graduate program, the number of intelligent students had better exceed the number of intelligent bureaucrats.

Last, while FSM needed to concern itself with winning support from just two publics, the students and the faculty, the administration found itself caught between many publics. The dilemmas of President Kerr illustrate the dilemmas of the administration at large. Recognizing that the student body is more liberal than the public at large, the president found it necessary to persuade the students that he himself is a liberal. So he took occasional note of his receipt of the Alexander Meiklejohn award for his contributions to academic freedom, though without indicating it was presented to him.[61] What is plaintive about such references is that as president of a state university dependent on broad public assistance Kerr sees one of his political problems as the need to escape his old designation as a liberal. Addressing the students, however, he had to defend himself against the suspicions or assertions of many of them that he was a fascist super-bureaucrat, a reactionary with no care for freedom of speech. In the same way, the administration in general found itself eyeing the voters of California, the state legislature, the governor, the Regents, the press, the American Civil Liberties Union, the police, the American Association of University Professors,—and the faculty and the students. Once the FSM had the support of a substantial minority of the students, the administration was able to do nothing without alienating the sympathy of at least one of its many publics.

In sum, the Free Speech Movement was able to survive the usual hazards of organizational birth because it drew from the start on a number of militant students joined by a previous network of social relations, experienced in protest work, and exceptionally sensitive to the deprivation of their traditional political rights on campus. The movement was able to grow to great size because it tapped the students' general propensities to rebelliousness, because the nature of campus life channels students into collective activity, because it had effective sources of legitimacy, and because it acquired leadership that was better adapted to triumph in a fluid situation than the university administration. With the support of about half the student body, it was able to carry out its promise to bring the campus to a halt: even large and durable centers of power, like university administrations, rule over what turn out to be surprisingly fragile empires.

NOTES

1. Except when noted, my account of the events of the free speech protest draws on "Three Months of Crisis," *California Monthly* (February 1965). "Three Months of Crisis" is an indispensable chronology which contains in addition to a summary of the events many quotations and paraphrases of speeches and documents. The chronology has been reprinted in S. M. Lipset and Sheldon S. Wolin, eds., *The Berkeley Student Revolt* (Garden City, 1965).
2. "The intensity of student reaction took the Berkeley campus and University-wide administration by surprise." Clark Kerr, "A Message to Alumni," *California Monthly* (February 1965), p. 94. Reprinted in Lipset and Wolin, eds., *The Berkeley Student Revolt.*
3. See Michael Rossman, "Some Background Notes on Civil Rights Activity and the Free Speech Movement," *Occident* (Berkeley, Fall 1964–65), esp. pp. 8–12; and Max Heirich and Sam Kaplan, "Yesterday's Discord," *California Monthly* (February 1965). "Yesterday's Discord" has been reprinted in Lipset and Wolin, eds., *The Berkeley Student Revolt.*
4. See Nathan Glazer, "What Happened at Berkeley," *Commentary* (February 1965), pp. 39–40; and Kerr, "A Message to Alumni," p. 95. "What Happened at Berkeley" has been reprinted in Lipset and Wolin, eds., *The Berkeley Student Revolt.*
5. Kerr, "A Message to Alumni," p. 94.
6. Rossman, "Some Background Notes . . . ," pp. 3–4, 14.
7. Slate is a student political party which prefers to be called radical rather than liberal.
8. Arthur Goldberg, as quoted in "Three Months of Crisis," p. 36.
9. Rossman, "Some Background Notes . . . ," p. 12. My emphasis.
10. Unnamed speaker, as quoted in "Three Months of Crisis," p. 38.
11. The introduction of historical factors will not, I trust, obscure the militantly sociological character of this paper.

12. *The Daily Californian* (September 18, 1958) commented that "it appears strange to us and a little bit disillusioning that any university should have to take such an effort to relocate speakers off campus."
13. Administrative efforts to relocate the tradition are themselves evidence that the university recognized and defended the tradition.
14. In 1956, for example, Adlai Stevenson was not allowed to speak on campus during his Presidential campaign. He did, however, avail himself of the Sather Gate tradition.
15. Samuel Stouffer, "Some Afterthoughts of a Contributor to 'The American Soldier,'" in Robert Merton and Paul Lazarsfeld, eds., *Continuities in Social Research* (Glencoe, 1950), esp. p. 199; and Samuel Stouffer *et al.*, *The American Soldier* (Princeton, 1949), 2v., esp. Vol. I, pp. 563–564 and also pp. 250–258.
16. *The Old Regime and the French Revolution* (Garden City, 1955), Stuart Gilbert, trans., pp. 176–177.
17. Elinor Barber, *The Bourgeoisie in Eighteenth Century France* (Princeton, 1955), pp. 139–140.
18. Crane Brinton, *The Anatomy of Revolution* (New York, 1957), pp. 66–67.
19. *Idem.*
20. *Ibid.*, pp. 34–36. Richard Hofstadter, *The Age of Reform* (New York, 1955), ch. iv, esp. pp. 131–137, has used relative deprivation to help account for the rise of reform movements among middle-class professionals in the United States at the start of this century.
21. Kerr, "A Message to Alumni," p. 95. Kerr goes on to say that "Most of the students of the time went about their regular affairs."
22. For example, Eugene Bardach *et al.*, "The Berkeley Free Speech Controversy (Preliminary Report)," (December 13, 1964), mimeographed, p. 8, report that on December 4, the second day of the strike, a Friday, the university's Office of Public Information called the strike 85 per cent effective, although later the office withdrew its estimate. Bardach *et al.*, p. 15 conclude that "Approximately 15,000 students stayed out of class from Thursday through Monday . . ." but give no source for their judgment. However, the FSM strike survey of Monday, December 7, found in a check of slightly more than 90 per cent of all scheduled classes that about half were not meeting at all; where classes were meeting, attendance was substantially reduced. These figures do not include the classes scheduled for the hours from 9 A.M. to noon, since these were officially cancelled by the administration for the convocation held at the Greek Theater. These assessments dovetail with the prediction by FSM, made

on the basis of a random telephone survey of 5000 students conducted on the weekend of December 5 and 6, that about 55 per cent of the student body intended to stay away from classes on the 7th. Further, newspaper accounts of the convocation at the Greek Theater on the 7th agree that about half of the audience, estimated at from 15,000 to 18,000, were hostile towards the speeches of President Kerr and Professor Robert Scalapino. The Berkeley *Gazette* (December 7, 1964, 2nd extra), p. 2, said that "about half of the audience arose and shouted, 'No! No!'" in response to the proposal by Kerr and Scalapino. The *Gazette, ibid.,* added that as the convocation began "More than half the audience stood up and cheered [Mario] Savio," the most prominent leader of the FSM.

23. The use of the word 'adolescent' has been changing in recent years. About 30 years ago it was used to refer to what is now more usually called 'the teen-age years.' Recent usage has expanded the meaning to include the teen-age years and the years thereafter, perhaps up to 25 for men and 21 for women. My usage reflects this newer definition.

24. Bennett M. Berger, "On the Youthfulness of Youth Cultures," *Social Research* (Autumn 1963), p. 321.

25. David Matza, "Subterranean Traditions of Youth," *The Annals* (November 1961), pp. 103, 116. Professor Matza has kindly offered several helpful suggestions in connection with this paper.

26. Two such assessments are Ruth Benedict, "Continuities and Discontinuities in Cultural Conditioning," *Psychiatry* (May 1938); and Talcott Parsons, *Essays in Sociological Theory* (New York, 1964, rev. ed.), ch. v, "Age and Sex in the Social Structure of the United States."

27. Parsons, "Age and Sex. . . . ," p. 94.

28. See Matza, "Subterranean Traditions of Youth," p. 103.

29. Or to those who are in some way, perhaps through friendship, brought into such kinds of behavior, whether or not they experience strain. See Berger, "On the Youthfulness of Youth Cultures," pp. 322–323.

30. See Gerhard Lenski, "Status Crystallization: A Non-Vertical Dimension of Social Status," *American Sociological Review* (August 1954).

31. See Gerald M. Swatez, "Kerr's Multiversity: The City of Intellect Under Pluralistic Industrialism," *The Graduate Student Journal* (Spring 1964), pp. 19, 27. See also Michael Young, *The Rise of the Meritocracy, 1870–2033* (Baltimore, 1961). But see as well Max Weber, "Bureaucracy," in *From Max Weber: Essays in Sociology,* Hans Gerth and C. Wright Mills, trans. and eds. (New York, 1958), pp. 221–224 and 235–237.

32. Simply to be at Berkeley apparently carries considerable cachet:

among 120,000 high school candidates for the National Merit Scholarship, Berkeley ranks fifth in popularity for the boys and fourth for the girls. *Newsweek* (February 15, 1965) p. 82.

33. Overheard by my wife in a freshman language class noted at that time as a sanctuary for dull students.

34. This must be a classic, both in length and solemnity, among graffiti, but then it appears on the wall of a library men's room at Berkeley.

35. Weber, "Bureaucracy," pp. 224–225.

36. I am grateful to Professor Bruce Hackett for this suggestion.

37. Quoted in full in "Three Months of Crisis," p. 60. Compare Savio's speech with: "If [an] injustice is part of the necessary friction of the machine of government, let it go, let it go . . . but if [the injustice] is of such a nature that it requires you to be the agent of injustice to another, then, I say, break the law. Let your life be a counter friction to stop the machine."— Thoreau, "On the Duty of Civil Disobedience."

38. Matza, "Subterranean Traditions of Youth," p. 117, suggests that the "larks and pranks" of fraternity life are part of a conventional Bohemianism. But see Note 45.

39. Here, once again, the frequent claim that student life at Berkeley and other large schools is oppressively lonely, that students are 'alienated' from one another, is called into doubt. Yet, what is to be made of students' convictions that they are lonely and just don't know *any*body? Gerald Swatez, to whom I am indebted for this and other suggestions, as well as for a patient editorial job on this paper, has proposed that students may feel isolated because they believe they ought to know *every*one— meaning everyone whom they consider as an insider. Since an undergraduate may define everyone in his living group and his several classes as an insider, the number of students he feels he ought to know may run to a few thousand. Knowing only a fraction of them, however, he feels cut off. For a student at a small college, the situation is rather different. He may know fewer of his fellows than the usual student at Berkeley knows of his, but because the number of insiders is much smaller he may feel that he knows everybody, perhaps even literally. Amherst College, for instance, has fewer students than the lecture meeting of Physics 10 at Berkeley.

40. Because they employ one or another emblem of that status: book bags, clipboards, fraternity pins, hair and clothing styles, diction, gestures, friends, all provide clues.

41. There are, of course, many variations within the student body that usually override the influences toward unity.

42. This same irregularity of life may provoke dissatisfaction at the same time.

43. The cautious university administrator who foresees his students

in permanent revolution may want, therefore, to plan future campuses with an eye to inhibiting, rather than facilitating, the formation of protest movements. The administrator might insist that the planning firm hire a Trotskyite, or safer, an ex-Trotskyite, as consultant. Did not Napoleon ensure that Parisian boulevards be straight and open for the benefit of artillery?

44. Some perspective may be gained on the likelihood of the eruption of loose crowd behavior on a college campus by contrasting the social contexts of the spectators at a professional football game. The spectators at a professional game ordinarily come from a wide area and travel separately to and from the game. Hence, during the course of the game, they constitute a fragmented mass without leadership. Once they start for their homes, they become too dispersed for a collective outburst. At a college game the students attend in their natural groups. Even while returning to their living quarters, passing over routes filled with other students, they maintain the fabric of group life. If they are exuberant in victory or frustrated in defeat, they can swiftly become a mob. And this opportunity occurs several times each autumn. In this light, it is the infrequency of student outbursts that seems the main puzzle.

45. Even panty raids, however, can generate real violence. One at Berkeley in 1956 apparently was nearly a riot.

46. See Seymour Martin Lipset, *Political Man* (Garden City, 1963), ch. 10, "American Intellectuals: Their Politics and Status," esp. pp. 336–338.

47. *FSM Newsletter* (December [misprinted as November] 10, 1964), p. 2, claimed that "900 out of 1200 Teaching Assistants declared themselves on strike, cancelling all their sections." Whether or not this estimate is exaggerated, it is clear that in many social science and humanities departments, a majority of assistants went on strike. See the *Daily Californian* (December 3, 1964), p. 1. It should be noted that graduate students experience status inconsistency even more than undergraduates, in part simply because they are older, in part because they are among those who have been most successful as undergraduates. Further, those already preparing for academic careers are apt to share the views of the faculty and hence were similarly subject to the moral appeals of the FSM.

The graduate students, especially the teaching and research assistants, are also in a strategic position to influence the faculty. From the faculty's perspective, they were a source of relatively reliable information and opinion; their attitudes toward the FSM instructed the faculty in the depth of student feelings; and when, finally, their assistants went on strike in December, some faculty cancelled their classes (often on the ground that public disorder made teaching impossible) to protect the strikers, who otherwise might have been subject to loss of pay and dismissal from their jobs. These cumulative effects both widened the strike and gave it additional legitimacy.

48. See Note 37.

49. After ten weeks of dispute, the mood of many students resembled that of one graduate student I know who said that he was tired and wanted to return to his studies. "But," he added, "if the administration finds it in its heart to do something stupid again, I guess I'll be able to find it in my heart to do something about it."

50. Philip Selznick, *Commentary* (March 1965), "Berkeley," p. 84, noting that the charges contained in the letters were reinstituted (from October 1 and 2), observes that students at Berkeley perceived the disciplinary attempt "as a sickness of soul." Reprinted in Lipset and Wolin, eds., *The Berkeley Student Revolt*.

51. "Statement by President Clark Kerr" (December 3, 1964), in "Appendix: Documents in the Free Speech Controversy," *California Monthly* (February 1965), p. 88.

52. President Kerr has recently resumed the attempt to identify the FSM as Communist-infiltrated, albeit in an indirect way. See Kerr, "A Message to Alumni," pp. 94, 95.

53. Like some other tactics of the administration, this one appeared to make many students feel that they were being wronged. It was not long after the strike that some students began wearing buttons that read: "I'm From Cal—Color Me Red." See Note 57.

54. Glazer, "What Happened at Berkeley," p. 43, has commented: "Everyone—arriving faculty members, arriving deans, visiting authorities—is astonished by the size of the administration at Berkeley, and in the statewide University of California."

55. Another kind of contemporary cant is the easy attack on bureaucracies as the source of our ills. Let us invoke C. Wright Mills, *White Collar* (New York, 1956), p. 78, "Descriptively, bureaucracy refers to a hierarchy of offices or bureaus, each with an assigned area of operation, each employing a staff having specialized qualifications. So defined, bureaucracy is the most efficient type of social organization yet devised." See also Weber, "Bureaucracy," pp. 214–216.

56. A revealing case in point, entirely internal in nature, is President Kerr's claim of December 3 that the students who sat in at the administration building the previous day had broken into the office of President-emeritus Robert Gordon Sproul and strewn its files about the room. This report was based on the inferences of a campus police officer who had made no effort to substantiate the culpability of the students by talking with President Sproul, his secretary, or any of the students. On December 4, the secretary reported that she detected no sign of

disruption; it turned out that she and President Sproul normally spread papers about the office. See Kerr, "Statement" (December 3, 1964), pp. 88–89.

57. Brinton, *The Anatomy of Revolution*, p. 36, has said: "Men may revolt partly or even mainly because they are hindered . . . in their economic activities; but to the world—and, save for a very few hypocrites, also to themselves—they must appear *wronged*. . . . Revolutions cannot do without the word 'justice' and the sentiments it arouses."

58. *Daily Californian* (October 20, 1964), p. 9. The advertisement was signed by nine professors, including one departmental chairman.

59. One way bureaucracies try to surmount the problems of rigidity is to create special bureaus which concern themselves with the ways the bureaucracy as a whole must change to adapt to external conditions. See Peter F. Drucker, *The Concept of the Corporation* (New York, 1964), pp. 66–67, 72–78. Perhaps the university administration needs to establish a kind of consumers research program to take the mood of its student clientele.

60. For example, students whose fathers had their own law firms or medical offices may have been more apt to support the FSM than those whose fathers worked in large law bureaucracies or in medical group practice.

61. For instance, see Kerr, "A Message to Alumni," p. 95.

The Student Movement: Some Impressions at Berkeley

HENRY F. MAY

Henry F. May has taught history since 1952 at the University of California in Berkeley. He is the author of Discontent of the Intellectuals, End of American Innocence *and* Protestant Churches and Industrial America.

THIS is not a historical survey of the Free Speech Crisis Berkeley. The events of the fall of 1964 have been well and repeatedly summarized. Here in Berkeley these events—

the sudden suspension of certain student political privileges, the defiance and violations, the attempted arrests and the blocking of the police car, the agreements and negotiations which always broke down, the concessions which came too late, the final student occupation of Sproul Hall, the resultant mass arrests and the ensuing strike—all these have become as familiar as the events that led up to the French and the Russian Revolutions. And like the events of these big revolutions, the events of our little one sound distressingly different in the versions given by equally honest men of differing political emotions.

Another thing this is not is an attempt to assess the blame for our conflict. The ineptness of the administration and the unwieldiness of our huge institution, both major causes of the trouble, have been dealt with again and again. Here, my sole concern is with the students. They were, as I saw it, the actors: faculty and administration merely reactors. They won major victories, they have great power here, and they are being watched—with anticipation or foreboding—on other campuses of the nation.

My approach toward the Free Speech Movement and its constituency is necessarily that of an outsider, although I have talked to members and sympathizers a good deal and attended a good many of the open rallies. To supplement what immediate knowledge I have, I must rely on two kinds of analogy. First, in the mid-thirties I was a student at Berkeley and cannot help comparing this generation of students to my own. Second, I am by profession a student and teacher of American intellectual history, and I cannot talk or think about any popular movement without other movements coming to my mind.

In some ways students in Berkeley have changed a lot since the thirties. They are more intelligent now. The University is harder to get into, and many enter from "enriched" high school courses. Telegraph Avenue, the "Left Bank" area near the campus, now offers an intellectual bill-of-fare of almost indigestible richness. It is easier to find Italian, French or Japanese movies than Hollywood products near the University. Bookstores offer everywhere overwhelming displays of the latest paperbacks in philosophy, religion and pornography. A wide range of magazines and newspapers of dissent, displayed everywhere around the campus, pleaded all possible and impossible causes.

Many students are nourished and stimulated by this fare. It is not surprising to find sophomores who read Sartre and Camus in the time they can spare from their assignments. Yet now, even more than in the thirties, range and excitement are commoner than intellectual discipline. Languages, including English, are seldom a bright student's strongest point. History, particularly European history, attracts great numbers, but this does not indicate that students are at all traditionalist. Institutions of the past make few claims on people who have not yet managed to feel any great identity with institutions in the present. Formal systems of thought—abandoned anyway in philosophy departments—attract no allegiance; the students are likely to be eclectic and experimental. The more rigid simplifications, including Marxist ones, fall apart under their uncommitted scrutiny.

The best quality of Berkeley students is their uncompromising effort to be honest with themselves and others. The defensive pseudosophisticated pursuit of intellectual fashion that plagues some colleges is the last thing one need worry about here. Whether one talks to our students about politics, religion or art, one feels that as they listen they are trying to decide, somewhat warily, what they believe and like—not what is In or Out. Despite all that has been said, justly but too simply, about the University's concentration on research, despite the heartbreaking problems of teaching undergraduates in such numbers, I know some faculty members who refuse high salaries elsewhere and stay in Berkeley not for prestige, libraries or climate, but for Berkeley's undergraduate students.

The nature of the student body in general has much to do with the shape of the radical movement that has grown up here. In the thirties, notoriously and also in actuality, the student movement was ranged in concentric circles around a Communist core. The Communists, open or secret—and there were both kinds—repelled most students by their pomposity of manner and language. Yet the causes of Communists espoused in those days of the "United Front" were everybody's causes: liberal unemployment relief, racial equality, and particularly international peace. In the late thirties, among "student leaders," it actually became fashionable and respectable to dabble a little in the movement. Thus there was a fairly clear series of stages or levels of radicalism, from fellow travelers to on-and-off sympathizers and beyond them to respectable but worried liberals. Beyond all these, of course, was a very large group—larger then than now—of students who were interested in dates and athletics and not at all in politics.

Today, a free-form figure, or even a mobile, has to be used instead of a system of concentric circles to symbolize the political makeup of the Berkeley campus. At the center there is still a group of dedicated, more or less full-time radical leaders. At the edge of the picture a large semistudent fringe fades by imperceptible shadings into the immediate background. And in between is a large and rapidly shifting mass of students, sometimes indifferent, but occasionally, in particular crises that involve their strong feelings, suddenly moved to dramatic action in thousands. Each of these three parts of our picture, the radical leadership, the semistudent fringe, and the shifting, potentially active mass needs separate definition before a pattern can even begin to emerge.

In discussing the full-time leadership, one is led, regrettably but inevitably, to the Communist question. In discussions of the F.S.M., as of other American radical movements, Communist influence has been both irresponsibly exaggerated and uncritically denied, and probably given too much importance in both cases. Grizzled and battle-scarred Stalinist veterans of the thirties are certainly on hand in Berkeley, as are shrill young devotees of Mao and Castro. A few of the leaders of the Free Speech Movement have themselves linked the student struggle with the Cuban Revolution and the supermilitant tactics of the Progressive Labor Movement. Yet insiders report that the orthodox Marxist minority in the movement has often opposed the direct-action tactics—to them unrealistic—that have proved so successful. It may be worth noting that demonstrations against American policy in Vietnam draw only a few hundred, whereas Free Speech demonstrations sometimes draw thousands. In the leadership, Communism exists but is probably unimportant. Various kinds of socialism, unaffiliated radicalism, and above all ultramilitant devotion to the Civil Rights movement are inextricably mixed together.

The relation between radical leadership of any kind and large-scale student support is very tenuous. It has been demonstrated that the thousand who occupied Sproul Hall were mostly without political affiliation or experience, and this is doubtless true also of the thousands more who supported the student strike. Yet it is not irrelevant that an experienced radical leadership has existed in Berkeley since long before the administrative mistakes that immediately produced the current crisis. At least since the so-called "San Francisco riots" of 1960 (the much misinterpreted protest against the House Un-American Activities Committee) Berkeley has been something of a radical Mecca. Some administrative quarters, here and elsewhere, have claimed that Berkeley is the first target of a deliberate nationwide drive which will later hit all major campuses. I have no knowledge whatever that this is (or is not) so, but more than one graduate student has told me frankly that he chose Berkeley partly because of the movement. Some former undergraduate leaders stay around and lend a hand.

Since 1960, the student movement has carried on guerrilla war with the Kerr administration over a set of presidential directives that then attempted, plausibly but unrealistically, to define the rights and duties of several distinct and complicated categories of undergraduate organizations. Since then, important concessions have been made and student victories won. By this fall, it was nonsense to talk about a "climate of oppression" in Berkeley. Students, by observing certain forms and rules, could *say* (although in theory they could not *do*) what they wanted. The climate was rather one of bureaucracy. It is particularly hard to explain to our students why a given kind of organization can have open meetings but not membership meetings on the campus, why Communism or free love may be advocated here but not there, as long as one has an associate or full professor—but not an assistant professor— as chairman. All these rules had their historical *raisons d'être*, but this kind of history is not a favorite subject here.

Last year, the movement's center of attention shifted with new intensity to the compelling cause of Civil Rights. Berkeley contributed a few students to Mississippi and many to militant demonstrations in the Bay Region. And finally, at the beginning of the fall term of 1964, before administration errors revived the question of campus political action, a publication of the left student organization called Slate seemed to suggest another major shift of emphasis, this time to the alleged outrages of the academic "system" itself. A Slate pamphlet called for "AN OPEN, FIERCE, AND THOROUGH-GOING REBELLION ON THIS CAMPUS," demanding that grades be eliminated in the social sciences and humanities, rules be abolished in university housing units, and negotiations undertaken about the question of examinations. Ways suggested to achieve these dazzling goals included civil disobedience at university public ceremonies and maybe "a mass student strike . . . something which seems unthinkable at present."

Thus, before the outbreak of the recent controversy and the formation of the Free Speech Movement, an experienced, tough, continuing radical leadership existed. The leadership of the new movement consisted partly of old-timers, partly of newcomers.

In one unpleasant way the Free Speech Movement seems more reminiscent of the Communist-led "United Front" movements of the thirties than it really is. These always started with lists of respectable constituent organizations and impeccable liberal objectives. The key posts, however, were always filled by the tried and true, who somehow ended in firm control. The F.S.M., formed this October to protest new political regulations, originally included representatives of radical, liberal and even conservative student groups, and also of student religious organizations. Before long, however, the moderate groups fell away, and it became obvious that the movement was dominated by militants. The process in the two instances was different. In the thirties, radical caucuses consciously arranged to run the "United Fronts." In the F.S.M., extreme tactics, derived from the Civil Rights movement, were, I believe, invoked without much planning in response to administration blunders. These tactics alienated moderates but drew sudden waves of student mass support which far outran, for short periods, the expectations of the most radical leaders.

Much has been said about the nonstudents, radical or Bohemian, who surround our campus in considerable numbers. Tourist buses stop near Telegraph Avenue, so that sightseers can goggle at the "beatniks," with their bare feet, beards and long dirty hair. With luck, they may even hear a speech, by a well-known nonstudent character, in favor of marijuana.

Nothing irritates the F.S.M. more than the newspaper charge that it is made up of a bunch of beatniks. During the height of the crisis some sitters-in and other protesters wrote to the local newspapers insisting angrily on their own high grades, clean clothes and bourgeois habits. Yet to some, beards and sandals do represent part of a general protest against confining restrictions. And people who *look* like extreme caricatures of nineteenth-century Bohemians appear at all demonstrations. The F.S.M. is indeed not Beat, but Beats favor, and perhaps slightly affect, the F.S.M.

Real Beats are usually nonstudents. Semistudents, a group more important here, may or may not be unconventional in behavior and dress. Many bright, attractive and serious young people, often from bourgeois families, cannot bring themselves to accept for long either the discipline of grades and requirements, or the professional goals these sometimes imply. Disaffected by the campus program but fascinated by campus life, many are in and out of the university.

Among those who are in, out and halfway, some students here and elsewhere suffer deeply, like many young people everywhere, from various kinds of psychic malaise. Resort to psychotherapy is almost as commonplace as getting treatment for mononucleosis. Student worries and even student neuroses are not peculiar to Berkeley or America. To some extent—I suspect a slight one—their immediate cause may indeed lie in the system of grades and examinations the student movement is always condemning. Students here take, as they took in the thirties, five courses at a time. Ambitious and even devoted professors have sometimes raised the requirements of individual courses to quite unrealistic levels. Thus students are harassed by too many examinations and papers—a fault that the crisis has brought to the university's attention and one that will be corrected. But it is hardly necessary to point out that student malaise comes from a whole range of causes, individual and cultural, which lie far beyond the power of the university to deal with.

The relation of psychic disorder to political unrest is complex. But I suspect that it is important, for the understanding of the Berkeley crisis, to remember that a considerable minority of young people here has withdrawn, in whole or in part, from conventional competition. These are, admirably in their way, impossible to deter by appeals for individual prudence. Fear of the security check and the police record has declined together with career ambition. For secession, some have paid a heavy price. Others are willing to pay it, and many more contemplate joining the seceders but keep one foot in respectability.

The main body of students who have supported the F.S.M. in action belongs neither to the radical core nor to any kind of semistudent fringe. Many are apparently well adjusted and highly successful students even in the most conventional terms of grades. Yet even among these, even among those least identifiable with any obvious source of unrest, many are asking ultimate questions in immediate and personal terms.

The most striking fact about the present generation, to me, is that large groups are both more idealistic and more alienated than any but a handful in the radical thirties. Not only is this student generation critical of the parents and the parental social order; it is often trained to be critical by the parents, themselves perplexed and somewhat guilty in their attitude toward their own times. Exposed early to a quite unprecedented range of ideas and committed to none, they will follow no leader consistently. But for the kind of immediate cause that stirs them, they will follow any leader who is going their way, and going fast enough.

The alienation of our students is social rather than political, and it is to this alienation that Mario Savio, far the most effective of the F.S.M. leaders, is best able to speak. Always extreme but never sectarian, at times Messianic and—to adult ears, often skirting the edges of the ridiculous—Savio is the only leader who seems to represent a new genre, as different from the Slate leaders of 1960 as from the Marxists of the thirties. Many students, he says, find "that for them to become part of society, to become lawyers, ministers, business men, people in government, very often they must compromise those principles which were most dear to them, they must suppress the most creative impulses that they have; this is a prior condition for being part of the system." In the thirties most students, and particularly the Marxists, took the "system" more for granted than this.

The sort of potential radicalism I am describing finds few easy outlets. Normally, I believe, our students are not much stirred by politics. They will turn out to work against laws that interfere with free speech or menace racial integration, and the Peace Corps offers one real outlet for their zeal for persona, concrete involvement with the problems of the world. President Johnson's profound political practicality fails to attract them; still less are most of them drawn toward the disciplined ruthlessness of the Communist world. I cannot imagine that sexual freedom presents, today, much of a fighting cause; the question now is more what to do with it than how to get it. Thus the Civil Rights movement is the one organized effort that can claim their complete allegiance; it is personal, immediate and revolutionary. The local sit-ins, shop-ins and the like roused much white resentment, but scored some undeniable successes in forcing the employment of Negroes. The high purpose of these efforts, their achievements, and also the courage they demanded gave them unrivaled prestige.

From Civil Rights to Free Speech proved to be an easy road. One participant in the Sproul Hall F.S.M. sit-in told me that he had long felt guilty about not participating in Civil Rights civil disobedience. Perhaps, he thought, because of his conventional upbringing he had never been able to persuade himself that real integration could be brought about in this manner. The Sproul Hall sit-in, on the other hand, took place in the name of Free Speech—a cause he had been taught to consider an absolute, and this gave him a chance to prove his courage. This honest self-analysis may well be representative. Many argue plausibly that the relation between the two causes is a more concrete one, that the restrictions on campus political action were tightened because of outside resentment at Civil Rights demonstrations. Some students devoutly believe that the efforts to suspend leaders of the demonstrations were intended to cripple the Civil Rights cause.

In my opinion the links between the movements should not be allowed to obscure the differences. Surely it is not the same thing to stay in a restaurant for the purpose of insisting on one's moral and even legal rights and to occupy a university building for the stated purpose of obtaining a "capitulation" on matters of university regulations. Defying a dean, or even risking academic units, does not call for the same kind of heroism—or the same degree of anger—as defying an Alabama sheriff and risking one's life.

No cause other than these two could have made so many students follow the F.S.M. leaders into the startling actions of this fall. And nothing but the cause of Free Speech—not even Civil Rights—could have drawn together the amorphous and shifting mass, together with some of the disaffected fringe, behind the experienced leadership. No other cause could have combined so many resentments, dispelled so many misgivings, and brought to the surface so much frustrated idealism.

If one looks, as I cannot help looking, to analogies in other times, one passes fairly quickly by the various forms of American proletarian radicalism. The I.W.W., with its free speech fights and its insistent toughness of language and manner, is closer than any kind of Marxism. But at its most effective, the F.S.M. speaks a language very different from the studied truculence of syndicalist revolt. Like other movements of youthful rebellion in America, the F.S.M. is far more deeply rooted in the national tradition than it seems, or than its members always realize.

In the person of Savio, the movement speaks with a voice that has been heard in America since the beginning, the voice of an exalted, quasi-religious romantic anarchism. For all of their toughness, some of the F.S.M. are crypto-transcendentalists and neo-antinomians. It is interesting that the movement has been patronized by some, although not all, of the Chris-

tian chaplains that surround our nonreligious campus like holy
wolves, waiting to pick off anyone who strays away from the
secularist campfire. One of the most eloquent and penetrating
early appraisals of the movement came from a Methodist minister who could not but approve moral outrage in the face of
depersonalization. Despite the F.S.M.'s frequent ugliness of
speech and action, this observer found to his own surprise
"a remarkable gentleness and sweetness of spirit which comes
out here and there as the life of the movement goes on."

In terms of standard American transcendentalism, Emerson
is obviously too decorous and optimistic to furnish much support. The American ancestor most nearly admitted is Thoreau.
In his wake Tolstoi and Gandhi, with their methods of passive
resistance and their hatred of the machine, obviously provide
some precedent for the sit-ins and also for the continual F.S.M.
denunciations of I.B.M. cards and factory methods. One of
the few relieving light moments in the tense day when students lay down around the police car, and hundreds of police
waited around the corner for the word of attack, occurred in
the name of the Indian saint. The harsh and unpleasantly
professional exhortations coming from the improvised speakers' stand on top of the car were interrupted by an announcement that it was Gandhi's birthday and the crowd, lying and
standing, responded by singing "Happy Birthday to You."
Actually the intensely individualistic discipline of Thoreau
contrasts sharply with the F.S.M.'s dependence on crowd
emotion. And Gandhi's insistence that in an unjust society
one must remain in jail is sharply different from the F.S.M.'s
confusing insistence that court punishment of demonstrators
is an outrage and a grievance.

In terms of religious and quasi-religious precedent, modern
existentialism seems closer than Tolstoyan nonviolence. What
Savio was demanding, when he urged in a peak of passion
that students throw their bodies on the administrative machine and bring it to a grinding halt, was something like an
existentialist *acte gratuit*, a gesture of self-identification.

Radical democracy, with its love of liberty and its dangers
of tyranny, its trust in the mass and its contempt for institutions, seems to me to pervade the movement as it has many

American movements. At times Whitman, that protean patron of American cranks and prophets, democrats and loners, furnishes texts that might well be used by the F.S.M.:

> I hear it was charged against me that I sought to destroy
> institutions
> But really I am neither for nor against institutions,
> (What indeed have I in common with them? Or what
> with the destruction of them?)
> Only I will establish . . .
> Without edifices or rules or trustees or any argument,
> The institution of the dear love of comrades.

The F.S.M. would agree with Walt about rules and trustees, and also about love, a word it often invokes. Joan Baez, the F.S.M.'s Maid in Armor, urged them to go into Sproul Hall with love in their hearts. And several of their leaflets have talked about the need for a "loving university," instead of a brutal and bureaucratic one.

Knowing that the movement proceeds partly from alienation, one is tempted to look to the 1920's for precedents. The literary rebels of that period interest our students, but they were very different. Sometimes frivolous, but often as serious as Savio, the writers of the twenties were more interested in literature than politics, sometimes inclined to dabble in Menckenian elitism, and concerned about Negroes mainly in terms of art and music. Perhaps significantly, the less completely alienated rebels of 1912 seem to offer a closer parallel. Their mixture of socialism and anarchism has its similarities to the present mood, especially when, as in the case of Randolph Bourne, it developed tragic implications.

One contemporary analogy that has often occurred to me I hesitate to bring up, because it is partly—only partly—misleading. This is the analogy to the Goldwater movement. When I hesitantly suggested this to a pro-F.S.M. graduate student of my acquaintance, he surprised me by saying that the same analogy had haunted his own dreams. The resemblance does not rest on the actual temporary cooperation between the Goldwaterites and leftists in the earliest days of the movement, when in protest against prohibition of certain kinds of political activities, students sang "Left and Right together, we shall Overcome." The relation I am speaking of is less direct and more lasting. Both the so-called conservative political movement and the radical student movement are protests against bigness, bureaucracy and official liberalism. Clark Kerr is actually a rather better symbol of the Liberal Establishment than is Lyndon Johnson, who has his archaic side. Both protest movements express vague wishes for immediate and simple solutions to complex problems. No statement could better summarize the whole F.S.M. defense of its methods than "In Defense of Liberty Extremism Is No Vice." And both movements appeal to the heart—by implication, sometimes, against the head.

So far I much prefer the anarchism of the left to that of the right. On the whole, the causes in which laws have been violated by the Bay Area Movement or the F.S.M. are to me noble causes, although I think their tactics have distorted these causes. And even discounting its disastrous "Southern" strategy, the Goldwater movement had far more hate and less love than the F.S.M., although skeptics have to expect harsh treatment from both.

All these analogies seem to me to help, and none to explain fully the student movement that came of age in Berkeley. To go further one must, in the first place, keep in mind the place and time, the American mass university in a time both of quickening intellectual life and collapsing patterns. And finally, one must admit that one never understands a new generation, although one deals with it every day.

Not understanding entirely, one may either accept or oppose the student movement. Perhaps one can defend certain boundaries against it. What one cannot do—and this one faculty group after another has learned with considerable cost—is to bargain or compromise. Essentially, the movement is absolutist. It is therefore very hard to fit into the habits or structure of our campus institutions, based, like all our institutions, on consensus or compromise.

What remains in doubt is not the existence of the student movement, although it will continue to have its ups and downs, or its militance, although this too will wax and wane.

It is rather its direction. Having won nearly everything it could ask in terms of campus free speech, will the movement turn its energies once more completely outward into Civil Rights or some other major cause, or inward into further university revolt? Some leaders call for the "Free University," a new kind of academic community without grades and rules, in which students share in all academic decisions. In Berkeley, moreover, faculty and administration have been so shaken that it is not clear that either has the moral authority or the will to draw clear lines and defend them if necessary. Like modern parents, deans and professors find it easy to sympathize with revolt, very hard to act their traditional roles.

Even if the program of the Free University collapses, as it may, for lack of support, and even if no further "internal" causes emerge, a student body so deeply committed to off-campus causes presents many subtle problems. In the midst of conflict, with slogans screaming from the placards and blaring from the loudspeakers on the edge of the campus, can the faculty insist on the values, never the easiest to defend in America, of precision and complexity and patience, even of humility before one's subject? How great will be the continuing appeal of subjects that have—at least on the surface—little to do with current controversy? American education has long been plagued by utilitarianism, and there is a utilitarianism of the left as well as of the Dewey-to-Kerr center.

A few years ago many professors, I among them, were deploring the passivity and complacency of American students and of American life, and wishing for a revival of campus radicalism. Somewhat wryly, we are forced to realize that radicalism never comes in the shape or size one has asked for. It is the breath of life, and it is full of danger. Our campus now is lively and dangerous. Divided between hope and anxiety, I can look for comfort only to the very considerable reserves, in Berkeley and elsewhere, of intelligence and honesty.

Berkeley and Beyond
IRVING HOWE

Irving Howe has taught at Stanford and Brandeis and is now Professor of English Literature at Hunter College. His latest book is A World More Attractive.

I WANT to posit the idea that almost every student who comes to an American university has somewhere in the back of his mind a true vision of what a university is supposed to be: that the university should serve as a center for disinterested learning; that it should be quick with the passions of controversy yet dedicated to those studies which the outer world may dismiss as esoteric; that it should be a sanctuary for opinion; and that in its precincts he should be able to encounter men who will serve as models of intellectual discipline and enthusiasm.

Now there are some American universities in which the student can find all of these, though it takes a bit of looking; but only rarely can he find them as the dominant voice of a university or find them uncontaminated by the grossness of utilitarian measurement and the calculations of the business ethic. Here is testimony from Clark Kerr, president of the University of California, who speaks as the agent of the prevailing drift:

The university has become a prime instrument of national purpose. . . . This is the essence of the transformation now engulfing our universities. Basic to this transformation is the growth of the "knowledge industry," which is coming to permeate government and business. . . . What the railroads did for the second half of the 19th Century and the automobile for the first half of this century, the knowledge industry may do for the second half of this century: that is, to serve as the focal point for national growth. And the university is at the center of the knowledge process.

There is the voice of dominant America: knowledge as "industry." And its style too: "the knowledge process." How old-fashioned, by contrast, is the view of Cardinal Newman that "knowledge is capable of being its own end," and how characteristically utopian of Lewis Mumford to write: "As the cloister of the monastery might be termed a passive university, so the university might be called an active cloister: its function is the critical reappraisal and renewal of the cultural heritage."

We have always, in our lust for self-congratulation, deluded ourselves as to the quality of American education, and we have never properly realized how deep is the conflict between the values of the free mind and the values of the marketplace. But partly the trouble has to do with something new in our society, the growth of "mass education" during the last 20 or 30 years. Whether more American boys and girls will go to college each year is no longer a question. The question is, what will happen to them once they arrive? For "mass education" is one of the more significant democratic experiments of our time: an experiment barely begun, and under circumstances that work heavily against its realization. Our society has stumbled into the possibilities of "mass education"—perhaps more accurately, it has been forced to confront these possibilities because of military and technological pressures. But it has not yet appropriated a small fraction of the talent, energy and resources needed to make "mass education" a success. Whether *this* society can do that is, to my mind, an open question. The difficulties would be staggering. Consider, for example, the recent expansion of our colleges and the consequent pressure to appoint to our faculties men who lack the necessary training and more important, the spirit of devotion and austerity which, at least occasionally, ought to characterize the scholar and intellectual. Fifty or sixty years ago, when the American university had a relatively well-defined role as the cultural training-ground for the country's upper strata, a decently mediocre professor was not likely to do much damage. As a carrier of the received culture, he might even do some good. Today, in an atmosphere of fevered expansion, lucrative busy-work and harsh uncertainty as to what a university should be, the decently mediocre professor tends all too often to be a disaster, because he cannot cope with the staggering tasks of convincing thousands of ill-prepared and poorly-motivated students that, quite apart from utilitarian or national ends, there is a value to the life of the mind. He cannot persuade his students that there is such a value because, more often than not, he does not know what the life of the mind is. Moreover, to make high claims for the life of the mind in a world devoted to accumulating money and bombs is either to indulge in a pious hypocrisy or to indicate to one's students that if they are to become serious intellectuals they must be ready to accept a measure of estrangement and perhaps deprivation.

The old-fashioned traditional scholar, sticking by his narrow specialty no matter who gets bombed or what freedom march occurs, may not be an intellectual hero or an inspiring model for the young, but at least he sustains the values of disinterested scholarship which are essential for the survival of a true university. Much more menacing, as it seems to me, is the professor-entrepreneur busy with a mess of grants, textbooks, institutes, conferences, consultations, indeed, with everything but serious teaching and intellectual work. I quote at some length from two quite moderate professors at the University of California at Berkeley, Sheldin Wolin and John Schaar:

For some time now, the students, especially the undergraduates, have felt themselves to be an alien presence within the multiversity, an "Other Academia" analogous to the "Other America," ill-fed, ill-housed and ill-clothed not in the material sense, but in the intellectual and spiritual senses. As the multiversity has climbed to higher and higher peaks of research productivity, material riches, and bureaucratic complexity, the students have fallen into deeper and deeper abysses of hostility and estrangement. The students' own favorite word for their condition is "alienation," by which they mean . . . a sense of not being valued members of a genuine intellectual and moral community. Their feeling is grounded in reality.

The architects of the multiversity simply have not solved the problem of how to build an institution which not only produces knowledge and knowledgeable people with useful skills, but which also enriches and enlightens the lives of its students—informing them with the values of the intellect, preparing them to serve as the guardians of the society's intellectual honesty and political health, arming them with the vision by which society seeks its own better future. . . .

By any reasonable standard, the multiversity has not taken its students seriously. At Berkeley, the educational environment of the undergraduate is bleak. He is confronted throughout his entire first two years with indifferent advising, endless bureaucratic routines, gigantic lecture courses, and a deadening succession of textbook assignments, and bluebook examinations testing his grasp of bits and pieces of knowledge. . . . It is possible to take a BA at Berkeley and never talk with a professor. To many of the students, the whole system seems a perversion of an educational community into a factory designed for the mass processing of men into machines.

This indictment is severe, but not, I am prepared to testify, excessive. Nor is it complete. A diagnosis of the malaise afflicting the American university would have to say a good deal about the increase in the size and power of administrative bureaucracies which regard the university as essentially "their" institution to be spared the troubles of restlessness and innovation. Something would have to be said about that prime vulgarity known as "publish or perish," a travesty of scholarship and common sense. And something more would have to be said, as I am glad to see the Berkeley students did, about the pressures faced by state universities from Boards of Regents heavily weighted toward conservative and business ideologies and almost always without faculty or student representation.

In short: the future of the American university, insofar as it will remain a university, is severely problematic; the ideal of the "active cloister" put forward by Mumford remains to be clarified and defended; and no one can do this as well as teachers and students together, for their interests, while not identical, are at least congruent.

Partly because the university has come to play a larger role in the socio-economic life of the country than ever before, hundreds of thousands of young people now spend larger portions of their lives in the universities than ever before. And not merely their lives as minors subject to institutional control, but also as young adults usually able to vote, expected to pay taxes, and liable to military service.

One consequence ought to be a serious effort to reconsider the relationship between university and student, the terms of which were originally set under radically different conditions. In regard to public discussion and the rights of political minorities, the American university remains, by and large, a stronghold of democratic freedom; but its inner life as an institution is usually far from democratic. The system of authority governing the American university ranges from the outright dictatorship of the "strong" president to academic control by a faculty conscious of its traditional privileges; in most cases there is an uneasy compromise between top administration and faculty, with an intervening bureaucracy slowly accumulating more and more power.

But as far as students are concerned, they are supposed to remain in and be content with a state of almost complete dependence. University administrators, brimming with rectitude, presume to supervise the private lives of students. Decisions concerning academic standards and procedures are generally made without so much as consulting students. This is not, I think, a healthy situation, and without indulging in any mystique about the spontaneous wisdom or virtue of the young, we ought to recognize the appropriateness of student consultation in academic affairs.

The doctrine by which administrators justify their supervision of student life is called *in loco parentis,* the institution acting in place of parents.

The usual attitude toward students is that they constitute a mixture of necessary consumer and irksome dependent. They pay their money (or receive their fellowships) and must then submit to whatever disciplines and routines the university proposes. Now there is a sense in which this seems quite proper: the student, being a novice, has come to learn from his superiors, and before the latter admit him to their ranks they have the obligation to test his competence. Yet this hardly justifies the present systematic refusal to consider seriously student opinion concerning such matters as teaching procedures, curriculum, course requirements, etc. (Actually, student opinion *is* taken into account, even about such sacrosanct matters as faculty tenure; but this happens in the worst possible way, through gossip, hearsay, comparison of class sizes, etc.)

At the graduate level the situation becomes still more galling. The graduate student, though presumed to be a serious person and often one who makes notable sacrifices to pursue his studies, is placed in a condition of dependency far more severe than that of the undergraduate. The whole career of the graduate student can be at the mercy or whim of a few professors, sometimes only one professor. Anyone who has taught in an American university knows how often the bright and lively undergraduate undergoes a depressing change in style soon after entering graduate school: he becomes professionally cautious, intellectually timid, concerned to please and adapt to professors. This is hardly a system calculated to encourage manliness and independence of spirit. Surely, without challenging the authority of the faculty or creating that state of "anarchy" which is said to haunt the dreams of educational administrators, it should be possible to consult systematically with graduate students concerning a wide range of educational policies.

Even to raise such a possibility is to provoke outcries from certain professors about the danger of reducing our universities to "banana republics" where over-politicized students would establish a terrorist reign of laxness. How far-fetched a fantasy this seems in the actual context of American university life! And besides, such fears would seem a bit more worthy if American professors had shown themselves proudly resistant against the real danger to their authority, which comes from the steady encroachments of academic bureaucracies.

What our more thoughtful and restless students are requesting is not that academic decisions be turned over to "student mobs," but that they be allowed, through democratic channels, to express their views about matters of the greatest concern to them. Often enough students are wrong in their opinions about academic life and educational policy, but then so too are the rest of us; and a supply of fresh mistakes might be invigorating. We professors ought to appreciate the value of constructive—even not so constructive—restlessness: for while it might make our lives less comfortable, it would surely make them more interesting.

At the height of the Berkeley struggle, the students were right to insist that questions about their leaders' politics could only distract attention from the urgencies of their campaign. Yet, in any larger perspective, it is obviously important to consider the motivating ideas of the student leaders. A significant number of them think of themselves as radicals. Their radicalism is vague and non-ideological; it places a heavy stress upon individual integrity, perhaps more than upon collective action; it seldom follows from any coherent theory of modern society. The campus radicals respond most strongly to immediate and morally unambiguous issues, such as Negro rights, free speech, etc., yet they also feel strongly that they are "alienated" from the prevalent norms and values of the society. Suspicious of older radicals, tending to dismiss (a little too casually, I think) the experience of the last forty years, properly hostile of what Orwell once called "smelly little orthodoxies," and sometimes a bit impatient with systematic thought, they cast about for a mode of socio-cultural criticism which will express their strong ethical revulsion from the outrages, deceits and vulgarities of our society. Frequently, their radicalism tends to be more a matter of personal life-style than a program for common activity: they react violently against the hypocrisies of "success" and worry about finding work and ways of life that seem to them authentic.

It is an encouraging development. We have badly needed such young people—devoted, passionate, educated—who will not be content with "the given." But the question must always arise in regard to student politics: how long, how deeply will this new generation persist? We are all familiar with the rhythm of a certain kind of campus radicalism. A sudden flare of political interest; a fury of activism, sometimes accompanied by premature ideological hardening and an impatience with those outside the campus who are regarded as insufficiently "revolutionary"; and then, often because the original commitment was not well thought-out, a slide into disillusionment, leading to the frenetic weariness of careerism, or the cautions of official liberalism, or literary reflections on the tragic limitations of mankind. Now this is, of course, a caricature, but it is a caricature based on more than a little reality.

Previous social movements, like the CIO in the thirties, and even the Negro liberation movement of our own day, can largely be seen as drawing their strength from the justified grievances of particular classes and groups. Radical intellectuals hoped that expressions of working-class discontent would lead to a larger effort toward social change; those under the influence of Marxism spoke of the proletariat's "historical mission" and its "inherent revolutionary potential." Right now, it is hard to think in these terms. We find ourselves, instead, wondering whether intelligent people, on various levels of the economic scale, can be drawn into a new politics based on their sense of responsibility, a vision of idealism, a wish to remake the world. If anything of the sort is ever to happen in the United States, it may well begin on the campus.

We can end only with questions. Will the energy of student rebellion be frittered away or will it grow into something stable, enduring and reflective? It is so hard for young people to wrench themselves away from our sticky world of "success" that when now and again they do become radicals, they tend

to think of their commitment mainly as an extreme posture—
a rebellion against the middle-class, a nose-thumbing at the
world of their fathers—rather than an effort to initiate a serious politics. And sometimes this difficulty leads to an un-
earned impatience, or even contempt, for the procedures of
democracy and an accompanying submission to the allure of
charismatic leaders and authoritarian ideologies. Still, the student rebels will have to work out their ideas for themselves,
and there is little reason why they should repeat the experience of an older generation, even that segment of an older
generation which may have learned something from its
experience.

Part One: WHAT HAPPENED AT BERKELEY

QUESTIONS FOR STUDY AND RESEARCH

1. Examine the "Chronology of the Berkeley Rebellion" and the
   other accounts of what happened at Berkeley between September 14, 1964, and January 3, 1965, and write a docu-
   mented paper describing in detail this sequence of incidents.
2. Consider Glazer's view that the issue at Berkeley was "not
   simply one of 'free speech.'" According to Glazer, what was
   the "real issue"? Examine Cass, Raskin and May, reading their
   essays carefully, and write a paper on the issues that divided
   the students and the administration.
3. Summarize the criticism directed toward the administration's
   handling of the Berkeley rebellion. Do you find this criticism
   justified? Defend your position.
4. By reference to the appropriate essays in this section, examine
   in some detail the role of the faculty in the Berkeley rebellion.
   Do you approve or disapprove of the faculty's role?
5. Cox's criticism of the faculty at Berkeley implies that faculties
   in British universities play a larger role in administration than
   do their American counterparts. Investigate the structure of

Oxford or Cambridge and compare it with that of the University of California.

6. Support or refute Sidney Hook's argument that a faculty's rejection of a student request to invite an extremist speaker has "nothing to do with questions of free speech or academic freedom" and that recognized student organizations should be permitted to invite *any* speaker to the campus.

7. According to Hook, "anything students can properly do for themselves as adults should be left to them." Write a paper describing those functions incidental to organized student life in your college that are entrusted to the student body. What kinds of student activities does Hook believe should be controlled by faculties? Do you agree or disagree? Consider Goodman's views on this point.

8. Consider Goodman's statement that middle-class youth "are the major exploited class" in America. Write a paper which clarifies Goodman's statement and which either refutes or supports his contention. Comment on the analogy implied by his use of such terms and phrases as "exploited," "speedup" and "organize their CIO."

9. Summarize Kaplan's "The Revolt of an Elite" and examine other essays in this section that support or weaken Kaplan's analysis.

10. On the basis of evidence found in the essays in this section and elsewhere, describe the leaders of the FSM and their student supporters. Is there any evidence that the movement was made up of "Beatniks"? If not, how would you explain this charge?

11. Support or refute the charge that the Berkeley rebellion was "Communist-inspired" or "Communist-dominated." In your paper, make use of the evidence as presented in the essays in this section. Also examine what some of the writers of these essays mean by the "New Radicalism."

12. Investigate the role of American college students in the recent civil rights movement and determine to what extent this involvement has prompted the Berkeley Free Speech Movement.

13. In several essays in this section, mention is made of Latin American and Asian university students (for example, students at the University of Caracas, Venezuela). Investigate this matter and determine why the Caracas example and others alarm Americans who are concerned about the Berkeley rebellion and student activism in general.

14. Write a characterization of Mario Savio, discussing his physical appearance, his views, his academic accomplishments and his role in the FSM.

15. From accounts of him in this section, write a characterization of Clark Kerr. Describe his views on his role in the Berkeley issue, and discuss his background as an administrator and an educator. In preparing your description, refer also to his analysis of the multiversity in his *The Uses of a University*.

READINGS FOR FURTHER STUDY AND RESEARCH

Abrams, Richard. "The Student Rebellion at Berkeley—An Interpretation," *Massachusetts Review* (Winter-Spring, 1965).

Alexander, Shana. "You Don't Shoot Mice with Elephant Guns," *Life* (January 15, 1965).

"Appendix: Documents in the Free Speech Controversy," *California Monthly* (February, 1965).

The Berkeley Student Revolt: Facts and Interpretations, edited by Seymour Martin Lipset and Sheldon S. Wolin, 1965.

"The California Uprising: Behind the Campus Revolt," *Look* (February 23, 1965).

"Chronology of Events: Three Months of Crisis," *California Monthly* (February, 1965).

Cleaveland, Bradford. "A Letter to Undergraduates," *Slate Supplement Report* (September, 1964).

"The Climate at Berkeley," *Time* (December 25, 1964).

Cousins, Norman. "Escalation in California," *Saturday Review* (January 30, 1965).

"Decentralization Is Proposed for the University of California," *New York Times* (May 16, 1965).

Feuer, Lewis S. "Inevitability and Institutes," *The New Leader* (January 18, 1965).

———. "Rebellion at Berkeley," *The New Leader* (December 21, 1965).

———. "A Reply," *The New Leader* (January 4, 1965).

Field, Mervin D. "The U. C. Student Protests: California Poll," *California Poll* (February 2, 1965).

"Free Speech Movement" (Documentary LP Record), Station KPFA, Berkeley.

"A Fresh Look at the University of California," *The New Republic* (July 3, 1965).

FSM: The "New Left" Uprising in Berkeley, edited by Hal Draper, 1965.

Glazer, Nathan. "Reply to Goodman," *The New York Review of Books* (February 11, 1965).

———. "Reply to Selznick," *Commentary* (March, 1965).

Harrison, Gilbert A. "Berkeley Riots," *The New Republic* (December 19, 1964).

Hechinger, Fred M. "Berkeley Story," *New York Times* (April 4, 1965).

Heireck, Max, and Kaplan, Sam. "Yesterday's Discord," *California Monthly* (February, 1965).

Hill, Gladwin. "Coast Regents Set Up Students' Code," *New York Times* (May 30, 1965).

Jacobs, Paul. "Dr. Feuer's Distortions," *The New Leader* (January 4, 1965).

Kelman, Steven. "Youth and Politics," *The New Leader* (February 1, 1965).

Kerr, Clark. "For the Record," *The New Leader* (January 18, 1965).

―――. "A Message to Alumni," *California Monthly* (February, 1965).

―――. "Rebuttal from Berkeley," in "Letters to the Editor," *Saturday Review* (March 6, 1965).

―――. "Reply to Wolin and Schaar," *The New York Review of Books* (April 8, 1965).

Lipset, Seymour M., and Seabury, Paul. "The Lesson of Berkeley," *The Reporter* (January 28, 1965).

Marine, Gene. "No Fair! The Student Strike at California," *The Nation* (December 21, 1964).

May, Henry F. "Statement," *California Monthly* (February, 1965).

Meyerson, Martin. "Statement by Acting Chancellor Martin Meyerson," *University Bulletin* (January 11, 1965).

Nelken, Michael. "My Mind Is Not Property," *The Graduate Student Journal* (Spring, 1965).

"New Man at Berkeley," *Time* (January 15, 1965).

Oppedahl, John, and Brandli, Bruno. "Mario Resigns FSM Leadership," *The Daily Californian* (April 27, 1965).

Peterson, William. "What's Left at Berkeley," *Columbia University Forum* (Spring, 1965).

Petras, James F., and Shute, Michael. "Berkeley '65," *Partisan Review* (Spring, 1965).

Pimsleur, Joe L. "Inside Sproul Hall," *News and Letters* (July, 1965).

"The Position of the Free Speech Movement on Speech and Political Activity," *California Monthly* (February, 1965).

The Regents, Berkeley, Free Speech Movement, 1965.

"Report of the Ad Hoc Committee on Student Conduct," *California Monthly* (February, 1965).

"Reports Clash on Red Influence on California Campus," *The Christian Science Monitor* (July 20, 1965).

Revolution at Berkeley: The Crisis in American Education, edited by Michael V. Miller and Susan Gilmore, 1965.

Rossman, Michael. "Some Background Notes on Civil Rights Activity and the Free Speech Movement," *Occident* (Fall, 1964–65).

Savio, Mario. "An End to History," *Humanity, an Arena of Critique and Commitment* (December, 1964).

Schwarz, Fred. "An Analysis of the Rebellion at the University of California as Applied Marxism-Leninism," *Christian Anti-Communism Crusade* (January 18, 1965).

"A Season of Discontent," *California Monthly* (February, 1965).

Selznick, Phillip. "Reply to Glazer," *Commentary* (March, 1965).

Stapp, Henry. "Reflections on the Crisis at Berkeley," *Daily Californian* (December 18, 1964).

Starobin, Robert. "Graduate Students and the Free Speech Movement," *Graduate Student Journal* (Spring, 1965).

Strong, Edward. "Statement Read at the Meeting of the Academic Senate, Berkeley Division," *University Bulletin* (December 14, 1964).

Text of the Special Byrne Report, Commissioned by the Forbes Committee of the Board of Regents, Proposing Reorganization of the University of California, Berkeley, 1965.

"Three Months of Crisis," *California Monthly* (February, 1965).

Trillin, Calvin. "Letter from Berkeley," *The New Yorker* (March 13, 1965).

Warshaw, Stephen. *The Trouble in Berkeley*, 1965.

Weinberg, Jack. "The Free Speech Movement and Civil Rights," *Campus Corelator* (January, 1965).

Weissman, Stephan. "What the Students Want," *The New Leader* (January 4, 1965).

White, Geoffrey. "The Student Revolt at Berkeley," *Spartacist* (May–June, 1965).

Wolin, Sheldon S., and Schaar, John H. "Berkeley and the Fate of the Multiversity," *The New York Review* (March 11, 1965).

2

Crisis on the Campus

Who Makes University Policy?

PAUL WOODRING

Paul Woodring is currently Education Editor of the Saturday
Review. A highly experienced educator himself, he has taught
at every level from the country grade school to the liberal arts
college and the university. He received his undergraduate degree at Bowling Green University and holds the Ph.D. from
Ohio State. He is the author of A Fourth of a Nation, New
Directions in Teacher Education and Let's Talk Sense About
Our Schools. Numerous articles by him have appeared in many
professional and general magazines.

COLLEGE students everywhere are on the march.
Though Berkeley has captured the headlines, students
on hundreds of other campuses are also in search of a cause
with which to identify and for which to fight. While some are
demonstrating against injustice in Alabama and throughout
the world, others are demanding freedom from adult control
over their personal behavior and still others are calling for
better teaching, less emphasis on research, and more attention
to undergraduates.

When their demands bring students into conflict with administrative authority, the faculty is prone to side with the
students—for professors everywhere are distrustful of administrators (Robert Maynard Hutchins was exaggerating only
slightly when he said that professors really prefer anarchy to
any form of government). But when students demand changes

147

in academic policy or control over it, when they ask for better teaching and less emphasis on research, or when they protest the dismissal or denial of promotion to a popular professor— as they have done at St. Johns University, Brooklyn College, Yale, and Tufts—they come into direct conflict with the faculty. It is the research-oriented faculty that is primarily responsible for the neglect of undergraduates, and on all but the most backward campuses a faculty committee rather than an administrator decides which professors shall be retained and promoted. If students are to have more influence over university affairs, faculty members will have less.

The recent student protests have reopened an ancient question: "Who runs the university?" There is no simple answer. A university is an enormously complex institution consisting of students, alumni, instructors, professors, administrators, and a vast array of supporting personnel—secretaries, clerks, accountants, and maintenance people. It differs from an undergraduate college in that it has not one but several faculties that preside over many professional and graduate schools. And it is responsible for the advancement of knowledge as well as for its dissemination—a fact that undergraduates critical of the research emphasis are prone to overlook.

By a tradition that dates from the Middle Ages, the faculty is the policy-making body. But the faculty of a contemporary American university shares its responsibility for policy with a board of trustees or regents which, in most cases, holds the final legal authority. The fact that a university president stands midway between these two policy-making bodies, each of which frequently wants more power at the expense of the other, makes his task far more difficult than that of the head of an industrial, governmental, or military organization in which power flows from the top downward.

To an undergraduate or a junior instructor, a university president, because he symbolizes authority, seems a natural target for attack from liberal groups. But, as Clark Kerr has pointed out in *The Uses of the University,* the president is primarily a mediator of countervailing forces. He has some control, or at least some influence, over the budget, usually he has a hand in the selection of deans and department heads, and he can use his office as a platform from which to persuade, but he has no real authority over the tenured faculty. His own job is always insecure. Not only can he be dismissed at any time by the board, but his resignation can be forced by a simple vote of no confidence from the faculty or by persistent protests from students, as was recently demonstrated at the University of California. After the president announced his intention to resign, both faculty and students conceded that the Kerr administration was their best defense against the forces from the outside that threaten freedom in the university. But if either faculty or the student body had continued to oppose him, Kerr's position would have been untenable.

The fact that university administrators must face enormous responsibilities with only limited authority is inherent in the nature of academic institutions. The obligation of a university to push back the frontiers of knowledge requires that both students and faculty be free to inquire, to challenge, and to examine critically all the assumptions and beliefs that society holds most dear. Inevitably, a strong academic institution will harbor individuals who hold divergent and unpopular views. An institution of higher learning ceases to be effective when the administrator attempts to exert the kinds of control considered normal in a non-academic institution of similar size and complexity.

Professors, when frustrated by administrative decisions that have gone against them, sometimes dream of a university without presidents or deans and are prone to point to the medieval university as a model. Perhaps such an institution might survive if professors were willing to take vows of poverty and if students were willing to forego credits and degrees. But in a world in which professors demand salaries and fringe benefits, in which credits are deemed necessary, and in which education requires expensive libraries and laboratories, there is no way to run a university without a highly skilled administration. And, if the university is to be better than second-rate, the administrator must be an intellectual leader with a clear sense of purpose and direction.

But he cannot be an autocrat. Policy in most of America's

great universities, as well as in the better small colleges, both public and private, is not made by administrators. Only in the broadest sense is it made by the board; it results from the interaction of countervailing forces. The board reflects the public conscience and acts as a buffer between the university and the larger community that supports it. The faculty, through its elected representatives—a faculty senate, council, or committees—has the primary responsibility for academic policy. It decides what kinds of students may be admitted, what courses and curricula shall be offered, and what the standards for graduation shall be. The administration clarifies and enunciates policy, reconciles conflicting points of view, mediates disputes, protects students and faculty against threats from outside the institution, and tries to keep the institution solvent. In a few universities the alumni play a part in policy-making but, in the majority, its major activities consist of making annual financial contributions and attending homecoming games. The minority of alumni who would like to play a larger and more intellectual role have not yet made their voices heard.

This leaves the students. What part do they play? Traditionally, not very much so far as academic policy is concerned. In past decades their major protests have been against unsuccessful coaches (who are routinely hanged in effigy), dormitory regulations (which are universally held to be too restrictive), and faculty control of the student press. On only a few campuses have students expressed concern for educational quality, for the competence of the faculty, or for the content of the curriculum—until recently. But now all this is changing. And because it is changing, faculties must now decide how much responsibility they should give to undergraduates. They will find the decision painful.

A properly organized student body with responsible leadership can play a useful role in making policy on matters of student discipline, since regulations governing student behavior should reflect the mores of the current college generation as well as those of the larger community. Students accused of violations have the same obligation to demand their constitutional rights, including due process, as do other citizens.

But students who deny that either university officials or public law enforcement officers have jurisdiction over their personal behavior take an untenable position; the fact of being a student does not exempt one from the law. And, if the university is to fulfill its purpose, it cannot avoid the necessity for some regulations of its own.

The greatest potential contribution of students—and the one most threatening to the faculty—is that of rating the competence of professors as classroom teachers. Students who sit through entire courses know much more about the effectiveness of teachers than do professors who rarely visit the classrooms of their colleagues. The judgment of any individual student may reflect his own biases, but if entire classes are polled anonymously, as they now are in a number of universities, the combined judgment cannot safely be ignored. Final decisions about promotion, however, cannot be made by students because they must include consideration of research and other professional obligations as well as teaching.

Though a university should provide open channels of communication to allow students to express their views on all matters of concern to them, a faculty would be most unwise to transfer to undergraduates the responsibility for such basic academic policy as curriculum-making, course content, or the determination of the long-range goals of the institution. Such decision requires a vast array of scholarly information, long years of experience, and maturity of judgment. Given time, a bright student can, of course, acquire the information, gain the experience, and achieve the maturity. But by the time he has done so he will no longer be a student. He will be a professor or, if fate is unkind, a university president.

The Idea of a Multiversity

CLARK KERR

During the past decade, Clark Kerr has emerged as one of the
nation's most distinguished university administrators. Educated at Swarthmore, Stanford and the University of California, he has had an active career in higher education, government, administration and business. Recently he was cited for
his outstanding contribution to the cause of academic freedom
by the American Association of University Professors. He is
now the President of the University of California and during
the Free Speech Movement in the fall of 1964 he remained
in the center of the controversy. His latest book, The Uses of
a University, from which the following excerpt is taken, has
been widely read and carefully studied by those who share a
concern for the role of the modern American university in a
rapidly changing world. He has written several other books,
including Unions, Management and the Public. He has also
contributed articles to many scholarly journals and various
outstanding periodicals, often replying boldly to critics who
have opposed his views and policies.

THE university started as a single community—a community of masters and students. It may even be said
to have had a soul in the sense of a central animating principle. Today the large American university is, rather, a whole
series of communities and activities held together by a common name, a common governing board, and related purposes.
This great transformation is regretted by some, accepted by

many, gloried in, as yet, by few. But it should be understood by all.

The university of today can perhaps be understood, in part, by comparing it with what it once was—with the academic cloister of Cardinal Newman, with the research organism of Abraham Flexner. Those are the ideal types from which it has derived, ideal types which still constitute the illusions of some of its inhabitants. The modern American university, however, is not Oxford nor is it Berlin; it is a new type of institution in the world. As a new type of institution, it is not really private and it is not really public; it is neither entirely of the world nor entirely apart from it. It is unique.

"The Idea of a University" was, perhaps, never so well expressed as by Cardinal Newman when engaged in founding the University of Dublin a little over a century ago. His views reflected the Oxford of his day whence he had come. A university, wrote Cardinal Newman, is "the high protecting power of all knowledge and science, of fact and principle, of inquiry and discovery, of experiment and speculation; it maps out the territory of the intellect, and sees that . . . there is neither encroachment nor surrender on any side." He favored "liberal knowledge," and said that "useful knowledge" was a "deal of trash."

Newman was particularly fighting the ghost of Bacon who some 250 years before had condemned "a kind of adoration of the mind . . . by means whereof men have withdrawn themselves too much from the contemplation of nature, and the observations of experience, and have tumbled up and down in their own reason and conceits." Bacon believed that knowledge should be for the benefit and use of men, that it should "not be as a courtesan, for pleasure and vanity only, or as a bond-woman, to acquire and gain to her master's use; but as a spouse, for generation, fruit and comfort."

To this Newman replied that "Knowledge is capable of being its own end. Such is the constitution of the human mind, that any kind of knowledge, if it really be such, is its own reward." And in a sharp jab at Bacon he said: "The Philosophy of Utility, you will say, Gentlemen, has at least done its work; and I grant it—it aimed low, but it has fulfilled its aim." Newman felt that other institutions should carry on research, for "If its object were scientific and philosophical discovery, I do not see why a University should have any students"—an observation sardonically echoed by today's students who often think their professors are not interested in them at all but only in research. A University training, said Newman, "aims at raising the intellectual tone of society, at cultivating the public mind, at purifying the national taste, at supplying true principles to popular enthusiasm and fixed aims to popular aspirations, at giving enlargement and sobriety to the ideas of the age, at facilitating the exercise of political powers, and refining the intercourse of private life." It prepares a man "to fill any post with credit, and to master any subject with facility."

This beautiful world was being shattered forever even as it was being so beautifully portrayed. By 1852, when Newman wrote, the German universities were becoming the new model. The democratic and industrial and scientific revolutions were all well underway in the western world. The gentleman "at home in any society" was soon to be at home in none. Science was beginning to take the place of moral philosophy, research the place of teaching.

"The Idea of a Modern University," to use Flexner's phrase, was already being born. "A University," said Flexner in 1930, "is not outside, but inside the general social fabric of a given era. . . . It is not something apart, something historic, something that yields as little as possible to forces and influences that are more or less new. It is on the contrary . . . an expression of the age, as well as an influence operating upon both present and future."

It was clear by 1930 that "Universities have changed profoundly—and commonly in the direction of the social evolution of which they are part." This evolution had brought departments into universities, and still new departments; institutes and ever more institutes; created vast research libraries; turned the philosopher on his log into a researcher in his laboratory or the library stacks; taken medicine out of the hands of the profession and put it into the hands of the scientists; and much more. Instead of the individual student, there were the needs of society; instead of Newman's eternal "truths in the natural order," there was discovery of the new; instead of the generalist, there was the specialist. The university became, in the words of Flexner, "an institution consciously devoted to the pursuit of knowledge, the solution of problems, the critical appreciation of achievement and the training of men at a really high level." No longer could a single individual "master any subject"—Newman's universal liberal man was gone forever.

But as Flexner was writing of the "Modern University," it, in turn, was ceasing to exist. The Berlin of Humboldt was being violated just as Berlin had violated the soul of Oxford. The universities were becoming too many things. Flexner himself complained that they were "secondary schools, vocational schools, teacher-training schools, research centers, 'uplift' agencies, businesses—these and other things simultaneously." They engaged in "incredible absurdities," "a host of inconsequential things." They "needlessly cheapened, vulgarized and mechanized themselves." Worst of all, they became " 'service stations' for the general public."

Even Harvard. "It is clear," calculated Flexner, "that of Harvard's total expenditures not more than one-eighth is devoted to the *central* university disciplines at the level at which a university ought to be conducted." He wondered: "Who has forced Harvard into this false path? No one. It does as it pleases; and this sort of thing pleases." It obviously did not please Flexner. He wanted Harvard to disown the Graduate School of Business and let it become, if it had to survive it all, the "Boston School of Business." He would also have banished all Schools of Journalism and Home Economics, football, correspondence courses, and much else.

It was not only Harvard and other American universities, but also London. Flexner asked "in what sense the University of London is a university at all." It was only "a federation."

By 1930, American universities had moved a long way from Flexner's "Modern University" where "The heart of a university is a graduate school of arts and sciences, the solidly professional schools (mainly, in America, medicine and law) and certain research institutes." They were becoming less and less like a "genuine university," by which Flexner meant "an organism, characterized by highness and definiteness of aim, unity of spirit and purpose." The "Modern University" was as nearly dead in 1930 when Flexner wrote about it, as the old Oxford was in 1852 when Newman idealized it. History moves faster than the observer's pen. Neither the ancient classics and theology nor the German philosophers and scientists could set the tone for the really modern university—the multiversity.

"The Idea of a Multiversity" has no bard to sing its praises; no prophet to proclaim its vision; no guardian to protect its sanctity. It has its critics, its detractors, its transgressors. It also has its barkers selling its wares to all who will listen—and many do. But it also has its reality rooted in the logic of history. It is an imperative rather than a reasoned choice among elegant alternatives.

President Nathan Pusey wrote in his latest annual report to the members of the Harvard Board of Overseers that the average date of graduation of the present Board members was 1924; and much has happened to Harvard since 1924. Half of the buildings are new. The faculty has grown five-fold, the budget nearly fifteen-fold. "One can find almost anywhere one looks similar examples of the effect wrought in the curriculum and in the nature of the contemporary university by widening international awareness, advancing knowledge, and increasingly sophisticated methods of research. . . . Asia and Africa, radio telescopes, masers and lasers and devices for interplanetary exploration unimagined in 1924—these and other developments have effected such enormous changes in the contemporary university as to have made the university we knew as students now seem a strangely underdeveloped, indeed a very simple and an almost unconcerned kind of institution. And the pace of change continues."

Not only at Harvard. The University of California last year had operating expenditures from all sources of nearly half a billion dollars, with almost another 100 million for construction; a total employment of over 40,000 people, more than IBM and in a far greater variety of endeavors; operations in over a hundred locations, counting campuses, experiment stations, agricultural and urban extension centers, and projects abroad involving more than fifty countries; nearly 10,000 courses in its catalogues; some form of contact with nearly every industry, nearly every level of government, nearly every person in its region. Vast amounts of expensive equipment were serviced and maintained. Over 4,000 babies were born in its hospitals. It is the world's largest purveyor of white mice. It will soon have the world's largest primate colony. It will soon also have 100,000 students—30,000 of them at the graduate level; yet much less than one third of its expenditures are directly related to teaching. It already has nearly 200,000 students in extension courses—including one out of every three lawyers and one out of every six doctors in the state. And Harvard and California are illustrative of many more.

Newman's "Idea of a University" still has its devotees—chiefly the humanists and the generalists and the undergraduates. Flexner's "Idea of a Modern University" still has its supporters—chiefly the scientists and the specialists and the graduate students. "The Idea of a Multiversity" has its practitioners—chiefly the administrators, who now number many of the faculty among them, and the leadership groups in society at large. The controversies are still around in the faculty clubs and the student coffee houses; and the models of Oxford and Berlin and modern Harvard all animate segments of what was once a "community of masters and students" with a single vision of its nature and purpose. These several competing visions of true purpose, each relating to a different layer of history, a different web of forces, cause much of the malaise in the university communities of today. The university is so many things to so many different people that it must, of necessity, be partially at war with itself.

How did the multiversity happen? No man created it; in fact, no man visualized it. It has been a long time coming about and it has a long way to go. What is its history? How is it governed? What is life like within it? What is its justification? Does it have a future?

THE STRANDS OF HISTORY

The multiversity draws on many strands of history. To the extent that its origins can be identified, they can be traced to the Greeks. But there were several traditions even then. Plato had his Academy devoted to truth largely for its own sake, but also truth for the philosophers who were to be kings. The Sophists, whom Plato detested so much that he gave them an evil aura persisting to this day, had their schools too. These schools taught rhetoric and other useful skills—they were more interested in attainable success in life than they were in the unattainable truth. The Pythagoreans were concerned, among other things, with mathematics and astronomy. The modern academician likes to trace his intellectual forebears to the groves of Academe; but the modern university with its professional schools and scientific institutes might look equally to the Sophists and the Pythagoreans. The humanists, the professionals, and the scientists all have their roots in ancient times. The "Two Cultures" or the "Three Cultures" are almost as old as culture itself.

Despite its Greek precursors, however, the university is, as Hastings Rashdall wrote, "a distinctly medieval institution." In the Middle Ages it developed many of the features that prevail today—a name and a central location, masters with a degree of autonomy, students, a system of lectures, a procedure for examinations and degrees, and even an administrative structure with its "faculties." Salerno in medicine, Bologna in law, and Paris in theology and philosophy were the great pacesetters. The university came to be a center for the professions, for the study of the classics, for theological and philosophical disputes. Oxford and Cambridge, growing out of Paris, developed in their distinctive ways with their particular emphasis on the residential college instead of the separate faculties as the primary unit.

By the end of the eighteenth century the European universities had long since become oligarchies, rigid in their subject matter, centers of reaction in their societies—opposed, in large part, to the Reformation, unsympathetic to the spirit of creativity of the Renaissance, antagonistic to the new science. There was something almost splendid in their disdain for contemporary events. They stood like castles without windows, profoundly introverted. But the tides of change can cut very deep. In France the universities were swept away by the Revolution, as they almost had been in England at the time of Cromwell.

It was in Germany that the rebirth of the university took place. Halle had dropped teaching exclusively in Latin in 1693; Göttingen had started the teaching of history in 1736; but it was the establishment of Berlin by Wilhelm von Humboldt in 1809 from his vantage point in the Prussian Ministry that was the dramatic event. The emphasis was on philosophy and science, on research, on graduate instruction, on the freedom of professors and students (*Lehrfreiheit* and *Lernfreiheit*). The department was created, and the institute. The professor was established as a great figure within and without the university. The Berlin plan spread rapidly throughout Germany, which was then entering a period of industrialization and intense nationalism following the shock of the defeat at the hands of Napoleon. The university carried with it two great new forces: science and nationalism. It is true that the German university system later bogged down through its uncritical reliance on the great professorial figure who ruled for life over his department and institute, and that it could be subverted by Hitler because of its total dependence on the state. But this does not vitiate the fact that the German university in the nineteenth century was one of the vigorous new institutions in the world.

In 1809 when Berlin was founded, the United States already had a number of colleges developed on the model of the colleges at Oxford and Cambridge. They concentrated on Calvinism for the would-be preacher and classics for the young gentleman. Benjamin Franklin had had other ideas for the University of Pennsylvania, then the College of Philadelphia, in the 1750's. Reflecting Locke, he wanted "a *more useful* culture of young minds." He was interested in training people for agriculture and commerce; in exploring science. Education should "serve mankind." These ideas were not to take root for another century. Drawing on the French Enlightenment, Jefferson started the University of Virginia with a broad curriculum including mathematics and science, and with the electives that Eliot was to make so famous at Harvard half a century later. He put great emphasis on a library—an almost revolutionary idea at the time. Again the application of the ideas was to be long delayed.

The real line of development for the modern American university began with Professor George Ticknor at Harvard in 1825. He tried to reform Harvard on the model of Göttingen where he had studied, and found that reforming Harvard must wait for an Eliot with forty years and the powers of the presidency at his disposal. Yale at the time was the great center of reaction—its famous faculty report of 1828 was a ringing proclamation to do nothing, or at least nothing that had not always been done at Yale or by God. Francis Wayland at Brown in the 1850's made a great fight for the German system, including a program of electives, as did Henry Tappan at Michigan—both without success.

Then the breakthrough came. Daniel Coit Gilman, disenchanted with the then grim prospects at California, became the first president of the new university of Johns Hopkins in 1876. The institution began as a graduate school with an emphasis on research. For Flexner, Gilman was the great herofigure—and Johns Hopkins "the most stimulating influence that higher education in America had ever known." Charles W. Eliot at Harvard followed the Gilman breakthrough and Harvard during his period (1869 to 1909) placed great emphasis on the graduate school, the professional school, and research—it became a university. But Eliot made his own particular contribution by establishing the elective system permitting students to choose their own courses of study. Others quickly followed—Andrew Dickson White at Cornell, James B. Angell at Michigan, Frederick Barnard at Columbia, William W. Folwell at Minnesota, David Starr Jordan at Stanford, William Rainey Harper at Chicago, Charles K. Adams at Wisconsin, Benjamin Ide Wheeler at California. The state universities, just then expanding, followed the Hopkins idea. Yale and Princeton trailed behind.

The Hopkins idea brought with it the graduate school with exceptionally high academic standards in what was still a rather new and raw civilization; the renovation of professional education, particularly in medicine; the establishment of the pre-eminent influence of the department; the creation of research institutes and centers, of university presses and learned journals and the "academic ladder"; and also the great proliferation of courses. If students were to be free to choose their courses (one aspect of the *Lernfreiheit* of the early nineteenth-century German university), then professors were free to offer their wares (as *Lehrfreiheit,* the other great slogan of the developing German universities of a century and a half ago, essentially assured). The elective system, however, came more to serve the professors than the students for whom it was first intended, for it meant that the curriculum was no longer controlled by educational policy as the Yale faculty in 1828 had insisted that it should be. Each professor had his own interests, each professor wanted the status of having his own special course, each professor got his own course—and university catalogues came to include 3,000 or more of them. There was, of course, as a result of the new research, more knowledge to spread over the 3,000 courses; otherwise the situation would have been impossible. In any event, freedom for the student to choose became freedom for the professor to invent; and the professor's love of specialization has become the students' hate of fragmentation. A kind of bizarre version of academic laissez-faire has emerged. The student, unlike Adam Smith's idealized buyer, *must* consume—usually at the rate of fifteen hours a week. The modern university was born.

Along with the Hopkins experiment came the land grant movement—and these two influences turned out to be more compatible than might at first appear. The one was Prussian, the other American; one elitist, the other democratic; one academically pure, the other sullied by contact with the soil and the machine. The one looked to Kant and Hegel, the other to Franklin, Jefferson, and Lincoln. But they both served an industrializing nation and they both did it through research and the training of technical competence. Two strands of history were woven together in the modern American university. Michigan became a German-style university and Harvard a land grant type of institution, without the land.

The land grant movement brought schools of agriculture and engineering (in Germany relegated to the *Technische Hochschulen*), of home economics and business administration; opened the doors of universities to the children of farmers and workers, as well as of the middle and upper classes; introduced agricultural experiment stations and service bureaus. Allan Nevins in commenting on the Morrill Act of 1862 said: "The law annexed wide neglected areas to the domain of instruction. Widening the gates of opportunity, it made democracy freer, more adaptable and more kinetic."

A major new departure in the land grant movement came before World War I when the land grant universities extended their activities beyond their campus boundaries. "The Wisconsin Idea" came to flower under the progressivism of the first Roosevelt and the first La Follette. The University of Wisconsin, particularly during the presidency of Charles Van Hise (1903 to 1918), entered the legislative halls in Madison with reform programs, supported the trade union movement through John R. Commons, developed agricultural and urban extension as never before. The university served the whole state. Other state universities did likewise. Even private universities, like Chicago and Columbia, developed important extension programs.

New contacts with the community were created. University athletics became, particularly in the 1920's, a form of public entertainment, which is not unknown even in the 1960's, even in the Ivy League. Once started, university spectator sports could not be killed even by the worst of teams or the best of de-emphasis; and few universities seriously sought after either.

A counterrevolution against these developments was occasionally waged. A. Lawrence Lowell at Harvard (1909 to 1934) emphasized the undergraduate houses and concentration of course work, as against the graduate work and electives of Eliot. It is a commentary not just on Harvard but also on the modern American university that Eliot and Lowell could look in opposite directions and the same institution could follow them both and glory in it. Universities have a unique capacity for riding off in all directions and still staying in the same place, as Harvard has so decisively demonstrated. At Chicago, long after Lowell, Robert M. Hutchins tried to take the university back to Cardinal Newman, to Thomas Aquinas, and to Plato and Aristotle. He succeeded in reviving the philosophic dialogue he loves so well and practices so expertly; but Chicago went on being a modern American university.

Out of the counterreformation, however, came a great new emphasis on student life—particularly undergraduate. Earnest attempts were made to create American counterparts of Oxford and Cambridge; residence halls, student unions, intramural playfields, undergraduate libraries, counseling centers sprang up in many places during the thirties, forties, and fifties. This was a long way from the pure German model, which had provided the student with only the professor and the classroom, and which had led Tappan to abolish dormitories at Michigan. British influence was back, as it was also with the introduction of honors programs, tutorials, independent study.

Out of all these fragments, experiments, and conflicts a kind of unlikely consensus has been reached. Undergraduate life seeks to follow the British, who have done the best with it, and an historical line that goes back to Plato; the humanists often find their sympathies here. Graduate life and research follow the Germans, who once did best with them, and an historical line that goes back to Pythagoras; the scientists lend their support to all this. The "lesser" professions (lesser than law and medicine) and the service activities follow the American pattern, since the Americans have been best at them, and an historical line that goes back to the Sophists; the social scientists are most likely to be sympathetic. Lowell found his greatest interest in the first, Eliot in the second, and James Bryant Conant (1934 to 1954) in the third line of development and in the synthesis. The resulting combination does not seem plausible but it has given America a remarkably effective educational institution. A university anywhere can aim no higher than to be as British as possible for the sake of the undergraduates, as German as possible for the sake of the graduates and the research personnel, as American as possible for the sake of the public at large—and as confused as possible for the sake of the preservation of the whole uneasy balance.

What Is a University?

JOHN HENRY NEWMAN

John Henry Newman (1801–1890) was ordained in the
Church of England and became one of the leaders of the Oxford Movement within that church. His concern over matters
of doctrine led him to become a Roman Catholic, and eventually he was made a Cardinal. His famous autobiography
Apologia pro Vita Sua is a defense of his action in leaving the
Church of England. Among his other books are Lyra Apostolica
and The Dream of Gerontius, books of poetry, and The Idea of
a University.

IF I were asked to describe as briefly and popularly as I
could, what a University was, I should draw my answer
from its ancient designation of a *Studium Generale* or "School
of Universal Learning." This description implies the assemblage of strangers from all parts in one spot;—*from all parts;*
else, how will you find professors and students for every department of knowledge? and *in one spot;* else, how can there
be any school at all? Accordingly, in its simple and rudimental
form, it is a school of knowledge of every kind, consisting of
teachers and learners from every quarter. Many things are
requisite to complete and satisfy the idea embodied in this
description; but such as this a University seems to be in its
essence, a place for the communication and circulation of
thought, by means of personal intercourse, through a wide
extent of country.

164

There is nothing far-fetched or unreasonable in the idea thus presented to us; and if this be a University, then a University does but contemplate a necessity of our nature, and is but one specimen in a particular medium, out of many which might be adduced in others, of a provision for that necessity. Mutual education, in a large sense of the word, is one of the great and incessant occupations of human society, carried on partly with set purpose, and partly not. One generation forms another; and the existing generation is ever acting and reacting upon itself in the persons of its individual members. Now, in this process, books, I need scarcely say, that is, the *litera scripta*, are one special instrument. It is true; and emphatically so in this age. Considering the prodigious powers of the press, and how they are developed at this time in the never-intermitting issue of periodicals, tracts, pamphlets, works in series, and light literature, we must allow there never was a time which promised fairer for dispensing with every other means of information and instruction. What can we want more, you will say, for the intellectual education of the whole man, and for every man, than so exuberant and diversified and persistent a promulgation of all kinds of knowledge? Why, you will ask, need we go up to knowledge, when knowledge comes down to us? The Sibyl wrote her prophecies upon the leaves of the forest, and wasted them; but here such careless profusion might be prudently indulged, for it can be afforded without loss, in consequence of the almost fabulous fecundity of the instrument which these latter ages have invented. We have sermons in stones, and books in the running brooks; works larger and more comprehensive than those which have gained for ancients an immortality, issue forth every morning, and are projected onwards to the ends of the earth at the rate of hundreds of miles a day. Our seats are strewed, our pavements are powdered, with swarms of little tracts; and the very bricks of our city walls preach wisdom, by informing us by their placards where we can at once cheaply purchase it.

I allow all this, and much more; such certainly is our popular education, and its effects are remarkable. Nevertheless, after all, even in this age, whenever men are really serious about getting what, in the language of trade, is called "a good article," when they aim at something precise, something refined, something really luminous, something really large, something choice, they go to another market; they avail themselves, in some shape or other, of the rival method, the ancient method, of oral instruction, of present communication between man and man, of teachers instead of learning, of the personal influence of a master, and the humble initiation of a disciple, and, in consequence, of great centres of pilgrimage and throng, which such a method of education necessarily involves. This, I think, will be found to hold good in all those departments or aspects of society, which possess an interest sufficient to bind men together, or to constitute what is called "a world." It holds in the political world, and in the high world, and in the religious world; and it holds also in the literary and scientific world.

If the actions of men may be taken as any test of their convictions, then we have reason for saying this, viz.—that the province and the inestimable benefit of the *litera scripta* is that of being a record of truth, and an authority of appeal, and an instrument of teaching in the hands of a teacher; but that, if we wish to become exact and fully furnished in any branch of knowledge which is diversified and complicated, we must consult the living man and listen to his living voice. I am not bound to investigate the cause of this, and anything I may say will, I am conscious, be short of its full analysis— perhaps we may suggest, that no books can get through the number of minute questions which it is possible to ask on any extended subject, or can hit upon the very difficulties which are severally felt by each reader in succession. Or again, that no book can convey the special spirit and delicate peculiarities of its subject with that rapidity and certainty which attend on the sympathy of mind with mind, through the eyes, the look, the accent, and the manner, in casual expressions thrown off at the moment, and the unstudied turns of familiar conversation. But I am already dwelling too long on what is but an incidental portion of my main subject. Whatever be the cause, the fact is undeniable. The general principles of any study you may learn by books at home; but the detail, the colour, the tone, the air, the life which makes it live in us, you must catch all these from those in whom it lives already. You must imitate the student in French or German, who is not content with his grammar, but goes to Paris or Dresden: you must take example from the young artist, who aspires to visit the great Masters in Florence and in Rome. Till we have discovered some intellectual daguerreotype, which takes off the course of thought, and the form, lineaments, and features of truth, as completely and minutely, as the optical instrument reproduces the sensible object, we must come to the teachers of wisdom to learn wisdom, we must repair to the fountain, and drink there. Portions of it may go from thence to the ends of the earth by means of books; but the fulness is in one place alone. It is in such assemblages and congregations of intellect that books themselves, the masterpieces of human genius, are written, or at least originated.

The principle on which I have been insisting is so obvious, and instances in point are so ready, that I should think it tiresome to proceed with the subject, except that one or two illustrations may serve to explain my own language about it, which may not have done justice to the doctrine which it has been intended to enforce.

For instance, the polished manners and high-bred bearing which are so difficult of attainment, and so strictly personal when attained,—which are so much admired in society, from society are acquired. All that goes to constitute a gentleman— the carriage, gait, address, gestures, voice; the ease, the self-possession, the courtesy, the power of conversing, the talent of not offending; the lofty principle, the delicacy of thought, the happiness of expression, the taste and propriety, the generosity and forbearance, the candour and consideration, the openness of hand;—these qualities, some of them come by nature, some of them may be found in any rank, some of them are a direct precept of Christianity; but the full assemblage of them, bound up in the unity of an individual character, do we expect they can be learned from books? Are they not necessarily acquired, where they are to be found, in high society? The very nature of the case leads us to say so; you cannot fence without an antagonist, nor challenge all comers in disputation before you have supported a thesis; and in like manner, it stands to reason, you cannot learn to converse till you have the world to converse with; you cannot unlearn your natural bashfulness, or awkwardness, or stiffness, or other besetting deformity, till you serve your time in some school of manners. Well, and is it not so in matter of fact? The metropolis, the court, the great houses of the land, are the centres to which at stated times the country comes up, as to shrines of refinement and good taste; and then in due time the country goes back again home, enriched with a portion of the social accomplishments, which those very visits serve to call out and heighten in the gracious dispensers of them. We are unable to conceive how the "gentlemanlike" can otherwise be maintained; and maintained in this way it is.

And now a second instance: and here too I am going to speak without personal experience of the subject I am introducing. I admit I have not been in Parliament, any more than I have figured in the *beau monde;* yet I cannot but think that statesmanship, as well as high breeding, is learned, not by books, but in certain centres of education. If it be not presumption to say so, Parliament puts a clever man *au courant* with politics and affairs of state in a way surprising to himself. A member of the Legislature, if tolerably observant, begins to see things with new eyes, even though his views undergo no change. Words have a meaning now, and ideas a reality, such they had not before. He hears a vast deal in public speeches and private conversation, which is never put into print. The bearings of measures and events, the action of parties, and the persons of friends and enemies, are brought out to the man who is in the midst of them with a distinctness, which the most diligent perusal of newspapers will fail to impart to them. It is access to the fountain-heads of political wisdom and experience, it is daily intercourse, of one kind or another, with the multitude who go up to them, it is familiarity with business, it is access to the contributions of fact and opinion thrown together by many witnesses from many quarters, which does this for him. However, I need not account for a fact, to which it is sufficient to appeal; that the

Houses of Parliament and the atmosphere around them are a sort of University of politics.

As regards the world of science, we find a remarkable instance of the principle which I am illustrating, in the periodical meetings for its advance, which have arisen in the course of the last twenty years, such as the British Association. Such gatherings would to many persons appear at first sight preposterous. Above all subjects of study, Science is conveyed, is propagated, by books, or by private teaching; experiments and investigations are conducted in silence; discoveries are made in solitude. What have philosophers to do with festive celebrities, and panegyrical solemnities with mathematical and physical truth? Yet on a closer attention to the subject, it is found that not even scientific thought can dispense with the suggestions, the instruction, the stimulus, the sympathy, the intercourse with mankind on a large scale, which such meetings secure. A fine time of year is chosen, when days are long, skies are bright, the earth smiles, and all nature rejoices; a city or town is taken by turns, of ancient name or modern opulence, where buildings are spacious and hospitality hearty. The novelty of place and circumstance, the excitement of strange, or the refreshment of well-known faces, the majesty of rank or of genius, the amiable charities of men pleased both with themselves and with each other; the elevated spirits, the circulation of thought, the curiosity; the morning sections, the outdoor exercise, the well-furnished, well-earned board, the not ungraceful hilarity, the evening circle; the brilliant lecture, the discussions or collisions or guesses of great men one with another, the narratives of scientific processes, of hopes, disappointments, conflicts, and successes, the splendid eulogistic orations; these and the like constituents of the annual celebration, are considered to do something real and substantial for the advance of knowledge which can be done in no other way. Of course they can but be occasional; they answer to the annual Act, or Commencement, or Commemoration of a University, not to its ordinary condition; but they are of a University nature; and I can well believe in their utility. They issue in the promotion of a certain living and, as it were, bodily communication of knowledge from one to another, of a general interchange of ideas, and a comparison and adjustment of science with science, of an enlargement of mind, intellectual and social, of an ardent love of the particular study, which may be chosen by each individual, and a noble devotion to its interests.

Such meetings, I repeat, are but periodical, and only partially represent the idea of a University. The bustle and whirl which are their usual concomitants, are in ill keeping with the order and gravity of earnest intellectual education. We desiderate means of instruction which involve no interruption of our ordinary habits; nor need we seek it long, for the natural course of things brings it about, while we debate over it. In every great country, the metropolis itself becomes a sort of necessary University, whether we will or no. As the chief city is the seat of the court, of high society, of politics, and of law, so as a matter of course is it the seat of letters also; and at this time, for a long term of years, London and Paris are in fact and in operation Universities. . . . The newspapers, magazines, reviews, journals, and periodicals of all kinds, the publishing trade, the libraries, museums, and academies there found, the learned and scientific societies, necessarily invest [London] with the functions of a University; and that atmosphere of intellect, which is a former age hung over Oxford or Bologna or Salamanca, has, with the change of times, moved away to the centre of civil government. Thither come up youths from all parts of the country, the students of law, medicine, and the fine arts, and the *employés* and *attachés* of literature. There they live, as chance determines; and they are satisfied with their temporary home, for they find in it all that was promised to them there. They have not come in vain, as far as their own object in coming is concerned. They have not learned any particular religion, but they have learned their own particular profession well. They have, moreover, become acquainted with the habits, manners, and opinions of their place of sojourn, and done their part in maintaining the tradition of them. We cannot then be without virtual Universities; a metropolis is such: the simple question is, whether the education sought and given should be based on principle, formed upon rule, directed to the highest ends, or left to the random succession of masters and schools, one after another, with a melancholy waste of thought and an extreme hazard of truth.

Religious teaching itself affords us an illustration of our subject to a certain point. It does not indeed seat itself merely in centres of the world; this is impossible from the nature of the case. It is intended for the many not the few; its subject matter is truth necessary for us, not truth recondite and rare; but it concurs in the principle of a University so far as this, that its great instrument, or rather organ, has ever been that which nature prescribes in all education, the personal presence of a teacher, or, in theological language, Oral Tradition. It is the living voice, the breathing form, the expressive countenance, which preaches, which catechises. Truth, a subtle, invisible, manifold spirit, is poured into the mind of the scholar by his eyes and ears, through his affections, imagination, and reason; it is poured into his mind and is sealed up there in perpetuity, by propounding and repeating it, by questioning and requestioning, by correcting and explaining, by progressing and then recurring to first principles, by all those ways which are implied in the word "catechising." In the first ages, it was a work of long time; months, sometimes years, were devoted to the arduous task of disabusing the mind of the incipient Christian of its pagan errors, and of moulding it upon the Christian faith. The Scriptures indeed were at hand for the study of those who could avail themselves of them; but St. Irenæus does not hesitate to speak of whole races, who had been converted to Christianity, without being able to read them. To be unable to read or write was in those times no evidence of want of learning: the hermits of the desert were, in this sense of the word, illiterate; yet the great St. Anthony, though he knew not letters, was a match in disputation for the learned philosophers who came to try him. Didymus again, the great Alexandrian theologian, was blind. The ancient discipline, called the *Disciplina Arcani*, involved the same principle. The more sacred doctrines of Revelation were not committed to books but passed on by successive tradition. The teaching on the Blessed Trinity and the Eucharist appears to have been so handed down for some hundred years; and when at length reduced to writing, it has filled many folios, yet has not been exhausted.

But I have said more than enough in illustration; I end as I began—a University is a place of concourse, whither students come from every quarter for every kind of knowledge. You cannot have the best of every kind everywhere; you must go to some great city or emporium for it. There you have all the choicest productions of nature and art all together, which you find each in its own separate place elsewhere. All the riches of the land, and of the earth, are carried up thither; there are the best markets, and there the best workmen. It is the centre of trade, the supreme court of fashion, the umpire of rival talents, and the standard of things rare and precious. It is the place for seeing galleries of first-rate pictures, and for hearing wonderful voices and performers of transcendent skill. It is the place for great preachers, great orators, great nobles, great statesmen. In the nature of things, greatness and unity go together; excellence implies a centre. And such, for the third or fourth time, is a University; I hope I do not weary out the reader by repeating it. It is the place to which a thousand schools make contributions; in which the intellect may safely range and speculate, sure to find its equal in some antagonist activity, and its judge in the tribunal of truth. It is a place where inquiry is pushed forward, and discoveries verified and perfected, and rashness rendered innocuous, and knowledge with knowledge. It is the place where the professor becomes eloquent, and is a missionary and a preacher, displaying his science in its most complete and most winning form, pouring it forth with the zeal of enthusiasm, and lighting up his own love of it in the breasts of his hearers. It is the place where the catechist makes good his ground as he goes, treading in the truth day by day into the ready memory, and wedging and tightening it into the expanding reason. It is a place which wins the admiration of the young by its celebrity, kindles the affections of the middle-aged by its beauty, and rivets the fidelity of the old by its associations. It is a seat of wisdom, a light of the world, a minister of the faith, an Alma Mater of the rising generation. It is this and a great deal more, and demands a somewhat better head and hand than mine to describe it well.

Such is a University in its idea and in its purpose . . .

Universities and Their Function

ALFRED NORTH WHITEHEAD

One of the most venerated twentieth-century philosophers, Alfred North Whitehead (1861–1947) was educated at Cambridge and became Professor of Philosophy at Harvard in 1924. He is the author of many important philosophical and mathematical works, including Science and the Modern World, Religion in the Making *and* Process and Reality.

THE expansion of universities is one marked feature of life in the present age. All countries have shared in this movement, but more especially America, which thereby occupies a position of honor. It is, however, possible to be overwhelmed even by the gifts of good fortune; and this growth of universities, in number of institutions, in size, and in internal complexity of organisation, discloses some danger of destroying the very sources of their usefulness, in the absence of a widespread understanding of the primary functions which universities should perform in the service of a nation. These remarks, as to the necessity for reconsideration of the function of universities, apply to all the more developed countries. They are only more especially applicable to America, because this country has taken the lead in a development which, under wise guidance, may prove to be one of the most fortunate forward steps which civilisation has yet taken.

This article will only deal with the most general principles, though the special problems of the various departments in any university are, of course, innumerable. But generalities require illustration, and for this purpose I choose the business school of a university. This choice is dictated by the fact that business schools represent one of the newer developments of university activity. They are also more particularly relevant to the dominant social activities of modern nations, and for that reason are good examples of the way in which the national life should be affected by the activities of its universities. Also at Harvard, where I have the honour to hold office, the new foundation of a business school on a scale amounting to magnificence has just reached its completion.

There is a certain novelty in the provision of such a school of training, on this scale of magnitude, in one of the few leading universities of the world. It marks the culmination of a movement which for many years past has introduced analogous departments throughout American universities. This is a new fact in the university world; and it alone would justify some general reflections upon the purpose of a university education, and upon the proved importance of that purpose for the welfare of the social organism.

The novelty of business schools must not be exaggerated. At no time have universities been restricted to pure abstract learning. The University of Salerno in Italy, the earliest of European universities, was devoted to medicine. In England, at Cambridge, in the year 1316, a college was founded for the special purpose of providing "clerks for the King's service." Universities have trained clergy, medical men, lawyers, engineers. Business is now a highly intellectualised vocation, so it well fits into the series. There is, however, this novelty: the curriculum suitable for a business school, and the various modes of activity of such a school, are still in the experimental stage. Hence the peculiar importance of recurrence to general principles in connection with the moulding of these schools. It would, however, be an act of presumption on my part if I were to enter upon any consideration of details, or even upon types of policy affecting the balance of the whole training. Upon such questions I have no special knowledge, and therefore have no word of advice.

II

The universities are schools of education, and schools of research. But the primary reason for their existence is not to be found either in the mere knowledge conveyed to the students or in the mere opportunities for research afforded to the members of the faculty.

Both these functions could be performed at a cheaper rate, apart from these very expensive institutions. Books are cheap, and the system of apprenticeship is well understood. So far as the mere imparting of information is concerned, no university has had any justification for existence since the popularisation of printing in the fifteenth century. Yet the chief impetus to the foundation of universities came after that date, and in more recent times has even increased.

The justification for a university is that it preserves the connection between knowledge and the zest of life, by uniting the young and the old in the imaginative consideration of learning. The university imparts information, but it imparts it imaginatively. At least, this is the function which it should perform for society. A university which fails in this respect has no reason for existence. This atmosphere of excitement, arising from imaginative consideration, transforms knowledge. A fact is no longer a bare fact: it is invested with all its possibilities. It is no longer a burden on the memory: it is energising as the poet of our dreams, and as the architect of our purposes.

Imagination is not to be divorced from the facts: it is a way of illuminating the facts. It works by eliciting the general principles which apply to the facts, as they exist, and then by an intellectual survey of alternative possibilities which are consistent with those principles. It enables men to construct an intellectual vision of a new world, and it preserves the zest of life by the suggestion of satisfying purposes.

Youth is imaginative, and if the imagination be strengthened by discipline this energy of imagination can in great measure be preserved through life. The tragedy of the world is that those who are imaginative have but slight experience, and those who are experienced have feeble imaginations. Fools act on imagination without knowledge; pedants act on knowledge without imagination. The task of a university is to weld together imagination and experience.

The initial discipline of imagination in its period of youthful vigor requires that there be no responsibility for immediate action. The habit of unbiased thought, whereby the ideal variety of exemplifications is discerned in its derivation from general principles, cannot be acquired when there is the daily task of preserving a concrete organisation. You must be free to think rightly and wrongly, and free to appreciate the variousness of the universe undisturbed by its perils.

These reflections upon the general functions of a university can be at once translated in terms of the particular functions of a business school. We need not flinch from the assertion that the main function of such a school is to produce men with a greater zest for business. It is a libel upon human nature to conceive that zest for life is the product of pedestrian purposes directed toward the narrow routine of material comforts. Mankind by its pioneering instinct, and in a hundred other ways, proclaims falsehood of that lie.

In the modern complex social organism, the adventure of life cannot be disjoined from intellectual adventure. Amid simpler circumstances, the pioneer can follow the urge of his instinct, directed toward the scene of his vision from the mountain top. But in the complex organisations of modern business the intellectual adventure of analysis, and of imaginative reconstruction, must precede any successful reorganisation. In a simpler world, business relations were simpler, being based on the immediate contact of man with man and on immediate confrontation with all relevant material circumstances. To-day business organisation requires an imaginative grasp of the psychologies of populations engaged in differing modes of occupation; of populations scattered through cities, through mountains, through plains; of populations on the ocean, and of populations in mines, and of populations in forests. It requires an imaginative grasp of conditions in the tropics, and of conditions in temperate zones. It requires an imaginative grasp of the interlocking interests of great organisations, and of the reactions of the whole complex to any change in one of its elements. It requires an imaginative understanding of laws of political economy, not merely in the abstract, but also with the power to construe them in terms of the particular circumstances of a concrete business. It requires some knowledge of the habits of government, and of the variations of those habits under diverse conditions. It requires an imaginative vision of the binding forces of any human organisation, a sympathetic vision of the limits of human nature and of the conditions which evoke loyalty of service. It requires some knowledge of the laws of health, and of the laws of fatigue, and of the conditions for sustained reliability. It requires an imaginative understanding of the social effects of the conditions of factories. It requires a sufficient conception of the rôle of applied science in modern society. It requires that discipline of character which can say "yes" and "no" to other men, not by reason of blind obstinacy, but with firmness derived from a conscious evaluation of relevant alternatives.

The universities have trained the intellectual pioneers of our civilisation—the priests, the lawyers, the statesmen, the doctors, the men of science, and the men of letters. They have been the home of those ideals which lead men to confront the confusion of their present times. The Pilgrim Fathers left England to found a state of society according to the ideals of their religious faith; and one of their earlier acts was the foundation of Harvard University in Cambridge, named after that ancient mother of ideals in England, to which so many of them owed their training. The conduct of business now requires intellectual imagination of the same type as that which in former times has mainly passed into those other occupations; and the universities are the organisations which have supplied this type of mentality for the service of the progress of the European races.

In early mediaeval history the origin of universities was obscure and almost unnoticed. They were a gradual and natural growth. But their existence is the reason for the sustained, rapid progressiveness of European life in so many fields of activity. By their agency the adventure of action met the adventure of thought. It would not have been possible antecedently to have divined that such organisations would have been successful. Even now, amid the imperfections of all things human, it is sometimes difficult to understand how they succeed in their work. Of course there is much failure in the work of universities. But, if we take a broad view of history, their success has been remarkable and almost uniform. The cultural histories of Italy, of France, of Germany, of Holland, of Scotland, of England, of the United States, bear witness to the influence of universities. By "cultural history" I am not chiefly thinking of the lives of scholars; I mean the energising of the lives of those men who gave to France, to Germany, and to other countries that impress of types of human achievement which, by their addition to the zest of life, form the foundation of our patriotism. We love to be members of society which can do those things.

There is one great difficulty which hampers all the higher types of human endeavour. In modern times this difficulty has even increased in its possibilities for evil. In any large organisation the younger men, who are novices, must be set to jobs which consist in carrying out fixed duties in obedience to orders. No president of a large corporation meets his youngest employee at his office door with the offer of the most responsible job which the work of that corporation includes. The young men are set to work at a fixed routine, and only occasionally even see the president as he passes in and out of the building. Such work is a great discipline. It imparts knowledge, and it produces reliability of character; also it is the only work for which the young men, in that novice stage, are fit, and it is the work for which they are hired. There can be no criticism of the custom, but there may be an unfortunate effect —prolonged routine work dulls the imagination.

The result is that qualities essential at a later stage of a career are apt to be stamped out in an earlier stage. This is only an instance of the more general fact, that necessary technical excellence can only be acquired by a training which is apt to damage those energies of mind which should direct the technical skill. This is the key fact in education, and the reason for most of its difficulties.

The way in which a university should function in the preparation for an intellectual career, such as modern business or one of the older professions, is by promoting the imaginative consideration of the various general principles underlying that career. Its students thus pass into their period of technical apprenticeship with their imaginations already practised in connecting details with general principles. The routine then receives its meaning, and also illuminates the principles which give it that meaning. Hence, instead of a drudgery issuing in a blind rule of thumb, the properly trained man has some hope of obtaining an imagination disciplined by detailed facts and by necessary habits.

Thus the proper function of a university is the imaginative acquisition of knowledge. Apart from this importance of the imagination, there is no reason why business men, and other professional men, should not pick up their facts bit by bit as they want them for particular occasions. A university is imaginative or it is nothing—at least nothing useful.

III

Imagination is a contagious disease. It cannot be measured by the yard, or weighed by the pound, and then delivered to the students by members of the faculty. It can only be communicated by a faculty whose members themselves wear their learning with imagination. In saying this, I am only repeating one of the oldest of observations. More than two thousand years ago the ancients symbolised learning by a torch passing from hand to hand down the generations. That lighted torch is the imagination of which I speak. The whole art in the organisation of a university is the provision of a faculty whose learning is lighted up with imagination. This is the problem of problems in university education; and unless we are careful the recent vast extension of universities in number of students and in variety of activities—of which we are so justly proud—will fail in producing its proper results, by the mishandling of this problem.

The combination of imagination and learning normally requires some leisure, freedom from restraint, freedom from harassing worry, some variety of experiences, and the stimulation of other minds diverse in opinion and diverse in equipment. Also there is required the excitement of curiosity, and the self-confidence derived from pride in the achievements of the surrounding society in procuring the advance of knowledge. Imagination cannot be acquired once and for all, and then kept indefinitely in an ice box to be produced periodically in stated quantities. The learned and imaginative life is a way of living, and is not an article of commerce.

It is in respect to the provision and utilisation of these conditions for an efficient faculty that the two functions of education and research meet together in a university. Do you want your teachers to be imaginative? Then encourage them to research. Do you want your researchers to be imaginative? Then bring them into intellectual sympathy with the young at the most eager, imaginative period of life, when intellects are just entering upon their mature discipline. Make your researchers explain themselves to active minds, plastic and with the world before them; make your young students crown their period of intellectual acquisition by some contact with minds gifted with experience of intellectual adventure. Education is discipline for the adventure of life; research is intellectual adventure; and the universities should be homes of adventure shared in common by young and old. For successful education there must always be a certain freshness in the knowledge dealt with. It must either be new in itself or it must be invested with some novelty of application to the new world of new times. Knowledge does not keep any better than fish. You may be dealing with knowledge of the old species, with some old truth; but somehow or other it must come to the students, as it were, just drawn out of the sea and with the freshness of its immediate importance.

It is the function of the scholar to evoke into life wisdom and beauty which, apart from his magic, would remain lost in the past. A progressive society depends upon its inclusion of three groups—scholars, discoverers, inventors. Its progress also depends upon the fact that its educated masses are composed of members each with a tinge of scholarship, a tinge of discovery, and a tinge of invention. I am here using the term "discovery" to mean the progress of knowledge in respect to truths of some high generality, and the term "invention" to mean the progress of knowledge in respect to the application of general truths in particular ways subservient to present needs. It is evident that these three groups merge into each other, and also that men engaged in practical affairs are properly to be called inventors so far as they contribute to the progress of society. But any one individual has his own limitation of function, and his own peculiar needs. What is important for a nation is that there shall be a very close relation between all types of its progressive elements, so that the study may influence the market place, and the market place the study. Universities are the chief agencies for this fusion of progressive activities into an effective instrument of progress. Of course they are not the only agencies, but it is a fact that to-day the progressive nations are those in which universities flourish.

It must not be supposed that the output of a university in the form of original ideas is solely to be measured by printed papers and books labeled with the names of their authors. Mankind is as individual in its mode of output as in the substance of its thoughts. For some of the most fertile minds composition in writing, or in a form reducible to writing, seems to be an impossibility. In every faculty you will find that some of the more brilliant teachers are not among those who publish. Their originality requires for its expression direct intercourse with their pupils in the form of lectures, or of personal discussion. Such men exercise an immense influence; and yet, after the generation of their pupils has passed away, they sleep among the innumerable unthanked benefactors of humanity. Fortunately, one of them is immortal—Socrates.

Thus it would be the greatest mistake to estimate the value of each member of a faculty by the printed work signed with his name. There is at the present day some tendency to fall into this error; and an emphatic protest is necessary against an attitude on the part of authorities which is damaging to efficiency and unjust to unselfish zeal.

But, when all such allowances have been made, one good test for the general efficiency of a faculty is that as a whole it shall be producing in published form its quota of contributions of thought. Such a quota is to be estimated in weight of thought, and not in number of words.

This survey shows that the management of a university faculty has no analogy to that of a business organisation. The public opinion of the faculty, and a common zeal for the purposes of the university, form the only effective safeguards for the high level of university work. The faculty should be a band of scholars, stimulating each other, and freely determining their various activities. You can secure certain formal requirements, that lectures are given at stated times and that instructors and students are in attendance. But the heart of the matter lies beyond all regulation.

The question of justice to the teachers has very little to do with the case. It is perfectly just to hire a man to perform any legal services under any legal conditions as to times and salary. No one need accept the post unless he so desires.

The sole question is, what sort of conditions will produce the type of faculty which will run a successful university? The danger is that it is quite easy to produce a faculty entirely unfit—a faculty of very efficient pedants and dullards. The general public will only detect the difference after the university has stunted the promise of youth for scores of years.

The modern university system in the great democratic countries will only be successful if the ultimate authorities exercise singular restraint, so as to remember that universities cannot be dealt with according to the rules and policies which apply to the familiar business corporations. Business schools are no exception to this law of university life. There is really nothing to add to what the presidents of many American universities have recently said in public on this topic. But whether the effective portion of the general public, in America or other countries, will follow their advice appears to be doubtful. The whole point of a university, on its educational side, is to bring the young under the intellectual influence of a band of imaginative scholars. There can be no escape from proper attention to the conditions which—as experience has shown—will produce such a band.

IV

The two premier universities of Europe, in age and in dignity, are the University of Paris and the University of Oxford.

I will speak of my own country because I know it best. The University of Oxford may have sinned in many ways. But, for all her deficiencies, she has throughout the ages preserved one supreme merit, beside which all failures in detail are as dust in the balance: for century after century, throughout the long course of her existence, she has produced bands of scholars who treated learning imaginatively. For that service alone, no one who loves culture can think of her without emotion.

But it is quite unnecessary for me to cross the ocean for my examples. The author of the Declaration of Independence, Mr. Jefferson, has some claim to be the greatest American. The perfection of his various achievements certainly places him among the few great men of all ages. He founded a university, and devoted one side of his complex genius to placing that university amid every circumstance which could stimulate the imagination—beauty of buildings, of situation, and every other stimulation of equipment and organisation.

There are many other universities in America which can point my moral, but my final example shall be Harvard—the representative university of the Puritan movement. The New England Puritans of the seventeenth and eighteenth centuries were the most intensely imaginative people, restrained in their outward expression, and fearful of symbolism by physical beauty, but, as it were, racked with the intensity of spiritual truths intellectually imagined. The Puritan faculties of those centuries must have been imaginative indeed, and they produced great men whose names have gone round the world. In later times Puritanism softened, and, in the golden age of literary New England, Emerson, Lowell, and Longfellow set their mark upon Harvard. The modern scientific age then gradually supervenes, and again in William James we find the typical imaginative scholar.

To-day business comes to Harvard; and the gift which the University has to offer is the old one of imagination, the lighted torch which passes from hand to hand. It is a dangerous gift, which has started many a conflagration. If we are timid as to that danger, the proper course is to shut down our universities. Imagination is a gift which has often been associated with great commercial peoples—with Greece, with Florence, with Venice, with the learning of Holland, and with the poetry of England. Commerce and imagination thrive together. It is a gift which all must pray for their country who desire for it that abiding greatness achieved by Athens:

Her citizens, imperial spirits,
Rule the present from the past.

For American education no smaller ideal can suffice.

Freedom of Learning and Teaching

CARL LOTUS BECKER

Carl Becker (1873–1945) was a leading American historian. Among his writings are such outstanding works as Progress and Power, The Declaration of Independence *and* Modern Democracy. *A gifted essayist as well as an influential historian, he often expressed ideas which prompted other historians to revise their own thoughts and attitudes.*

Knowledge and learning generally diffused through a community being essential to the preservation of a free government, . . . it shall be the duty of the general assembly . . . to provide by law for a system of education, ascending in regular gradation from township schools to a State university, wherein tuition shall be gratis, and equally open to all.

CONSTITUTION OF INDIANA (1816)

F REEDOM of learning and teaching is an essential part of what I have called freedom of the mind. It might be said, indeed, that freedom of the mind and freedom of learning and teaching are indistinguishable—that they are one and the same thing; and in theory and logic that is true. But the terms "learning" and "teaching" have by long custom come to be associated with learning and teaching of a particular sort—the learning and teaching that go on under specially prepared conditions at a certain age in the life of the individual as distinct from the learning and teaching that go on during the rest of his life. Freedom of learning and teaching has to do, therefore, with the formal education, in schools and colleges, that society thinks it desirable to provide for young men and women as a preparation for what is called "real life." This sort of learning and teaching is commonly regarded as of fundamental importance in a democratic society, and it is for this reason that I have thought it worth while to deal with it in a separate lecture.

From time immemorial men have commonly regarded learning as inherently dangerous, and have instinctively understood that, so far as schools are concerned, the danger could be met in one of two ways—either by not having any schools, or by preventing the schools from teaching any but familiar and accepted ideas. William Berkeley, Governor of Virginia in the seventeenth century, preferred the first way. "Thank God," he said, "there are no free schools or printing; . . . for learning has brought disobedience and heresy . . . into the world, and printing has divulged them. . . . God keep us from both." But most men, in Virginia and elsewhere, being either less pessimistic or more courageous than Governor Berkeley, have preferred the second way; have believed that the danger inherent in learning could best be met by schools under proper control teaching the right things—the ideas and beliefs, whether true or not, that would tend to confirm rather than to undermine the established social system. In the long history of civilization there have been relatively few systems of government that accepted in theory and applied in practice the dangerous notion that learning and teaching should be perfectly free. Modern liberal democracy is one of the few. In theory at least, however much or little it may apply the theory in practice, it rests upon the right of the individual to freedom of learning and teaching. On what ground can the right be justified?

In our constitutions and elsewhere the right has commonly been justified both for philosophical and for practical reasons. In all of our constitutions it is declared, by implication at least, to be one of the natural, God-given, and therefore imprescriptible rights of man. And from colonial times and almost by common consent it has been taken for granted that, as the Indiana Constitution of 1816 puts it, "knowledge and learning generally diffused through a community [are] essential for the preservation of a free government." The subject of freedom of learning and teaching may well be considered, therefore, from these two points of view—first from the philosophical and then from the practical point of view.

2

Jefferson and his contemporaries were quite sure that God had created the universe on a rational plan for man's special convenience, and that he had endowed men with reason in order that they might, by progressively discovering the invariable laws of nature, know what they were intended to be and to do. Freedom of the mind, freedom of learning and teaching, could therefore be regarded by them as an imprescriptible right because it was God's appointed way by which men could read the divine revelation and shape their conduct and institutions in accordance with God's will.

This simple philosophy has lost much of its validity for us. We are no longer sure that the universe was created by a beneficent intelligence, or by any intelligence at all. We are not sure that the universe is anything more than the product of blind material forces that for a certain time and for reasons that are obscure happen to be active, and that may after a certain time and for reasons equally obscure become quiescent. We are not sure that man is more than a peculiarly active chance deposit on the surface of a world as indifferent to him as to itself, or that the mind of man is more than a cause useful to it in finding its way around in a hostile environment, or that human reason is more than the perception of discordant experience pragmatically adjusted to a particular purpose and for the time being. Since this may be so, we can no longer with any confidence justify freedom of the mind, freedom of learning and teaching, by saying that it is a God-given imprescriptible right. We can justify it, if at all, not by reference to its antecedents, but only by reference to its consequences. Let us then, keeping whatever private faith we may still have in God or nature, turn to the record of history to see if it can provide us with any good reason for believing that freedom of learning and teaching has some fundamental and enduring significance in the life of man.

Man is not the only creature capable of learning, but he is the only one capable of appropriating for his own use the learning of others; and this garnered knowledge—knowledge of the past and of distant places—enables him, compels him indeed, to create an ideally extended environment beyond the narrow confines of what is immediately perceived and experienced. Primitive men in "prehistoric" times knew very well the region in which they lived, and what their fathers and grandfathers could tell them of events occurring before they were born. But beyond this narrow world of the matter-of-fact was the outer void of space and time, of nature and history. What this void contained the primitive man did not know, but he realized that it must contain something that it was desirable for him to know, since it might aid or thwart his purposes. Inevitably, therefore, the primitive man enlarged his narrow world of matter-of-fact experience imaginatively, projecting into the outer void of nature a complicated structure of magic, and into the outer void of the long time past an epic story of the doings of gods and heroes since the beginning of created things.

Many primitive peoples never passed beyond this imaginary account of nature and history. But some five or six thousand years ago certain peoples were forced, against their will as one may say, to learn something more. For reasons which it is unnecessary to examine here, they developed a more complex and unstable social structure in which the sharp differentiation of classes presented conflicts and inequities too obvious to be ignored and too flagrant to be accepted without question. In due course written records disclosed the disconcerting fact that the event as recorded differed from the event as remembered, that customs once regarded as sacred no longer prevailed, and that, while empires once powerful had disappeared, cities formerly insignificant had acquired great renown. Thus made aware that the life of man is precarious, that his knowledge is limited and his destiny insecure, certain exceptional individuals—a Buddha or a Confucious, a Solomon or a Socrates—were impelled to ask and to attempt to answer all the fundamental questions. What is the true nature of man and the meaning of life? What are the gods that man should be mindful of them? What are the real activities behind appearance in the outward world of nature? What is fact and what fancy in the epic story? What is conventional and passing and what is permanent and desirable in social arrangements and individual behavior?

With these questions once posed, learning could no longer be confined to the preservation and transmission of what was accepted as true. For certain exceptional individuals it became an end in itself—an attempt to distinguish the true from the false in the inherited tradition and to add something more to the accumulated store of verifiable or more rationally grounded knowledge. Philosophy and mathematics, history and the social studies, literature and the arts, natural science and technology, as they have developed during the ages, are but corrections and elaborations of primitive magic and the epic story—progressive efforts to find out what exists and is occurring in the outer void of the physical universe, and what has existed and has occurred in the outer void of the long time past. And the general result of this progressive effort, during the last five or six thousand years, has been to substitute for the medicine man's magic the matter-of-fact structure of natural science, and for the poet's epic story the historian's verified account of man's origin and activities.

All of our superiority is in this accumulated and transmitted store of learning and the consequent power it confers upon us. The native intelligence of the modern man is probably no greater than that of the primitive man—certainly no greater than that of the ancient Sumerians or Greeks. Nor was it any less possible for Plato than it is for Einstein to make an

ideal extension of his environment beyond the limits of immediate experience, or to conceive of a universe infinitely
extended in space and without beginning or end in time. But
the accumulated store of learning at the command of the
modern man enables him to fill in the outer void of nature
and history with more things and more familiar things—
with stars and atoms of measurable mass and movement; with
an endless succession of generations of men like himself, inspired with like motives, who brought to pass a series of related and credible events from remote times to the present.
The ideally extended environment of the modern man is thus
of the same texture as that of his immediate experience. Within
this extended environment he can therefore move freely and
without apprehension, so that however far he may wander in
the outer void of nature or times past he finds himself at
home because he meets with no alien men or strange inexplicable events.

It is this accumulated knowledge about the outer world of
nature and the past history of mankind that places the modern man in a position to emancipate himself from bondage
to ignorance and superstition, to subdue the physical world to
his needs, and to shape his life in closer accord with the essential nature of men and things. Whether all this has been
worth while, whether modern man is any happier than primitive man, whether modern civilization is superior or inferior
to Greek civilization, may no doubt be debated. But it is beside the point. The point is that the impulse to know seems
to be an inherent and ineradicable human trait. Since prehistoric times the impulse has persisted, and with every advance in knowledge the impulse has become stronger and
more consciously directed. With or without the support or
approval of established authority, by accident or in response
to practical needs or as the result of deliberate purpose, the
realm of verifiable matter-of-fact knowledge has been slowly
enlarged, the realm of myth and insubstantial belief has been
slowly restricted. Without any doubt this process will go
on. Whether it makes us any happier or results in a better
ordered world or not, it is our only resource. If we can find
neither intelligence nor purpose in the universe at large, we

must perforce rely upon our own. It is true that intelligence and purpose are not in themselves sufficient; they need to be restrained by integrity and good will. But integrity and good will are of little avail unless directed by intelligence, and the foundation of intelligence is knowledge—knowledge of what is true.

And so we arrive at our philosophical justification of freedom of learning and teaching—if you can call the justification philosophical. If we cannot justify freedom of the mind, and therefore freedom of learning and teaching, by saying that it is a God-given imprescriptible right, we can at least justify it by saying that the impulse to know what is true is an inherent human trait, that it has been the principal source of whatever happiness and ordered life man has been able to achieve, and that it is his only hope for a life better ordered and a happiness more general and more secure.

3

The practical justification of freedom of learning and teaching in a democracy is to be found in the fact that democratic government is self-government: in it the people decide for themselves what shall be done to secure happiness and the well-ordered life, and it is obvious that they cannot make these momentous decisions to the best advantage unless the majority may be intelligent and informed, that, as the Indiana constitution puts it, knowledge and learning may be generally diffused through the community, educational institutions are established—schools for the masses, colleges and universities for the leaders. It is commonly agreed that learning and teaching in schools and universities should be free in the sense that teachers should be free to teach and pupils to learn what is generally accepted by the community as true. But the practical question (always the difficult question) is what subjects should be taught, and just how free teachers should be to employ these subjects to indoctrinate pupils with ideas or theories that the majority of the people do not accept; theories that are still matters of dispute in the learned world and in any case may be no more than suggestive hypotheses rather than propositions capable of ever being proved either true or false.

This question does not arise in the primary or grade schools. No one denies that two and two equal four. The majority of the people would probably agree, at least if it were clearly pointed out to them, that "he has went" is not, strictly speaking, the preferred grammatical form. Nor is anyone, unless maybe the father of Huck Finn, likely to question the value of learning and teaching these useful truths. In high schools the question need not but sometimes does arise. The function of high schools is to teach immature minds what is known rather than to undertake the critical examination of the foundations of what is accepted in the hope of learning something new. What subjects should be taught is indeed a problem, and a difficult one; but whatever subjects may be chosen —mathematics, physics, biology, literature, history and civics, economics, mechanical drawing, first aid, plain cooking or the proper care of babies—the elements of what is definitely known about any of these subjects is sufficient, and could be taught, one might suppose, without serious offense to the morals and prejudices of the community.

One might suppose so, but in fact it cannot always be done. It depends in part on the discretion and common sense of the teacher, but chiefly on the intelligence and common sense of the people of the community—as, indeed, in the last analysis everything concerned with democracy does. During the last war, to take an example, an Iowa judge (I am sorry to have to say an Iowa judge, because I was born and brought up in that greatest of all states) announced publicly his considered opinion that American history and institutions, if taught at all in the schools, should always be taught in such a way as to demonstrate their obvious superiority to the history and institutions of all other countries. No doubt you will agree with me that this is nonsense. I hope you will agree with me that teachers should teach and pupils should learn, so far as possible, the essential facts of American history and institutions, and be allowed, like other citizens, to form their own opinions about the significance and value of that history and those institutions. But if the people of the great state of Iowa should agree with the Iowa judge (which they have not yet done), there is nothing anyone could do about it except to hope that the people of the great state of Iowa might in time become less hysterical and better informed.

Some years ago, to take another instance, the author of a high-school textbook on modern history was denounced in the newspapers as a Communist (that he was a well-known Communist could be proved, it was said, by "records in the Library of Congress") because he had set forth in his textbook the principal ideas of Karl Marx about history and society. That the ideas of Marx were correctly set forth was not denied, but it was maintained that the author must share the ideas of Marx, since he did not denounce them. But the main point was that nothing at all, true or false, should be taught in high schools about Karl Marx, because Communist ideas were dangerous and high-school pupils might, if they learned what those ideas were, become infected with them. For similar reasons the teaching of the German language was forbidden in many schools during the last war. The logic of all this seems to be that it is all right for young people in a democracy to learn about any civilization or social theory that is not dangerous, but that they should remain entirely ignorant of any civilization or social theory that might be dangerous, on the ground that what you don't know can't hurt you. It is a weird species of logic in itself, and, what is more to the point, it is a complete denial of the democratic principle that the general diffusion of knowledge and learning through the community is essential to the preservation of free government.

Attempts such as these to interfere with freedom of teaching in high schools are deplorable, but it is easy to make too much of them. They are, if we take into account all the high schools and all the subects taught, comparatively rare after all; and even these rare attempts are often enough inspired by other than the professed motives. The Iowa judge was probably less interested in the way American history should be taught than in showing that he was not to be outdone by anyone in patriotic hatred of the Hun. The protest against the teaching of Marxism was a local affair, and it turned out to be a political maneuver staged to discredit the superintendent of schools, who was a Republican, in the hope that some deserving Democrat might get his place.

But, aside from all that, it is a sound instinct on the part of parents to ask whether their children go to high school in order to be indoctrinated with interesting but debatable social theories. It must be remembered that high-school students are adolescents, and it is at least reasonable to maintain that the chief task of high-school teachers is to furnish the immature minds of their pupils with solid factual information. Whether the system of capitalist democracy is no more than a conditioned reflex induced by the factors of production is a fascinating and important question, but one may well doubt the ability of high-school students to arrive at any valid answer to the question, or even to discuss it intelligently, until they have learned what the factors of production are, besides a lot of other things. Nor is there much point in discussing with high-school students the meaning and significance of American history if they do not first know, for example, that California was not one of the original thirteen states, or that Washington did not deliver the Gettysburg address, or that the Gettysburg address was not a street number in Gettysburg where Lincoln once lived. That high-school students should learn something they or their parents do not know is admitted—admitted that they should be taught to think intelligently about what they learn. But by and large it may well be maintained that the primary task of the high-school teacher is to furnish immature minds with something solid to think about, rather than to present them with ready-made theories or interpretations of facts that they have not yet learned or cannot recall in their proper relations with any degree of accuracy.

If the general diffusion of knowledge and learning through a community is essential to the preservation of free government, then few things are more important than the sort of education that is provided in our high schools. But of the many and difficult problems that now confront high-school teachers and administrators, freedom of learning and teaching is by no means the most important. What subjects should be taught? Should all students be given essentially the same training, or should the students be provided with quite different courses of study according to their native aptitudes and their prospective occupations? What can be done to prepare students for the responsibilities of citizenship? Above all, what can be done to confer on the teaching profession the prestige, the privileges, and the rewards that will attract to it men and women of first-rate ability?

These are some of the principal problems that arise in connection with high-school education. They arise also in connection with education in colleges and universities. But in colleges and universities freedom of learning and teaching, unhampered by the prevailing ideas and prejudices of the community, is fundamental, since without it colleges and universities lose their chief reason for existence.

Universities are commonly called centers of learning, and the origin of universities as we know them is commonly traced back to the twelfth century—to the parent universities of Paris and Bologna. But, disregarding names, the thing itself is much older. For the universities of Paris and Bologna were originally little more than groups of exceptional men surrounded by their pupils and engaged with them in the disinterested and systematic attempt to learn what is true. In a very real sense, therefore, the origin of universities as centers of learning carries us back to those exceptional individuals who first asked and attempted to answer all the fundamental questions about man and the world in which he finds himself.

One of the earliest, and perhaps the most famous, of these early centers of learning was established by Socrates at Athens in the fifth century B.C., and for the moment we may take it as an ideal or model university. It had no organization. It was limited to the essentials. It consisted of one professor and such students as he could beguile, at any time or place, to engage in discussing with him and with each other such questions as the meaning of virtue and justice, the nature of the gods, and what is essential to the good life. The value of this university was due entirely to the qualities of its professor, Socrates, who had the virtue that all professors should in some measure have—the virtue of being concerned above all things with the disinterested search for truth. The defect that professors and universities are prone to, Socrates managed to avoid: never, fortunately, having discovered any final truth, he was never in a position to rest on his laurels and abandon the search for it.

I am fully aware that this is an oversimplification of the virtues and defects of universities as we know them. The university of Socrates was a one-man affair, with relatively few commitments to the community. But universities as they have existed since the twelfth century have been institutionalized centers of learning, thoroughly warped into the social structure by their vested interests and loyalties, their traditions, and their rights and obligations as defined by the laws and customs of the land. Whether privately endowed or church- or state-controlled, they have always been explicitly or tacitly under bond to the community to provide for a select group of the rising generation what is called a "liberal education" —an education primarily designed to fit those who receive it for leadership in the community. Our own universities and colleges certainly devote the greater part of their endowment, their time, and their energies to what is called "teaching" rather than to what is called "research"—that is to say, to the transmission of what is known rather than to the critical examination of what is known and the expansion of the frontiers of knowledge. Nevertheless, the two functions of teaching and research cannot be divorced without loss to both. The education of college students for leadership in the community, if it be not constantly based on the results of current critical research, tends to become conventional and dogmatic and to leave the student with a body of information learned by rote and housed in a closed and incurious mind; while research, carried on by professors secure in their tenure and under no obligation to concern themselves with the social significance of learning and teaching, tends to run into a barren antiquarianism, as harmless and diverting, and just about as socially useful, as crossword puzzles or contract bridge.

In an ideal world the two functions of research and teaching would always supplement and reinforce each other: the new truth would always be immediately and painlessly assimilated to the old. In the world as it is the assimilation is always going on, but not always painlessly. There are always areas of danger—fields of knowledge and belief in which the new facts and the theories offered to explain them are apt to be regarded by the community as destructive of morality, vested interests, or public order. The classic example of this conflict is to be found in the trial of Socrates and the sentence of death inflicted upon him by the men of Athens because in their view his atheistical teachings were corrupting the youth of the city. The conflict symbolized by this famous event is perennial, and the community always holds the cup of hemlock, in one form or another, in reserve for those who teach too ardently or conspicuously facts or doctrines that are commonly regarded as a menace to the social order. The danger areas shift from time to time and from place to place, and the conflict may be more embittered and disastrous in one place or at one time than another. But in general it may be said that learning and teaching will be relatively free, and universities will for that reason be important centers for the advancement of knowledge, during those times when the political community and the fraternity of scholars are not in too flagrant disagreement in respect to the fundamentals of learning and the life of man.

This favorable situation exists either because the people do not know or take no interest in what is going on in the scholarly world, or because the political community (that is to say, those who control political action) have no sustaining convictions about morality and the good life, or because the basic assumptions of their political ideology are not essentially for the promotion of knowledge. In fifth-century Greece the case of Socrates was exceptional. At that time scholars were for the most part free from political oppression; and apart from a peculiar conjunction of circumstances and personal animosities Socrates himself might well have lived out his life without molestation. During the Hellenic age scholars in the Alexandrian schools were mainly concerned with aspects of natural science or antiquarian historical research that had little bearing on politics or religion, and in any case they pursued their activities at a time when rulers and politicians were, either from skepticism or indifference, less inclined to attach importance to the ideas than to the utility of scholars. The Romans contributed little to the advancement of knowledge except in the realm of law and politics; and the Roman emperors, ruling over many and diverse peoples, were for reasons of political policy forced to be tolerant and to accept the view that all religions and ideologies were (in Gibbon's famous phrase) "considered by the people, as equally true; by the philosopher, as equally false; and by the magistrate, as equally useful." When the Christian philosophy of history and morality arose to threaten the basic conceptions of classical civilization the emperors attempted to suppress it; failing to do that, they adopted it as the state religion and closed the schools of Athens and Alexandria; and with the collapse of the Roman Empire knowledge and learning virtually disappeared in Western Europe until the revival of the eleventh century.

Mediaeval universities present us with an arresting paradox: they appear to us to have been singularly bound and yet curiously free. We know that the mediaeval Church suppressed heresy with a ruthless hand, and yet nearly all the great scholars, from Abélard to William of Occam, were associated with some university sponsored by the Church and appear to have been quite free to learn what they could and to teach whatever they thought to be true. The key to this enigma is that at that time the common man, the constituted authorities, and the fraternity of scholars all accepted the Christian faith—the Christian story of man's origin and destiny—as the necessary basis of all knowledge and all ordered and virtuous living. The mediaeval scholar did not expect to find anything true that did not conform to the Christian story, any more than the modern scholar expects to find anything true that does not conform to the natural law of cause and effect. He could therefore contribute to the advancement of knowledge without offending the Church, because there was still plenty of room within the framework of the Christian story to learn again what the Greeks had known and the Arabs knew; and he felt no constraint so long as it was possible, by an ingenious use of logic, dialectic, and symbolism, to reconcile the new knowledge (new to Western Europe) with the Christian faith. After some two centuries, however, accumulated knowledge made the reconciliation of what was known with what must be believed too formidable, and the further advance of knowledge called for other premises and a different technique.

From the fifteenth to the eighteenth century other premises and a different technique were gradually adopted. The leading scholars turned from theology and philosophy to natural science and history; in place of logic and dialectic and symbolism they adopted the technique of observation, experiment, and the literal record of events; and in place of the Christian story of man's origin and destiny as the necessary premise in the search for truth, they accepted the modern conception of a universal natural law of cause and effect.

The result of all this was an unprecedented expansion of accumulated and verifiable knowledge—knowledge of the structure and behavior of the physical world and of the history of man's origin and activities. But the New Learning, except in so far as it was primarily antiquarian and without apparent bearing on the Christian story, could not be freely promoted in the established universities. The reason is that the Christian story was still accepted by the people as the foundation of the social order and the good life; the rulers of states, whether Protestant or Catholic, could maintain their power only by maintaining the religion acceptable to their subjects; and natural science and the interpretation of history, in so far as they denied, or were thought to deny, the validity of the Christian story, were therefore excluded from the universities altogether or admitted only with restrictions intended to make them innocuous. Of the thirty or forty leading scholars, from Erasmus to Gibbon, who rank highest in the history of learning, only a few were associated with any university, and of those few Kepler was driven out of Tübingen, Galileo was forced to recant his teachings, and Giordano Bruno, wandering from one university to another and welcomed in none, was finally burned at the stake. The scholars who contributed most to the advancement of knowledge were for the most part members of what Bayle called "the invisible college"; the visible colleges for the most part became, either through inertia or social compulsion, servile instruments of state policy, whose function, in effect if not in intention, was to support the authority of kings and defend the established religion.

This conflict between the political community and the fraternity of scholars was in theory ended, and in practice much abated, by the liberal-democratic revolution of the eighteenth and nineteenth centuries. The revolution was directed against the arbitrary authority of kinds, the class privileges of nobles and priests, and the regimentation of opinion by church and state. In order to justify the revolution, political philosophers derived from the theory of natural law, which had long been accepted by scholars as the necessary premise in the search for truth, the natural and imprescriptible rights of men to the very liberties the revolution sought to win, and made these liberties the foundation of religion, morality, and public authority. In so far as the revolution succeeded, the old divergence between learning and politics was thus, in theory, ended. Both the political community and the fraternity of scholars professed to believe that the disinterested search for truth was essential to knowledge and the good life. Both professed to believe that the truth, so far from being something divinely revealed, was a progressive discovery negotiated by the open competition of individual judgments freely arrived at by the application of reason to the knowledge available. Both were therefore committed to the principle of freedom of learning and teaching, and by implication to the support of universities as places where the advancement of knowledge could be promoted without censorship or control by the state.

In theory the conflict was ended, but in practice the principle of freedom of learning and teaching enshrined in our political philosophy was not all at once, or ever completely, realized in administration of our colleges and universities. The ancient conflict between science and theology lingered on until science had contributed so much to business and to the convenience of the community that it was raised to the level of a religious faith. The conflict between vested interests and economic theory proved more enduring; and one must record the fact that, among those who made outstanding contributions to knowledge in the nineteenth century, Thorstein Veblen (to mention only one) was more or less politely elbowed out of academic centers of learning, and that many other men have found, and still find, their academic position precarious or untenable on account of their economic or political opinions.

I record the fact and deplore it. But if we compare the universities of Europe and America as they functioned in the nineteenth and early twentieth centuries, and as they still function in free countries, with the fate that has overtaken them in countries committed to an antidemocratic philosophy and practice, we cannot well miss the main point. The main point is that during the last three centuries there has been a close correlation between the spread of democratic government, the emancipation of the individual from restraints on freedom of learning and teaching, and the revival and expansion of colleges and universities as effective centers for the advancement of knowledge.

4

I have discussed, in separate categories, the philosophical and the practical justifications for freedom of learning and teaching. You may think that I have somewhat confused the categories. That may well be, for the philosophical and the practical reasons for freedom cannot really be separated, since they come to the same thing in the end.

In the last analysis democracy rests on the assumption that men have or may acquire sufficient intelligence and integrity to govern themselves better than any one or any few can do it for them—sufficient intelligence and integrity to manage their affairs with a minimum of compulsion, by free discussion and reasonable compromises voluntarily entered into and faithfully maintained. If this assumption is valid, then freedom of learning and teaching is essential, because it is obvious that the better informed the people are the more likely it is that the ends they desire will be wise and the measures taken to attain them effective. If the assumption is not valid, or is not valid in the long run, then democracy is no more than a temporary phase—a luxury, as one may say, available only to those fortunate people who live in new and undeveloped countries, or countries endowed by peculiar and temporary circumstances with unaccustomed wealth, or small countries upon which nature or fortune have for the time being conferred some special felicities. In any case the only alternative to democracy is government by the one or by the few— government in which the many are subject to the will of the one or of the few; government in which it is for the one or the few to decide how much freedom of learning and teaching there shall be, how much the many shall be permitted to know, and what special mixture of truth and falsehood is best designed to keep them servile and contented.

For some years now we have been permitted, have indeed been forced, to contemplate and assess this unpalatable alternative. We have been told that democracy is no more than government by the few, no more than plutocracy, and that, having failed to provide for the welfare of the many, it is bound to be superseded by some more efficient system. We have seen these more efficient systems in action. We have seen, in Russia, the one-man and the one-party dictatorship suppress what little political freedom and freedom of opinion there may have been, and organize the economic life of the country without regard to the will of the people. We have seen, in Italy and Germany, the one-man and the one-party dictatorship, professing to represent the historic destiny of the nation or the right of the master race, embark on the conquest of Europe with a ruthless and scientifically calculated brutality and deception the like of which has never before been known. And we have been assured that this represents the "wave of the future"—a "new order" that will endure for a thousand years.

But we have seen something else—something that reassures us. We have seen this scientific systematization of force and fraud arouse first the loathing, then the fear, and at last the united resistance of the independent and the conquered and devastated nations of the world; and it is now clear that the new order that was to have lasted for a thousand years is already broken and will shortly be destroyed. Nevertheless, we need something more than superior force and military victory to assure us that democracy as we know it is not a passing phase—that democracy itself, in whatever altered form, represents the "wave of the future."

We may, I think, find some measure of assurance in the fact that democracy accepts in theory, and realizes in practice better than other forms of government, the humane and rational values of life, and that it is to that extent in harmony with the age-long human impulse to know that which is true and to follow that which is good—the impulse that throughout the ages, although often frustrated and sometimes defeated, has been the determining factor in lifting mankind above the life that, as Hobbes said, is "nasty, brutish and short." In all times past this inherent and indefeasible impulse has proved to be, with whatever reverses, the wave of the future; in the time that is before us, I think it will likewise prove to be, with whatever reverses, the wave of the future.

For the moment we are living in one of the periods of reverses, in a time when, as the poet Jeffers says, we seem to feel "a gathering in the air of something that hates humanity." Something that hates humanity and, for that reason, the truth too. The best case for democracy, and our best reason for having faith in the freedom of learning and teaching which it fosters, is that in the long history of civilization humanity has proved stronger than hate, and falsehood less enduring than truth.

The College Grad
Has Been Short-Changed
ANDREW HACKER

Andrew Hacker was born in New York and received his Ph.D. at Princeton. Now a Professor of Government at Cornell University, he has also taught at the Salzburg Seminar in American Studies, Salzburg, Austria. He is the author of Political Theory: Philosophy, Ideology, Science; Social Theories of Talcott Parsons; *and* The Uses of Power. *He contributes articles frequently to* The Reporter, Commentary, Commonweal, *the* New York Times Magazine *and various other publications.*

HARDLY a commencement or baccalaureate address this week will not contain at least one allusion, however veiled, to the fact that this was the Year of the Demonstration. If some campus protests have been political while others have exemplified educational discontents, it remains to say that students at schools as widely contrasted as Berkeley, St. John's and Yale have rallied, marched, signed and sat in displays of vehemence and in numbers not equaled in this generation.

A major reason for these stirrings is that not a few American undergraduates have become convinced that they are being short-changed. Feeling cheated on the educational end, especially at the larger institutions, they are ripe for any demonstration against authority in general and campus officialdom in particular. Nevertheless, it must be recorded that the protests over the quality of higher education are foredoomed to failure. They are outcries against conditions which will become even further entrenched in the years to come.

What is distressing is that so many students, faculty members and observers of the educational scene still think that serious reforms are possible. For this reason the facts of modern university life deserve to be catalogued, if only because so many of us will have to live with them.

In the first place, colleges and universities will become larger, and consequently more bureaucratic and impersonal. Within a generation, only a minor fraction of the student population will be attending small, independent colleges. Already 6 out of every 10 students are in institutions having enrollments of over 5,000, whereas a dozen years ago, less than half were in schools of that size.

The reason for this is not that small colleges are going out of business—hardly any do—but that most of them are becoming larger. This is especially the case with publicly supported institutions. Whereas every state used to have its network of normal and A.&M. schools, these are now being transformed into universities with no ceilings foreseen for their enrollments. What was once a teachers' college in Carbondale is now Southern Illinois University, with over 17,-000 students. Plans are being made to expand New York's old normal schools—like Brockport, Fredonia, Geneseo, New Paltz, Oneonta, Potsdam—so they can absorb the tens of thousands of students in search of a college education. And except for a handful of Amhersts and Swarthmores, virtually all of the small private colleges are anxious to raise their enrollments, sometimes for financial reasons but also for purposes of prestige.

It is easy to give publicity to projects and experiments intended to counter this trend. About 10 years ago, for example, California declared that it would make its Riverside campus the "Amherst" of the system, with an enrollment limited to about 1,000 liberal arts majors. As of now, Riverside has grown to some 3,000 and its plans are to have as many as

14,000 students on the campus by 1980, many of them working for advanced degrees. So much for the "Amherst" idea.

Now we are hearing about the new Santa Cruz campus, this time to be the "Oxford" of the Coast, having a series of small colleges, each with its own professors giving tutorials, on a prominence above the Pacific. It is impossible to see how such an educational luxury can survive, especially in a state with so many teen-agers knocking on college doors. The Santa Cruz plan, like Riverside's before it, is expensive in fact and undemocratic in theory. These are two powerful strikes against intimate education, public or private.

Larger enrollments mean larger classes. In a small school, only 15 students would elect medieval history and a professor would be assigned to teach them. In a large place, 150 sign up for such a course—and the professor lectures to them en masse. (Why not have 10 professors, each teaching a class of 15? The answer, apart from the fact that no department has 10 medievalists, is that such an arrangement is outrageously expensive. That is why colleges are expanding their enrollments to begin with.) One result is that students will come to know fewer and fewer professors on a personal basis. But if they will have less to do with the faculty, they are destined for many more encounters with the administration.

On every campus, students find they must spend more and more time dealing with an expanding bureaucracy. Regular visits must be paid to administrative purlieus to fill in forms in triplicate, to be photographed in duplicate (face and lungs), to appeal, to petition, to ask permission. They must not fold, multilate, staple or spindle the I.B.M. cards representing their studenthood; they must secure prior approval for all manner of social, political and domestic arrangements if they are to ensure that their existence does not violate the rules contained in the thick handbooks of codes and regulations. (One might ask if this is not the case in every sphere of modern organized life. The answer is that a university is supposed to be a realm of scholars, a community of ideas and hence to be spared such encumbrances.)

The ranks of the administrators have been expanding much faster than those of the teaching faculty and this trend will doubtless continue. I have yet to learn of a single college or university where the growth rate of its administrative corps is less than that of the professoriat. Educational administrators, like their counterparts elsewhere, are adept at discovering new services they can perform, new committees they can create, new reports they can write.

They have an advantage over the professors in this respect, for they possess both the will and the skill for arrogating new powers and functions to themselves. And they have, after all, a sweet reasonableness on their side. Would anyone care to suggest that a college could operate without registrars, controllers, deans of men, housemothers, public-relations emissaries, guidance counselors, activities advisers, residence managers, proctors, pastors, research coordinators, placement officers, clinic technicians and development directors?

Every day these officials find new ways to intrude their presence into student life. It may well be that undergraduates are looked after better than ever before: they are ministered with food and housing, counseling and recreation, medicine and religion, career guidance and financial assistance. Yet if undergraduates are driven into the arms of the burgeoning bureaucracies this is partly because the professors are so seldom at home.

Much has been written and said about the retreat from the classroom, about the increasing unwillingness of professors to teach or otherwise to meet with students. No elaboration is needed here, except to say that the charges are true. This is the age of the foundation grant, of prolonged academic travel, of frequent leaves. It is also the era of conferences, workshops and symposia that draw professors (all expenses paid) away from the campus, frequently in the middle of classes. The mere murmuring of the sacred incantation "research" is sufficient excuse to bow out of introductory courses, to confine one's offerings to graduate seminars, to depart for another institution where more grandiose projects will be more generously underwritten.

But the focus here is on the future of higher education and it is relevant to consider the rising generation of professors. These young men are being suitably indoctrinated even while in graduate school. For one thing, they learn the dominant fashions in their disciplines and commit themselves intellectually (if that is the word) to the going trends. This is especially necessary for the less talented (in other words the majority) for the rising tide of fashion offers the safest haven for mediocre minds.

Just a few months ago I was lecturing at a liberal arts college, a small upstate institution, with a strong teaching tradition. I was told by several department chairmen of their great difficulties in attracting new faculty members. The men they interviewed, most of them in their middle 20's, all wanted to be assured about research funds, abbreviated teaching schedules, grants, leaves and the other prerequisites they are coming to expect. Even undergraduate colleges are being forced to match these demands if they are to recruit for their faculty—and what amounts to a part-time faculty at that.

Most of the new professors like to think of themselves primarily as scholars, and this attitude is held even by those incapable of making more than a quite minimal contribution to human knowledge. This being the case, who is going to do the teaching? This question would be a pressing one even if the every-man-a-researcher fetish did not exist.

Assuming that one professor is needed for every 10 students, for every million undergraduates we add to our college rolls—and we are currently adding a million every three years—100,000 more teachers will be needed. Yet fewer than 15,000 Ph.D.'s are produced annually in this country—and not all of these go into teaching. And of those who do, not all are exactly excited over the prospect of spending their careers in the classroom.

At the same time, there is no indication that reputable colleges or universities are willing to sign up, on a permanent basis, people with lesser degrees. The chasm between the

M.A. and the Ph.D. is a yawning one. After all, kindergarten teachers have M.A.'s. The notion that each college will establish a separate "teaching faculty," unencumbered by the publish-or-perish test, is illusory. The Ph.D. standard has been set, and nowadays even independent undergraduate schools find themselves going through the motions of expecting research and publication from their faculty.

The result will be larger classes, more machine-graded examinations and more televised instruction. (The "solution" of less classroom work and more "independent" study is another delusion; it takes a professor far more time to supervise and evaluate the independent work of students than it does to teach them in groups.) It is fruitless to discuss the wisdom of developments such as electronic education. They are going to come, like it or not, and whatever is inevitable ceases to be a worthwhile issue for discussion. If three million new places are going to be created for students over the coming decade, the 300,000 new professors who will be needed to teach them are nowhere in sight. And those who are recruited will spend less time in actual teaching than ever before.

Does all this really trouble most of today's and tomorrow's students? I suspect that it does not. When all is said and done, the vast majority of American undergraduates are not greatly concerned with the quality of the education they are receiving. The millions of teen-agers filling up our colleges and universities are there for career purposes. They know, better than their parents, that a degree is absolutely necessary for financial and social success; and they are willing to spend four not-too-arduous years to become properly accredited. Most undergraduates have enrolled for eminently practical majors—business and engineering for the boys and education for the girls. Those doing liberal arts subjects are the minority, and very few of these have any illusions that they are engaged in learning for its own sake.

Most of today's students are not intellectuals, nor are they capable of becoming so. They do not object to large, anonymous classes. They have no ideas of their own to put forward and they want to be told what they have to know. Eight out of 10 students discover that they have nothing to say at such times as they *do* meet with a real professor at close range. Hence their preference for fraternities and sororities, activities and athletics, and the nonacademic chit-chat with guidance counselors, activity directors and religious advisers.

Once we admit that most young Americans have no genuine interest in or talent for the intellectual life, the problem of quality in education begins to recede. It may even cease to be a problem.

Certainly, this year's protesters and demonstrators were not representative of their classmates, and it is instructive how quickly their ranks have tended to dwindle away after the first flamboyant outbursts. So long as a school will give an undergraduate his passport into the upper-middle-class without demanding more than he can give with 15 weekly hours of studying, few are going to complain.

Perhaps the root of the trouble lies in the tendency to compare American colleges of today with those of earlier generations or with their European counterparts. At the turn of the century, only 4 per cent of the 18-to-21 age group was enrolled in colleges and universities, and even in Europe today only about 10 per cent are in institutions of higher learning.

The United States, in contrast, has committed itself to higher education for almost half of those of college age and the proportion may well rise to 70 per cent. If the consequence is mass production, this is bound to happen when a nation tries to give the best of everything to everyone.

The only possible way to reintroduce quality into higher education would be to deny college places of any sort to three out of four who are now applying. But a democracy cannot tell its citizens—who are, after all, articulate taxpayers and awakened voters—that their children will have to make do with lesser credentials. An aristocratic posture makes sense only when the masses admit to their inferior status and defer to their betters.

When, as in America, the majority is affluent and self-confident, people come to feel entitled to all manner of things that were once the exclusive privileges of a minority. Admission to a college, with the opportunities it opens for ascending careers, can no longer be confined to a small fraction of the population. Having chosen to be a democracy we must accept its consequences.

Colleges and universities as constituted at present have too many contented constituents for them to change their ways. Most of the students, at least half of the professors and all of the educational administrators are faring better than ever before and are experiencing opportunities that only a favored few knew in earlier days. The dissenting members of the academic community are setting themselves against the combined forces of democracy in education and technology in learning. Like many rebels they are nostalgic for a society they never knew and a world they can never know.

American Idealism, 1965

HAROLD TAYLOR

Harold Taylor, a Canadian by birth, has concerned himself with American education since coming to this country in 1939. He was educated at the University of Toronto and the University of London, where he received the Ph.D. He served as President of Sarah Lawrence College and has been a faculty member of several other institutions. Among his writings are On Education and Freedom *and* Art and Intellect.

If we're going to stay in the Movement, we've got to watch ourselves, we've got to control ourselves all the time. It's like a war.—*Mississippi civil rights demonstrator, 1962.*

I N THE 1930's, the war that university students cared about was the Spanish Civil War. In the 1960's it is Vietnam and Mississippi, the moral equivalent of war, where the nature of a bigger world can be seen on a personal scale and public events can be directly known and acted upon.

The Spanish war was ideologically close and physically distant. Mississippi and Alabama are physically close, emotionally real, and have little to do with abstractions. Political action there is personal. The names are known, the ideology has given way to the politics of personal commitment. And that of course, is exactly what today's students are seeking— a sense of involvement with history.

Between Spain and Mississippi lies a stretch of time that has changed the response of the West to the occasions demanding moral sympathy. Few would now volunteer for an ideological war. The idealist's protest is against war itself, as in Vietnam, and ideological reasons are insufficient to condone the possibility of enormous disasters. The context of moral decision has shifted. The situation of the American Negro and the American poor in the 1920s and 1930s was worse than it is now, yet the strongest rallying point for liberal thought and action was not at home in the South but in Spain, where the abstract forces of history each had their public representatives in the field—fascists, Communists, anti-Communists, militarists, capitalists, clericalists, anti-clericalists, progressives, reactionaries.

In the 1920s and 1930s, those among the young who were alienated from middle-class white America went to Europe to write, to paint, to compose, to study, to fight, to be free from an America they had come to condemn for its cultural and social impurities. In the 1960s the young go to Africa, Asia, or Latin America for the Peace Corps, they teach in Mississippi, demonstrate in Alabama, tutor in Chicago slums. They do the work they are doing, not in support of an abstract idea, but for the sake of the people they are able to help.

The liberal ideology of the 1930s, which linked together students, trade unionists, Negroes, the poor, the unemployed, the teachers, anti-Fascists, and political radicals, no longer exists. Teachers are nonpolitical members of guilds and associations, the unions are conservative in social philosophy, some are anti-liberal. The tension between labor and capital that gave an ideological flavor and a moral content to political and social action has disappeared into a dialectic of bargaining strategies supported by economic and social ambitions on both sides.

The leadership has accordingly shifted away from the older generation, into the hands of the young, whose style is that of the Peace Corps volunteer, the SNCC worker, the CORE activist, the Berkeley Free Speech student whose slogan is "You can't trust anyone over thirty." The term "white liberal" becomes in these quarters a label for middle-class compromisers—the faculty member who calls for orderly discussion instead of demonstrations, the social worker who plans poverty programs for the poor instead of joining rent strikes, the Democrat who supports American foreign policy while expressing doubts about it.

The younger generation has inherited the tougher traditions of the Depression years and of those who then fought the battles of the sharecroppers, the Negro, and the poor. The problems of the Depression were never solved. They were absorbed into the mobilization for war. After the war they were hidden from view in a society almost totally concerned with achieving political and militarly security against Communism and obtaining material prosperity for an expanding middle class.

That the Depression issues have now broken the surface of the public mind in an explosion of consciousness is due, in the area of its beginning, to the courage, initiative, and steady moral sense of young Southern Negroes in the late 1950s. Against the warnings of their parents, their teachers, and the Negro leaders in their own communities, the boys and girls quietly began their lunch-counter demonstrations to achieve a limited objective of almost unlimited symbolic value—the right to be served at a lunch counter, the peoples' eating place. Lacking in political inhibition, knowing little of political strategy, strong in comradeship, they formed their own small band of witnesses and suffered reprisals with a dignity plain for all to see.

Through the mass media, the youth of the country, white and black, saw at that time the members of their generation beaten, jailed, molested, bombed, shot at, set upon by dogs, jabbed by cattle prods, threatened by bullies, and denied the simple rights and forms of justice that Americans have come to take for granted. The quickening of conscience from that experience has set in motion a stream of ideas and acts among the young which almost no one foresaw.

Until then, the youth of America had known little of the problems of the Thirties, or even of the Fifties. Depressions, Fascists, poverty, social justice were seldom mentioned. In R. H. Tawney's words, ". . . the agonies of peoples [had] become the exercise in the schools." The young had been taught, not the reality of their age, but the simple notions of cold war politics in which friends were those who would fight Communists and enemies were those who thought otherwise.

Colleges had in fact become a refuge into which the young could escape, by the possession of sufficient funds and sufficient grades, to find a shelter from the immediacy of finding a job, serving in the military, finding a place in society. College already was a place in society, one in which rewards were assigned to the educated; education was defined as academic skill, and the college student was both a symbol and a hostage of the organized establishment.

Then the message of the Negro broke through. The drama of his struggle was publicly enacted, often on the campuses themselves, as in the Meredith case, and the moral issue for members of the younger generation was sharply raised in the context of their personal lives. Students began to see, in ways they had never seen before, that the situation of the Negro was the situation of the victim everywhere and that it was linked to poverty, unemployment, inequality, and injustice in a society they had been told was affluent and just.

Out of that awakening a new leadership was formed among the young, resulting in a movement with a character of its own and a new coalition of social forces. During the 1950s a class division had begun consciously to develop within the society and among the young. It was not the European class-consciousness of workers and owners, or even rich and poor, but a class division between the young ineducables—dropouts, delinquents, draftees, wage-earners and hotrodders—those who did not or could not go to college, and those who could and did—the Merit Scholars, fraternity men, straight-A students, pre-medical, pre-law, pre-professionals of all kinds, and the rest who went to Fort Lauderdale. In one dimension the division was between the middle-class whites and the poor whites and Negroes. In another it was between the political sophisticates and the noncommitted. In another, it was between affluent, white middle-class America and the poverty-stricken colored races of the world.

The new liberal coalition finds a common base among the young by rejecting the idea of a half-affluent society, that is to say the idea of a class society composed of two classes, the white well-to-do and the others. The coalition of young Negroes and whites is founded on the commitment to an equalitarian ethic that can act on a world scale. There is the same sense of alienation from white middle-class society that marked the liberal movement of the 1930s, but a new sense of identity by the liberal with the poor, the uneducated, and the unemployed. The white youth in the movement find in the character of the Negro people the qualities basic to a new democratic culture. The music, the songs, the humor, the wit, and the style of the Negro community have an authenticity they find lacking in their own lives.

These are the young who wish to get out of the middle class if they are in it, and to move, not into a hierarchy above or below, but into the classless society of those to whom the acquisition of money, property, or social position does not matter. In becoming social activists they draw their parents and the members of the older generation into the swirl of social consequence. They go first to the South from the North, to be followed, months later, by clergymen, doctors, lawyers, and older-generation liberals who then march in Alabama with the established Negro leaders. The transaction between the generations has shifted the moral authority to the young who act first and explain later.

Their explanations are precise and far-reaching. They are against war because it is literally a dead end and solves nothing. They are for international cooperation, disarmament, international peace controls, and negotiation of conflict since these constitute the alternative to war. They are for equality in education and in economic and social opportunity, and they take practical steps to bring it about. They have few slogans, few ringing statements about democratic values. It is as if, having seen hypocrisy in the proclamations of politics and having examined the nature of the political process, they have decided to proceed by individual acts bearing witness to beliefs, rather than by public statements about belief.

Political action by the idealist of the 1930s was marked by the prevalence of liberal propaganda and public statement, an emphasis on mass movements organized around political strategies and tactics set by the leadership. The young activists of that time were in rebellion against an older generation and its conservative values, against a generation which had failed to stop war, cure poverty, prevent the rise of fascism. But the young joined political movements organized by their elders.

The activitists of the present generation have not rebelled. They have simply bypassed the older generation and its political apparatus and have acted on their own, calling upon certain of their elders to help them if they cared to. They are skeptical of heroes; they owe allegiance to those with whom they work and to the people they are trying to help. In voter-registration projects, Freedom Schools, community organization, tutoring programs, they are acting outside the organized institutions of society, inventing their own curricula as teachers, often withdrawing from school and college to work in the field of education and social change.

They have also developed new forms of organization for themselves, in which the older patterns of the liberal movements have been replaced by loose membership arrangements and a casual kind of leadership marked by an easy interchange of members and leaders. The character of the leadership depends on the nature of the job to be done.

The new generation does its own research in foreign policy, economic reform, disarmament, education. When volunteers return from Peace Corps service abroad, they bring with them bodies of knowledge derived from direct experience; they have knowledge unavailable to any except those who have served in the field. They are impatient with a society that takes its knowledge and values at second hand. As a result, they are often misunderstood by those of the older generation, especially among the educators, who have not themselves had the experience of direct involvement with the situation of the world and who have not entered, either directly or in imagination, into the lives of the younger generation. Were they to enter into them, they would discover how far behind they have fallen in understanding the nature of contemporary social change and the role of youth in bringing it about.

They would understand that the demand of youth for a share in the reform of the universities is part of a larger demand for the achievement of democratic rights and the reconstruction of society through education. They would also understand that the reason so many of the young reformers seem radical in social philosophy and intransigent in social action is that there are almost no radicals in the older generation to compare them with, and that the complacency, conservatism, and paternalism of the educators give them a reference point too distant from the reality of the student to make informed judgment of student thought and action even remotely possible.

The universities of the United States are not only the center of the knowledge industry. They are certainly that. But they must also be centers of creative thought on matters having to do with public policy. The leaders of the liberal movement among students know this. They have learned through experience in Mississippi and the slums that the secret of social power lies in possessing the right to make decisions about matters affecting one's own situation. They claim that right to decision in the context of their own education and their own place in the society, and they claim the right not only for themselves but for everyone else.

It is a sign of the failure of higher education in America that it has had in the past so little to do with the needs of the Negro, the poor, the deprived, and the socially depressed, and so much to do with the success of the money-making classes. It is another sign of failure that, rather than taking leadership in the political and social education of the student, the university has done everything possible to insulate him from direct confrontation with the reality of his society by hedging him around with prohibitions on political and educational action, by treating the educational process as if it were simply a matter of academic busy-work.

The time has come for a change in all this. The younger generation has won, in the field, the right to represent the forces of intellectual and liberal reform. It is entitled, in this gallant endeavor, to the respect and support of those who control the universities.

Don't Tell Them to Play It Safe
WILLIAM SLOANE COFFIN, JR.

William Sloane Coffin, Jr., Yale's outspoken chaplain, has served in the CIA and the Peace Corps. In 1961 he was jailed as a freedom rider in Alabama.

IN the 1950s students generally were agreeing their way through life. Instead of using their education, they were trading on it. Pledged more to security and comfort than to truth, they were for the most part silent—and were simply imitating the vast majority of their parents.

The majority of their professors were silent too, silent in the face of McCarthyism and silent in the face of the massive resistance that arose to the 1954 Supreme Court decision. I can still remember one student's sour comment: "We are called the 'Silent Generation.' Can you blame us? After all, we sit at the feet of those who make a fetish of their silence."

But the national complacency of the '50s has been shaken in the '60s. Part of the credit must go to the cold war. More of the credit, I think, must go to the Southern Negro students who, in the early years of the decade, set off the wave of sit-ins, stand-ins, wade-ins and kneel-ins. In the process they persuaded a sufficient number of their white fellow students to join them to make the struggle in essence not black against white, but black and white against injustice.

The first student demonstrators were only demanding of Americans what America claimed already to have given. These students believed in America as the "cradle of liberty" and as the "land of equal opportunity"; they believed in the ballot box and the courts as proper procedures for the redress of grievances. If they departed from these procedures, it was for the sake of these procedures—because they had broken down —and not because they didn't believe in them. The majority of protesting students today have little quarrel with the American way of life as a whole. But a sizable minority do.

The developments of the decade have forced students to probe more deeply and to ask: What is freedom from oppression if it is not accompanied by freedom from want? What is equality of opportunity if in an automated age access to this opportunity is denied those of inferior education?

As the questioning has deepened, so has it broadened. To many of these students, their parents' lives look pretty meaningless. "My old man's in a rat race. And even if you win a rat race, you're still a rat." American culture too looks pretty empty, distracting from rather than giving meaning to life. Perceptive students wonder if Peter De Vries' fictional character might not have been speaking about the entire country when she said, "Deep down, he's shallow."

This type of questioning may displease parents but it delights professors. For now students are really beginning to use their education. True, many professors received a rude jolt this year when students used their education to question education itself.

The new complaints are mainly these. Just as students are beginning to get more and more interested in learning, their teachers are getting more and more interested in research. The social-minded students object also to the social neutrality of universities. "Why didn't university presidents publicly support the passage of the 1964 civil rights bill?" As for the professors, while they talk about problems, they don't live with them, and thus classrooms become terrains for the great game of intellectual volleyball—"let's bat this one around."

Students feel alienated because they have no say in the conduct of important university affairs. Serious students have only contempt for student governments. They term them "sandbox" governments because they deal only with the "Mickey Mouse" of education, not with the real issue of the quality of their education.

But what is going to be most upsetting—if it is not already —to professors, parents, the American public at large, and most certainly to university administrators, is, I suspect, the emergence of the so-called "New Radicals." Although few in number as yet, their influence is bound to increase. To idealize the New Radicals would be a mistake, for they have many "handups" and it is often hard to tell when their actions are prompted more by psychological needs than by intellectual convictions. But to dismiss them as mere "kooks" would be a much greater mistake, for among them are able leaders with great insight. To call them Communists would likewise be foolish, for their solutions are far too tentative to warrant any neat ideological label.

By far their most constructive work to date has been community organization in the rural and urban slums. Here, with a patience untypical of youth, they have labored not so much to get the poor out of the slums as the slums out of the poor. These New Radicals, of course, will sometimes appear destructive because they are disenchanted with normal democratic procedures that seem to lead to tokenism or hypocrisy, and they are often opposed to immediate progress on the grounds that it is only superficial change.

If there is an ominous ring in all this, then let it be heard. But there is hope, too, when students get excited about things worth getting excited about. And there is always the hope that errors can be corrected. So here, for whatever they are worth, are a few suggestions.

To university administrators and professors:

► Trust students more, and listen to them more carefully. Universities as a rule are less interested in what students are complaining about than in how to stop their complaining.

► Do not be timid about activism. Activism does not always mean a lower form of intellectualism. It may be what Whitehead meant when he said: "The success of language in conveying information is vastly overrated, especially in learned circles. . . . Nothing can supply the defect of firsthand experience."

► Nourish, encourage and promote good teachers.

► Speak out on important issues, for a university should not only serve a community but lead it as well.

To the parents of protesting students:

► Do not be blind to their faults, but do not be blind either to their insights. As St. Benedict reminded us, "God often reveals what is better to the younger." Whatever you do, don't tell your sons and daughters to play it safe. Personally, I would be far more worried about a son or daughter who was *not* protesting.

Finally, to the protesting students:

► You are right in believing that we must think as men of action. But while we are thinking as men of action, we must also live as men of thought, which means thinking constructively. Remember, it is easier to hate evil than to love good, easier also to swing a sledgehammer than to build a new carburetor; and, of course, it is desperately difficult while hating the sin to keep loving the sinner. But keep on loving we must, for our quarrel with America is indeed a lover's quarrel, and we shall have nothing to contribute if it degenerates into a dirty and purposeless grudge fight.

Students Speak

Here four student leaders explain why they have joined what they call "the movement," a title which encompasses all of their protests and crusades.

STEVEN BLOCK, Williams College

WE'RE a new generation of people, developed in precarious times. There's the cold war, and the civil rights movement—which has made us aware of some glaring problems in our own country. Also we have been fairly well off—even the poorest among us has had material advantages which our parents and grandparents did not have. So it's interesting that while many of us have not gone through a war or had to fight through a long depression, more and more of us are getting very upset about the world around us.

Today most people look at students who are involved in protest as though we were still searching for an identity and not yet adjusting to our social situation. They see us as "not quite balanced." My parents, for example, still think I'm going through a phase. This common view of what we are all about is wrong—it completely misses the point.

Many of us *have* found an identity. What we are trying to do now is to make our identity realizable. We've found possibilities for a brotherhood—for understanding a lot of things that people kind of feel are corny. Brotherhood is something you talk about in rhetoric, but in everyday life brotherhood and love and understanding are things that people get squeamish if you talk about. We believe that there are some very fundamental problems in Western society. They have to do with our orientation toward consumption, toward materialism that doesn't account for truly human considerations. When we talk about people making decisions and participating in the world and experiencing some sense of control over their destiny—when we talk about human happiness—we believe that it is discovering what our real needs are and acting upon them that is important.

One problem we have right now is automation. I think that our economy is flexible enough so that we can always develop new products to employ people in one fashion or another. But maybe that is not what we want. I believe that working on an assembly line is a debilitating experience for anybody. A man does it only to get enough money to clothe his kids, to have a roof over his head, to get a television set and a car, but it is in no way a vocation—a calling—which he pursues to fulfill himself in any real sense. Maybe we should consciously attempt to automate in order to release people from this kind of work.

That will mean free people—the leisure bit. So the question is, what do you do with it? Well, the way people behave today, the answer is that they'll bowl a lot, play golf a lot and watch television a lot. And I think that's very scary.

I worry about the passivity business. We have cultural passivity. We watch television. We attend plays and concerts. I think plays and concerts are good, but to me culture means participation in some sense. Why aren't more people involved in community kinds of productions?

Religion, too, is passive. We go off to church on Sunday and somebody preaches to us and that's our religion. We go home and it has no effect on our daily lives. I think politics is also passive. Voting is our way of being in politics. What baloney! Decisions are made for us.

The thing for me right now is the movement. That's an

interesting word, if you think about it—movement. Because it is people in motion. It's not an end; it's not static. That's a very apt word for what we are doing.

GARRETT LAMBREV, Stanford University

I don't believe in the American ideal. Everything around me contradicts it. Our system is not democratic—it's each man for himself and the people get left behind. I am a socialist. That's the only democratic system, but it has never been given a chance. In a capitalistic society I don't think there is opportunity for the man at the bottom, or for the man at the top. It's a dead end.

Gandhi's doctrine is best: truth is force. Gandhi showed us the true value of every human being and he showed us that pacifism is practical.

I am not a Communist. But the Vietnamese don't think that they are Communists either. We are fighting on the wrong level, the military level. Instead we should provide a framework so countries in need can develop viable systems by themselves. But I don't think the capitalistic system can provide that. I don't apologize for capitalism in the U.S. but here we have always had freedom, culture and sophisticated traditions.

Sure, we want to get arrested when we demonstrate. We want to make it clear to the public that we are serious. And we want to show our immediate concern toward our neighbors. Nonviolence shows concern, not so much for your friend as for your enemy. When we demonstrate, our nonviolence shows that we can disobey and alter without harming the individual. At least I hope that's what we show.

HOWARD ROMAINE, University of Virginia

In this country you seem to need credentials—a degree, white skin and two cars in the garage—before you are allowed to think. I think anyone, even a student, who sees the injustice of the South's segregation system cannot help but realize what is wrong and act. Segregation distorts and twists the minds of fundamentally good people. I can't stand it. I feel I must do something about it.

People in civil rights groups are not interested in football, dances or school spirit. These are games and lots of us don't want to play them. We want to deal with life and reality. In a time when loads of people are uncertain about nearly everything, we can identify with the Negro cause and know it is right.

Companies hire people who will be docile and do as they are told. They don't want someone who challenges the system. So a lot of students don't get involved with us because it might threaten their careers—though they do join us in "acceptable" causes like Selma. It may be true that life is full of compromise but it is for others to compromise, not me. I'm not interested in filling one of society's niches—to be an ordinary guy, go to school, get a good safe job and shut up when something seems wrong. When I get discouraged I think about doing this—taking the easy way out—but then I feel pretty sick at the thought. People ask me what I am going to do when the civil rights cause runs out. I tell them it is not just a cause we arbitrarily picked out just to do something. It is a feeling about humanity—any color, anywhere. And that won't change.

DAVID SMITH, Tufts University

We are trying to change society. In the '50s, the beat generation ran away from it. My generation knows we have to strike at the system to make it respond.

The system my father was part of, and is part of, said that a white colonial 14-room house, roast beef instead of hash, and college education for his kids demanded that he not do what he wanted to do, but what the system made him do.

Most middle-class students see their role as going back to supplant Daddy when he retires. Our whole society is moving in a direction that will mean an end to questioning. I hear very little re-evaluation, very little challenge of accepted values.

What I want is a world where people are free to make the decisions that affect their own lives, a world in which they're not trapped on a vast merry-go-round of concealed power, not forced into situations where the choice is already made for them. I want a "participatory democracy" where I, for one, am involved in the workings of the system I'm living in. I want a nonexploited system in which no one's making money off another man's work. I want people to be happy, too. More than anything else, I want a world where we're free to be human to each other.

I feel the university could be a fantastically exciting place in which to begin to create this kind of society. It's the only place that places a premium on skepticism, on questioning. But I'd like to see the university *in* the society, rather than be a function of society—to come to grips with the problems we have to face today. I don't think the university does that, but the potential is there.

Why the Students Revolt

BILL WARD

Bill Ward, Assistant Professor of Journalism at Syracuse University, was formerly on the news staff of the Minneapolis Tribune *and the San Bernardino (Calif.)* Sun-Telegram.

IT WAS just a small demonstration of student disapproval, hardly violent enough to cause a ripple in the nation's press. The students were unhappy about the dates for Christmas vacation, so a few thousand of them (estimated from 2,000 to 5,000 by crowd counters) gathered in front of the campus chapel to protest. Radio and television brought along their cameras, hoping for the worst, and the local newspaper reporters were there. But the press got just two newsworthy facts: The chancellor of the university again said No, the students could not have an extra two and a half days of vacation; some of the students jeered the chancellor's talk.

Out in Berkeley, students were staging a sit-down-drag-out battle with authorities, but here at Syracuse University the protest was mainly verbal and not disruptive at all. It was typical of dozens of such demonstrations on campuses across the nation this year and last—and typical of more to come in this age of "action" campuses.

For their confrontation of authority, the student body at Syracuse got bad publicity. First of all, the motive on the surface was barely supportable. It was not obviously a matter of high principle to demand a longer vacation. And the booing shocked people who didn't realize that the speech, not the chancellor, was being booed. The students were supposed to show proper respect, to know their place and keep it.

And that, in a nutshell, is the reason for the demonstrations. The college student does indeed know the place allotted to him—and he doesn't like it. That is why the constrained demonstration at Syracuse in December is symbolic of the changing attitudes of today's college students.

For three weeks, student leaders and official student organizations had been pressing the administration for a vacation to start on December 18, rather than December 23. A number of reasons were given, but all the petitions were politely turned down. Then, as a last resort, a mass meeting was called for a Monday afternoon, and to everyone's surprise thousands turned out. Something was happening to student attitude; for once there was no apathy. At 3:30, as promised, the chancellor made a personal appearance, held his ground and was rudely received.

In succeeding days, student leaders tried picketing (no support from students) and called for a boycott of classes (a little more support). Then it was time for vacation and the issue died.

After the students had left for Christmas, theories began to develop among members of the faculty about the "real" significance of the demonstration. An explanation went free with every cup of coffee. One of the most popular was immaturity—too many students still live in an adolescent stage of parent rejection, and if a university insists on maintaining its role of parental substitute, it must be prepared to face rebellious offspring.

Another theory posed demagogues at work. At emotional times of the school year, such as near the end of a term, the hounds can bay at the uneasy herd and send it into quick fighting. Battling for power, a few student leaders hope to usurp the chancellor's authority, and one way to bring down the monarch is to rouse the rabble.

But no single, all-encompassing theory fits neatly—particularly to such minor movements as the Christmas demonstrations at Syracuse, where the causes were obviously plural. The students who jeered the chancellor, or stood quietly listening to the speeches, or who packed up and went home whenever they damn well felt like it had a variety of motives. Here follows a "Who's Who" of a demonstration:

1. Some of the most vociferous hecklers found in the movement self-justification for academic failure. The semester was nearing completion, final grades had become apparent, and those who faced failure enthusiastically jumped into the demonstrations. One boy was heard to say after the chancellor's speech, "Well, it just proves all over again that I'm lucky to get out of here."

Most colleges don't publish their annual dropout rate, but it is considerable. The greater the pressures to get in, the easier it is to be flunked out. And as more students need excuses, campus dissatisfaction will more easily be whipped up.

One of the students in the front lines at Syracuse is well known to me. He has twice dropped courses, hoping to trim his academic load to manageable proportions, but he still fails. As his anger grows, he looks lightning and mouths thunder. One professor has it in for him; another just doesn't know how to teach. "I don't know about that cat," he said one day. "He dips me no end." I have watched this youngster for two semesters and never seen him smile. He won't be given a chance to return to summer school again to make up deficiencies, so he must have his excuses ready. And there he was, in the front lines, booing the chancellor, a girl friend gripping his hand and crying bitterly.

On a campus of 10,000 students, hundreds are headed straight for failure. They provide a desperate army, ready to strike for revenge.

2. Where there are malcontents, there are some demagogues. On college campuses they often are popularly elected student leaders who look about them and see precious few to lead. A few decades ago, student government became a vogue, a device to make students feel a part of things. But relatively little power went with office. Now, student leaders, ambitious and hating the hypocrisy of their position, frequently demand power. And many of them have studied 20th-century power techniques and know how to amass strength. This is particularly true of those who come from metropolitan backgrounds. The rural student enjoys elbowroom and independence and feels little need to head a power structure. The urban student, raised in crowds, often feels compelled to stand out. He can be ruthless.

When student support is not satisfactory, the leader may draw upon emotional words. One is "apathetic." If a student were to get an honor point every time he is called "apathetic" today, he would easily be graduated *cum laude*. Leaders know that the word bites, so if few undergraduates show up at a rally, the campus is "apathetic." Students are never thought of as being in their rooms, trying to study for examinations; they are "apathetic" to the cause. They are never conceded to be out of sympathy with a nifty maneuver designed to aggrandize student government; they are "apathetic." They are never called self-reliant or self-thinking, never sensible about controversy; they are instead always "apathetic." To defend themselves against the charge, students must rally behind their young leaders and besiege the administration building.

Not that all student rebellions are provoked by impure motives, but demagogy is in the air. The desire for followers is producing a group of touring campus leaders, who move from campus to campus, somewhat like circuit parsons, churning student spirit. Power becomes additive, and one flock is becoming not enough for these leaders.

3. Students undergoing the pressures of today's schooling struggle from vacation to vacation, like a desert tribe moving hopefully from oasis to oasis. Vacations provide time to catch up on work (books and term papers), to catch up on sleep (no staying up until 3 A.M. to finish reports). Vacations mean a chance to unwind nerves, a chance to eat noninstitutional food, a chance to get away from the monster university. "If I can hold out three more weeks, it'll be time for vacation. Then I can make it to intersession." Their schedule for survival is so closely planned that every day of vacation is significant. The school-weary students—in need of a booster day —turned out en masse at Syracuse, but generally they were not the hecklers. Instead, at the chancellor's firm no, they shook their heads and trudged back to the residences for one more stay-awake pill.

4. And, of course, a demonstration is exciting. College campuses, despite their reputation for antisocial behavior, are notoriously strait-laced and decorous. They would be havens for adult moderates, but for thousands of young people they are flat wastes of tedium. Life is kept lean and dry. For example, at home most college-age girls can stay out past midnight without causing alarm, but at most colleges the girls must be in at 10:30 P.M., except for a midnight curfew on Saturdays and an occasional 2 A.M. special pass. The university campus is an urban community with a rural ethic, one of the final homes of the Puritan code. To many students, the most exciting event of the week is a party called TGIF: Thank God, it's Friday; time for beers in celebration. Some overdo the rejoicing, but academic competition is too tough to allow much license. Colleges are knife-quick to dismiss the laggards. In fact, when newspapers editorialize about orgiastic life on—or off—the campuses, or when a new book exposes the depravity of college students, no one laughs more bitterly than the students themselves. The life just doesn't exist; a few incidents are parlayed into a bestseller. So most students welcome excitement on campus, even if they disapprove of jeering the chancellor and wouldn't do so.

5. Finally, there is the constant fear of being buried alive in what has been called "the sprawling multiversity." The desire for physical growth in most colleges is insatiable. More money is always needed—more contributions from alumni, more endowments, more profit-making groups within the university, more students paying higher tuitions, more federal grants, more research dollars from the foundations. Growth. Power. Numbers. Dollars. The most important man on campus is the one who brings in the most funds. In the past, it was the authority on Shakespeare who received a standing ovation at the conclusion of his final lecture. Not today. A teacher cannot be measured numerically, but the man of money can— he always stands so high in dollars and cents.

Students swiftly and surely sense any change in campus values. They suspect that they, too, have been displaced. The university is not quite the city of mind that they had been taught to expect. It is in part a materialistic city of research, of growth, of grinding out profit and interest to be put back into expansion. The tuition fee—the student's contribution— is not of primary importance. In state colleges, taxes carry the load; in private colleges, outside funds meet the bills. The student, feeling somewhat like a welfare case, fears losing even more of his position.

At lunch the other day, an intelligent and mature student described the problem. "They always seem to be wanting to make me into a number. I won't let them. I have a name and am important enough to be known by it. No numbers for me— or anything else that threatens my identity and position. I'll join any movement that comes along to help me. The faculty can give up and be digits if they want to. But not me!" He became effusive. "This is my school. I figure I am just as important to the school as it is important to me. My education is the significant thing here and that is the source of my allegiance to the school." Therefore, he is willing to rebel against any power that threatens to submerge him.

For these reasons and others, most campuses today are increasingly vulnerable to student demonstrations. Last year at Syracuse, for instance, food service was boycotted ("The double Jello caper"); civil right issues led to a series of picketings, parades and boycotts.

But several elements must be present to unite the disparate groups on campus into one "action." First, the issue should be morally and socially defensible in the eyes of the public (which generally means parents and friends back home). Free speech at Berkeley; allegedly substandard food; disregard of a religious holiday; racial equality; unjust suspension of students for minor infractions of campus rules—if the issue has the sanction of morality and common sense, however heavily disguised, students will risk going into action. At Syracuse, an attempt was made to criticize students by pointing out that a sizable portion of these are Jewish and presumably indifferent to Christmas. Jewish students answered hotly, "We can be Jewish and still participate in the spirit of the Christmas holidays." Proper observance of Christmas was defensible cause.

Second, the issue must have direct effect on most students. A change in regulations thus would affect all students and can easily be whipped into a movement. A contradiction arises here: student quickness to react against change, in the name of "action," helps assure the *status quo*.

Third, and perhaps most important, "action" must confront the generations in charge: those elders who control society, and in the minds of most students make a bad job of it. Here one comes upon the "why" of rebellion.

Every college generation has supposedly challenged its elders, but never before has it been quite like this. In the 1920s, expatriation was a popular form of rebellion; for others gin and joy provided escape. In the 1930s, the fight was economic and political and the college group pinched by depression was very small. In the 1940s, all energies were burned up by war. In the 1950s, refugees from depression and war, students refused to face issues and wanted, instead, security and moderation.

The present generation is different. Its energies cannot be drafted into a war for either economic or political survival. Students today refuse to escape like their fathers, and they refuse to settle for materialistic security like their older brothers and sisters. They see American history in this century as a series of mistakes—a blundering from one war, supposed to end all wars, right into another. They view the depression as the result of economic and political stupidity. They see weapons of mass destruction as the most prevailing instruments to come out of the atomic age.

A columnist for one of the Syracuse newspapers criticized students at Syracuse University for their demonstration at Christmas and suggested they gird themselves for greater sacrifices, rather than gain. As an illustration of sacrifice, he used an incident from World War I, when he and his buddies willingly spent one holiday digging latrines for a group of dysentery patients. The column caused amusement on campus. The modern college student—"the best educated and the healthiest"—could not understand the moral of the anecdote. He believes man must have greater hopes and purposes and values. To survive college is to aspire to far more useful sacrifices, if need be. After all, this college generation largely fills the ranks of the Peace Corps.

Harping on war merely convinces the student of the incapacity of the elder generations to govern wisely. Better give over the controls, or at least accept a younger copilot! As the editor of the student newspaper at Syracuse wrote: "If today's demonstration proves nothing else, it must at least show the administration we are here and we care what it thinks about us. We are not ones to be ignored or taken lightly."

There is then this matter of superior education; the modern student willingly agrees that he is superior and believes that therefore he sees more clearly, carries proper banners, is better able to undertake correct and elevating action. He grants that he is young but is convinced that his superiority to previous college generations equips him to lead at a much earlier age. He is also a creative thinker (teachers of English constantly attack his inability to spell and punctuate, but they say little against his creativity); he sees all the old problems in new perspective. For his own survival, he must get control soon, an impulse that is setting campus leaders to a faster timetable. After all, their idol John F. Kennedy became President in his 40s. If one of today's students exerts enough pressure and keeps his elders sufficiently unnerved, he too may become the youngest President, and may have a world to take care of.

To the other generations, Kennedy was a good President, but he was not as warmly held as FDR or Eisenhower. But to the college generation, Kennedy was more than political leader; he was physically, intellectually, ideologically and ethically the perfect symbol of all their dreams. A professor friend of mine inadvertently pointed this out recently. He was uncertain whether to show a movie based on a Kennedy press conference. "They will all start crying again," he said.

Today's college students could not vote for Kennedy, and they contributed little to his acceleration to power, but they identified totally with him. They even believe he was sent to them. With President Kennedy, who understood their aspirations, they would have reformed the world—and thus saved man from mass suicide. After all, this generation was born as Hiroshima died.

What better evidence of their loyalty than the brilliant expositions which appeared in college and high school newspapers after the President's death—in general showing much greater depth of loss than did the adult press, even though the students were more uncertain in style. The students pin the assassination mercilessly to the older generations. The act was fully characteristic of the genius for destruction.

The prosecution sums up: "You set off the atomic bomb. You were complacent until Dachau. Your Depression wasn't so Great. You got trapped in Korea. Now, you want to threaten my life in some place like Vietnam. You assassinated Kennedy and gave me in his place a professional politician from Texas. Your generation has failed us and yourselves utterly. We are much better equipped to make decisions and to take control."

That is why, when a chancellor says he has made a decision, that it is final, and that he expects all loyal students to abide by it, he gets jeered. The older generation represents to them dogmatism and self-righteousness that have produced two world wars, a depression, a political inquisition, a rising crime rate and a dehumanization of city ethics, among other things. To prevent further blunders, they refuse to extend blind loyalty, even though they may revere personally the man who asks for it. "If only he had given us a reason we could accept," said students after the demonstrations at Syracuse.

Mississippi is still another symbol of the perfidy of the elders. Many students spent the summer there and have returned to Northern campuses to exert greater pressures against any society that tolerates a Mississippi in its midst. The attitude toward rights has led to consistent interracial dating on campuses, to great enthusiasm for civil rights groups, for pickets and sit-ins and parades. These students consider themselves the true warriors of the times, fighters in new, nonviolent terms.

Another thing that angers the college student is the feeling that he has been belittled by his elders. He is misunderstood, for instance, when he confronts established authority and is accused of falling in, blindly or otherwise, with Communists or other demagogues. He is misunderstood when he demonstrates against the House Un-American Activities Committee, not because that group is anti-Communist but because many times it has been anti-student. He is misunderstood by the new President. The student tried to transfer allegiance from Kennedy but discovered that Johnson talked down to him, patted him on the head, used him for such political showpieces as convention dancing girls.

Even in college, he feels patronized. He is in search of enriched intellect and too often finds himself treated like a youngster. He is fobbed off with graduate students as teachers. He is governed by a bourgeois ethic that is fundamentally caste and many times alien to his own background. He is given too many cut-and-paste assignments. He is lectured at and rarely reasoned with. He feels creativity blunted and stunted at every turn. His health and morality are fretted over, but rarely his intellect. He feels like his teen-age hero-victim, Holden Caulfield, arrested in his years, seeking the ideal and hating to accept the real.

The student sometimes feels robbed of his heritage. He has been told again and again that his path has been cleared of obstacles by the elders. He can live his life in leisure and luxury because the affluent utopia is here and now. Unfortunately this student has been so well educated that his mind needs mission, not materialism. He can live without the TV Westerns and continental wardrobes and souped-up Bentleys that his older brothers and sisters settled for. That is one reason why he joins the Peace Corps and tramps off to poverty and underprivilege.

At times, in desperation, he tries to escape his frustration by challenging morality—by reading, for instance, great gobs of Rechy and Henry Miller and Styron. He dances the Watusi and the monkey because that makes the elders squirm, but these are angry reactions; they do not truly represent the student.

So "action" may be just a little jeering of a university president (most students feel badly about it and some write the president to apologize). More seriously, it may be violence as at Berkeley and at Buffalo. It will be manifested in many other ways this year and next. The point is, this college generation will not be shoved aside or await its seniority. They are not kids, as one columnist wrote recently, whose main problem is still acne. They come from a generation that sees the world much differently than do its predecessors. And, although not necessarily the offspring of Dr. Frankenstein, they are beginning to feel a compulsion to power, a need to rise up against elder authority—for their own preservation and the world's.

Roots of Student Discontent

MERVIN B. FREEDMAN

Mervin B. Freedman is Assistant Dean of Undergraduate Education at Stanford University. Dr. Freedman holds a Ph.D. in psychology from the University of California, Berkeley, and has been a Fellow at the Center for Advanced Study in the Behavioral Sciences.

T HE Byrne Report to the Regents of the University of California renders valuable service to that institution and to higher education in general. It uncovers many of the defects in the structure and government of the university system in the state of California, and contains cogent observations on the students who have been involved in various uprisings at Berkeley during the last year. Among its many statements about students, the following is the most penetrating: "We conclude that the basic cause of unrest on the Berkeley campus was the dissatisfaction of a large number of students with many features of the society they were about to enter."

This pervasive sense of dissatisfaction with American society lies at the root of student discontent, protest and rebellion. The heart of the matter is that students are being educated to fit into a society they reject, at least in considerable part. This temper or mood must be recognized if the sources of unrest on the various campuses are to be understood. Explanations based on local issues alone—large classes at Michigan, rules governing the use of alcohol at Trinity College, women's social regulations and judicial procedures at Stanford, military service at Columbia or Cornell—are incomplete. Similarly, explanations based on traditional politics do not hold water. The social scientists or philosophers who discuss the Free Speech Movement in Berkeley in terms of political disputes and allegiances, after the fashion of the Trotsky-Stalin conflict of the 1930s, are maundering. The Byrne Report stresses that connections between political parties or political figures and the leaders of the Free Speech Movement were remote and tenuous.

The Byrne Report makes a significant start on a very badly needed task—the interpretation of the hopes, dreams and desires of college students to their parents, their teachers and the American public. Much more understanding of students is required, however, if disasters like the turmoil at Berkeley are not to be repeated. I have talked to students at Berkeley who have learned to their dismay that their parents and the friends of their parents still explain the difficulties on that campus as the work of agitators or beatniks. These citizens display no understanding of the college youth of their state, including their own children.

And college administrators and faculty members have hardly begun to appreciate what it is that makes students tick these days. Of course, until recent months, many faculty members and administrators were concerned with matters other than the undergraduate student—research and publications, for example, or expansion of undergraduate programs. But even when faculty members and administrators do turn their attention to the undergraduate, their descriptions and explanations almost invariably are wide of the mark.

To some extent, the feelings and behavior of students must also be interpreted to the students themselves. Many students are unconscious of, or but dimly perceive, the springs of their restlessness and rebellion. So it is that minor issues may become the focus of major conflict. A protest movement among students resembles an iceberg in respect to what is visible above the surface. Thus students may fall prey to leadership that does not serve them well. Inchoate dissatisfaction may be channeled into irrelevant outbursts. The analogy to psychoanalysis and psychotherapy is apposite here: the better students understand themselves, the freer they are to choose wisely among alternative actions, and the more likely they are to find suitable answers to their questions and suitable solutions to their problems.

Why are our students dissatisfied with so much of American society? Why are they reluctant to fit in? The answer is simple. The Industrial Revolution is ending in the United States; indeed, it may already be over. A new era—that of automation and cybernation—is upon us. And the consequences of the termination of the Industrial Revolution, for the individual and for society, are enormous.

Students are restless and dissatisfied because they recognize —not always consciously—that the education they are receiving is not functional to the world they will be inhabiting in ten or twenty years. Current educational practices and procedures are modeled on the images of men and of work bequeathed to us by the 19th century. Young people, thus, feel cheated by their elders and teachers.

I cannot anticipate all the consequences of the revolution of automation and cybernation. I can, however, discern that students are preparing for a different human and social condition. I quote J. Bronowski, the scientific and moral philosopher, on this point:

> The key to the action of living things then is this, that it is directed toward that future. They have a way of knowing what is going to happen next. Most of this knowledge is unconscious. We need not be astonished about this foresight, or at any rate we need not find it more astonishing than we find the rest of the world. For plainly it has always been the condition for the survival of living things, individually and in species. Unless they could adapt themselves to the future, and interpret its signals in advance, they were bound to perish.

Faculty members and college administrators also respond to these evolutionary pressures, but, being older, the forces of conservatism are strong within them. Youth is more responsive. Much unrest and conflict on college campuses may be explained as the attempt by students to bend educational procedures to their will and to influence faculty members and administrators for certain personal and social ends. These goals are fourfold: (1) the restoration of viable communities in colleges and universities and in society at large; (2) the introduction of unity into the intellect and the personality; (3) the establishment of the ethic of social service as a powerful motive in modern life; (4) the freeing of the impulse life of man—the release of what Henry Murray calls "the erotic imagination."

Students today are rebellious; they want less constraint by authority, and more autonomy. This is particularly true of the leaders of student movements. But rebelliousness and autonomy are by no means all that is involved. Students desire as well more affiliation with the faculty. They are demanding of administrators, and particularly of teachers, that they join with students to establish that "community of scholars" one hears so much about and so seldom sees. Students, I believe, are trying to restore to colleges and universities a sense of community that has somehow been lost on most campuses since World War II. Before the war, students shared certain things. Often these were not academic experiences, but rather fraternity and sorority life, football games, social events and the like which provided a feeling of belonging or participation that is not to be underestimated. Academic culture has made sharp inroads into that area of student life, and intellectual performance has accordingly been elevated—but often at the expense of elements of living which students, being human, find it difficult to do without.

Given the intense competition of contemporary academic life, a student rarely has the opportunity to cooperate with other people in a venture which has meaning for all the participants. Team sports are but lightly regarded by guardians of academic integrity, but they provide the student with one of his few opportunities to work with others toward a common end. Ideology aside, the teach-ins appeal to students because they are a chance to work cooperatively with faculty in an enterprise that cuts across traditional teacher-student relationships and activities. Students are attempting to counter the atmosphere of competitiveness and isolation which has prevailed on most campuses for the last two decades. This motive, of which they are often only vaguely aware, accounts for much behavior that on the surface appears to be simple rebellion.

The need for "adult" leadership, faculty leadership in particular, must not be overlooked. Much has been made of the statement, "you can't trust anyone over 30," which reputedly was one of the slogans of the Free Speech Movement. Yet the leaders of the movement wished to dedicate the steps of Sproul Hall on the Berkeley campus to the late Alexander Meikeljohn, the great civil libertarian, who was over 90 when he died last December. It is safe to say that no rebellion of consequence will occur on a campus on which the faculty displays moral force. At Berkeley, where the faculty in recent months has become actively involved in issues of the university community, potentially explosive issues—the "Filthy Speech Movement," for example, or controversial statements and actions on the part of the Regents of the university—have been, or are being, resolved with a minimum of public discord.

The Industrial Revolution diversified labor and knowledge. As the United States was rapidly industrialized in the decades after the Civil War, colleges became increasingly fragmented. Major fields of specialization, departments and divisions replaced a uniform curriculum and courses which emphasized the synthesis of subject matter. This tendency reached its height in the post-Sputnik era, when young people were urged to specialize in secondary school, or even earlier, so that they might get into the right undergraduate college, which would prepare them for the right graduate or professional school, which in turn would insure them entree to the more important professional or business positions.

College students are becoming increasingly dissatisfied with this atomizing process. They seek breadth and unity in their studies. At many colleges in the last few years the number of undergraduates who major in broadly defined fields—for example, literature, philosophy and history—has been increasing at a considerable rate. To be sure, such students more often than not are women. (There is the problem of sustenance. An undergraduate philosophy major does not readily convert to a job in business or industry.) But the trend holds for men as well. Although Stanford is very strong in engineering and sciences, the department today with the largest number of undergraduate majors is history, and at Stanford men outnumber women by about 2 to 1. I do not mean to imply that what Whitehead calls "expert knowledge in some special direction" will disappear at the undergraduate level. I do believe, however, that by majoring in broadly defined fields students are attempting to introduce a measure of unity or wholeness into their lives.

While it can hardly be said that the desire for material and worldly success has disappeared from the face of American campuses, activities such as the Peace Corps and the Civil Rights Movement demonstrate that an ethic of social service has in recent years assumed more moment in the lives of college students. As the Byrne Report indicates, the plight of the Negro in American life symbolized for many students the evil and hypocrisy of American society. The Puritan or Calvinist ethic of hard work and success in competitive struggle is on the wane, and to some extent the ethic of social service, which nourishes the hunger to be part of a community, is replacing it. The ethic of social service is a response as well, I believe, to an era of automation and an economy of affluence. If but little human energy is required to sustain human life in excellent material circumstances, a philosophy of life dominated by the aphorisms of Benjamin Franklin becomes dubious. In all events, it becomes increasingly difficult to make students respond to the traditional rewards of Western industrial society.

The freeing of the impulse life, or the freeing of Eros in Western civilization, has been taking place since the end of World War I. I quote from Henry Murray:

> It took World War I and the moral revolution of the 1920s to shatter the prohibitions of puritanism and Victorianism and open a wide vent for the eruption of the repressed instincts and emotions: sex chiefly, but also hatred of the dominant powers, plutocracy, mediocracy, and finally Mechos, the cold-blooded dragon of impersonal matter-of-factness and technics, of business, advertising, and upward mobility, of hollow showmen and spurious prestige. . . .

I wish to make it clear that by Eros I do not mean the sexual expression in its physical manifestations only. And I surely do not mean sexual promiscuity. Although sexual intercourse among engaged couples or among students who are seriously involved with each other is probably increasing at a slow rate, sexual promiscuity, in the sense of relations between students who have made little or no emotional commitment to each other, has probably declined on college campuses in recent years. Those individuals who talk of "proliferating promiscuity" or "the sexual revolution" should ask themselves why it is that college youth marry at an early age. The answer, of course, is that they do not wish to postpone sexual gratification until well into adult life, as Musgrove has pointed out in a perceptive article (*The Nation,* April 26, 1965), and on the other hand are not so insensitive as to indulge freely in sex relations outside the conventional ties of engagement and marriage. More generally on the subject of impulse, college students are increasingly unwilling to accept education as a grim, humorless, competitive affair. They want more zest, more gusto, more life than has been available at most colleges and universities in recent years. They want to mean it when they sing *Gaudeamus Igitur.*

The consequences of these desires and needs of students are enormous. No facet of personal or social life in the United States will be unaffected. I shall dwell briefly on some of the implications for higher education. The grading system and comparable procedures for judging students will be drastically altered. A movement to liberalize grading programs is now under way in American colleges. Antioch, for example, will dispense with grades in the freshman year, and Princeton has made it possible for students to receive pass or fail marks rather than letter grades outside their major fields. Princeton students may now "experiment" with courses and disciplines without fear of penalty by way of a lowered grade point average.

Similarly, students will not be dropped for reason of academic failure—at least not in the first several years of college. The system that will emerge is likely to resemble arrangements at the Universities of Oxford and Cambridge. After some period of time students will be required to demonstrate an appropriate degree of competence or mastery, but acceptance of the student by a college will mean a commitment to educate him. This commitment dictates retaining him within the confines of the institution, except as it may seem that his education would be better served by his leaving. In rare cases, when the presence of a student appears to threaten the welfare of a college, it may be necessary to expel him, but the present system in most colleges and universities, which really places students on trial, which demands that they measure up to standards under pain of dismissal, will disappear.

Current academic procedures and teaching and learning situations will be drastically altered. Much of the burden of conveying routine information—events of history, vocabulary and grammar of foreign languages, chemical and mathematical formulas and so on—will be assumed by programed instruction. Less faculty time will be devoted to these activities. The development of new knowledge, new ways of looking at things, will receive increasing attention. To such ends, small groups of faculty members, graduate students and undergraduates will work together. In such groups, age and status variations will be minimal, since the task of developing new knowledge, new concepts, new ways of thought will induce an appropriate humility and cooperative spirit among all the participants. Beginning in the autumn of 1965, a large number of seminars will be available to Stanford freshmen. They will be taught by all levels of faculty from teaching assistant to full professor. Each seminar will contain about six freshmen (perhaps fewer in the case of physical sciences) and in some instances an upper division undergraduate. The emphasis in these freshman seminars will be on subject matter and activities that are outside traditional curriculums and courses. A few illustrative titles: "Problems Facing the Contemporary Composer," "Authority in Organizations," "The University as a Social Institution."

Traditional departments and fields of study will assume less and less importance in higher education as time goes by. There will be more emphasis on activities and knowledge that combine and cut across disciplines. Many students will have no major subjects of concentration. The assumption that there is a finite body of information which each student in a field of study must absorb will go by the boards—to some extent because of concern with new ways of thought and with interdisciplinary programs that attempt to synthesize this thought, but also because the explosion of knowledge renders such universal expertise almost impossible. Curriculums suitable to the needs and desires of youth and the future are still in their infancy. In all events, it is certain that traditional major fields of study and courses of specialization are on their way out.

Consider the interest in creativity among educators and social scientists in recent years. The creative act is the leap of imagination that provides a wholeness which did not previously exist. As Bronowski has pointed out, the creation of unity out of variety is the same in science as in art. Newton's remarkable conjunction of apple and moon is of the same order as Keats's extraordinary association of beauty and truth. No one concerned to devise a curriculum that will foster creative expression is likely to confine his attention to the traditional departments and fields of specialization. The same is true of attempts to promote development of such qualities as independence of judgment, logical thinking or proficiency in communication.

Counseling activities—for example, counseling in the high schools for admission to college—and occupational counseling and guidance in the colleges, will undergo extensive modification of basic conception. By and large such counseling is now designed to make it possible for students to fit into one system or another as smoothly as possible. A high school student is aided in choosing the college in which he is likely to be successful—that is, likely to be graduated with good grades. A student is helped to choose an occupation or profession for which he has the requisite aptitudes and for which he seems to possess the appropriate interests—interests that resemble those of people who are successful in the field. The emphasis on development of new knowledge and the reduction of emphasis on grading and failure will change these patterns. Students will be encouraged to try new things; to go to a college, for example, where they will find colleagues of quite different values or personality; or to take courses which may interest them, even if they seem to have little aptitude or ability for them. Counselors, in short, will advise with an eye to the fullest development of individual personality rather than to the perpetuation of traditional professions and occupations. (See Robert Mathewson, "Manpower or Persons," *The Personnel and Guidance Journal*, December, 1964.)

The concept of self-development as a major goal of life will be a tremendous spur to liberal education in the classic sense. An affluent society in which the labor of young people is not needed will mean that they will be allowed longer time before committing themselves to a profession or comparable activity. Young adults will come to resemble the young men of the upper classes in the 19th century who were not expected to do much of anything before they were 30, except travel around and meditate and perhaps sow some wild oats. Basil Ransom in Henry James's *The Bostonians* is a good example of such a young man. Recently, an eminent foundation undertook to support a program wherein a number of students at a prominent men's college will interrupt their education for a year to live and observe—without any specified program or duties —in certain underdeveloped countries.

Some courses of study and corollary professions or occupations will benefit from the kinds of trends I have described—

the teaching profession, for one. Others, however, will suffer. Business, industry, medicine and the law are examples. The decline of material reward as a motive for entering occupations and professions and the interest in synthesis of knowledge and interdisciplinary study rather than in specialization will militate against students' adopting such careers. This will be particularly true of the brighter and livelier students. One hopes that major redefinition of these professions and activities will result. And by major redefinition I do not mean superficial alterations of public "image" designed to attract good students.

At least in the professions signs of change may be discerned. Law schools have traditionally attracted the more conservative and conventional students. The following news item is from *The Daily Californian*, May 20, 1965: "Ten Boalt Hall law students will participate in a civil rights clerk-ship program throughout the South this summer. Sponsored by the Law Students Civil Rights Research Council, they will be working as part of a team of 120 students from leading law schools in the nation." Inevitably such students will modify the ethos of the profession of law. Doctors are not noted for a disposition to contravene the *status quo* in American society. The general stodginess and lack of intellectual vivacity in the profession are among the reasons why many of the more intelligent and discerning undergraduates of recent years have chosen academic or research careers in various of the biological sciences in preference to attendance at medical school. Countervailing tendencies may be found—Dr. Spock's public pronouncements on foreign policy, for example, or the doctors who picketed the International Automobile Show in New York on behalf of greater automobile safety (*The Nation*, May 3, 1965). Medical schools will recapture their share of the best undergraduate students only to the extent that they can appeal to the humanitarian instincts and need for social contribution of these students.

One has but to skim the marriage columns in *The New York Times* to realize that a very high proportion of the well-educated sons and daughters of businessmen and industrialists do not enter business and industry. A surprising number are pursuing academic careers or are preparing for such. On the other hand, few sons and daughters of professional men and of those in academic pursuits seem disposed to enter business and industry. A research carried out by David Beardslee and Donald O'Dowd (*The American College,* edited by Nevitt Sanford) finds that liberal arts college students think businessmen less intelligent and more selfish than professional men. They also see them as emotionally more unstable. Does this mean that control of business and industry will pass gradually to more narrowly educated and less sophisticated individuals?

The education of women may recapture the educational initiative it formerly possessed. At one time women's colleges were pioneers in various educational ventures. They introduced courses in creative arts, as well as programs of study abroad. Of late, they have done little except exemplify Diana Trilling's dictum that women need to get an education as bad as men's in order to feel that they are not being discriminated against. At the very time that automation and cybernation and attendant economic and social changes are likely to produce widespread unemployment, increased leisure time and redefinition of work vs. leisure, college women and alumnae are encouraged by educators to realize themselves in the world of work after the manner of men. The situation is similar to that of the Negro in the United States. Now that there is little place for youth in the work force, Negro high school students are urged to take advantage of educational opportunities and thereby qualify for good jobs after graduation. Thus far, educated women have had the good sense not to enter male professions and occupations en masse. They seem to recognize instinctively that there are apt to be more valuable outlets for them than the weary and uninteresting rounds men have been pursuing for generations. New ways of living and of working are now needed, and educated women, divorced as they are from some of the traditional commitments of men, are in a unique position to provide them. I am not particularly sanguine that women's education will offer the educational leadership so badly needed. Faculty and administrators concerned with women's education are only too willing to emulate the education of men.

A discipline and a profession of college teacher or educator will emerge. It is ridiculous to suppose that a graduate degree in one field of study or another—chemistry, or French or psychology—is sufficient qualification for educating college students. A teacher should know something about college students, how and what they learn, how they are changed by educational experiences and the like.

Most research workers in the social sciences have not been interested in the study of whole human beings in real-life situations, but the need to understand college students may change this attitude. A classic example is the situation at the University of California. Although thousands upon thousands of students have served as research subjects for studies and experiments in the School of Education and in the Departments of Sociology and Psychology, with but very few exceptions no research workers were concerned with students as students or as whole human beings. Students were simply eyes for perception experiments, ears for auditory experiments, representatives of this or that reference group, etc. The turmoil at Berkeley suddenly galvanized a number of research workers into investigating the lives of their student colleagues.

As accurate and useful information about students and college experience becomes available, will educators be interested in it? A year ago I should have thought not. The attitude of most administrators and faculty members toward educational research is negative—or was until very recently. They have been disposed to dismiss such research as the product of second-rate minds of the kind that emphasize life adjustment or driver education at the expense of "real" education. But current student unrest may well change these views and impress upon educators the necessity for systematic observation and empirical study. Rhetoric about the glories and wonders of college education will no longer suffice. There will be much more interest in what actually goes on.

I do not suggest that my description of students is appropriate to the majority of American undergraduates. Most of them are conventional, bound by the traditional demands of American society and culture, dutiful and complaisant. The students I have described represent an *avant-garde* at the more prestigious colleges. But in the fashion of these things, we may be sure that what is a ripple today will be a wave tomorrow. Nor do I wish to convey a simple optimism about the future. Man and his society are complex, and I hardly believe that individual and human progress are inevitable. I am convinced, nevertheless, that if we can refrain from blowing ourselves up in the next decade or so, college youth will make this a much better world.

War of the Generations

LOUIS E. REIK

Louis E. Reik, psychiatrist in the University Health Service at Princeton University, is the author of various papers on the mental health of students.

BY the time a student reaches college age, he should be well launched on a good, brisk war of independence. His object is to express to his satisfaction the ferment of energy with which sometimes he is all but bursting. He no longer endows his elders with the godlike authority they had for him in the days of his helpless childhood. In fact, now that he has learned that even his parents are not so wealthy, wise and infallible as he had previously imagined them to be, he enters a phase when he exaggerates their shortcomings. Not infrequently, he feels constrained to apologize for them to his friends, or to express a blend of rebellious attitudes ranging from condescension to open hostility. At the point where cold war threatens to give way to a hot one in the home, he packs up and goes off to college, often to the immense relief of all concerned.

In its physical aspect, a college campus seems one of the most peaceful and beautiful places in the world. But behind this idyllic façade, the student continues to wage his war for independence. He has achieved a truce, if not a victory, in his struggle to free himself from those powerful despots in the home who had only to assert their wishes to establish them as family law. But at the university he is confronted with some of the same demands for unquestioning obedience to the seemingly arbitrary dictates of his elders and presumably his betters. It is true that at first he is ready to have more tolerance for these elders than for his parents, but the role of submissive neophyte in which he is cast, with its demands for subordinating private inclinations to an unrelenting succession of assignments, requirements and examinations inevitably stirs up the urge to revolt to a more or less intense degree. But while this urge is probably common to students everywhere, it remains for the most part covert and unnoticed, except in occasional times of riot. Students, obviously, have too much to lose to run the risk of open rebellion during their college days. Actually, there seems to be a clear and startling analogy between the educational customs of civilized people and the primitive initiation rites for adolescents practiced the world over from ancient times. The modern student, like his primitive brother, is faced with the necessity of submitting to an ordeal at the hands of his elders as the price he must pay for the privileges of adulthood. It is debatable which ordeal is worse—the student's with its prolonged psychological torments, or the primitive boy's with its relatively fleeting physical hardships. In any event, the student's initiation into the world of civilized men cannot be assumed, even under the most auspicious circumstances, to be an entirely painless affair, or to proceed without provoking conflict, hidden or expressed.

Both at home and in the university, there are confusing elements that prevent the average student from achieving independence, or even from recognizing clearly that this may be desirable. After all, it is undeniable that parents and teachers ostensibly have his own best interests at heart, so that filial duty and gratitude demand that he give up his own inclinations when they clash with theirs. Moreover, he is confronted with the additional difficulty of discriminating between what his elders in their wisdom unselfishly advocate for him and what they mistakenly imagine is best because it would be best for themselves. Henry Fielding observed long ago of this tendency of the older generation to confuse their children's identity with their own, thus making both parties completely miserable in the process: "Though it is almost universal in parents, [it] hath always appeared to me to be the most unaccountable of all the absurdities which ever entered into the brain of that strange prodigious creature man." Bernard Shaw, in one of his prefaces, went even further, presuming not only to find the cause of the absurdity but also to prescribe for its cure: "If adults will frankly give up their claim to know better than children what the purposes of the Life Force are, and treat the child as an experiment like themselves, and possibly a more successful one, and at the same time relinquish their monstrous parental claims to personal private property in children, the rest may be left to common sense." Just recently, the veteran child psychoanalyst, Gerald H. J. Pearson, in his monograph *Adolescence and the Conflict of Generations,* after convincingly tracing some of the hidden psychological origins of the conflict, concluded that since its main roots on both sides are so deeply anchored in a tangle of emotional attitudes, of which self-love is by no means the least important, he had small hope that either parents or adolescents could profit much from a generalized intellectual explanation of the affairs of the heart—which nevertheless he proceeded to give in his book.

These emotional affairs of the heart have such a distinct and primitive logic of their own that psychiatrists long before Freud have steadfastly and repeatedly observed that a man may be brilliantly endowed from the intellectual viewpoint and simultaneously an irresponsible child where his emotions are concerned. Or he may be the reverse: a genius when it comes to the affairs of the heart, but an intellectual moron as measured by his I.Q. In this connection, it is worth remembering that following the introduction of Binet's intelligence test in the early years of this century, situations in ordinary school and social life that before seemed baffling because someone was involved whose feeble-mindedness remained unrecognized, became clear and susceptible to control when approached with the new knowledge. Undoubtedly, some day we shall also have better indices of emotional development, a kind of E.Q., which will enable teachers and parents to take a more calm and realistic attitude towards problems posed by students that now seem inexplicable or of deliberate malevolent intent.

Meanwhile, we have outgrown old superstitions in the ruling power of witches, devils, planets and charms, but have still to discard the notions that emotional attitudes and motives are readily controlled by the intelligence, or that they depend only on external circumstances, or that they are utterly mysterious beyond comprehension. On the contrary, medical psychology, particularly during the last half-century, has been accumulating an impressive mass of clinical data, drawn from normal as well as abnormal subjects, that demonstrates something of the peculiar evolution and logic of the emotional life.

In college practice, for example, the psychiatrist has many opportunities for observing that a student's attitude towards his father seems to determine his attitude towards college authorities. A student who has been strongly attached to, and simultaneously overwhelmed by, the father is apt to view the college teacher as the embodiment of the wisdom of the ages. His war for intellectual independence does not go well because the more he admires his mentors the more he is inclined to be uncritically influenced by them and to belittle himself. Educators are familiar with students of this type, who are variously called "perfectionists," "overachievers" or "over-conscientious." The more they belittle themselves, the less capable they become of achieving self-assurance and spontaneous, original work. Their energies, instead, are used up in curbing natural impulse and in preoccupation with superficial detail.

One such student, for example, felt compelled to memorize the dates of withdrawal and return on the librarian's card in a book of assigned reading, to say nothing of a staggering mass of excerpts he had copied down. The psychiatrist sees this as a kind of self-defeating compromise, in which there has been no wholehearted acceptance of either the self or the father. Its object, essentially, is to keep the peace and to win rewards and esteem from parents and teachers for a kind of mechanical compliance characteristic of the rote-learning of childhood days, rather than to achieve satisfying growth and true self-expression. Deficient self-esteem and an exaggerated estimate of authority make such students slaves to duty and routine, a slavery which the world too frequently applauds, but which nevertheless defeats the aims of liberal education and provides fertile soil for private misery and neurotic symptoms, such as fatigue, insomnia, incapacitating tension, and sometimes despair.

Likewise, it is frequently observed that students who have been inclined to defy and underestimate the father are similarly inclined to belittle authority in general. In extreme form, their behavior is variously regarded as immature, abnormal, delinquent or even criminal, depending on how badly the community feels its interests have been violated and how it assesses the responsibility of the offender. As long ago as 1910, the psychiatrist Stewart Paton (who incidentally was the first to advocate a mental-health program for college students) is said to have been astonished when he first began his work at Princeton University to discover "students who had pronounced suicidal, homicidal impulses, sex perverts, those who stole, cheated, were exceedingly egotistical, aggressive and showed other signs of serious maladjustment." He saw no point in making "every attempt . . . to induce all, the unfit as well as the fit, to pass through the educational mill" which, he noted, is in sharp contrast to the more realistic policy in schools and colleges of preventing those with weak hearts or lungs from taking part in strenuous athletic pursuits. Since then, colleges have been paying more attention to the need for earlier recognition and more intelligent treatment of students with serious emotional disturbances.

When it comes to the less serious problems posed by rebellious but essentially healthy students, any good educator knows that the rebel is only confirmed in his defiance when he sees himself vindictively or scornfully treated with little, if any, concern as an individual, in spite of the professed brotherly love for him of the Christian community. The late psychoanalyst Fritz Wittels rightly pointed out the enormous difference in the effect on the culprit when punishment is administered by those who care for him, as by a father in childhood who wants to continue to love the naughty child, or by those in institutions or state who neither care for him nor are interested in his welfare. The wise father and the good teacher intuitively know that lasting repentance and ultimate self-discipline are not products of terror and force alone.

The student's war for independence does not, however, always display the more obvious forms of submission and rebellion described above. The majority of students seem to oscillate somewhere between these extremes, being on the whole perhaps more rebellious than submissive. Those who read standard histories of university life, where, as Rashdall observed, "the life of the virtuous student has no annals," are not surprised to find that they have been a rebellious lot from the beginning. Haskins in his informative *The Rise of the Universities* records that in 1317 the students at Bologna not only brought the townsmen to terms by threatening to go elsewhere, but also laid down strict regulations governing the teaching of their professors, who were subject to fines for absences and other controlling maneuvers. We also learn that in medieval Paris students went about armed with swords and knives, attacking citizens, abusing women and slashing off one another's fingers. Elsewhere, it is said that prior to the present century, outbreaks of violence against college officials and property were more extensive and frequent than they are today in American colleges, and were seemingly worst at the most puritanical colleges. On the other hand, it is well known that there have been periods when students submitted to a much more rigorous academic discipline than at present, at least in a physical sense. From the standpoint of the psychological relationship today between the older and younger generations, it would be an anomaly if in these more democratic times either generation were to revert to the attempts at physical domination of the feudal past. But he who looks will find that the conflict goes on in other less obvious ways. It has, so to speak, been driven underground.

For instance, a student complains of a perplexing inability to concentrate on academic material, yet emphasizes that he would like ultimately to follow his father's career in teaching; meanwhile, he feels tense and miserable *except* when engaged in extracurricular activities. Another has had extensive medical investigations, with entirely negative results, of his complaint of recurring digestive upset, which, on inquiry, is found to be associated particularly with times of stress and examination. A third, while professing to want to remain in the university from which his father graduated, is in danger of dismissal because he cuts classes from oversleeping, which he says he can neither correct nor understand.

Examples like these could be multiplied. But a recital of their bare outlines does not adequately convey the rich and subtle interplay of defensive and offensive maneuver that goes on. Often conflict is not ostensibly with authority at all, but with what we now recognize as its inner representative and ally, the conscience. The college psychiatrist encounters many instances where such inner warfare leads to apparently senseless dilemmas or pointless activities. These can only be understood when viewed in terms of the struggle within, reflecting in part a desire to yield to temptation and in part the scruples about it. Students can, of course, justify themselves with compelling logic and eloquence, recalling Shaw's observation that excellent reasons can be found "for every conceivable course of conduct, from dynamiting and vivisection to martyrdom." I share the feeling with colleagues that a university would be a dead and dusty place if all students were models of conformity. But I can also sympathize with the professor who once said that a university would be a wonderful place if there were no undergraduates in it.

When we turn to the strategies that the older generation employs to meet these offensive forays of students during the years of their rebellion, we find on the college campus that they gravitate toward two opposite extremes, neither of which seems sensible or practicable from a psychiatric or pedagogical point of view. At one extreme, there are those who rely heavily on impersonal disciplinary retaliation when students exhibit unusual behavior or become troublesome. These are the upholders of traditions and rules at all costs, the sensitive spirits who beneath an impersonal mask react to the offending student as though they had been personally affronted themselves. At the other extreme, there are those among the older generation so easily influenced by the student's point of view that if their attitude prevailed there would inevitably be chaos and ineffective leadership and education.

Both extremists view the psychiatrist's approach according to their own predilections. The disciplinarians assume that the psychiatrist is indubitably against any punishment whatsoever and thus favors anarchy on the campus. The opposite group tends to be so convinced of the basic stability and intellectual capacity of any student who has been admitted to college that it suspects the psychiatrist of magnifying mental pathology where none exists, or of wanting to substitute some dreary form of adjustment for all the excitement and color that rebellious youth brings to the campus. Both views miss the mark.

Concerning the disciplinarian viewpoint, it is now becoming well known that punishment must take into account the individual as well as his offense. In other words, we are beginning to realize that there are abnormal states which no amount of punishment can cure, but in fact may aggravate instead. Until the comparatively recent pioneer work of the psychiatrist William Healy, begun in 1908, the law, for example, was still operating under the assumption that the vast majority of juvenile delinquents are of essentially sound mind, can control perverse impulses and will respond favorably to punishment. Since then, through the work of juvenile courts and the psychological appraisal of offenders, society has been discovering, sometimes to its chagrin, that unwittingly it has been actively persecuting individuals who are so powerfully driven to antisocial behavior that they appear genuinely unable to restrain themselves as normal individuals can do, and so must be judged to be in some respects irresponsible and provided for in some other way than the law traditionally decrees.

On the campus, the very word "irresponsible" applied to a

student is apt to evoke the itch to punish rather than the urge to investigate. The college psychiatrist, for his part, has to distinguish between students whose perversities come against a background of reasonable stability, and those who are rendered "irresponsible" by some deeply ingrained intrapsychic disturbance. Take, for example, the phenomenon of examination anxiety. Because it is present in almost everyone to some degree, it is often assumed of little importance. Yet in a large university hardly a year goes by without several more or less serious psychiatric casualties during the final examination period. The large majority of students can meet and surmount this type of pressure without serious strain. But the problem, as the psychiatrist sees it, is to recognize that there are occasional students so vulnerable already that this added strain of examinations can cause a degree of incapacity well beyond the student's ability to control. Fortunately, these exaggerated reactions to examinations are not frequent nor are they always of serious import. But occasionally they are symptomatic of deeply entrenched and extensive emotional disturbances that should be recognized as early as possible.

In the past, the first reaction of disciplinarians everywhere to the student who complains of being rattled on an examination is to turn a deaf ear, or if, as occasionally happens, a blank examination paper has been turned in, to feel incensed and to think of maximum penalties. The student may at once be assumed to be disrespectful, dishonest or flagrantly lazy, the choice of diagnosis being more in line with the disciplinarian's pet preconception than with the facts, and the treatment being dictated more by fear that other students will become delinquent on examinations than by considerations of the educational development of the individual. The disciplinarian has often, therefore, been strangely reluctant to give the offending student careful and thoughtful scrutiny. Yet from both the psychiatric and educational points of view, an inquiry aimed at some understanding of whether the student is in good mental health has a more far-reaching significance than the specific offensive itself, or the question of whether to punish or not to punish. The student who says that during an important examination his mind becomes blank or behaves like a drunken man's is confessing to inner disorganization that may have important implications regarding not only his mental health but his future educational development as well. Besides, an attitude of inquiry that seeks to establish the facts of a student's inner life will do more to alleviate cold war on the campus than one that presupposes, or is intent on, arbitrary domination.

Those lenient souls who, on the other hand, regard student aberrations and rebellions with an overly benevolent eye—perhaps finding in them a source of vicarious excitement and secret pleasure—run the same risk as the disciplinarians of overlooking the educational value of having some understanding of the student's inner problems. I agree with Chancellor Lawrence A. Kimpton of the University of Chicago, who is recently reported to have said that a great university must also have the "excitement of rebellion, the maladjustment of youth," and "occasionally it should discipline itself in freedom by embracing and supporting a weird one just for his weirdness." But I have too much respect for the force and vitality of rebellious youth to share his fear that the university "would lose all its greatness if it were tortured into adjustment through analysis" by the psychiatrist or by anyone else. The student has something to say about whether he will submit to such analysis, and regardless of how desirable others may think such a course to be, he nevertheless holds a veto power. The psychiatrist would be a megalomaniac indeed if he believed he had the magic power sometimes attributed to him for making unwilling rebels lay down their arms. In fact, he would be inclined to wonder whether those who overlook this veto power of youth are not themselves overestimating the power of the older generation to influence, guide, and to create in its own image. In short, he would caution educators and parents, as he must constantly caution himself, against the illusions of omnipotence and omniscience.

Tension and conflict between the old and the young will presumably always exist. But the problem of whether the individual's aggressive energies will be expressed in useful or destructive ways has never before cast such a deep and terrible shadow over human life. The student today, for example, must learn that atomic energy is merely the concentrated projection of these inner energies, made possible by the unified efforts of many, and thus not rightfully subject to arbitrary individual control or caprice. That the days of unbridled individualism are gone is a lesson that, at bottom, no high-spirited young man wants to learn.

Faced with the mounting urgency of this difficult problem, college teachers and psychiatrists need to pool their efforts to promote a healthy understanding of the forces in the inner world. Up until the present century, man could enjoy the luxury of dismissing this inner problem and concentrating his energies on achieving mastery over the external world. He did so partly to avoid confronting himself with unpleasant aspects of his inner life, and partly because healthy and disciplined introspection is extraordinarily difficult in the face of conflicting feeling and impulse and the demands of the outside world. Thus the very word *introspection* continues to have unfavorable overtones, suggesting to many extreme subjectivism and even disease. The psychiatrist, however, recommends a kind of introspection that is based on more than the superficial data of inner thought. It must take into account not only what a student tells us in apparent sincerity about his motives, but must also square with what can be observed about his present behavior and his past tendencies. The author-physician Oliver Wendell Holmes perceived with remarkable intuitive clarity why accurate introspection is so elusive, as the following passage published when Sigmund Freud was a mere boy of fifteen illustrates:

There are thoughts that never emerge into consciousness, which yet make their influence felt among the perceptible mental currents, just as the unseen planets sway the movements of those which are watched and mapped by the astronomer. Old prejudices, that are ashamed to confess themselves, nudge our talking thought to utter magisterial veto. . . . The more we examine the mechanism of thought, the more we shall see that the automatic, unconscious action of the mind enters largely into all its processes.

Unusual students, and students who sometimes behave in unusual fashion, raise serious questions pertaining to the philosophy of education in a democratic society. They are complex questions that have long been discussed, such as the effect of coercion on students, the optimum conditions for teaching and learning, the fate of non-conforming students in a system of mass education, and many others. The psychiatrist cannot pretend to answer them. But he would feel that the solution of such thorny questions depends not so much on generalizations, or even on technical psychological knowledge, as on an attitude towards students similar to that of the physician towards his patients. This attitude derives from the great clinicians in medicine who over the centuries discovered that if physician and patients have learned from each other it has only been because they were able to unite their energies against a common enemy—disease. Moreover, it is an attitude that permits acceptance of the individual in spite of dislike or even loathing for his sickness. Ben Jonson remarked: "I know no disease of the soul but ignorance."

Against this common enemy, ignorance, the old and the young have long sought to join forces. But only in this revolutionary twentieth century have we begun to have glimmerings of the hidden source of much of the enemy's power. Once we recognize that it resides in ignorance of the deeper and more primitive emotional self, which can bring to naught the proudest intelligence, the campus cold war will take on a healthier and more worthwhile objective.

Salvation on the Campus:
Why Existentialism Is Capturing
the Students

J. GLENN GRAY

J. Glenn Gray, Chairman of the Philosophy Department at Colorado College, has written widely on German Existentialism and has been both a Fulbright Research Professor and a Guggenheim Fellow. His book The Warriors, Reflections on Men in Battle *was published in 1959. He studied at Juniata College, the University of Pittsburgh and Columbia University.*

O UR Tom looked like a bum when he came home for Christmas. His clothes were filthy, he was wearing a mandarin beard, and his hair hadn't been cut since September. Last fall we gave him permission to live alone off-campus and cook for himself. Now he has trench mouth, a bad case of athlete's foot, and some kind of mysterious virus."

Our neighbor was both exasperated and amused as she thus described her son, a senior at a famous Ivy League college. He is a superior student who had hitherto seemed anything but a beatnik. For years his parents have let him steer his own course and supported him financially at some sacrifice. What, then, is he rebelling against? Is this merely a ludicrous episode in his development or a sign of a severe disorder? His mother doesn't know.

Many other enlightened parents are equally perplexed by the bizarre actions of their college sons and daughters. Nor can professors and university administrators shed much light on the moods and motivations of students in the 'sixties. They have been baffled by the rioting at Berkeley last fall and other less publicized incidents elsewhere.

For today's student is a very different creature from his predecessors. In my own college days in the 'thirties, if I had come home at Christmas in Tom's condition, my parents would probably have had me committed to a different sort of institution. What lies behind the change?

For one thing, today's student is more affluent than we were, more comfortably housed, and better equipped with the materials of scholarship. But his college life is also more impersonal and competitive, less humane. It is harder for him to know his professors, the administration, or even his all too numerous fellow students. Learning is increasingly packaged and is sometimes referred to, shamelessly, as the "knowledge business." Knowledge itself expands at a rate that makes him feel like an impostor if he seeks to be broadly educated, and walls him off from others if he specializes. His professors are less attached to the institution where they teach and more to their disciplines. And they have less time to give him or the college. In this situation, the traditional college spirit— of either the rah-rah variety or the community of learners— may seem to the student as outmoded as the raccoon coat and the hip flask.

If he has reached the age of reflection, today's student is seeking above all to differentiate himself from the crowd. Thirty years ago it was distinctive merely to be a college man. Now he must struggle to be more than a grade-point average, an anonymous statistic with a college and home address. Often he expresses this yearning for uniqueness in ways that parents, administrators, professors, and other out-siders consider illegitimate. Well publicized are the bearded, sloppily dressed students, defiant of even minimal adminis-trative regulations, studious enough, but incontinent in their demands for alcoholic and sexual freedoms, fiercely insistent on leading their own lives.

Typical of this state of mind is a student's letter in a recent issue of our college newspaper.

The trouble is that they [administration and faculty] take it all as seriously as the rest of the piety we get about law and morality and the intellectual purpose of our existence. The most ironic thing on this campus is that they believe in their own hypocrisy. . . . One of the reasons that administration and much of the faculty alike draw grotesque pictures of students is that they probably have never talked with one, not that they'd listen if they did. For years the same situations occur, the same opinions are given, the same pleas are voiced, and the same nothing happens.

The desire for self-definition often goes hand in hand with an inner need—more or less conscious—for a compelling authority to make freedom meaningful. In the 'thirties, economic pressures for existence and our opposition to the fascist menace rescued us from this dilemma. In the 'forties there was the war and, afterward, the threat of the Bomb to distract attention from inner conflicts. For some students in the 'sixties the civil-rights struggle has become a Cause—a clear-cut issue on which to act and to argue. But as yet this movement has not reached anything like the numbers nor hit with anything like the impact that we experienced with fascism, communism, the war, and the Bomb.

Lacking an embracing cause and a fervent ideology, the student's search for a durable purpose is likely to become aggressive, extremist, at times despairing. It can easily turn into preoccupation with subjective feelings and plain egotism. As André Gide has put it, "Each human being who has only himself for aim suffers from a horrible void." Paradoxical as it sounds, the real problem of our college youth is to discover some authority, both private and public, that will make possible authentic individuality.

I have learned something about this search over the past fifteen years as one of the professors conducting a senior seminar called Freedom and Authority. Before generalizing, perhaps I should say a word about Colorado College, where I teach philosophy. It is a fairly typical small, private liberal-arts institution, founded in 1874 by New England Congregationalists before Colorado was a state. It has long since cut loose from church ties, drifting—like Grinnell, Carleton, Pomona, and others—into secularism. Our students are drawn from many states; after Colorado, California and Illinois contribute the most.

We are not as selective as the Ivy League colleges nor as equalitarian as the state institutions. Since—like those of most private colleges—our costs are high, our students come largely from upper-middle-class families. (Some are shockingly rich. A few years back when we banned automobiles for freshmen, a Texas girl wired our admissions committee, requesting in good faith that she be permitted to bring her private airplane.)

I was originally lured out here by a dean who painted an enticing picture of Back Bay Boston accents mixed with Western ranch drawls. But the percentage of students from ranches, farms, and the working class has steadily declined, and drawls are now rare. In sum, our students and their families are, economically and socially, very much like you who are reading this magazine. They represent an important—if not typical—sample of American college students.

Our Freedom and Authority seminar is a very freewheeling, wide-ranging course. Though we constantly change the readings, a few books have remained by nearly unanimous consent from the beginning. The first of these is Plato's account of the trial, imprisonment, and death of Socrates in the *Apology, Crito,* and end of *Phaedo.* These short dialogues, conveniently grouped in one paperback, are probably exerting a profounder influence on the campus today than such bestsellers as Golding, Salinger, and Baldwin, which bloom and fade in campus popularity.

Why does Socrates appeal to contemporary students? They respond to his fearless assertion of his right to determine his own conduct despite powerful opposition from the majority of his fellow citizens. The conflict between individual freedom and sociopolitical authority which he dramatizes expresses their own central dilemma. These students have outgrown the discipline of parents. In college, various authorities —the college administration, campus mores, and student cliques—vie for their allegiance. They are also uneasily conscious of the different standards of the professional and business worlds they are about to enter. The sensitive student, confused by these uncertain values, is thrilled when Socrates, the original rebel who became the "father" of philosophy, tells his fellow Athenians that he loves and cherishes them, but chooses to obey only his own vision of the right and good. Socrates' example can still engender a revolutionary fervor in youthful hearts. It was hardly an accident that the campus rebellions at Berkeley and earlier at the University of Colorado were led by philosophy majors.[1]

Less acceptable to my students than Socrates' idea of freedom is his concept of authority, which leads him to refuse a proffered escape from prison after he has been sentenced to death. He likens the laws of Athens to parents, who must always be obeyed even if they chastise their children unjustly. At this point, my students begin to protest, and their identification with Socrates is broken. As one of them put it last fall, "I can't imagine anything less comparable to my parents than the U.S. government."

There are exceptions. One girl, for example, last November reconciled the seeming contradictions in Socrates' philosophy in this fashion: "In the *Apology* individual determination of conduct challenges and defeats all other values, including Athenian law. However, the reverse is not what happens in the *Crito*. Here, Athenian law is weighted *with* his personal laws of conduct *against* a solitary value, his life. His natural desire to flee for his life, not his individualism, is challenged here. . . . As part of his personal conduct code, Socrates could not destroy Athenian law simply because it was being used to destroy a lesser value, his life on earth. 'To injure in turn when ill-treated' was against his moral structure also, so that his personal conduct code forced him to abide by Athenian law. Of the three values considered in the *Apology* and the *Crito*, Socrates held individual determination of conduct most important, Athenian law second, and his own life least important."

All of us blessed her, a rank beginner in philosophy, for the kind of insight that an unburdened mind often brings to a complex issue. In the ensuing discussion, her classmates were intellectually persuaded that Socrates' freedom was sustained by his lifelong membership in the community of Athens. But how could his example be helpful today? Since patriotism is hardly an operable emotion among contemporary students, Socratic freedom, though intellectually appealing, does not in the end provide a satisfying answer. After all, Socrates was an old man with secure roots in a small community, a situation quite opposite to that of young people in our huge, fast-changing, incredibly complex society.

As a contrast to Socrates, we study *The Death of Ivan Ilych*, Tolstoi's powerful short story in which a modern man must face an agonizing death with no resources save the polite conventions of an artificial society. Slowly dying, daily more isolated and desperate, Ivan asks:

"Then what does it mean? Why? It can't be that life is so senseless and horrible. But if it really has been so horrible and senseless, why must I die and die in agony? There is something wrong!

"Maybe I did not live as I ought to have done," it suddenly occurred to him. "But how could that be, when I did everything properly," he replied, and immediately dismissed from his mind this, the sole solution of all the riddles of life and death, as something quite impossible.

But he cannot dismiss these fears for long.

He lay on his back and began to pass his life in review in quite a new way. In the morning when he saw first his footman, then his wife, then his daughter, and then the doctor, their every word and movement confirmed to him the awful truth that had been revealed to him during the night. In them he saw himself—all that for which he had lived—and saw clearly that it was not real at all, but a terrible and huge deception which had hidden both life and death. This consciousness intensified his suffering tenfold.

In the end, Tolstoi rescues Ivan from utter meaninglessness and absurdity via his own (Tolstoi's) passionate faith in primitive Christianity. But this does little to alleviate the atmosphere of controlled terror and doom.

The story has a stunning impact on our students. If they find Socrates wholly admirable but a size larger than life, Ivan is all too human, the anonymous Everyman of our day, painfully contemporary. I have overheard more than one of my students breathe, "My God, he is just like my old man!" They do not identify with him for he is too much like adults they know and dislike—a portrait of what modern life may force them eventually to become. Though they hardly aspire to be heroes like Socrates, they desperately want to escape being victims like Ivan.

Ivan's "inauthentic" life has become a rich source for the Existentialists in their indictment of modern society. On the campus Existentialism—which is both a mood and a metaphysics—is compounded of anxiety about being lost in the crowd and the lack of closeness or intimacy with fellow students. Sometimes the despairing response to these feelings is sexual promiscuity; more often it is expressed in eccentric dress and flamboyant behavior. Such climates of opinion are contagious and often attract spurious reactions. These can be downright funny, as in the reported case of the student who used to telephone his girl friend and say, "Honey, I'm in the abyss again. How about going out for a beer?"

But in fact the underlying mood is quite different from the perennial depressions of late adolescence. These students are anxiously concerned with the problem of being themselves. Authenticity is the element of Existentialism that strikes the deepest note for them. The highest virtue is honesty with themselves and others while phoniness in whatever form is the greatest vice. "The thing that's wrong with this class," a senior burst out recently, "is that none of us is spontaneous. We're all trying to be so clever and to impress each other. I think we are simply afraid to be ourselves. I'm sick of my own pretending."

To be a genuine or authentic person is not primarily a moral matter, in the sense that older Americans think of morality. For Existentialists authenticity means freely choosing what is one's own in behavior, attitude, and mode of living, however singular these may appear to others. The kind of society we are building—or that is being built around us—is, for them, a major obstacle to the attainment of authentic individuality.

The difficult art of becoming oneself can hardly be more than begun by the age of twenty-two or twenty-three. Hence the important question is: How long does the search continue? Graduates of our Freedom and Authority seminar often write to their old professors and many of them return to campus annually, from as far away as Pennsylvania and California. We hold an informal seminar with them at Homecoming, usually based on a book which we have assigned in advance.

Surprises about the future development of one's students are the rule for a college professor. But I am still disconcerted when the students I counted on fail me and the least promising prove to be "late bloomers."

In the last category is a pretty Connecticut girl who seemed quite unremarkable when she left my seminar section a couple of years ago and proceeded to a government job in Washington. Soon afterward an FBI agent came to my office for a routine loyalty check and I gave him the expected replies. But meanwhile someone denounced her as an associate of Communists at college, and she was subjected to a thorough investigation. She secured help from the American Civil Liberties Union, an organization she had first heard of in our course. The investigation ended harmlessly at a hearing where one government agent testified that she was "an innocuous person."

When she returned to campus last spring for a visit this characterization was much on her mind. "That agent was right," she told me. "Up till now I have been just that, an innocuous person, but I intend to be innocuous no longer."

She asked me to support her application for law school, which she entered last fall. She had decided to become a defender of civil liberties in a private capacity, not to practice law. This winter she wrote me long letters displaying an unsuspected spirit and passion and marking her as a person who has attained security of mind. She has already resolved not to take the loyalty oath required of members of the bar in the state where she is studying, to make a court case of the matter. She has also become a militant pacifist. It was apparently the description of her as "innocuous" that triggered all these responses—all dormant in her college days.

The death of President Kennedy had a similar transforming effect on another unlikely student whose undistinguished college career included a troubled progress through my Freedom and Authority course. He married and went to work for a national soap company where he was rising rapidly. But the Kennedy assassination disrupted his world. Soon afterward he wrote to me asking for "a philosopher's point of view." "I felt a strong sense of identity with him," he wrote, expressing a feeling widespread at that time. "Perhaps this is because he was young, or because we shared similar political views (weak and irresolute as mine are) or because he was an 'intellectual' President, or because . . . I felt guilt because of his murder, and I feel dead because of his death."

He had tried, he said, to cope with the disaster, to reason it through, but in vain. "I usually end up saying 'God damn,' with an incredulous shake of the head. Surely there must be more grief written in people's hearts than what is written on their faces. Aside from a few hours at the funeral, all seems to be normal with the people I see and know. But for me this one act has made all other acts irrelevant and trivial; it has displaced time with paranoia, good with evil, relative simplicity with incomprehensibility, an ideal with dirt."

He could no longer remain in the business world. Despite his wife and children, he decided to return to graduate school to prepare himself for work in international education. He is now immersed in the study of foreign languages and Existentialism. Wearing a heavy beard, he has lost all resemblance to the young executive of a year ago. For the first time in his life, he told me recently, he is truly "engaged" in discovering the meaning of existence through commitment to thought and action rather than middle-class drift.

These two cases are, of course, exceptions. Relatively few of our young alumni have made much progress toward attaining a distinctive individuality after leaving college. The demands of business and professional life on the men, of homemaking and child-rearing on the women, tend either to halt the search or even to induce surrender to reigning values. It would seem that the very prosperity which permits college students to spend time pondering important issues of existence acts as a sedative in their early adulthood. Affluence, not religion, might be called the opiate of the 'sixties. The immediate requirements of making a living and getting ahead in the status race seem to dull the passions and despair which obsessed many of them in college. There is, of course, nothing surprising in this. Many of us escape the need to give meaning to our existence through the age-old expedient of producing the next generation and letting them struggle with the problem.

The Existentialist preoccupation with the Absurd, Nothingness, *Angst,* etc.—at least as metaphysical concepts—did not until recently have much of a grip on the English-speaking countries. When I first began teaching the leading Existentialists about 1950, interest in a Kierkegaard, Heidegger, or Sartre was likely to be a matter of either curiosity or fashion. Their very names were strange and most Americans had difficulty pronouncing the word Existentialism. In those years my colleagues frequently asked me to give a coffee-break explanation of the movement.

Now discussions are far more earnest and passionate. I conduct a Wednesday evening seminar on Existentialism at my home. Frequently I have to push the students out after several hours, if I am to simmer down and get any sleep that night. Often they continue heated arguments elsewhere till the small hours. In colleges all over America courses dealing with Existentialists are currently very popular to the disgust of the disciples of Language Analysis—an Oxford import—who once felt confident of dominating academic philosophy. The rapid availability of translations from German and French Existentialist writings and sales of large editions attest to the surprising new demand.

What accounts for it? Undeniably, there is a large element of the modish, for Americans have always been susceptible to philosophic imports from the Continent and England. (In philosophy, it has been said, we are still largely a colony of Europe.) I must also admit, rather shamefacedly, that even philosophy is not immune to the attraction of "the hottest thing in town." After the war it was Oxford Analysis, now it is Existentialism.

There is, however, much more to the matter. Existentialists draw their insights and inspiration from literature rather than science. They are concerned with the individual and with personal experience in an age that threatens to overwhelm individuality. This is why they attract so many American playwrights and novelists who have begun the process of Americanizing the European mood. Because the specific possibilities and frustrations of our everyday life are sharply different from those in France or Germany we were slow to accept the Existentialist mood and metaphysics. Now that our writers have succeeded in "translating" them into our American idiom, we are feeling their delayed impact.

The students I know best seem to have an intuitive grasp of what Heidegger and Sartre mean when they write of man's exposure to Nothingness. In a few extreme cases Nothingness means a profound feeling of disengagement with American culture, if not Western civilization itself. Other students who say in the privacy of my office, "I am at the end of my rope," are feeling only a temporary despair, perhaps little more than the romantic storm and stress of late adolescence. Sometimes I respond with a gentle joshing, and refuse to take them too seriously. With others I am far from sure.

The latter group includes students who often do superb work in my classes but who are quite as likely to be on academic probation as on the Dean's list. (One of them recently spent three semesters in the near-failing and three in the excellent category.)

These are brilliant, alienated young people. Generally, they do not care for Karl Jaspers, the Existentialist who identifies himself most closely with conventional philosophy. They respond to the philosophers radically at odds with the whole tradition of modern culture. They want Kierkegaard's either-or—the leap of faith or gross sensuality; Sartre's good faith or self-deception; Heidegger's nearness to Being or nihilism.

The ablest student I ever taught at Colorado College was of this kind. He wrote better commentaries on these philosophers than are found in the published literature. His poems, which I alone was allowed to see, were also first-rate. But it was a trial to keep him in college from one semester to another. Again and again he would disappear into the mountains, by himself for days. My wife and I constantly feared his suicide. When he finally graduated I easily secured fellowships for him to three graduate schools. He turned down all of them and proceeded to wander over the country, supporting himself at odd jobs. In his college years I was, in effect, struggling with him for his very soul; it is now sadly clear that I lost.

In an earlier day, before the disillusionment with communism, some such students found release in action, in attachment to a utopian authority which gave them a feeling of belonging. For others, the crude menace of Hitler served to unite them with Western values. Today a few find a sense of belonging in Southern racism. Others in the civil-rights movement or in the Peace Corps with its opportunities for genuine service.

What these students need above all is action, not further study, yet how can I counsel them to give up their studies before the degree? To serve with any significance in our specialized society they will need more formal schooling than they have or want before they have "found" themselves. The plight of dropouts on the lower academic rungs is well known. Equally poignant is the problem of those at the top —often even in graduate school—who do not know where they are headed nor whether they should stay in college at all.

Ironically, our technological society appears to widen the

spheres of freedom while making it even harder to escape from the toils of "the system" as students call it. Students today travel far more than we did in the 'thirties and 'forties; learn and see more and participate in a much larger range of activities. At an early stage the choice of many different careers is open to them. But once they have chosen anything specific, whether it be a "major" or marriage, they are soon past the point of no return.

In this situation Existentialism appeals. Its deepest conviction is that through his choices each individual makes himself. Its emphasis is not only on the absurd character of social reality, in some cases, of the world as a whole, but also on Possibility. In an inner sense everyone determines his own course. He can choose to lead an authentic existence or choose to be lost in the crowd. If the overwhelming majority opt for the latter condition, this does not prevent the exceptional person from standing alone as an authentic "single one." To a man, Existentialists are against group activities. They never tire of reminding us that "existence" literally means to "stand out from."

"I have decided that I am simply different from all the others," a brilliant youth told me the other day, explaining how even his close friends saw no point whatever to his poetry. "I must think and write for myself from now on." Both resolution and pathos were in his voice.

I doubt that Existentialist philosophy can ultimately satisfy the search for authority. So far, few of these thinkers have provided guidelines for social or political action, though all of them stress the necessity for individual commitment. However, for students who are not yet able or ready to act, Existentialism offers a great deal. At the least it presents an escape from the morass of conformity, *la dolce vita*, boredom, and the meaningless competitiveness in which they see so many of their elders caught.

Furthermore, those who go behind Sartre to the Danish and German originators of this movement discover a choice between an absurd or tragic view of human destiny. The absurd view is that existence is finally meaningless and futile, a defiant if admirable gesture in a void. The tragic conviction acknowledges the fragile and exposed character of individuality but discovers meaning and purpose in the individual's struggle to locate himself in nature and society. Though his personal life is of short duration, and subject to chance and misfortune while it lasts, his actions are of great importance in the moral sum of things. Tragedy links us to what has been in the history of our species and binds us in faith to the future. It teaches that there are things worth living and dying for, ideas, ancestors, and descendants.

On the other hand, the metaphysical idea that "life is a tale told by an idiot, full of sound and fury, signifying nothing" can do none of these things. The conviction of absurdity cuts all ties to history and nature and with them the nerve of meaningful action. Which version of Existentialism will be accepted by students in the rest of the 'sixties?

The answer will be important. It has been a favorite taunt of European critics that in America there are no tragedies, only mistakes. The quality of current experience is rapidly dissipating any remaining truth in this ancient charge. Yet young people inevitably find it hard to learn the price in pain and suffering necessary to pay for the tragic vision. Falling into a persuasion of absurdity and meaninglessness is, on the surface at least, much easier. The polar choices again are between the life of Socrates and that of Ivan Ilych.

That the tragic and absurd should be competing for students' minds in the 'sixties is not surprising, when one remembers that many of their parents were fighting World War II while they were infants and that they have grown up in a world changing at an incredible pace. Indeed, were young people not constitutionally adaptable and preoccupied with the immediate present, they would be in a much worse plight than they are. The wonder is that so many are sane and resilient.

Nevertheless, there has hardly been a time, in my experience, when students needed more attention and patient listening to by experienced professors than today. The pity is that so many of us retreat into research, government contracts, and sabbatical travel, leaving counsel and instruction to junior colleagues and graduate assistants. In so doing we deepen the rift between the generations and at the same time increase the sense of impersonality, discontinuity, and absence of community that makes college life less satisfactory in this decade than it used to be. What is needed are fewer books and articles by college professors and more cooperative search by teacher and taught for an authority upon which to base freedom and individuality.

After surviving so many turbulent decades of this century, some of us may feel a certain confidence that the present will prove no harder than the past has been. But we should remind ourselves that peace and affluence have their own perils as surely as do wars and depressions. Though our students increasingly come to us better prepared in the traditions of Western civilization, how many of them care more deeply about these traditions than did students in the bad old days? My pessimistic sense of catastrophe has lessened somewhat since 1960, but I find that deep uneasiness about the course of American higher education has grown. Nowadays nearly everyone looks to education for salvation as once we looked to religion or to a political ideology. But before we succeed in building the great society, we shall need to resolve the doubt and bafflement about its validity and worth in the minds of those now in college who should serve as leaders. Many of the harassed young men and women I teach, at any rate, have not yet decided what sense, if any, their existence has.

NOTES

1. Similarly, the unprecedented student demonstration at Yale in March was a protest against the administration's failure to give tenure to an admired philosophy teacher.

Student Life in the Middle Ages
HASTINGS RASHDALL

Hastings Rashdall (1858–1924), moral philosopher, theologian and historian, was born in London and educated at Oxford. His reputation as a historical scholar was established with the publication of The Universities of Europe in the Middle Ages, *in three volumes. He wrote a number of other works, including* The Theory of Good and Evil, Ideas and Ideals *and* God and Man.

THE WILDER SIDE OF UNIVERSITY LIFE[1]

The boundaries of the city of Paris had been extended by Philip Augustus so as to include the suburb south of the river. The western portion of this transpontine region formed the students' quarter, in which were situated most of the buildings used by the university and most of the colleges and hostels inhabited by the scholars. This *quartier latin* (as it came to be called) extended from the Cathedral of Notre Dame on the island *cité* to the western wall near the site now occupied by the palace of the Institute. Medieval Paris, like medieval London, was surrounded by a belt of monasteries, whose abbots exercised a feudal jurisdiction over the districts surrounding their churches. Just outside the city wall, to the west of the students' quarter, stood the great abbey of S. Germain. Outside the abbey walls was an open meadow or waste

ground which had from time immemorial been the prome-
nade of the elder and the playground of the younger students.
When the university had assumed the form of a definite corporation, that body or rather its faculty of arts claimed the
Pré-aux-clercs as its freehold property. The property, or at
least the free use of it, was recognized as belonging to the
university by the statutes of the cardinal legate, Robert Cur-
zon, in 1215. The monks, however, contended that the property had anciently been theirs and had been unlawfully alienated by one of the secular abbots in the ages of confusion;
and the decision of the legate appears to have left at all events
a boundary dispute between the abbey and the university
unsettled. The unfortunate scholars were in consequence exposed to much annoyance, and at times to violent and organized attacks from the monks and their retainers. The first recorded outrage of this description occurred in 1278. At the
morrow of the Translation of S. Nicholas, the patron saint of
scholars, the fields were crowded with the clerks, when the
abbey bell was heard summoning the tenants and servants of
the abbot and convent. By order of their black-robed masters
an armed guard took possession of the three city gates which
opened on to the Pré, so as to cut off the retreat of the scholars,
while to the sound of horns and trumpets and with shouts of
'death to the clerks' the convent and its retainers, headed by
their provost, sallied forth upon the unarmed and defenceless
boys and masters, and fell upon them with bow and arrow,
club, sword, or iron-tipped stave. Many were badly wounded,
some mortally, but they were nevertheless dragged off to the
'horrible dungeons' of the abbey. Those who fled (a doctor of
divinity and a doctor of medicine were among the number)
were pursued far and wide over the country.

It is significant of the lawlessness of the times that the ordinary course of justice seems to have been quite incapable of
reaching ruffianism of this kind when committed by such offenders as the abbot and convent of S. Germain. The abbey
claimed the 'justice' of the Pré; and was exempt from all episcopal or metropolitan jurisdiction. The university had no resource but to lay their complaint before the king and the papal
legate, and to threaten a 'cessation' if redress were not granted
within fifteen days. The abbot and the provost were deprived

of their offices, but the penalties imposed were, as usual in such cases, mainly corporate. The monks were required to found and endow two chaplaincies, one in the church of Sainte-Catherine, the other in the chapel of Saint-Martin-des-Orges close to the walls of the abbey, with annual stipends of £20. At these chapels mass was to be said for the benefit of scholars 'before play-time'. These chaplaincies were to be in the gift of the university, and formed the nucleus of the considerable patronage (chiefly in Paris) eventually acquired by the university. The brutality of the monks was not, however, by any means effectually repressed by this humiliation. They were especially sensitive about the claim to fish in the city moat which divided the abbey grounds from the domain of the university. In 1318 it was necessary to procure a papal Bull empowering the bishops of Soissons and Noyon to investigate and punish an outrage upon some priests and other clerks who were enjoying this favourite amusement.

In 1304 the provost of Paris hanged a scholar and gibbeted his body in flagrant contempt of the privileges of the university, and (as we are assured by a contemporary historian) unjustly to boot. A cessation of lectures compelled the king to punish the provost. The offender was required, besides suing for absolution at Avignon, to found two chaplaincies and present the advowson to the offended corporation. In addition to this substantial penalty, the wounded honour of the clerks was appeased by two characteristically medieval impositions. The provost was compelled to cut down the corpse, which had been hanging on the gibbet for some months, and kiss it; while all the clergy of Paris were solemnly convened by the official (the see being vacant) to march in procession with their respective flocks, each with cross and holy water, to the house of the offending magistrate, and there throw stones against it and utter a solemn exorcism or imprecation against the devil who was supposed to inhabit the building.

Another celebrated outrage on scholars occurred in 1404. The university was now at the height of its power, and the penalties which befell its oppressor were in consequence still more exemplary. A university procession was on its way to the church of Sainte Catherine, the patroness of scholars, to intercede for the peace of the church and realm and the health of the king. A party of pages and others in the service of the king's chamberlain, Charles of Savoisy, on their way towards the Seine to water their horses, met the procession, and, instead of waiting for it to pass, rode in among the scholars. A riot took place in which stones were thrown and some of the boys got trampled on by the horses of their assailants. Savoisy's retainers were not, however, satisfied with the results of the unpremeditated fray; but, retiring to their master's hotel, procured bows and arrows and other weapons, with which they made a deliberate and still more murderous onslaught upon the scholars, pursuing some of them into a neighbouring church where mass was being celebrated. A crowd of indignant clerks, headed by the rector, proceeded at once to the king, and threatened to leave Paris in a body if justice were not done. The amplest satisfaction was promised; but a suspension of lectures and sermons for six weeks was necessary before it was obtained. Eventually, the master of the truculent household was sentenced to pay a fine of 1,000 *livres* to the victims, another 1,000 to the university, and to create a rent-charge of the annual value of 100 *livres* for the endowment of five chaplaincies which were to be in the gift of the university and to be held by masters. Finally, the chamberlain was dismissed from all his employments, banished from court, and his hotel ordered to be razed to the ground. The latter part of the sentence, we are told by the official record of the proceedings in Parlement, was executed by a great number of the triumphant scholars 'promptly and almost before it was pronounced.' Formal evidence having been given that Savoisy was a clerk, he was exempted from making 'amende honorable' in person, but three of his servants (who were apparently the actual offenders) were ordered to go as penitents to three churches clad in their shirts only, and there carrying lighted tapers in their hands to be publicly flogged on behalf of their master.

Another often-quoted illustration of academical morals in the thirteenth century is the proclamation of the official of Paris in 1269 in which he denounces a class of scholars, or pretended scholars, who 'by day and night atrociously wound and slay many, carry off women, ravish virgins, break into houses', and commit 'over and over again robberies and many other enormities hateful to God'. Such were the kind of crimes in which the clerical tonsure enabled the Parisian scholar to indulge without the smallest fear of the summary execution which would have been the fate of an apprentice or a 'sturdy beggar' who essayed such pranks. As a means of preventing such outrages in future the official has nothing more deterrent to hold over the offender's head than the ineffectual threat of excommunication.

If we turn to Oxford, perhaps the best evidence which comes to our hand is contained in the records of coroner's inquisitions. Over and over again occurs the dismal record, 'Such and such jurors on their oaths present that M or N, clerk, killed A or B, citizen or clerk (as the case might be—to do him justice it was nearly as often a brother-clerk as a citizen) with a sword or a pole-axe or a knife or an arrow; that he has fled and that there are no goods left' which can be distrained upon. Rarely is the entry varied by the statement that the accused was obliged to take sanctuary, and after so many days abjured the realm. In those rare cases the culprit might be put to the inconvenience of continuing his studies abroad. In the majority of cases nothing worse happened to them than being compelled to go to Cambridge.

Another illustration may be drawn from the annals of Orleans. In the year 1387, Jean Rion, a citizen of Orleans, employed two ruffians to waylay a bachelor of the civil law named Guillaume Entrant. Catching him on horseback outside the town, they threw him from his horse, and were only prevented from killing him by the arrival of timely succour. On another occasion they were more successful, wounded him 'atrociously and inhumanly in the head and other parts of the body', cut off a finger and left an arm hanging by 'a slender strip of skin' (*pellicula*). Finally they 'tyrannically' pulled out an eye, and left him for dead. Summoned before the Parlement of Paris, Rion pleaded that the scholar had seduced his wife, and continued the intrigue after having been forgiven and having solemnly pledged himself to abandon it. The fact was notorious and was not denied. The enormous damages claimed by the victim were considerably reduced by the Court. Nevertheless, Rion was condemned to pay 300 *livres tournois* by way of compensation, a fine of 100, and to make 'amende honorable' to the Court, the plaintiff, and the proctor for the university on bended knee and clad only in his shirt. The sentence led to a general outburst of rage and indignation against the scholars. Another scholar was beaten and mutilated 'so that he is expected to die rather than live'. At last there was a regular raid on the scholars 'to the ringing of bells and the sound of trumpets'. Houses were broken open, and scholars dragged out to the town prison. The citizens threatened that all the scholars should die. Nevertheless they do not appear to have done much in execution of their threats beyond beating a scholar's servant and pillaging a house. The scholars, however, fled the town *en masse*. The captain of the city guard rode through the suburbs with his men, shouting 'death to the scholars'. One noble youth was so frightened as to hide in a sewer 'for a long time'. The offenders—chiefly, it would seem, royal officials—were condemned to do penance and make 'amende honorable' to the university in the usual way, and to a fine, part of which was to be expended on a picture representing the offenders on their knees before the rector and other scholars.

Yet another story from Toulouse. In the year 1332 five brothers of the noble family de la Penne lived together in a *hospicium* at Toulouse as students of the civil and canon law. One of them was provost of a monastery, another archdeacon of Albi, another an archpriest, another canon of Toledo. A bastard son of their father, named Peter, lived with them as squire to the canon. On Easter Day, Peter, with another squire of the household named Aimery Béranger and other students, having dined at a tavern, were dancing with women, singing, shouting, and beating 'metallic vessels and iron culinary instruments' in the street before their masters' house. The provost and the archpriest were sympathetically watching the jovial scene from a window, until it was disturbed by the appearance of a capitoul and his officers, who summoned some of the party to surrender the prohibited arms which they were wearing. 'Ben Senhor, non fassat' was the impudent reply. The capitoul attempted to arrest one of the offenders; whereupon the ecclesiastical party made a combined attack upon the official. Aimery Béranger struck him in the face with a poignard, cutting off his nose and part of his chin and lips, and knocking out or breaking no less than eleven teeth. The surgeons deposed that if he recovered (he eventually did recover) he would never be able to speak intelligibly. One of the watch was killed outright by Peter de la Penne. That night the murderer slept, just as if nothing had happened, in the house of his ecclesiastical masters. The whole household, masters and servants alike, were, however, surprised by the other capitouls and a crowd of 200 citizens and led off to prison, and the house is alleged to have been pillaged. The archbishop's official demanded their surrender. In the case of the superior ecclesiastics, this after a short delay was granted. But Aimery, who dressed like a layman in 'divided and striped clothes' and wore a long beard, they refused to treat as a clerk, though it was afterwards alleged that the tonsure was plainly discernible upon his head until it was shaved by order of the capitouls. Aimery was put to the torture, admitted his crime, and was sentenced to death. The sentence was carried out by hanging, after he had had his hand cut off on the scene of the crime, and been dragged by horses to the place of execution. The capitouls were then excommunicated by the official, and the ecclesiastical side of the quarrel was eventually transferred to the Roman Court. Before the Parlement of Paris the university complained of the violation of the royal privilege exempting scholar's servants from the ordinary tribunals. The capitouls were imprisoned, and after a long litigation sentenced to pay enormous damages to the ruffian's family and erect a chapel for the good of his soul. The city was condemned for a time to the forfeiture of all its privileges. The body was cut down from the gibbet on which it had been hanging for three years, and accorded a solemn funeral. Four capitouls bore the pall, and all fathers of families were required to walk in the procession. When they came to the schools, the citizens solemnly begged pardon of the university, and the cortège was joined by 3,000 scholars. Finally, it cost the city 15,-000 *livres tournois* or more to regain their civic privileges.

It must be remembered that the violent scenes which crowd the records of a medieval university are only an extreme development of the violence which characterizes medieval life in general. It is, however, not so much the violence which distinguishes medieval society from modern as the status and position of the persons who abused, insulted, challenged, and fought each other like 'roughs' or small boys at school. At the present day party feeling sometimes runs high, but we do not hear of an ex-mayor of Cambridge wishing to fight the chancellor. Scenes of disorder occur in modern universities, but the rectors and professors, heads and tutors take no part in them. Sometimes, too, violence of this kind was not merely the act of isolated individuals, however eminent, but the concerted resolution of grave assemblies. We have seen how at Oxford the bell of S. Mary's was wont to summon the gownsmen to do battle with the town when the bell of S. Martin's was set going by the mayor. At Paris we find the scholars of the Norman nation taking a vote in 'a congregation' as to the propriety of an attack upon another nation. The attack was voted, with the result that 'one was killed and another mutilated'. Our knowledge of the fact comes to us from a 'dispensation from irregularity' granted to a clergyman, afterwards beneficed, who had voted for what is justly described as 'the war'.

NOTES

1. In what follows Rashdall gives instances of more or less organized turbulence. Another and more normal aspect of "the wilder side of university life" at Paris is described in a vivacious chapter of P. Champion's *François Villon: sa vie et son temps* (Paris, 1915), i. 65–129.

Part Two: CRISIS ON THE CAMPUS

QUESTIONS FOR STUDY
AND RESEARCH

1. What is Woodring's answer to the question "Who makes university policy?" Show how "the interaction of countervailing forces" at Berkeley resulted in the working of policy, and how the President at Berkeley was "primarily a mediator" of these countervailing forces.
2. Compare Newman's description of the ideal university with Kerr's modern multiversity. Summarize Kerr's historical explanation of the growth of the multiversity. From the comments made by the essayists in Part One, demonstrate how the size and structure of the University of California contributed to the Berkeley conflict.
3. Summarize Whitehead's "general principles" pertaining to the ideal university. How does Whitehead agree or disagree with Newman's "idea" of a university? Compare Whitehead's ideal university with the multiversity.
4. In his essay in Part One, Irving Howe refers to the depth of the "conflict between the values of the free mind and the values of the marketplace." In this regard compare Kerr's multiversity with Newman's "idea of the university." What is the relevance of Whitehead's views to this conflict?
5. Investigate the structure of your college or university and compare it with that of the modern multiversity. Determine whether the students at your school have the grievances that the Berkeley students claim to have had.
6. Define "academic freedom" by reference to Becker's essay and Hook's remarks. Consider Goodman's view that the Berkeley students wanted "to extend the concept of academic freedom . . . to include *Lernfreiheit.*" What is Hook's argument concerning this extension of academic freedom?
7. According to Becker, what are the philosophical and practical justifications for freedom of learning and teaching? How does the Berkeley controversy illustrate Becker's reference to "the conflict between the political community and the fraternity of scholars"? Does Rashdall's essay support Becker's remark on this subject?
8. Examine the criticisms directed by the FSM students and by those in "Students Speak" against contemporary American education; show how the aspects of American education which are criticized violate Whitehead's "general principles."
9. Interview a number of faculty members on your campus. Ask their opinions on the Berkeley rebellion, on Kerr's book *The Uses of a University* and on the current pressures upon faculty

members to do research. What does Whitehead say about this last point? Compare Hacker's criticism of university professors with the criticisms you hear others make.

10. Summarize Hacker's pessimistic view of education in a democratic society. Do you agree with his criticism of university teachers? Of university students? Contrast Hacker's analysis with Freedman's.

11. Examine the statements made by the four students in "Students Speak" for verification of Taylor's definition of American idealism in 1965. Do the actions and statements of the FSM students support Taylor's contentions? Illustrate.

12. According to Coffin, "students feel alienated because they have no say in the conduct of important university affairs." In your college or university how much "say" does the student body have in "important" affairs? Do you believe that there should be any limit to the degree of student participation in policymaking? Do these limitations create "alienation"?

13. Both Freedman and Reik analyze unusual behavior of students by the application of psychiatric principles. Compare the two analyses, demonstrating how they are similar, different. Comment on the validity of the generational conflict as an explanation of current student rebellions.

14. Examine Freedman's analysis of the roots of student discontent. Which of these are supported by specific statements made by students quoted in these first two groups of essays?

15. Write a paper in which you employ Gray's analysis of youth and existentialism to support May's statement that "in terms of religious and quasi-religious precedent, modern existentialism" explains a great deal about the FSM. Examine the comments made by students in the essays in Parts One and Two for evidence of existentialism.

16. Examine the *Carmina Burana*, a collection of lyrics composed by anonymous, dissident students during the Middle Ages (see J. A. Symonds, *Wine, Women and Song*, London, 1907, or H. Waddell, *The Wandering Scholars*, London, 1932). Read selections from the *Carmina* and determine what medieval students and modern students have in common, how they differ. Also, consult C. H. Haskins, *The Rise of the Universities*, for instances of student rebellions in the Middle Ages.

READINGS FOR FURTHER STUDY AND RESEARCH

Academic Freedom and Civil Liberties of Students in Colleges and Universities, American Civil Liberties Union (November, 1963).

Babbidge, Homer D., and Rosenzweig, Robert M. *The Federal Interest in Higher Education*, 1962.

Barton, R. D. "Militant Latin Campus," *The Nation* (August 12, 1961).

Brademas, J. "Freedom and the University in Latin America," *Vital Speeches* (July 15, 1961).

Brown, Kenneth I. "The Terrible Responsibility of the Teacher," *The Christian Scholar* (March, 1953).

Burton, Ernest DeWitt. *Education in a Democratic World*, 1927.

"Campus Agitation versus Education," *Life* (January 22, 1965).

"Campus Causes: '62: Integration and Survival," *The Nation* (May 19, 1962).

Care, Norman S. "Yale's Tenure Trouble," *The New Republic* (March 27, 1965).

"The Careful Young Men," *The Nation* (March 9, 1957.).

"The Class of '58 Speaks Up," *The Nation* (May 17, 1958).

Codification of Policy, United States National Student Association, 1960–61.

"College Pressure," *Life* (January 8, 15, 22, 1965).

Conant, James B. *The Citadel of Learning*, 1956.

———. *Education and Liberty*, 1953.

Crowther, Geoffrey. "English and American Education," *The Atlantic Monthly* (April, 1960).

———. "Two Heresies," *Michigan Alumnus Quarterly Review* (Summer, 1960).

Daiches, David. "Education in a Democratic Society," *Commentary* (April, 1957).

Degler, Carl N. "Academic Casualty," *The New Republic* (July 10, 1965).

Devane, William Clyde. *Higher Education in Twentieth-Century America*, 1965.

Dewey, John. "The Democratic Faith and Education," *The Antioch Review* (Summer, 1944).

———. *School and Society*, 1900.

Dunkel, Harold B. *Whitehead on Education*, 1965.

Eddy, Edward D., Jr. "Paradox in Parenthesis," *The Nation* (May 16, 1959).

Feuer, Lewis S. "Pornopolitics and the University," *The New Leader* (April, 1965).

Fischer, John. "Is There a Teacher on the Faculty?" *Harper's* (February, 1965).

Fitch, Robert Elliot. *Odyssey of the Self-Centered Self*, 1961.

Flexner, Abraham. *Universities, American, English, German*, 1930.

Friedenberg, Edgar Z. *Coming of Age in America: Growth and Acquiescence*, 1965.

Fromm, Erich. *Escape from Freedom*, 1941.

Gilbert, Eugene. "Why Today's Teen-Agers Seem So Different," *Harper's* (November, 1959).

Gilbert, Richard. "A Good Time at UCLA," *Harper's* (April, 1965).
Gilson, Etienne, "Education and Higher Learning," in *A Gilson Reader*, 1957.
Goodman, Paul. *The Community of Scholars*, 1962.
————. "For a Reactionary Experiment in Education," *Harper's* (November, 1962).
————. *Growing Up Absurd*, 1960.
————. *People or Personnel*, 1965.
Hale, Dennis, and Miller, Peter. "Bureaucracy and Protest at Oberlin," *News and Letters* (May, 1965).
Hechinger, Fred M. "Education: Activism on Campus," *New York Times* (June 6, 1965).
————. "Why's of the Student Revolts," *New York Times* (May 2, 1965).
Heimberger, Frederic. "The Grass Roots of Campus Freedom," *Saturday Review* (July 17, 1965).
Hentoff, Nat, and Harrington, Michael. "Is There a New Radicalism?" *Partisan Review* (Spring, 1965).
Higher Education: Some Newer Developments, edited by Samuel Baskin, 1965.
Howe, Irving, and Rousseas, Stephen. "The New Radicalism: Round II," *Partisan Review* (Summer, 1965).
Hutchins, Robert M. *Education for Freedom*, 1943.
————. *The Higher Learning in America*, 1936.
————. "The Meaning and Significance of Academic Freedom," *The Annals of the American Academy of Political and Social Sciences* (July, 1955).
————. *Some Observations on American Education*, 1956.
————. *The University of Utopia*, 1953.
Huxley, Aldous. "Over-Organization," *Brave New World Revisited*, 1958.
Issues in University Education, edited by Charles Frankel, 1959.
Jacobs, Phillip E. *Changing Values in College*, 1957.
Jaffe, Natalie. "Protest Leaders on Campus Hailed: Five-Year Study at Eight Colleges Finds Demonstrators Are the Best Academically," *New York Times* (September 7, 1965).
Johnson, Gerald W. "An Outburst of Servility," *The New Republic* (February 8, 1960).
Kassof, Allen. *The Soviet Youth Program: Regimentation and Rebellion*, 1965.
Kelman, Steven. "Youth and Politics," *The New Leader* (February 1, 1965).
Kerr, Clark. *Industrialism and Industrial Man*, 1960.
————. *The Uses of a University*, 1963.
Kibre, Paul. *The Nations in the Medieval Universities*, 1948.
Lazarsfeld, Paul F., and Thielens, Wagner, Jr. *The Academic Mind*, 1958.
Littell, Franklin H. "Is the University Done For?" *Union Seminary*

Quarterly Review (November, 1964).

MacLeish, Archibald. "What Is a True University?" *Saturday Review* (January 31, 1959).

Meland, B. E. *Higher Education and the Human Spirit,* 1953.

Millet, John D. *The Academic Community—An Essay on Organization,* 1962.

Moberly, Walter. *The Crisis in the University,* 1949.

Musgrove, F. *Youth and the Social Order,* 1965.

Nash, Arnold. *The University and the Modern World,* 1944.

Newman, John Henry. *The Idea of a University,* 1959.

Niebuhr, Reinhold. *Moral Man and Immoral Society,* 1932.

Parsons, Talcott, and Shils, Edward. *Toward a General Theory of Action,* 1951.

Presthus, Robert. "University Bosses: The Executive Conquest of Academe," *The New Republic* (February 20, 1965).

Rashdall, Hastings. *The Universities of Europe in the Middle Ages,* 1936.

"Rebels with Cause," *The New Republic* (May 1, 1965).

"Rebels with a Hundred Causes," *The Nation* (May 27, 1961).

Riesman, David. "Where is the College Generation Headed?" *The Atlantic Monthly* (April, 1961).

"Rising Unrest," *New York Times* (April 4, 1965).

Rosenberg, Morris. *Society and the Adolescent Self-Image,* 1965.

Savio, Mario. "The University Has Become a Factory," *Life* (February 26, 1965).

Sears, Laurence. "Liberals and Conservatives," *The Antioch Review* (Fall, 1953).

Swatez, Gerald M. "Kerr's Multiversity: The City of Intellect Under Pluralistic Industrialism," *The Graduate Student Journal* (Spring, 1964).

Taylor, Harold. "The Academic Industry: A Discussion of Clark Kerr's *The Uses of a University,*" *Commentary* (December, 1964).

Ten Hoor, Martin. "Education for Privacy," *The American Scholar* (Winter, 1953–54).

"Tension Beneath Apathy," *The Nation* (May 16, 1959).

Ways, Max. "On the Campus: a Troubled Reflection of the U.S.," *Fortune* (September, October, 1965).

White, E. B. "Freedom," *One Man's Meat,* 1938.

Whitehead, Alfred North. *The Aims of Education,* 1957.

Wilson, Woodrow. "What Is College For?" *Scribner's* (November, 1909).

Wriston, Henry M. "Publish or Perish," *Saturday Review* (July 17, 1965).

3

The Tradition of Liberty and Responsibility

Fido (handwritten)

From The ~~Crito~~

PLATO

Although he lived almost 2,500 years ago, Plato (427?–347 B.C.) has remained influential ever since. A Greek philosopher as well as a pupil and friend of Socrates, he was the teacher of Aristotle and the founder of the Academy. He advocated government by an oligarchy of intellectuals whose primary assumption was that virtue is knowledge. He is the author of The Republic.

CR. . . . But, oh! my beloved Socrates, let me entreat you once more to take my advice and escape. For if you die I shall not only lose a friend who can never be replaced, but there is another evil: people who do not know you and me will believe that I might have saved you if I had been willing to give money, but that I did not care. Now, can there be a worse disgrace than this—that I should be thought to value money more than the life of a friend? For the many will not be persuaded that I wanted you to escape, and that you refused.

SOC. But why, my dear Crito, should we care about the opinion of the many? Good men, and they are the only persons who are worth considering, will think of these things truly as they occurred.

Translated by Benjamin Jowett.

CR. But you see, Socrates, that the opinion of the many must be regarded, for what is now happening shows that they can do the greatest evil to any one who has lost their good opinion.

SOC. I only wish it were so, Crito; and that the many could do the greatest evil; for then they would also be able to do the greatest good—and what a fine thing this would be! But in reality they can do neither; for they cannot make a man either wise or foolish; and whatever they do is the result of chance.

CR. Well, I will not dispute with you; but please tell me, Socrates, whether you are not acting out of regard to me and your other friends: are you not afraid that if you escape from prison we may get into trouble with the informers for having stolen you away, and lose either the whole or a great part of our property; or that even a worse evil may happen to us? Now, if you fear on our account, be at ease; for in order to save you, we ought surely to run this, or even a greater risk; be persuaded, then, and do as I say.

SOC. Yes, Crito, that is one fear which you mention, but by no means the only one.

CR. Fear not—there are persons who are willing to get you out of prison at no great cost; and as for the informers, they are far from being exorbitant in their demands—a little money will satisfy them. My means, which are certainly ample, are at your service, and if you have a scruple about spending all mine, here are strangers who will give you the use of theirs; and one of them, Simmias the Theban, has brought a large sum of money for this very purpose; and Cebes and many others are prepared to spend their money in helping you to escape. I say, therefore, do not hesitate on our account, and do not say, as you did in the court, that you will have a difficulty in knowing what to do with yourself anywhere else. For men will love you in other places to which you may go, and not in Athens only; there are friends of mine in Thessaly, if you like to go to them, who will value and protect you, and no Thessalian will give you any trouble. Nor can I think that you are at all justified, Socrates, in betraying your own life when you might be saved; in acting thus you are playing into the hands of your enemies, who are hurrying on your destruction. And further I should say that you are deserting your own children; for you might bring them up and educate them; instead of which you go away and leave them, and they will have to take their chance; and if they do not meet with the usual fate of orphans, there will be small thanks to you. No man should bring children into the world who is unwilling to persevere to the end in their nurture and education. But you appear to be choosing the easier part, not the better and manlier, which would have been more becoming in one who professes to care for virtue in all his actions, like yourself. And indeed, I am ashamed not only of you, but of us who are your friends, when I reflect that the whole business will be attributed entirely to our want of courage. The trial need never have come on, or might have been managed differently; and this last act, or crowning folly, will seem to have occurred through our negligence and cowardice, who might have saved you, if we had been good for anything; and you might have saved yourself, for there was no difficulty at all. See now, Socrates, how sad and discreditable are the consequences, both to us and you. Make up your mind then, or rather have your mind already made up, for the time of deliberation is over, and there is only one thing to be done, which must be done this very night, and if we delay at all will be no longer practicable or possible; I beseech you therefore, Socrates, be persuaded by me, and do as I say.

soc. Dear Crito, your zeal is invaluable, if a right one; but if wrong, the greater the zeal the greater the danger; and therefore we ought to consider whether I shall or shall not do as you say. For I am and always have been one of those natures who must be guided by reason, whatever the reason may be which upon reflection appears to me to be the best; and now that this chance has befallen me, I cannot repudiate my own words: the principles which I have hitherto honoured and revered I still honour, and unless we can at once find other and better principles, I am certain not to agree with you; no, not even if the power of the multitude could inflict many more imprisonments, confiscations, deaths, frightening us like children with hobgoblin terrors. What will be the fairest way of considering the question? Shall I return to your old argument about the opinions of men?—we are saying that some of them are to be regarded, and others not. Now were we right in maintaining this before I was condemned? And has the argument which was once good now proved to be talk for the sake of talking—mere childish nonsense? That is what I want to consider with your help, Crito:—whether, under my present circumstances, the argument appears to be in any way different or not; and is to be allowed by me or disallowed. That argument, which, as I believe, is maintained by many persons of authority, was to the effect, as I was saying, that the opinions of some men are to be regarded, and of other men not to be regarded. Now you, Crito, are not going to die to-morrow—at least, there is no human probability of this—and therefore you are disinterested and not liable to be deceived by the circumstances in which you are placed. Tell me then, whether I am right in saying that some opinions, and the opinions of some men only, are to be valued, and that other opinions, and the opinions of other men, are not to be valuable. I ask you whether I was right in maintaining this?

CR. Certainly.

SOC. The good are to be regarded, and not the bad?

CR. Yes.

SOC. And the opinions of the wise are good, and the opinions of the unwise are evil?

CR. Certainly.

SOC. And what was said about another matter? Is the pupil who devotes himself to the practice of gymnastics supposed to attend to the praise and blame and opinion of every man, or of one man only—his physician or trainer, whoever he may be?

CR. Of one man only.

SOC. And he ought to fear the censure and welcome the praise of that one only, and not of the many?

CR. Clearly so.

SOC. And he ought to act and train, and eat and drink in the way which seems good to his single master who has understanding, rather than according to the opinion of all other men put together?

CR. True.

SOC. And if he disobeys and disregards the opinion and approval of the one, and regards the opinion of the many who have no understanding, will he not suffer evil?

CR. Certainly he will.

SOC. And what will the evil be, whither tending and what affecting, in the disobedient person?

CR. Clearly, affecting the body; that is what is destroyed by the evil.

SOC. Very good; and is not this true, Crito, of other things which we need not separately enumerate? In questions of just and unjust, fair and foul, good and evil, which are the subjects of our present consultation, ought we to follow the opinion of the many and to fear them; or the opinion of the one man who has understanding? ought we not to fear and reverence him more than all the rest of the world: and if we desert him shall we not destroy and injure that principle in us which may be assumed to be improved by justice and deteriorated by injustice;—there is such a principle?

CR. Certainly there is, Socrates.

SOC. Take a parallel instance:—if, acting under the advice of those who have no understanding, we destroy that which is improved by health and is deteriorated by disease, would life be worth having? And that which has been destroyed is—the body?

CR. Yes.

SOC. Could we live, having an evil and corrupted body?

CR. Certainly not.

SOC. And will life be worth having, if that higher part of man be destroyed, which is improved by justice and depraved by injustice? Do we suppose that principle, whatever it may be in man, which has to do with justice and injustice, to be inferior to the body?

CR. Certainly not.

SOC. More honourable than the body?

CR. Far more.

SOC. Then, my friend, we must not regard what the many

say of us: but what he, the one man who has understanding of just and unjust, will say, and what the truth will say. And therefore you begin in error when you advise that we should regard the opinion of the many about just and unjust, good and evil, honourable and dishonourable,—'Well,' some one will say, 'but the many can kill us.'

CR. Yes, Socrates; that will clearly be the answer.

SOC. And it is true: but still I find with surprise that the old argument is unshaken as ever. And I should like to know whether I may say the same of another proposition—that not life, but a good life, is to be chiefly valued?

CR. Yes, that also remains unshaken.

SOC. And a good life is equivalent to a just and honourable one—that holds also?

CR. Yes, it does.

SOC. From these premises I proceed to argue the question whether I ought or ought not to try and escape without the consent of the Athenians: and if I am clearly right in escaping, then I will make the attempt; but if not, I will abstain. The other considerations which you mention, of money and loss of character and the duty of educating one's children, are, I fear, only the doctrines of the multitude, who would be as ready to restore people to life, if they were able, as they are to put them to death—and with as little reason. But now, since the argument has thus far prevailed, the only question which remains to be considered is, whether we shall do rightly either in escaping or in suffering others to aid in our escape and paying them in money and thanks, or whether in reality we shall not do rightly; and if the latter, then death or any other calamity which may ensue on my remaining here must not be allowed to enter into the calculation.

CR. I think that you are right, Socrates; how then shall we proceed?

SOC. Let us consider the matter together, and do you either refute me if you can, and I will be convinced; or else cease, my dear friend, from repeating to me that I ought to escape against the wishes of the Athenians: for I highly value your attempts to persuade me to do so, but I may not be persuaded against my own better judgment. And now please to consider my first position, and try how you can best answer me.

CR. I will.

SOC. Are we to say that we are never intentionally to do wrong, or that in one way we ought and in another we ought not to do wrong, or is doing wrong always evil and dishonourable, as I was just now saying, and as has been already acknowledged by us? Are all our former admissions which were made within a few days to be thrown away? And have we, at our age, been earnestly discoursing with one another all our life long only to discover that we are no better than children? Or, in spite of the opinion of the many, and in spite of consequences whether better or worse, shall we insist on the truth of what was then said, that injustice is always an evil and dishonour to him who acts unjustly? Shall we say so or not?

CR. Yes.

SOC. Then we must do no wrong?

CR. Certainly not.

SOC. Nor when injured injure in return, as the many imagine; for we must injure no one at all?

CR. Clearly not.

SOC. Again, Crito, may we do evil?

CR. Surely not, Socrates.

SOC. And what of doing evil in return for evil, which is the morality of the many—is that just or not?

CR. Not just.

SOC. For doing evil to another is the same as injuring him?

CR. Very true.

SOC. Then we ought not to retaliate or render evil for evil to any one, whatever evil we may have suffered from him. But I would have you consider, Crito, whether you really mean what you are saying. For this opinion has never been held, and never will be held, by any considerable number of persons; and those who are agreed and those who are not agreed upon this point have no common ground, and can only despise one another when they see how widely they differ. Tell me, then, whether you agree with and assent to my first principle, that neither injury nor retaliation nor warding off evil by evil is ever right. And shall that be the premiss of our argument? Or do you decline and dissent from this? For so I have ever thought, and continue to think; but, if you are of another opinion, let me hear what you have to say. If, however, you remain of the same mind as formerly, I will proceed to the next step.

CR. You may proceed, for I have not changed my mind.

SOC. Then I will go on to the next point, which may be put in the form of a question:—Ought a man to do what he admits to be right, or ought he to betray the right?

CR. He ought to do what he thinks right.

SOC. But if this is true, what is the application? In leaving the prison against the will of the Athenians, do I wrong any? or rather do I not wrong those whom I ought least to wrong? Do I not desert the principles which were acknowledged by us to be just—what do you say?

CR. I cannot tell, Socrates; for I do not know.

SOC. Then consider the matter in this way:—Imagine that I am about to play truant (you may call the proceeding by any name which you like), and the laws and the government come and interrogate me: 'Tell us, Socrates,' they say, 'what are you about? are you not going by an act of yours to overturn us—the laws, and the whole state, as far as in you lies? Do you imagine that a state can subsist and not be overthrown, in which the decisions of law have no power, but are set aside and trampled upon by individuals?' What will be our answer, Crito, to these and the like words? Any one, and especially a rhetorician, will have a good deal to say on behalf of the law which requires a sentence to be carried out. He will argue that this law should not be set aside; and shall we reply, 'Yes; but the state has injured us and given an unjust sentence.' Suppose I say that?

CR. Very good, Socrates.

SOC. 'And was that our agreement with you?' the law would answer; 'or were you to abide by the sentence of the state?' And if I were to express my astonishment at their words, the law would probably add: 'Answer, Socrates, instead of opening your eyes—you are in the habit of asking and answering questions. Tell us,—What complaint have you to make against us which justifies you in attempting to destroy us and the state? In the first place did we not bring you into existence? Your father married your mother by our aid and begat you. Say whether you have any objection to urge against those of us who regulate marriage?' None, I should reply. 'Or against those of us who after birth regulate the nurture and education of children, in which you also were trained? Were not the laws, which have the charge of education, right in command-ing your father to train you in music and gymnastic?' Right, I should reply. 'Well then, since you were brought into the world and nurtured and educated by us, can you deny in the first place that you are our child and slave, as your fathers were before you? And if this is true you are not on equal terms with us; nor can you think that you have a right to do to us what we are doing to you. Would you have any right to strike or revile or do any other evil to your father or your master, if you had one, because you have been struck or reviled by him, or received some other evil at his hands?— you would not say this? And because we think right to destroy you, do you think that you have any right to destroy us in return, and your country as far as in you lies? Will you, O professor of true virtue, pretend that you are justified in this? Has a philosopher like you failed to discover that our country is more to be valued and higher and holier far than mother or father or any ancestor, and more to be regarded in the eyes of the gods and of men of understanding? Also to be soothed, and gently and reverently entreated when angry, even more than a father, and either to be persuaded, or if not persuaded, to be obeyed? And when we are punished by her, whether with imprisonment or stripes, the punishment is to be endured in silence; and if she leads us to wounds or death in battle, thither we follow as is right; neither may any one yield or retreat or leave his rank, but whether in battle or in a court of law, or in any other place, he must do what his city and his country order him; or he must change their view of what is just: and if he may do no violence to his father or mother, much less may he do violence to his country.' What answer shall we make to this, Crito? Do the laws speak truly, or do they not?

CR. I think that they do.

SOC. Then the laws will say, 'Consider, Socrates, if we are speaking truly that in your present attempt you are going to do us an injury. For, having brought you into the world, and nurtured and educated you, and given you and every other citizen a share in every good which we had to give, we further proclaim to any Athenian by the liberty which we allow him, that if he does not like us when he has become of age and has seen the ways of the city, and made our acquaintance, he may go where he pleases and take his goods with him. None of us laws will forbid him or interfere with him. Any one who does not like us and the city, and who wants to emigrate to a colony or to any other city, may go where he likes, retaining his property. But he who has experience of the manner in which we order justice and administer the state, and still remains, has entered into an implied contract that he will do as we command him. And he who disobeys us is, as we maintain, thrice wrong; first, because in disobeying us he is disobeying his parents; secondly, because we are the authors of his education; thirdly, because he has made an agreement with us that he will duly obey our commands; and he neither obeys them nor convinces us that our commands are unjust; and we do not rudely impose them, but give him the alternative of obeying or convincing us;—that is what we offer, and he does neither.

'These are the sort of accusations to which, as we were saying, you, Socrates, will be exposed if you accomplish your intentions; you, above all other Athenians.' Suppose now I ask, why I rather than anybody else? they will justly retort upon me that I above all other men have acknowledged the agreement. 'There is clear proof,' they will say, 'Socrates, that we and the city were not displeasing to you. Of all Athenians you have been the most constant resident in the city, which, as you never leave, you may be supposed to love. For you never went out of the city either to see the games, except once when you went to the Isthmus, or to any other place unless when you were on military service; nor did you travel as other men do. Nor had you any curiosity to know other states or their laws: your affections did not go beyond us and our state; we were your special favourites, and you acquiesced in our government of you; and here in this city you begat your children, which is a proof of your satisfaction. Moreover, you might in the course of the trial, if you had liked, have fixed the penalty at banishment; the state which refuses to let you go now would have let you go then. But you pretended that you preferred death to exile, and that you were not unwilling to die. And now you have forgotten these fine sentiments, and pay no respect to us the laws, of whom you are the destroyer; and are doing what only a miserable slave would do, running away and turning your back upon the compacts and agreements which you made as a citizen. And first of all answer this very question: Are we right in saying that you agreed to be governed according to us in deed, and not in word only? Is that true or not?' How shall we answer, Crito? Must we not assent?

CR. We cannot help it, Socrates.

SOC. Then will they not say: 'You, Socrates, are breaking the covenants and agreements which you made with us at your leisure, not in any haste or under any compulsion or deception, but after you have had seventy years to think of them, during which time you were at liberty to leave the city, if we were not to your mind, or if our covenants appeared to you to be unfair. You had your choice, and might have gone either to Lacedaemon or Crete, both which states are often praised by you for their good government, or to some other Hellenic or foreign state. Whereas you, above all other Athenians, seemed to be so fond of the state, or, in other words, of us her laws (and who would care about a state which has no laws?), that you never stirred out of her; the halt, the blind, the maimed were not more stationary in her than you were. And now you run away and forsake your agreements. Not so, Socrates, if you will take our advice; do not make yourself ridiculous by escaping out of the city.

'For just consider, if you transgress and err in this sort of way, what good will you do either to yourself or to your

friends? That your friends will be driven into exile and deprived of citizenship, or will lose their property, is tolerably
certain; and you yourself, if you fly to one of the neighboring
cities, as, for example, Thebes or Megara, both of which are
well governed, will come to them as an enemy, Socrates, and
their government will be against you, and all patriotic citizens
will cast an evil eye upon you as a subverter of the laws, and
you will confirm in the minds of the judges the justice of
their own condemnation of you. For he who is a corrupter of
the laws is more than likely to be a corrupter of the young
and foolish portion of mankind. Will you then flee from well-
ordered cities and virtuous men? and is existence worth having on these terms? Or will you go to them without shame,
and talk to them, Socrates? And what will you say to them?
What you say here about virtue and justice and institutions
and laws being the best things among men? Would that be
decent of you? Surely not. But if you go away from well-
governed states to Crito's friends in Thessaly, where there is
great disorder and licence, they will be charmed to hear the
tale of your escape from prison, set off with ludicrous particulars of the manner in which you were wrapped in a goatskin
or some other disguise, and metamorphosed as the manner is
of runaways; but will there be no one to remind you that in
your old age you were not ashamed to violate the most
sacred laws from a miserable desire of a little more life?
Perhaps not, if you keep them in a good temper; but if they
are out of temper you will hear many degrading things; you
will live, but how?—as the flatterer of all men, and the servant
of all men; and doing what?—eating and drinking in Thessaly, having gone abroad in order that you may get a dinner.
And where will be your fine sentiments about justice and
virtue? Say that you wish to live for the sake of your children
—you want to bring them up and educate them—will you
take them into Thessaly and deprive them of Athenian citizenship? Is this the benefit which you will confer upon them?
Or are you under the impression that they will be better cared
for and educated here if you are still alive, although absent
from them; for your friends will take care of them? Do you
fancy that if you are an inhabitant of Thessaly they will take

care of them, and if you are an inhabitant of the other world that they will not take care of them? Nay; but if they who call themselves friends are good for anything, they will—to be sure they will.

'Listen, then, Socrates, to us who have brought you up. Think not of life and children first, and of justice afterwards, but of justice first, that you may be justified before the princes of the world below. For neither will you nor any that belong to you be happier or holier or juster in this life, or happier in another, if you do as Crito bids. Now you depart in innocence, a sufferer and not a doer of evil; a victim, not of the laws but of men. But if you go forth, returning evil for evil, and injury for injury, breaking the covenants and agreements which you have made with us, and wronging those whom you ought least of all to wrong, that is to say, yourself, your friends, your country, and us, we shall be angry with you while you live, and our brethren, the laws of the world below, will receive you as an enemy; for they will know that you have done your best to destroy us. Listen, then, to us and not to Crito.'

This, dear Crito, is the voice which I seem to hear murmuring in my ears, like the sound of the flute in the ears of the mystic; that voice, I say, is humming in my ears, and prevents me from hearing any other. And I know that anything more which you may say will be vain. Yet speak, if you have anything to say.

CR. I have nothing to say, Socrates.

SOC. Leave me then, Crito, to fulfil the will of God, and to follow whither he leads.

From The Politics

ARISTOTLE

Aristotle (384–322 B.C.), along with Plato, is regarded as the source of some of the most important ideas to have been expressed in the Western tradition. Representing the best of the classical Greek philosophers, he wrote The Physics, The Ethics, The Poetics *and* The History of Animals.

---

1. THE SUMMUM BONUM FOR INDIVIDUALS AND STATES[1]

He who would duly inquire about the best form of a state ought first to determine which is the most eligible life; while this remains uncertain the best form of the state must also be uncertain; for, in the natural order of things, those may be expected to lead the best life who are governed in the best manner of which their circumstances admit. We ought therefore to ascertain, first of all, which is the most generally eligible life, and then whether the same life is or is not best for the state and for individuals.

Assuming that enough has been already said in discussions outside the school concerning the best life, we will now only repeat what is contained in them. Certainly no one will dispute the propriety of that partition of goods which separates them into three classes, viz. external goods, goods of the body,

---

Translated by Benjamin Jowett.

. and goods of the soul, or deny that the happy man must have all three. For no one would maintain that he is happy who has not in him a particle of courage or temperance or justice or prudence, who is afraid of every insect which flutters past him, and will commit any crime, however great, in order to gratify his lust of meat or drink, who will sacrifice his dearest friend for the sake of half-a-farthing, and is as feeble and false in mind as a child or a madman. These propositions are almost universally acknowledged as soon as they are uttered, but men differ about the degree or relative superiority of this or that good. Some think that a very moderate amount of virtue is enough, but set no limit to their desires of wealth, property, power, reputation, and the like. To whom we reply by an appeal to facts, which easily prove that mankind do not acquire or preserve virtue by the help of external goods, but external goods by the help of virtue, and that happiness, whether consisting in pleasure or virtue, or both, is more often found with those who are most highly cultivated in their mind and in their character, and have only a moderate share of external goods, than among those who possess external goods to a useless extent but are deficient in higher qualities; and this is not only matter of experience, but, if reflected upon, will easily appear to be in accordance with reason. For, whereas external goods have a limit, like any other instrument, and all things useful are of such a nature that where there is too much of them they must either do harm, or at any rate be of no use, to their possessors, every good of the soul, the greater it is, is also of greater use, if the epithet useful as well as noble is appropriate to such subjects. No proof is required to show that the best state of one thing in relation to another corresponds in degree of excellence to the interval between the natures of which we say that these very states are states: so that, if the soul is more noble than our possessions or our bodies, both absolutely and in relation to us, it must be admitted that the best state of either has a similar ratio to the other. Again, it is for the sake of the soul that goods external and goods of the body are eligible at all, and all wise men ought to choose them for the sake of the soul, and not the soul for the sake of them.

Let us acknowledge then that each one has just so much of happiness as he has of virtue and wisdom, and of virtuous and wise action. God is a witness to us of this truth, for he is happy and blessed, not by reason of any external good, but in himself and by reason of his own nature. And herein of necessity lies the difference between good fortune and happiness; for external goods come of themselves, and chance is the author of them, but no one is just or temperate by or through chance. In like manner, and by a similar train of argument, the happy state may be shown to be that which is best and which acts rightly; and rightly it cannot act without doing right actions, and neither individual nor state can do right actions without virtue and wisdom. Thus the courage, justice, and wisdom of a state have the same form and nature as the qualities which give the individual who possesses them the name of just, wise, or temperate.

Thus much may suffice by way of preface: for I could not avoid touching upon these questions, neither could I go through all the arguments affecting them; these are the business of another science.

Let us assume then that the best life, both for individuals and states, is the life of virtue, when virtue has external goods enough for the performance of good actions. If there are any who controvert our assertion, we will in this treatise pass them over, and consider their objections hereafter.

There remains to be discussed the question, Whether the happiness of the individual is the same as that of the state, or different? Here again there can be no doubt—no one denies that they are the same. For those who hold that the well-being of the individual consists in his wealth, also think that riches make the happiness of the whole state, and those who value most highly the life of a tyrant deem that city the happiest which rules over the greatest number; while they who approve an individual for his virtue say that the more virtuous a city is, the happier it is. Two points here present themselves for consideration: first (1), which is the more eligible life, that of a citizen who is a member of a state, or that of an alien who has no political ties; and again (2), which is the best form of constitution or the best condition of a state, either on the supposition that political privileges are desirable for all, or for a majority only? Since the good of the state and not of the individual is the proper subject of political thought and speculation, and we are engaged in a political discussion, while the first of these two points has a secondary interest for us, the latter will be the main subject of our inquiry.

Now it is evident that the form of government is best in which every man, whoever he is, can act best and live happily. But even those who agree in thinking that the life of virtue is the most eligible raise a question, whether the life of business and politics is or is not more eligible than one which is wholly independent of external goods, I mean than a contemplative life, which by some is maintained to be the only one worthy of a philosopher. For these two lives—the life of the philosopher and the life of the statesman—appear to have been preferred by those who have been most keen in the pursuit of virtue, both in our own and in other ages. Which is the better is a question of no small moment; for the wise man, like the wise state, will necessarily regulate his life according to the best end. There are some who think that while a despotic rule over others is the greatest injustice, to exercise a constitutional rule over them, even though not unjust, is a great impediment to a man's individual well-being. Others take an opposite view; they maintain that the true life of man is the practical and political, and that every virtue admits of being practised, quite as much by statesmen and rulers as by private individuals. Others, again, are of opinion that arbitrary and tyrannical rule alone consists with happiness; indeed, in some states the entire aim both of the laws and of the constitution is to give men despotic power over their neighbours. And, therefore, although in most cities the laws may be said generally to be in a chaotic state, still, if they aim at anything, they aim at the maintenance of power: thus in Lacedaemon and Crete the system of education and the greater part of the laws are framed with a view to war. And in all nations which are able to gratify their ambition military power is held in esteem, for example among the Scythians and Persians and Thracians and Celts. In some nations there are even laws tending to stimulate the warlike virtues, as at Carthage, where we are told that men obtain the honour of wearing as many armlets as they have served campaigns. There was once a law in Macedonia that he who had not killed an enemy should wear a halter, and among the Scythians no one who had not slain his man was allowed to drink out of the cup which was handed round at a certain feast. Among the Iberians, a warlike nation, the number of enemies whom a man has slain is indicated by the number of obelisks which are fixed in the earth round his tomb; and there are numerous practices among other nations of a like kind, some of them established by law and others by custom. Yet to a reflecting mind it must appear very strange that the statesman should be always considering how he can dominate and tyrannize over others, whether they will or not. How can that which is not even lawful be the business of the statesman or the legislator? Unlawful it certainly is to rule without regard to justice, for there may be might where there is no right. The other arts and sciences offer no parallel; a physician is not expected to persuade or coerce his patients, nor a pilot the passengers in his ship. Yet most men appear to think that the art of despotic government is statesmanship, and what men affirm to be unjust and inexpedient in their own case they are not ashamed of practising towards others; they demand just rule for themselves, but where other men are concerned they care nothing about it. Such behaviour is irrational; unless the one party is, and the other is not, born to serve, in which case men have a right to command, not indeed all their fellows, but only those who are intended to be subjects; just as we ought not to hunt mankind, whether for food or sacrifice, but only the animals which may be hunted for food or sacrifice, this is to say, such wild animals as are eatable. And surely there may be a city happy in isolation, which we will assume to be well-governed (for it is quite possible that a city thus isolated might be well-administered and have good laws); but such a city would not be constituted with any view to war or the conquest of enemies—all that sort of thing must be excluded. Hence we see very plainly that warlike pursuits, although generally to be deemed honourable, are not the supreme end of all things, but only means. And the good lawgiver should inquire how states and races of men and communities may participate in a good life, and in the happiness which is attainable by them. His enactments will not be always the same; and where there are neighbours he will have to see what sort of studies should be practised in relation to their several characters, or how the measures appropriate in relation to each are to be adopted. The end at which the best form of government should aim may be properly made a matter of future consideration.

Let us now address those who, while they agree that the life of virtue is the most eligible, differ about the manner of practising it. For some renounce political power, and think that the life of the freeman is different from the life of the statesman and the best of all; but others think the life of the statesman best. The argument of the latter is that he who does nothing cannot do well, and that virtuous activity is identical with happiness. To both we say: 'you are partly right and partly wrong.' The first class are right in affirming that the life of the freeman is better than the life of the despot; for there is nothing grand or noble in having the use of a slave, in so far as he is a slave; or in issuing commands about necessary things. But it is an error to suppose that every sort of rule is despotic like that of a master over slaves, for there is as great a difference between the rule over freemen and the rule over slaves as there is between slavery by nature and freedom by nature, about which I have said enough at the commencement of this treatise. And it is equally a mistake to place inactivity above action, for happiness is activity, and the actions of the just and wise are the realization of much that is noble.

But perhaps some one, accepting these premises, may still maintain that supreme power is the best of all things, because the possessors of it are able to perform the greatest number of noble actions. If so, the man who is able to rule, instead of giving up anything to his neighbour, ought rather to take away his power; and the father should make no account of his son, nor the son of his father, nor friend of friend; they should not bestow a thought on one another in comparison with this higher object, for the best is the most eligible and 'doing well' is the best. There might be some truth in such a view if we assume that robbers and plunderers attain the chief good. But this can never be; their hypothesis is false. For the actions of a ruler cannot really be honourable, unless he is as much superior to other men as a husband is to a wife, or a father to his children, or a master to his slaves. And therefore he who violates the law can never recover by any success, however great, what he has already lost in departing from virtue. For equals the honourable and the just consist in sharing alike, as is just and equal. But that the unequal should be given to equals, and the unlike to those who are like, is contrary to nature, and nothing which is contrary to nature is good. If therefore, there is any one superior in virtue and in the power of performing the best actions, him we ought to follow and obey, but he must have the capacity for action as well as virtue.

If we are right in our view, and happiness is assumed to be virtuous activity, the active life will be the best, both for every city collectively, and for individuals. Not that a life of action must necessarily have relation to others, as some persons think, nor are those ideas only to be regarded as practical which are pursued for the sake of practical results, but much more the thoughts and contemplations which are independent and complete in themselves; since virtuous activity, and therefore a certain kind of action, is an end, and even in the case of external actions the directing mind is most truly said to act. Neither, again, is it necessary that states which are cut off from others and choose to live alone should be inactive; for activity, as well as other things, may take place by sections; there are many ways in which the sections of a state act upon one another. The same thing is equally true of every individual. If this were otherwise, God and the universe, who have no external actions over and above their own energies, would be far enough from perfection. Hence it is evident that the same life is best for each individual, and for states and for mankind collectively.

2. THE CHARACTER OF THE CITIZENS[2]

Having spoken of the number of the citizens, we will proceed to speak of what should be their character. This is a subject which can be easily understood by any one who casts his eye on the more celebrated states of Hellas, and generally on the distribution of races in the habitable world. Those who live in a cold climate and in Europe are full of spirit, but wanting in intelligence and skill; and therefore they retain comparative freedom, but have no political organization, and are incapable of ruling over others. Whereas the natives of Asia are intelligent and inventive, but they are wanting in spirit, and therefore they are always in a state of subjection and slavery. But the Hellenic race, which is situated between them, is likewise intermediate in character, being high-spirited and also intelligent. Hence it continues free, and is the best-governed of any nation, and, if it could be formed into one state, would be able to rule the world. There are also similar differences in the different tribes of Hellas; for some of them are of a one-sided nature, and are intelligent or courageous only, while in others there is a happy combination of both qualities. And clearly those whom the legislator will most easily lead to virtue may be expected to be both intelligent and courageous. Some say that the guardians should be friendly towards those whom they know, fierce towards those whom they do not know. Now, passion is the quality of the soul which begets friendship and enables us to love; notably the spirit within us is more stirred against our friends and acquaintances than against those who are unknown to us, when we think that we are despised by them; for which reason Archilochus, complaining of his friends, very naturally addresses his soul in these words,

For surely thou art plagued on account of friends.

The power of command and the love of freedom are in all men based upon this quality, for passion is commanding and invincible. Nor is it right to say that the guardians should be fierce towards those whom they do not know, for we ought not to be out of temper with any one; and a lofty spirit is not fierce by nature, but only when excited against evil-doers. And this, as I was saying before, is a feeling which men show most strongly towards their friends if they think they have received a wrong at their hands: as indeed is reasonable; for, besides the actual injury, they seem to be deprived of a benefit by those who owe them one. Hence the saying,

Cruel is the strife of brethren,

and again,

They who love in excess also hate in excess.

Thus we have nearly determined the number and character of the citizens of our state, and also the size and nature of their territory. I say 'nearly,' for we ought not to require the same minuteness in theory as in the facts given by perception.

3. The Education of Youth[3]

No one will doubt that the legislator should direct his attention above all to the education of youth; for the neglect of education does harm to the constitution. The citizen should be moulded to suit the form of government under which he lives. For each government has a peculiar character which originally formed and which continues to preserve it. The character of democracy creates democracy, and the character of oligarchy creates oligarchy; and always the better the character, the better the government.

Again, for the exercise of any faculty or art a previous training and habituation are required; clearly therefore for the practice of virtue. And since the whole city has one end, it is manifest that education should be one and the same for all, and that it should be public, and not private—not as at present, when every one looks after his own children separately, and gives them separate instruction of the sort which he thinks best; the training in things which are of common interest should be the same for all. Neither must we suppose that any one of the citizens belongs to himself, for they all belong to the state, and are each of them a part of the state, and the care of each part is inseparable from the care of the whole. In this particular as in some others the Lacedaemonians are to be praised, for they take the greatest pains about their children, and make education the business of the state.

That education should be regulated by law and should be an affair of state is not to be denied, but what should be the character of this public education, and how young persons should be educated, are questions which remain to be considered. As things are, there is disagreement about the subjects. For mankind are by no means agreed about the things to be taught, whether we look to virtue or the best life. Neither is it clear whether education is more concerned with intellectual or with moral virtue. The existing practice is perplexing; no one knows on what principle we should proceed—should the useful in life, or should virtue, or should the higher knowledge, be the aim of our training; all three opinions have been entertained. Again, about the means there is no agreement; for different persons, starting with different ideas about the nature of virtue, naturally disagree about the practice of it. There can be no doubt that children should be taught those useful things which are really necessary, but not all useful things; for occupations are divided into liberal and illiberal; and to young children should be imparted only such kinds of knowledge as will be useful to them without vulgarizing them. And any occupation, art, or science, which makes the body or soul or mind of the freeman less fit for the practice or exercise of virtue, is vulgar; wherefore we call those arts vulgar which tend to deform the body, and likewise all paid employments, for they absorb and degrade the mind. There are also some liberal arts quite proper for a freeman to acquire, but only in a certain degree, and if he attend to them too closely, in order to attain perfection in them, the same evil effects will follow. The object also which a man sets before him makes a great difference; if he does or learns anything for his own sake or for the sake of his friends, or with a view to excellence, the action will not appear illiberal; but if done for the sake of others, the very same action will be

thought menial and servile. The received subjects of instruction, as I have already remarked, are partly of a liberal and
partly of an illiberal character.

NOTES

1. From Book VII, Chapters 1, 2 and 3.
2. From Book VII, Chapter 7.
3. From Book VIII, Chapters 1 and 2.

What Is Enlightenment?

IMMANUEL KANT

---

*Immanuel Kant (1724–1804), a German philosopher whose
ideas influenced poets and other philosophers for nearly a century after his death, was among the first Europeans to formulate the theory of transcendentalism which later occupied
Thomas Carlyle, Ralph Waldo Emerson and Henry David
Thoreau. Among his important works are* Critique of Pure
Reason, Critique of Practical Reason *and* Critique of Judgment.

ENLIGHTENMENT is man's release from his self-incurred
tutelage. Tutelage is man's inability to make use of
his understanding without direction from another. Self-incurred is this tutelage when its cause lies not in lack of reason
but in lack of resolution and courage to use it without direction from another. *Sapere aude!* [1] "Have courage to use your
own reason!"—that is the motto of enlightenment.

Laziness and cowardice are the reasons why so great a portion of mankind, after nature has long since discharged them
from external direction (*naturaliter maiorennes*), nevertheless remains under lifelong tutelage, and why it is so easy for
others to set themselves up as their guardians. It is so easy

not to be of age. If I have a book which understands for me, a pastor who has a conscience for me, a physician who decides my diet, and so forth, I need not trouble myself. I need not think, if I can only pay—others will readily undertake the irksome work for me.

That the step to competence is held to be very dangerous by the far greater portion of mankind (and by the entire fair sex)—quite apart from its being arduous—is seen to by those guardians who have so kindly assumed superintendence over them. After the guardians have first made their domestic cattle dumb and have made sure that these placid creatures will not dare take a single step without the harness of the cart to which they are confined, the guardians then show them the danger which threatens if they try to go alone. Actually, however, this danger is not so great, for by falling a few times they would finally learn to walk alone. But an example of this failure makes them timid and ordinarily frightens them away from all further trials.

For any single individual to work himself out of the life under tutelage which has become almost his nature is very difficult. He has come to be fond of this state, and he is for the present really incapable of making use of his reason, for no one has ever let him try it out. Statutes and formulas, those mechanical tools of the rational employment or rather misemployment of his natural gifts, are the fetters of an everlasting tutelage. Whoever throws them off makes only an uncertain leap over the narrowest ditch because he is not accustomed to that kind of free motion. Therefore, there are only few who have succeeded by their own exercise of mind both in freeing themselves from incompetence and in achieving a steady pace.

But that the public should enlighten itself is more possible; indeed, if only freedom is granted, enlightenment is almost sure to follow. For there will always be some independent thinkers, even among the established guardians of the great masses, who, after throwing off the yoke of tutelage from their own shoulders, will disseminate the spirit of the rational appreciation of both their own worth and every man's vocation for thinking for himself. But be it noted that the public, which has first been brought under this yoke by their guardians, forces the guardians themselves to remain bound when it is incited to do so by some of the guardians who are themselves capable of some enlightenment—so harmful is it to implant prejudices, for they later take vengeance on their cultivators or on their descendants. Thus the public can only slowly attain enlightenment. Perhaps a fall of personal despotism or of avaricious or tyrannical oppression may be accomplished by revolution, but never a true reform in ways of thinking. Rather, new prejudices will serve as well as old ones to harness the great unthinking masses.

For this enlightenment, however, nothing is required but freedom, and indeed the most harmless among all the things to which this term can properly be applied. It is the freedom to make public use of one's reason at every point.[2] But I hear on all sides, "Do not argue!" The officer says: "Do not argue but drill!" The tax-collector: "Do not argue but pay!" The cleric: "Do not argue but believe!" Only one prince in the world says, "Argue as much as you will, and about what you will, but obey!" Everywhere there is restriction on freedom.

Which restriction is an obstacle to enlightenment, and which is not an obstacle but a promoter of it? I answer: The public use of one's reason must always be free, and it alone can bring about enlightenment among men. The private use of reason, on the other hand, may often be very narrowly restricted without particularly hindering the progress of enlightenment. By the public use of one's reason I understand the use which a person makes of it as a scholar before the reading public. Private use I call that which one may make of it in a particular civil post or office which is intrusted to him. Many affairs which are conducted in the interest of the community require a certain mechanism through which some members of the community must passively conduct themselves with an artificial unanimity, so that the government may direct them to public ends, or at least prevent them from destroying those ends. Here argument is certainly not allowed—one must obey. But so far as a part of the mechanism regards himself at the same time as a member of the whole community or of a society of world citizens, and thus in the role of a scholar who addresses the public (in the proper sense of the word) through his writings, he certainly can argue without hurting the affairs for which he is in part responsible as a passive member. Thus it would be ruinous for an officer in service to debate about the suitability or utility of a command given to him by his superior; he must obey. But the right to make remarks on errors in the military service and to lay them before the public for judgment cannot equitably be refused him as a scholar. The citizen cannot refuse to pay the taxes imposed on him; indeed, an impudent complaint at those levied on him can be punished as a scandal (as it could occasion general refractoriness). But the same person nevertheless does not act contrary to his duty as a citizen when, as a scholar, he publicly expresses his thoughts on the inappropriateness or even the injustice of these levies. Similarly a clergyman is obligated to make his sermon to his pupils in catechism and his congregation conform to the symbol of the church which he serves, for he has been accepted on this condition. But as a scholar he has complete freedom, even the calling, to communicate to the public all his carefully tested and well-meaning thoughts on that which is erroneous in the symbol and to make suggestions for the better organization of the religious body and church. In doing this, there is nothing that could be laid as a burden on his conscience. For what he teaches as a consequence of his office as a representative of the church, this he considers something about which he has no freedom to teach according to his own lights; it is something which he is appointed to propound at the dictation of and in the name of another. He will say, "Our church teaches this or that; those are the proofs which it adduces." He thus extracts all practical uses for his congregation from statutes to which he himself would not subscribe with full conviction but to the enunciation of which he can very well pledge himself because it is not impossible that truth lies hidden in them, and, in any case, there is at least nothing in them contradictory to inner religion. For if he believed he had found such in them, he could not conscientiously discharge the duties of his office; he would have to give it up. The use, therefore, which an appointed teacher makes of his reason before his congregation is merely private, because this congregation is only a domestic one (even if it be a large gathering); with respect to it, as a priest, he is not free, nor can he be free, because he carries out the orders of another. But as a scholar, whose writings speak to his public, the world, the clergyman in the public use of his reason enjoys an unlimited freedom to use his own reason and to speak in his own person. That the guardians of the people (in spiritual things) should themselves be incompetent is an absurdity which amounts to the eternalization of absurdities.

But would not a society of clergymen, perhaps a church conference or a venerable classis (as they call themselves among the Dutch), be justified in obligating itself by oath to a certain unchangeable symbol in order to enjoy an unceasing guardianship over each of its members and thereby over the people as a whole, and even to make it eternal? I answer that this is altogether impossible. Such a contract, made to shut off all further enlightenment from the human race, is absolutely null and void even if confirmed by the supreme power, by parliaments, and by the most ceremonious of peace treaties. An age cannot bind itself and ordain to put the succeeding one into such a condition that it cannot extend its (at best very occasional) knowledge, purify itself of errors, and progress in general enlightenment. That would be a crime against human nature, the proper destination of which lies precisely in this progress; and the descendants would be fully justified in rejecting those decrees as having been made in an unwarranted and malicious manner.

The touchstone of everything that can be concluded as a law for a people lies in the question whether the people could have imposed such a law on itself. Now such a religious compact might be possible for a short and definitely limited time, as it were, in expectation of a better. One might let every citizen, and especially the clergyman, in the role of scholar, make his comments freely and publicly, i.e., through writing, on the erroneous aspects of the present institution. The newly introduced order might last until insight into the nature of these things had become so general and widely approved that through uniting their voices (even if not unanimously)

they could bring a proposal to the throne to take those congregations under protection which had united into a changed
religious organization according to their better ideas, without,
however, hindering others who wish to remain in the order.
But to unite in a permanent religious institution which is not
to be subject to doubt before the public even in the lifetime
of one man, and thereby to make a period of time fruitless
in the progress of mankind toward improvement, thus working to the disadvantage of posterity—that is absolutely forbidden. For himself (and only for a short time) a man can
postpone enlightenment in what he ought to know, but to renounce it for himself and even more to renounce it for posterity is to injure and trample on the rights of mankind.

And what a people may not decree for itself can even less
be decreed for them by a monarch, for his lawgiving authority rests on his uniting the general public will in his own.
If he only sees to it that all true or alleged improvement
stands together with civil order, he can leave it to his subjects
to do what they find necessary for their spiritual welfare.
This is not his concern, though it is incumbent on him to
prevent one of them from violently hindering another in determining and promoting this welfare to the best of his
ability. To meddle in these matters lowers his own majesty,
since by the writings in which his subjects seek to present
their views he may evaluate his own governance. He can do
this when, with deepest understanding, he lays upon himself
the reproach, *Caesar non est supra grammaticos*. Far more
does he injure his own majesty when he degrades his supreme
power by supporting the ecclesiastical despotism of some
tyrants in his state over his other subjects.

If we are asked, "Do we now live in an *enlightened age?*"
the answer is, "No," but we do live in an *age of enlightenment*.[3] As things now stand, much is lacking which prevents
men from being, or easily becoming, capable of correctly using their own reason in religious matters with assurance and
free from outside direction. But, on the other hand, we have
clear indications that the field has now been opened wherein
men may freely deal with these things and that the obstacles
to general enlightenment or the release from self-imposed tute-

lage are gradually being reduced. In this respect, this is the age of enlightenment, or the century of Frederick.

A prince who does not find it unworthy of himself to say that he holds it to be his duty to prescribe nothing to men in religious matters but to give them complete freedom while renouncing the haughty name of *tolerance,* is himself enlightened and deserves to be esteemed by the grateful world and posterity as the first, at least from the side of government, who divested the human race of its tutelage and left each man free to make use of his reason in matters of conscience. Under him venerable ecclesiastics are allowed, in the role of scholars, and without infringing on their official duties, freely to submit for public testing their judgments and views which here and there diverge from the established symbol. And an even greater freedom is enjoyed by those who are restricted by no official duties. This spirit of freedom spreads beyond this land, even to those in which it must struggle with external obstacles erected by a government which misunderstands its own interest. For an example gives evidence to such a government that in freedom there is not the least cause for concern about public peace and the stability of the community. Men work themselves gradually out of barbarity if only intentional artifices are not made to hold them in it.

I have placed the main point of enlightenment—the escape of men from their self-incurred tutelage—chiefly in matters of religion because our rulers have no interest in playing the guardian with respect to the arts and sciences and also because religious incompetence is not only the most harmful but also the most degrading of all. But the manner of thinking of the head of a state who favors religious enlightenment goes further, and he sees that there is no danger to his lawgiving in allowing his subjects to make public use of their reason and to publish their thoughts on a better formulation of his legislation and even their open-minded criticisms of the laws already made. Of this we have a shining example wherein no monarch is superior to him whom we honor.

But only one who is himself enlightened, is not afraid of shadows, and has a numerous and well-disciplined army to assure public peace can say: "Argue as much as you will, and about what you will, only obey!" A republic could not dare say such a thing. Here is shown a strange and unexpected trend in human affairs in which almost everything, looked at in the large, is paradoxical. A greater degree of civil freedom appears advantageous to the freedom of mind of the people, and yet it places inescapable limitations upon it; a lower degree of civil freedom, on the contrary, provides the mind with room for each man to extend himself to his full capacity. As nature has uncovered from under this hard shell the seed for which she most tenderly cares—the propensity and vocation to free thinking—this gradually works back upon the character of the people, who thereby gradually become capable of managing freedom; finally, it affects the principles of government, which finds it to its advantage to treat men, who are now more than machines, in accordance with their dignity.

NOTES

1. "Dare to know!" (Horace, *Ars poetica*).
2. It is this freedom Kant claimed later in his conflict with the censor, deferring to the censor in the "private" use of reason, i.e., in his lectures.
3. "Our age is, in especial degree, the age of criticism, and to criticism everything must submit" (*Critique of Pure Reason*, Preface to first ed. [Smith trans.]).

From Reflections on the Revolution in France

EDMUND BURKE

Edmund Burke (1729–1797) was an influential British states-man whose conservative point of view has become a standard among spokesmen of twentieth-century American conserva-tism. His writings represent something of a classical model to those who advocate moderation and balance in government and society. He is the author of A Philosophical Inquiry into the Sublime and the Beautiful, Thoughts on the Present Dis-content, On American Taxation *and* On Conciliation with the Colonies.

---

1. The Real Rights of Men

Far am I from denying in theory, full as far is my heart from withholding in practice, (if I were of power to give or to withhold,) the *real* rights of men. In denying their false claims of right, I do not mean to injure those which are real, and are such as their pretended rights would totally destroy. If civil society be made for the advantage of man, all the advantages for which it is made become his right. It is an institution of beneficence; and law itself is only be-neficence acting by a rule. Men have a right to live by that rule; they have a right to do justice, as between their fellows, whether their fellows are in public function or in ordinary occupation. They have a right to the fruits of their industry; and to the means of making their industry fruitful. They have a right to the acquisitions of their parents; to the nourishment and improvement of their offspring; to instruction in life, and to consolation in death. Whatever each man can separately do, without trespassing upon others, he has a right to do for himself; and he has a right to a fair portion of all which society, with all its combinations of skill and force, can do in his favour. In this partnership all men have equal rights; but not to equal things. He that has but five shillings in the partnership, has as good a right to it, as he that has five hundred pounds has to his larger proportion. But he has not a right to an equal dividend in the product of the joint stock; and as to the share of power, authority, and direction which each individual ought to have in the management of the state, that I must deny to be amongst the direct original rights of man in civil society; for I have in my contemplation the civil social man, and no other. It is a thing to be settled by convention.

If civil society be the offspring of convention, that convention must be its law. That convention must limit and modify all the descriptions of constitution which are formed under it. Every sort of legislative, judicial, or executory power are its creatures. They can have no being in any other state of things; and how can any man claim under the conventions of civil society, rights which do not so much as suppose its existence? rights which are absolutely repugnant to it? One of the first motives to civil society, and which becomes one of its fundamenal rules, is, *that no man should be judge in his own cause.* By this each person has at once divested himself of the first fundamental right of unconvenanted man, that is, to judge for himself, and to assert his own cause. He abdicates all right to be his own governor. He inclusively, in a great measure, abandons the right of self-defence, the first law of nature. Men cannot enjoy the rights of an uncivil and of a civil state together. That he may obtain justice, he gives up his right of determining what it is in points the most essential to him. That he may secure some liberty, he makes a surrender in trust of the whole of it.

Government is not made in virtue of natural rights, which

may and do exist in total independence of it; and exist in much greater clearness, and in a much greater degree of abstract perfection; but their abstract perfection is their practical defect. By having a right to everything they want everything. Government is a contrivance of human wisdom to provide for human *wants*. Men have a right that these wants should be provided for by this wisdom. Among these wants is to be reckoned the want, out of civil society, of a sufficient restraint upon their passions. Society requires not only that the passions of individuals should be subjected, but that even in the mass and body, as well as in the individuals, the inclinations of men should frequently be thwarted, their will controlled, and their passions brought into subjection. This can only be done *by a power out of themselves;* and not, in the exercise of its function, subject to that will and to those passions which it is its office to bridle and subdue. In this sense the restraints on men, as well as their liberties, are to be reckoned amongst their rights. But as the liberties and the restrictions vary with times and circumstances, and admit of infinite modifications, they cannot be settled upon any abstract rule; and nothing is so foolish as to discuss them upon that principle.

The moment you abate anything from the full rights of men, each to govern himself, and suffer any artificial, positive limitation upon those rights, from that moment the whole organization of government becomes a consideration of convenience. This it is which makes the constitution of a state, and the due distribution of its powers, a matter of the most delicate and complicated skill. It requires a deep knowledge of human nature and human necessities, and of the things which facilitate or obstruct the various ends, which are to be pursued by the mechanism of civil institutions. The state is to have recruits to its strength, and remedies to its distempers. What is the use of discussing a man's abstract right to food or medicine? The question is upon the method of procuring and administering them. In that deliberation I shall always advise to call in the aid of the farmer and the physician, rather than the professor of metaphysics.

The science of constructing a commonwealth, or renovating

it, or reforming it, is like every other experimental science, not to be taught *a priori*. Nor is it a short experience that can instruct us in that practical science; because the real effects of moral causes are not always immediate; but that which in the first instance is prejudicial may be excellent in its remoter operation; and its excellence may arise even from the ill effects it produces in the beginning. The reverse also happens: and very plausible schemes, with very pleasing commencements, have often shameful and lamentable conclusions. In states there are often some obscure and almost latent causes, things which appear at first view of little moment, on which a very great part of its prosperity or adversity may most essentially depend. The science of government being therefore so practical in itself, and intended for such practical purposes, a matter which requires experience, and even more experience than any person can gain in his whole life, however sagacious and observing he may be, it is with infinite caution that any man ought to venture upon pulling down an edifice, which has answered in any tolerable degree for ages the common purposes of society, or on building it up again, without having models and patterns of approved utility before his eyes.

These metaphysic rights entering into common life, like rays of light which pierce into a dense medium, are, by the laws of nature, refracted from their straight line. Indeed in the gross and complicated mass of human passions and concerns, the primitive rights of men undergo such a variety of refractions and reflections, that it becomes absurd to talk of them as if they continued in the simplicity of their original direction. The nature of man is intricate; the objects of society are of the greatest possible complexity: and therefore no simple disposition or direction of power can be suitable either to man's nature, or to the quality of his affairs. When I hear the simplicity of contrivance aimed at and boasted of in any new political constitutions, I am at no loss to decide that the artificers are grossly ignorant of their trade, or totally negligent of their duty. The simple governments are fundamentally defective, to say no worse of them. If you were to contemplate society in but one point of view, all these simple modes of polity are infinitely captivating. In effect each would answer its single end much more perfectly than the more complex is able to attain all its complex purposes. But it is better that the whole should be imperfectly and anomalously answered, than that, while some parts are provided for with great exactness, others might be totally neglected, or perhaps materially injured, by the over-care of a favourite member.

The pretended rights of these theorists are all extremes: and in proportion as they are metaphysically true, they are morally and politically false. The rights of men are in a sort of *middle*, incapable of definition, but not impossible to be discerned. The rights of men in governments are their advantages; and these are often in balances between differences of good; in compromises sometimes between good and evil, and sometimes between evil and evil. Political reason is a computing principle; adding, subtracting, multiplying, and dividing, morally and not metaphysically, or mathematically, true moral denominations.

By these theorists the right of the people is almost always sophistically confounded with their power. The body of the community, whenever it can come to act, can meet with no effectual resistance; but till power and right are the same the whole body of them has no right inconsistent with virtue, and the first of all virtues, prudence. Men have no right to what is not reasonable, and to what is not for their benefit; for though a pleasant writer said, *Liceat perire poetis*, when one of them, in cold blood, is said to have leaped into the flames of a volcanic revolution, *Ardentem frigidus Ætnam insiluit*, I consider such a frolic rather as an unjustifiable poetic licence, than as one of the franchises of Parnassus; and whether he were poet, or divine, or politician, that chose to exercise this kind of right, I think that more wise, because more charitable, thoughts would urge me rather to save the man, than to preserve his brazen slippers as the monuments of his folly.

2. SOCIETY A CONTRACT

To avoid therefore the evils of inconstancy and versatility, ten thousand times worse than those of obstinacy and the blindest prejudice, we have consecrated the state, that no man should approach to look into its defects or corruptions but with due caution; that he should never dream of beginning its reformation by its subversion; that he should approach to the faults of the state as to the wounds of a father, with pious awe and trembling solicitude. By this wise prejudice we are taught to look with horror on those children of their country, who are prompt rashly to hack that aged parent in pieces, and put him into the kettle of magicians, in hopes that by their poisonous weeds, and wild incantations, they may regenerate the paternal constitution, and renovate their father's life.

Society is indeed a contract. Subordinate contracts for objects of mere occasional interest may be dissolved at pleasure —but the state ought not to be considered as nothing better than a partnership agreement in a trade of pepper and coffee, calico or tobacco, or some other such low concern, to be taken up for a little temporary interest, and to be dissolved by the fancy of the parties. It is to be looked on with other reverence; because it is not a partnership in things subservient only to the gross animal existence of a temporary and perishable nature. It is a partnership in all science; a partnership in all art; a partnership in every virtue, and in all perfection. As the ends of such a partnership cannot be obtained in many generations, it becomes a partnership not only between those who are living, but between those who are living, those who are dead, and those who are to be born. Each contract of each particular state is but a clause in the great primæval contract of eternal society, linking the lower with the higher natures, connecting the visible and invisible world, according to a fixed compact sanctioned by the inviolable oath which holds all physical and all moral natures, each in their appointed place. This law is not subject to the will of those, who by an obligation above them, and infinitely superior, are bound to submit their will to that law. The municipal corporations of that universal kingdom are not morally at liberty at their pleasure, and on their speculations of a contingent improvement, wholly to separate and tear asunder the bands of their subordinate community, and to dissolve it into an unsocial, uncivil, unconnected chaos of elementary principles.

It is the first and supreme necessity only, a necessity that is not chosen, but chooses, a necessity paramount to deliberation, that admits no discussion, and demands no evidence, which alone can justify a resort to anarchy. This necessity is no exception to the rule; because this necessity itself is a part too of that moral and physical disposition of things, to which man must be obedient by consent or force: but if that which is only submission to necessity should be made the object of choice, the law is broken, nature is disobeyed, and the rebellious are outlawed, cast forth, and exiled, from this world of reason, and order, and peace, and virtue, and fruitful penitence, into the antagonist world of madness, discord, vice, confusion, and unavailing sorrow.

3. CONSERVATIVE REFORM

At once to preserve and to reform is quite another thing. When the useful parts of an old establishment are kept, and what is superadded is to be fitted to what is retained, a vigorous mind, steady, persevering attention, various powers of comparison and combination, and the resources of an understanding fruitful in expeditions, are to be exercised; they are to be exercised in a continued conflict with the combined force of opposite vices, with the obstinacy that rejects all improvement, and the levity that is fatigued and disgusted with everything of which it is in possession. But you may object—"A process of this kind is slow. It is not fit for an assembly, which glories in performing in a few months the work of ages. Such a mode of reforming, possibly, might take up many years." Without question it might; and it ought. It is one of the excellencies of a method in which time is amongst the assistants, that its operation is slow, and in some cases almost imperceptible. If circumspection and caution are a part of wisdom, when we work only upon inanimate matter, surely they become a part of duty too, when the subject of our demolition and construction is not brick and timber, but sentient beings, by the sudden alteration of whose state, condition, and habits, multitudes may be rendered miserable. But it seems as if it were the prevalent opinion in Paris, that an unfeeling heart, and an undoubting confidence, are the sole

qualifications for a perfect legislator. Far different are my
ideas of that high office. The true lawgiver ought to have a
heart full of sensibility. He ought to love and respect his
kind, and to fear himself. It may be allowed to his tempera-
ment to catch his ultimate object with an intuitive glance;
but his movements towards it ought to be deliberate. Political
arrangement, as it is a work for social ends, is to be only
wrought by social means. There mind must conspire with
mind. Time is required to produce that union of minds which
alone can produce all the good we aim at. Our patience will
achieve more than our force. If I might venture to appeal
to what is so much out of fashion in Paris, I mean to experience, I should tell you, that in my course I have known, and,
according to my measure, have co-operated with great men;
and I have never yet seen any play which has not been mended
by the observations of those who were much inferior in
understanding to the person who took the lead in the business.
By a slow but well-sustained progress, the effect of each step
is watched; the good or ill success of the first gives light to
us in the second; and so, from light to light, we are conducted
with safety through the whole series. We see that the parts of
the system do not clash. The evils latent in the most promising
contrivances are provided for as they arise. One advantage is
as little as possible sacrificed to another. We compensate, we
reconcile, we balance. We are enabled to unite into a consistent whole the various anomalies and contending principles
that are found in the minds and affairs of men. From hence
arises, not an excellence in simplicity, but one far superior,
an excellence in composition. Where the great interests of
mankind are concerned through a long succession of generations, that succession ought to be admitted into some share in
the councils which are so deeply to affect them. If justice
requires this, the work itself requires the aid of more minds
than one age can furnish. It is from this view of things that
the best legislators have been often satisfied with the establishment of some sure, solid, and ruling principle in government;
a power like that which some of the philosophers have called
a plastic nature; and having fixed the principle, they have
left it afterwards to its own operation.

To proceed in this manner, that is, to proceed with a presiding principle, and a prolific energy, is with me the criterion of profound wisdom. What your politicians think the marks of a bold, hardy genius, are only proofs of a deplorable want of ability. By their violent haste and their defiance of the process of nature, they are delivered over blindly to every projector and adventurer, to every alchymist and empiric. They despair of turning to account anything that is common. Diet is nothing in their system of remedy. The worst of it is, that this their despair of curing common distempers by regular methods, arises not only from defect of comprehension, but, I fear, from some malignity of disposition. Your legislators seem to have taken their opinions of all professions, ranks, and offices, from the declamations and buffooneries of satirists; who would themselves be astonished if they were held to the letter of their own descriptions. By listening only to these, your leaders regard all things only on the side of their vices and faults, and view those vices and faults under every colour of exaggeration. It is undoubtedly true, though it may seem paradoxical; but in general, those who are habitually employed in finding and displaying faults, are unqualified for the work of reformation: because their minds are not only unfurnished with patterns of the fair and good, but by habit they come to take no delight in the contemplation of those things. By hating vices too much, they come to love men too little. It is therefore not wonderful, that they should be indisposed and unable to serve them. From hence arises the complexional disposition of some of your guides to pull everything in pieces. At this malicious game they display the whole of their *quadrimanous* activity. As to the rest, the paradoxes of eloquent writers, brought forth purely as a sport of fancy, to try their talents, to rouse attention and excite surprise, are taken up by these gentlemen, not in the spirit of the original authors, as means of cultivating their taste and improving their style. These paradoxes become with them serious grounds of action, upon which they proceed in regulating the most important concerns of the state. Cicero ludicrously describes Cato as endeavouring to act, in the commonwealth, upon the school paradoxes, which exercised the wits of the junior students in the Stoic philosophy. If this was true of Cato, these gentlemen copy after him in the manner of some persons who lived about his time—*pede nudo Catonem*. Mr. Hume told me that he had from Rousseau himself the secret of his principles of composition. That acute though eccentric observer had perceived, that to strike and interest the public, the marvellous must be produced; that the marvellous of the heathen mythology had long since lost its effects; that giants, magicians, fairies, and heroes of romance which succeeded, had exhausted the portion of credulity which belonged to their age; that now nothing was left to the writer but that species of the marvellous which might still be produced, and with as great an effect as ever, though in another way; that is, the marvellous in life, in manners, in characters, and in extraordinary situations, giving rise to new and unlooked-for strokes in politics and morals. I believe, that were Rousseau alive, and in one of his lucid intervals, he would be shocked at the practical phrensy of his scholars, who in their paradoxes are servile imitators, and even in their incredulity discover an implicit faith.

4. TRUE LIBERTY

The effects of the incapacity shown by the popular leaders in all the great members of the commonwealth are to be covered with the "all-atoning name" of liberty. In some people I see great liberty indeed; in many, if not in the most, an oppressive, degrading servitude. But what is liberty without wisdom, and without virtue? It is the greatest of all possible evils; for it is folly, vice, and madness, without tuition or restraint. Those who know what virtuous liberty is, cannot bear to see it disgraced by incapable heads, on account of their having high-sounding words in their mouths. Grand, swelling sentiments of liberty I am sure I do not despise. They warm the heart; they enlarge and liberalize our minds; they animate our courage in a time of conflict. Old as I am, I read the fine raptures of Lucan and Corneille with pleasure. Neither do I wholly condemn the little arts and devices of popularity. They facilitate the carrying of many points of moment; they keep the people together; they refresh the mind in its exertions; and they diffuse occasional gaiety over the severe brow of moral freedom. Every politician ought to sacrifice to the graces; and to join compliance with reason. But in such an undertaking as that in France, all these subsidiary sentiments and artifices are of little avail. To make a government requires no great prudence. Settle the seat of power; teach obedience: and the work is done. To give freedom is still more easy. It is not necessary to guide; it only requires to let go the rein. But to form a *free government;* that is, to temper together these opposite elements of liberty and restraint in one consistent work, requires much thought, deep reflection, a sagacious, powerful, and combining mind. This I do not find in those who take the lead in the National Assembly. Perhaps they are not so miserably deficient as they appear. I rather believe it. It would put them below the common level of human understanding. But when the leaders choose to make themselves bidders at an auction of popularity, their talents, in the construction of the state, will be of no service. They will become flatterers instead of legislators; the instruments, not the guides, of the people. If any of them should happen to propose a scheme of liberty, soberly limited, and defined with proper qualifications, he will be immediately outbid by his competitors, who will produce something more splendidly popular. Suspicions will be raised of his fidelity to his cause. Moderation will be stigmatized as the virtue of cowards; and compromise as the prudence of traitors; until, in hopes of preserving the credit which may enable him to temper, and moderate, on some occasions, the popular leader is obliged to become active in propagating doctrines, and establishing powers, that will afterwards defeat any sober purpose at which he ultimately might have aimed.

But am I so unreasonable as to see nothing at all that deserves commendation in the indefatigable labours of this Assembly? I do not deny that, among an infinite number of acts of violence and folly, some good may have been done. They who destroy everything certainly will remove some grievance. They who make everything new, have a chance that they may establish something beneficial. To give them credit for what they have done in virtue of the authority they have usurped, or which can excuse them in the crimes by which that authority has been acquired, it must appear, that the same things could not have been accomplished without producing such a revolution. Most assuredly they might; because almost every one of the regulations made by them, which is not very equivocal, was either in the cession of the king, voluntarily made at the meeting of the states, or in the concurrent instructions to the orders. Some usages have been abolished on just grounds; but they were such, that if they had stood as they were to all eternity, they would little detract from the happiness and prosperity of any state. The improvements of the National Assembly are superficial, their errors fundamental.

Whatever they are, I wish my countrymen rather to recommend to our neighbours the example of the British constitution, than to take models from them for the improvement of our own. In the former they have got an invaluable treasure. They are not, I think, without some causes of apprehension and complaint; but these they do not owe to their constitution, but to their own conduct. I think our happy situation owing to our constitution; but owing to the whole of it, and not to any part singly; owing in a great measure to what we have left standing in our several reviews and reformations, as well as to what we have altered or superadded. Our people, will find employment enough for a truly patriotic, free, and independent spirit, in guarding what they possess from violation. I would not exclude alteration neither; but even when I changed, it should be to preserve. I should be led to my remedy by a great grievance. In what I did, I should follow the example of our ancestors. I would make the reparation as nearly as possible in the style of the building. A politic caution, a guarded circumspection, a moral rather than a complexional timidity, were among the ruling principles of our forefathers in their most decided conduct. Not being illuminated with the light of which the gentlemen of France tell us they have got so abundant a share, they acted under a strong impression of the ignorance and fallibility of mankind. He that had made them thus fallible, rewarded them for having in their conduct attended to their nature. Let us imitate their caution, if we wish to deserve their fortune, or to retain their bequests. Let us add, if we please, but let us preserve what they have left: and standing on the firm ground of the British constitution, let us be satisfied to admire, rather than attempt to follow in their desperate flights, the aëronauts of France.

I have told you candidly my sentiments. I think they are not likely to alter yours. I do not know that they ought. You are young; you cannot guide, but must follow the fortune of your country. But, hereafter they may be of some use to you, in some future form which your commonwealth may take. In the present it can hardly remain; but before its final settlement it may be obliged to pass, as one of our poets says, "through great varieties of untried being," and in all its transmigrations to be purified by fire and blood.

I have little to recommend my opinions but long observation and much impartiality. They come from one who has been no tool of power, no flatterer of greatness; and who in his last acts does not wish to belie the tenour of his life. They come from one, almost the whole of whose public exertion has been a struggle for the liberty of others; from one in whose breast no anger durable or vehement has ever been kindled, but by what he considered as tyranny; and who snatches from his share in the endeavours which are used by good men to discredit opulent oppression, the hours he has employed on your affairs; and who in so doing persuades himself he has not departed from his usual office; they come from one who desires honours, distinctions, and emoluments, but little; and who expects them not at all; who has no contempt for fame, and no fear of obloquy; who shuns contention, though he will hazard an opinion; from one who wishes to preserve consistency, but who would preserve consistency by varying his means to secure the unity of his end; and, when the equipoise of the vessel in which he sails may be endangered by overloading it upon one side, is desirous of carrying the small weight of his reasons to that which may preserve its equipoise.

From On Liberty

JOHN STUART MILL

*John Stuart Mill (1806–1873) was one of the leading think-
ers in England during the nineteenth century. Highly influential and varied in his interests and abilities, he can be regarded as an outstanding political and social philosopher, an
economist, a social reformer or a brilliant man of letters. He
was a proponent of utilitarianism and political freedom and
the author of* A System of Logic, Utilitarianism *and* Autobiography.

T HE subject of this Essay is not the so-called Liberty of
the Will, so unfortunately opposed to the misnamed
doctrine of Philosophical Necessity; but Civil, or Social Liberty: the nature and limits of the power which can be legiti-
mately exercised by society over the individual. A question
seldom stated, and hardly ever discussed, in general terms,
but which profoundly influences the practical controversies of
the age by its latent presence, and is likely soon to make itself
recognized as the vital question of the future. It is so far
from being new, that, in a certain sense, it has divided mankind, almost from the remotest ages; but in the stage of progress into which the more civilized portions of the species have
now entered, it presents itself under new conditions, and requires a different and more fundamental treatment.

The struggle between Liberty and Authority is the most conspicuous feature in the portions of history with which we are earliest familiar, particularly in that of Greece, Rome, and England. But in old times this contest was between subjects, or some classes of subjects, and the Government. By liberty, was meant protection against the tyranny of the political rulers. The rulers were conceived (except in some of the popular governments of Greece) as in a necessarily antagonistic position to the people whom they ruled. They consisted of a governing One, or a governing tribe or caste, who derived their authority from inheritance or conquest, who, at all events, did not hold it at the pleasure of the governed, and whose supremacy men did not venture, perhaps did not desire, to contest, whatever precautions might be taken against its oppressive exercise. Their power was regarded as necessary, but also as highly dangerous; as a weapon which they would attempt to use against their subjects, no less than against external enemies. To prevent the weaker members of the community from being preyed upon by innumerable vultures, it was needful that there should be an animal of prey stronger than the rest, commissioned to keep them down. But as the king of the vultures would be no less bent upon preying on the flock than any of the minor harpies, it was indispensable to be in a perpetual attitude of defence against his beak and claws. The aim, therefore, of patriots was to set limits to the power which the ruler should be suffered to exercise over the community; and this limitation was what they meant by liberty. It was attempted in two ways. First, by obtaining a recognition of certain immunities, called political liberties or rights, which it was to be regarded as a breach of duty in the ruler to infringe, and which, if he did infringe, specific resistance, or general rebellion, was held to be justifiable. A second, and generally a later expedient, was the establishment of constitutional checks, by which the consent of the community, or of a body of some sort, supposed to represent its interests, was made a necessary condition to some of the more important acts of the governing power. To the first of these models of limitation, the ruling power, in most European countries, was compelled, more or less, to submit. It was not so with the second; and, to attain this, or when already in some degree possessed, to attain it more completely, became everywhere the principle object of the lovers of liberty. And so long as mankind were content to combat one enemy by another, and to be ruled by a master, on condition of being guaranteed more or less efficaciously against his tyranny, they did not carry their aspirations beyond this point.

A time, however, came, in the progress of human affairs, when men ceased to think it a necessity of nature that their governors should be an independent power, opposed in interest to themselves. It appeared to them much better that the various magistrates of the State should be their tenants or delegates, revocable at their pleasure. In that way alone, it seemed, could they have complete security that the powers of government would never be abused to their disadvantage. By degrees this new demand for elective and temporary rulers became the prominent object of the exertions of the popular party, wherever any such party existed; and superseded, to a considerable extent, the previous efforts to limit the power of rulers. As the struggle proceeded for making the ruling power emanate from the periodical choice of the ruled, some persons began to think that too much importance had been attached to the limitation of the power itself. *That* (it might seem) was a resource against rulers whose interests were habitually opposed to those of the people. What was now wanted was, that the rulers should be identified with the people; that their interest and will should be the interest and will of the nation. The nation did not need to be protected against its own will. There was no fear of its tyrannizing over itself. Let the rulers be effectually responsible to it, promptly removable by it, and it could afford to trust them with power of which it could itself dictate the use to be made. Their power was but the nation's own power, concentrated, and in a form convenient for exercise. This mode of thought, or rather perhaps of feeling, was common among the last generation of European liberalism, in the Continental section of which it still apparently predominates. Those who admit any limit to what a government may do, except in the case of such governments as they think ought not to exist, stand out as brilliant exceptions among the political thinkers of the Continent. A similar tone of sentiment might by this time have been prevalent in our own country, if the circumstances which for a time encouraged it, had continued unaltered.

But, in political and philosophical theories, as well as in persons, success discloses faults and infirmities which failure might have concealed from observation. The notion, that the people have no need to limit their power over themselves, might seem axiomatic, when popular government was a thing only dreamed about, or read of as having existed at some distant period of the past. Neither was that notion necessarily disturbed by such temporary aberrations as those of the French Revolution, the worst of which were the work of an usurping few, and which, in any case, belonged, not to the permanent working of popular institutions, but to a sudden and convulsive outbreak against monarchical and aristocratic despotism. In time, however, a democratic republic came to occupy a large portion of the earth's surface, and made itself felt as one of the most powerful members of the community of nations; and elective and responsible government became subject to the observations and criticisms which wait upon a great existing fact. It was now perceived that such phrases as 'self-government,' and 'the power of the people over themselves,' do not express the true state of the case. The 'people' who exercise the power are not always the same people with those over whom it is exercised; and the 'self-government' spoken of is not the government of each by himself, but of each by all the rest. The will of the people, moreover, practically means the will of the most numerous or the most active *part* of the people; the majority, or those who succeed in making themselves accepted as the majority; the people, consequently, *may* desire to oppress a part of their number; and precautions are as much needed against this as against any other abuse of power. The limitation, therefore, of the power of government over individuals loses none of its importance when the holders of power are regularly accountable to the community, that is, to the strongest party therein. This view of things, recommending itself equally to the intelligence of thinkers and to the inclination of those important classes in European society to whose real or supposed interests democracy is adverse, has had no difficulty in establishing itself; and in political speculations 'the tyranny of the majority' is now generally included among the evils against which society requires to be on its guard.

Like other tyrannies, the tyranny of the majority was at first, and is still vulgarly, held in dread, chiefly as operating through the acts of the public authorities. But reflecting persons perceived that when society is itself the tyrant—society collectively, over the separate individuals who compose it—its means of tyrannizing are not restricted to the acts which it may do by the hands of its political functionaries. Society can and does execute its own mandates: and if it issues wrong mandates instead of right, or any mandates at all in things with which it ought not to meddle, it practises a social tyranny more formidable than many kinds of political oppression, since, though not usually upheld by such extreme penalties, it leaves fewer means of escape, penetrating much more deeply into the details of life, and enslaving the soul itself. Protection, therefore, against the tyranny of the magistrate is not enough: there needs protection also against the tyranny of the prevailing opinion and feeling; against the tendency of society to impose, by other means than civil penalties, its own ideas and practices as rules of conduct on those who dissent from them; to fetter the development, and if possible, prevent the formation, of any individuality not in harmony with its ways, and compel all characters to fashion themselves upon the model of its own. There is a limit to the legitimate interference of collective opinion with individual independence: and to find that limit, and maintain it against encroachment, is as indispensable to a good condition of human affairs, as protection against political despotism.

But though this proposition is not likely to be contested in general terms, the practical question, where to place the limit—how to make the fitting adjustment between individual independence and social control—is a subject on which nearly everything remains to be done. All that makes existence valuable to any one, depends on the enforcement of restraints upon the actions of other people. Some rules of conduct, therefore, must be imposed, by law in the first place, and by opinion on many things while are not fit subjects for the operation of law. What these rules should be, is the principal question in human affairs; but if we except a few of the most obvious cases, it is one of those which least progress has been made in resolving. No two ages, and scarcely any two countries, have decided it alike; and the decision of one age or country is a wonder to another. Yet the people of any given age and country no more suspect any difficulty in it, than if it were a subject on which mankind had always been agreed. The rules which obtain among themselves appear to them self-evident and self-justifying. This all but universal illusion is one of the examples of the magical influence of custom, which is not only, as the proverb says, a second nature, but is continually mistaken for the first. The effect of custom, in preventing any misgiving respecting the rules of conduct which mankind impose on one another, is all the more complete because the subject is one on which it is not generally considered necessary that reasons should be given, either by one person to others, or by each to himself. People are accustomed to believe, and have been encouraged in the belief by some who aspire to the character of philosophers, that their feelings, on subjects of this nature, are better than reasons, and render reasons unnecessary. The practical principle which guides them to their opinions on the regulation of human conduct, is the feeling in each person's mind that everybody should be required to act as he, and those with whom he sympathizes, would like them to act. No one, indeed, acknowledges to himself that his standard of judgement is his own liking; but an opinion on a point of conduct, not supported by reasons, can only count as one person's preference; and if the reasons, when given, are a mere appeal to a similar preference felt by other people, it is still only many people's liking instead of one. To an ordinary man, however, his own preference, thus supported, is not only a perfectly satisfactory reason, but the only one he generally has for any of his notions of morality, taste, or propriety, which are not expressly written in his religious creed; and his chief guide in the interpretation even of that. Men's opinions, accordingly, on what is laudable or blameable, are affected by all the multifarious causes which influence their wishes in regard to the conduct of others, and which are as numerous as those which determine their wishes on any other subject. Sometimes their reason—at other times their prejudices or superstitions: often their social affections, not seldom their antisocial ones, their envy or jealousy, their arrogance or contemptuousness: but most commonly, their desires or fears for themselves—their legitimate or illigitimate self-interest. Wherever there is an ascendant class, a large portion of the morality of the country emanates from its class interests, and its feelings of class superiority. The morality between Spartans and Helots,[1] between planters and negroes, between princes and subjects, between nobles and roturiers, between men and women, has been for the most part the creation of these class interests and feelings: and the sentiments thus generated, react in turn upon the moral feelings of the members of the ascendant class, in their relations among themselves. Where, on the other hand, a class, formerly ascendant, has lost its ascendancy, or where its ascendancy is unpopular, the prevailing moral sentiments frequently bear the impress of an impatient dislike of superiority. Another grand determining principle of the rules of conduct, both in act and forbearance, which have been enforced by law or opinion, has been the servility of mankind towards the supposed preferences or aversions of their temporal masters, or of their gods. This servility, though essentially selfish, is not hypocrisy; it gives rise to perfectly genuine sentiments of abhorrence; it made men burn magicians and heretics. Among so many baser influences, the general and obvious interests of society have of course had a share, and a large one, in the direction of the moral sentiments: less, however, as a matter of reason, and on their own account, than as a consequence of the sympathies and antipathies which grew out of them: and sympathies and antipathies which had little or nothing to do with the interests of society, have made themselves felt in the establishment of moralities with quite as great force.

The likings and dislikings of society, or of some powerful

portion of it, are thus the main thing which has practically determined the rules laid down for general observance, under the penalties of law or opinion. And in general, those who have been in advance of society in thought and feeling, have left this condition of things unassailed in principle, however, they may have come into conflict with it in some of its details. They have occupied themselves rather in inquiring what things society ought to like or dislike, than in questioning whether its likings or dislikings should be a law to individuals. They preferred endeavouring to alter the feelings of mankind on the particular points on which they were themselves heretical, rather than make common cause in defence of freedom, with heretics generally. The only case in which the higher ground has been taken on principle and maintained with consistency, by any but an individual here and there, is that of religious belief: a case instructive in many ways, and not least so as forming a most striking instance of the fallibility of what is called the moral sense: for the *odium theologicum,*[2] in a sincere bigot, is one of the most unequivocal cases of moral feeling. Those who first broke the yoke of what called itself the Universal Church, were in general as little willing to permit difference of religious opinion as that church itself. But when the heat of the conflict was over, without giving a complete victory to any party, and each church or sect was reduced to limit its hopes to retaining possession of the ground it already occupied; minorities, seeing that they had no chance of becoming majorities, were under the necessity of pleading to those whom they could not convert, for permission to differ. It is accordingly on this battle-field, almost solely, that the rights of the individual against society have been asserted on broad grounds of principle, and the claim of society to exercise authority over dissentients, openly controverted. The great writers to whom the world owes what religious liberty it possesses, have mostly asserted freedom of conscience as an indefeasible right, and denied absolutely that a human being is accountable to others for his religious belief. Yet so natural to mankind is intolerance in whatever they really care about, that religious freedom has hardly anywhere been practically realized, except where religious indifference, which dislikes to have its peace disturbed by theological quarrels, has added its weight to the scale. In the minds of almost all religious persons, even in the most tolerant countries, the duty of toleration is admitted with tacit reserves. One person will bear with dissent in matters of church government, but not of dogma; another can tolerate everybody, short of a Papist or a Unitarian;[3] another, every one who believes in religion; a few extend their charity a little further, but stop at the belief in a God and in a future state. Wherever the sentiment of the majority is still genuine and intense, it is found to have abated little of its claim to be obeyed.

In England, from the peculiar circumstances of our political history, though the yoke of opinion is perhaps heavier, that of law is lighter, than in most other countries of Europe; and there is considerable jealousy of direct interference, by the legislative or the executive power, with private conduct; not so much from any just regard for the independence of the individual, as from the still subsisting habit of looking on the government as representing an opposite interest to the public. The majority have not yet learnt to feel the power of the government their power, or its opinions their opinions. When they do so, individual liberty will probably be as much exposed to invasion from the government, as it already is from public opinion. But, as yet, there is a considerable amount of feeling ready to be called forth against any attempt of the law to control individuals in things in which they have not hitherto been accustomed to be controlled by it; and this with very little discrimination as to whether the matter is, or is not, within the legitimate sphere of legal control; insomuch that the feeling, highly salutary on the whole, is perhaps quite as often misplaced as well grounded in the particular instances of its application. There is, in fact, no recognized principle by which the propriety or impropriety of government interference is customarily tested. People decide according to their personal preferences. Some, whenever they see any good to be done, or evil to be remedied, would willingly instigate the government to undertake the business; while others prefer to bear almost any amount of social evil, rather than add one to the departments of human interests amenable to governmental control. And men range themselves on one or the other side in any particular case, according to this general direction of their sentiments; or according to the degree of interest which they feel in the particular thing which it is proposed that the government should do, or according to the brief they entertain that the government would, or would not, do it in the manner they prefer; but very rarely on account of any opinion to which they consistently adhere, as to what things are fit to be done by a government. And it seems to me that in consequence of this absence of rule or principle, one side is at present as often wrong as the other; the interference of government is, with about equal frequency, improperly invoked and improperly condemned.

The object of this Essay is to assert one very simple principle, as entitled to govern absolutely the dealings of society with the individual in the way of compulsion and control, whether the means used be physical force in the form of legal penalties, or the moral coercion of public opinion. That principle is, that the sole end for which mankind are warranted, individually or collectively, in interfering with the liberty of action of any of their number, is self-protection. That the only purpose for which power can be rightfully exercised over any member of a civilized community, against his will, is to prevent harm to others. His own good, either physical or moral, is not a sufficient warrant. He cannot rightfully be compelled to do or forbear because it will be better for him to do so, because it will make him happier, because, in the opinions of others, to do so would be wise, or even right. These are good reasons for remonstrating with him, or reasoning with him, or persuading him, or entreating him, but not for compelling him, or visiting him with any evil in case he do otherwise. To justify that, the conduct from which it is desired to deter him, must be calculated to produce evil to some one else. The only part of the conduct of any one, for which he is amenable to society, is that which concerns others. In the part which merely concerns himself, its independence is, of right, absolute. Over himself, over his own body and mind, the individual is sovereign.

It is, perhaps, hardly necessary to say that this doctrine

is meant to apply only to human beings in the maturity of their faculties. We are not speaking of children, or of young persons below the age which the law may fix as that of manhood or womanhood. Those who are still in a state to require being taken care of by others, must be protected against their own actions as well as against external injury. For the same reason, we may leave out of consideration those backward states of society in which the race itself may be considered as in its nonage. The early difficulties in the way of spontaneous progress are so great, that there is seldom any choice of means for overcoming them; and a ruler full of the spirit of improvement is warranted in the use of any expedients that will attain an end, perhaps otherwise unattainable. Despotism is a legitimate mode of government in dealing with barbarians, provided the end be their improvement, and the means justified by actually effecting that end. Liberty, as a principle, has no application to any state of things anterior to the time when mankind have become capable of being improved by free and equal discussion. Until then, there is nothing for them but implicit obedience to an Akbar [4] or a Charlemagne,[5] if they are so fortunate as to find one. But as soon as mankind have attained the capacity of being guided to their own improvement by conviction or persuasion (a period long since reached in all nations with whom we need here concern ourselves), compulsion, either in the direct form or in that of pains and penalties for non-compliance, is no longer admissible as a means to their own good, and justifiable only for the security of others.

It is proper to state that I forgo any advantage which could be derived to my argument from the idea of abstract right, as a thing independent of utility. I regard utility as the ultimate appeal on all ethical questions; but it must be utility in the largest sense, grounded on the permanent interests of man as a progressive being. Those interests, I contend, authorize the subjection of individual spontaneity to external control, only in respect to those actions of each, which concern the interest of other people. If any one does an act hurtful to others, there is a prima facie case for punishing him, by law, or, where legal penalties are not safely applicable, by general disapprobation. There are also many positive acts for the benefit of others, which he may rightfully be compelled to perform; such as, to give evidence in a court of justice; to bear his fair share in the common defence, or in any other joint work necessary to the interest of the society of which of which he enjoys the protection; and to perform certain acts of individual beneficence, such as saving a fellow creature's life, or interposing to protect the defenceless against ill-usage, things which whenever it is obviously a man's duty to do, he may rightfully be made responsible to society for not doing. A person may cause evil to others not only by his actions but by his inaction, and in either case he is justly accountable to them for the injury. The latter case, it is true, requires a much more cautious exercise of compulsion than the former. To make any one answerable for doing evil to others, is the rule; to make him answerable for not preventing evil, is, comparatively speaking, the exception. Yet there are many cases clear enough and grave enough to justify that exception. In all things which regard the external relations of the individual, he is *de jure*[6] amenable to those whose interests are concerned, and if need be, to society as their protector. There are often good reasons for not holding him to the responsibility; but these reasons must arise from the special expediencies of the case: either because it is a kind of case in which he is on the whole likely to act better, when left to his own discretion, than when controlled in any way in which society have it in their power to control him; or because the attempt to exercise control would produce other evils, greater than those which it would prevent. When such reasons as these preclude the enforcement of responsibility, the conscience of the agent himself should step into the vacant judgement-seat, and protect those interests of others which have no external protection; judging himself all the more rigidly, because the case does not admit of his being made accountable to the judgement of his fellow creatures.

But there is a sphere of action in which society, as distinguished from the individual, has, if any, only an indirect interest; comprehending all that portion of a person's life and conduct which affects only himself, or if it also affects others, only with their free, voluntary, and undeceived consent and participation. When I say only himself, I mean directly, and in the first instance: for whatever affects himself, may affect others through himself; and the objection which may be grounded on this contingency will receive consideration in the sequel. This, then, is the appropriate region of human liberty. It comprises, first, the inward domain of consciousness; demanding liberty of conscience, in the most comprehensive sense; liberty of thought and feeling; absolute freedom of opinion and sentiment on all subjects, practical or speculative, scientific, moral, or theological. The liberty of expressing and publishing opinions may seem to fall under a different principle, since it belongs to that part of the conduct of an individual which concerns other people; but, being almost of as much importance as the liberty of thought itself, and resting in great part on the same reasons, is practically inseparable from it. Secondly, the principle requires liberty of tastes and pursuits; of framing the plan of our life to suit our own character; of doing as we like, subject to such consequences as may follow: without impediment from our fellow creatures, so long as what we do does not harm them, even though they should think our conduct foolish, perverse, or wrong. Thirdly, from this liberty of each individual, follows the liberty, within the same limits, of combination among individuals; freedom to unite, for any purpose not involving harm to others: the persons combining being supposed to be of full age, and not forced or deceived.

No society in which these liberties are not, on the whole, respected, is free, whatever may be its form of government; and none is completely free in which they do not exist absolute and unqualified. The only freedom which deserves the name, is that of pursuing our own good in our own way, so long as we do not attempt to deprive others of theirs, or impede their efforts to obtain it. Each is the proper guardian of his own health, whether bodily, or mental and spiritual. Mankind are greater gainers by suffering each other to live as seems good to themselves, than by compelling each to live as seems good to the rest.

Though this doctrine is anything but new, and, to some

persons, may have the air of a truism, there is no doctrine which stands more directly opposed to the general tendency of existing opinion and practice. Society has expended fully as much effort in the attempt (according to its lights) to compel people to conform to its notions of personal, as of social excellence. The ancient commonwealths thought themselves entitled to practise, and the ancient philosophers countenanced, the regulation of every part of private conduct by public authority, on the ground that the State had a deep interest in the whole bodily and mental discipline of every one of its citizens; a mode of thinking which may have been admissible in small republics surrounded by powerful enemies, in constant peril of being subverted by foreign attack or internal commotion, and to which even a short interval of relaxed energy and self-command might so easily be fatal, that they could not afford to wait for the salutary permanent effects of freedom. In the modern world, the greater size of political communities, and, above all, the separation between spiritual and temporal authority (which placed the direction of men's consciences in other hands than those which controlled their worldly affairs), prevented so great an interference by law in the details of private life; but the engines of moral repression have been wielded more strenuously against divergence from the reigning opinion in self-regarding, than even in social matters; religion, the most powerful of the elements which have entered into the formation of moral feeling, having almost always been governed either by the ambition of a hierarchy, seeking control over every department of human conduct, or by the spirit of Puritanism. And some of those modern reformers who have placed themselves in strongest opposition to the religions of the past, have been no way behind either churches or sects in their assertion of the right of spiritual domination: M. Comte,[7] in particular, whose social system, as unfolded in his *Système de politique positive*, aims at establishing (though by moral more than by legal appliances) a despotism of society over the individual, surpassing anything contemplated in the political ideal of the most rigid disciplinarian among the ancient philosophers.

Apart from the peculiar tenets of individual thinkers, there is also in the world at large an increasing inclination to stretch unduly the powers of society over the individual, both by the force of opinion and even by that of legislation: and as the tendency of all the changes taking place in the world is to strengthen society, and diminish the power of the individual, this encroachment is not one of the evils which tend spontaneously to disappear, but, on the contrary, to grow more and more formidable. The disposition of mankind, whether as rulers or as fellow citizens, to impose their own opinions and inclinations as a rule of conduct on others, is so energetically supported by some of the best and by some of the worst feelings incident to human nature, that it is hardly ever kept under restraint by anything but want of power; and as the power is not declining, but growing, unless a strong barrier of moral conviction can be raised against the mischief, we must expect, in the present circumstances of the world, to see it increase.

It will be convenient for the argument, if, instead of at once entering upon the general thesis, we confine ourselves in the first instance to a single branch of it, on which the principle here stated is, if not fully, yet to a certain point, recognized by the current opinions. This one branch is the Liberty of Thought: from which it is impossible to separate the cognate liberty of speaking and of writing. Although these liberties, to some considerable amount, form part of the political morality of all countries which profess religious toleration and free institutions, the grounds, both philosophical and practical, on which they rest, are perhaps not so familiar to the general mind, nor so thoroughly appreciated by many even of the leaders of opinion, as might have been expected. Those grounds, when rightly understood, are of much wider application than to only one division of the subject, and a thorough consideration of this part of the question will be found the best introduction to the remainder. Those to whom nothing which I am about to say will be new, may therefore, I hope, excuse me, if on a subject which for now three centuries has been so often discussed, I venture on one discussion more.

NOTES

1. The Helots were serfs, or slaves, attached to the landed estates in ancient Sparta; they could not be sold, and could be freed only by the state.
2. The enmity peculiar to contending theologians.
3. *Unitarian:* a member of a religious body that affirms the single personality of the Godhead, as opposed to believers in the Trinity.
4. Akbar Khan, the great Mogul emperor of Hindustan, who reigned from 1556 to 1605.
5. Charlemagne (742–814), king of the Franks (768), emperor of the West (800).
6. 'by (lawful) right.'
7. Auguste Comte (1798–1857) was the chief exponent of the positivist philosophy, which excludes metaphysics and religion, and substitutes the religion of humanity and sociological ethics. His *Système de politique positive* (1851–54) attempts to frame a positivist religion, on the pattern of Roman Catholicism, with sacraments, prayers, etc.

From Democracy

THOMAS CARLYLE

Thomas Carlyle (1795–1881) is ranked among the leading writers of the nineteenth century. He was born in Scotland and prepared for the ministry there. But instead of a preacher he became an essayist and historian. He wrote Sartor Resartus; The French Revolution; *and* On Heroes, Hero-Worship, and the Heroic in History, *all of which were controversial books during his lifetime and remain controversial today.*

LIBERTY? The true liberty of a man, you would say, consisted in his finding out, or being forced to find out the right path, and to walk thereon. To learn, or to be taught, what work he actually was able for; and then by permission, persuasion, and even compulsion, to set about doing of the same! That is his true blessedness, honor, "liberty" and maximum of wellbeing; if liberty be not that, I for one have small care about liberty. You do not allow a palpable madman to leap over precipices; you violate his liberty, you that are wise; and keep him, were it in strait-waistcoats, away from the precipices! Every stupid, every cowardly and foolish man is but a less palpable madman: his true liberty were that a wiser man, that any and every wiser man, could, by brass collars, or in whatever milder or sharper way, lay hold of him when he was going wrong, and order and compel him to go a little righter. O, if thou really art my *Senior*, Seigneur, my *Elder*, Presbyter or Priest,—if thou art in very deed my *Wiser*, may a beneficent instinct lead and impel thee to "conquer" me, to command me! If thou do know better than I what is good and right, I conjure thee in the name of God, force me to do it; were it by never such brass collars, whips and handcuffs, leave me not to walk over precipices! That I have been called, by all the Newspapers, a "free man" will avail me little, if my pilgrimage have ended in death and wreck. O that the Newspapers had called me slave, coward, fool, or what it pleased their sweet voices to name me, and I had attained not death, but life!—Liberty requires new definitions.

A conscious abhorrence and intolerance of Folly, of Baseness, Stupidity, Poltroonery and all that brood of things, dwells deep in some men: still deeper in others an *un*conscious abhorrence and intolerance, clothed moreover by the beneficent Supreme Powers in what stout appetites, energies, egoisms so-called, are suitable to it;—these latter are your Conquerors, Romans, Normans, Russians, Indo-English; Founders of what we call Aristocracies. Which indeed have they not the most "divine right" to found;—being themselves very truly Αριστοι, BRAVEST, BEST; and conquering generally a confused rabble of WORST, or at lowest, clearly enough, of WORSE? I think their divine right, tried, with affirmatory verdict, in the greatest Law-Court known to me, was good! A class of men who are dreadfully exclaimed against by Dryasdust; of whom nevertheless beneficent Nature has oftentimes had need; and may, alas, again have need.

When, across the hundredfold poor scepticisms, trivialisms and constitutional cobwebberies of Dryasdust, you catch any glimpse of a William the Conqueror, a Tancred of Hauteville [1] or suchlike,—do you not discern veritably some rude outline of a true God-made King; whom not the Champion of England cased in tin, but all Nature and the Universe were calling to the throne? It is absolutely necessary that he get thither. Nature does not mean her poor Saxon children to perish, of obesity, stupor or other malady, as yet: a stern Ruler and Line of Rulers therefore is called in,—a stern but most beneficent *perpetual House-Surgeon* is by Nature herself called in, and even the appropriate *fees* are provided for him! Dryasdust talks lamentably about Hereward [2] and the Fen Counties; fate of Earl Waltheof; Yorkshire and the North reduced to ashes: all which is undoubtedly lamentable.[3] But even Dryasdust apprises me of one fact: "A child, in this William's reign, might have carried a purse of gold from end to end of England." My erudite friend, it is a fact which outweights a thousand! Sweep away thy constitutional, sentimental and other cobwebberies; look eye to eye, if thou still have any eye, in the face of this big burly William Bastard: thou wilt see a fellow of most flashing discernment, of most strong lion-heart;—in whom, as it were, within a frame of oak and iron, the gods have planted the soul of "a man of genius"! Dost thou call that nothing? I call it an immense thing!—Rage enough was in this Willelmus Conquæstor, rage enough for his occasions;—and yet the essential element of him, as of all such men, is not scorching *fire,* but shining illuminative *light.* Fire and light are strangely interchangeable; nay, at bottom, I have found them different forms of the same most godlike "elementary substance" in our world: a thing worth stating in these days. The essential element of this Conquæstor is, first of all, the most sun-eyed perception of what *is* really what on this God's Earth;—which, thou wilt find, does mean at bottom "Justice," and "Virtues" not a few: *Conformity* to what the Maker has seen good to make; that, I suppose, will mean Justice and a Virtue or two?—

Dost thou think Willelmus Conquæstor would have tolerated ten years' jargon, one hour's jargon, on the propriety of killing Cotton-manufacturers by partridge Corn-Laws? I fancy, this was not the man to knock out of his night's-rest with nothing but a noisy bedlamism in your mouth! "Assist us still better to bush the partridges; strangle Plugson who spins the shirts?—*"Par la Splendeur de Dieu!"* ⁴—Dost thou think Willelmus Conquæstor, in this new time, with Steam-engine Captains of Industry on one hand of him, and Joe-Manton ⁵ Captains of Idleness on the other, would have doubted which *was* really the BEST; which did deserve strangling, and which not?

I have a certain indestructible regard for Willelmus Conquæstor. A resident House-Surgeon, provided by Nature for her beloved English People, and even furnished with the requisite fees, as I said; for he by no means felt himself doing Nature's work, this Willelmus, but his own work exclusively! And his own work withal it was; informed *"par la Splendeur de Dieu."*—I say, it is necessary to get the work out of such a man, however harsh that be! When a world, not yet doomed for death, is rushing down to ever-deeper Baseness and Confusion, it is a dire necessity of Nature's to bring in her ARISTOCRACIES, her BEST, even by forcible methods. When their descendants or representatives cease entirely to *be* the Best, Nature's poor world will very soon rush down again to Baseness; and it becomes a dire necessity of Nature's to cast them out. Hence French Revolutions, Five-point Charters, Democracies, and a mournful list of *Etceteras,* in these our afflicted times.

To what extent Democracy has now reached, how it advances irresistible with ominous, ever-increasing speed, he that will open his eyes on any province of human affairs may discern. Democracy is everywhere the inexorable demand of these ages, swiftly fulfilling itself. From the thunder of Napoleon battles, to the jabbering of Openvestry in St. Mary Axe, all things announce Democracy. . . .

. . . It may be admitted that Democracy, in all meanings of the word, is in full career; irresistible by any Ritter Kauderwälsch or other Son of Adam as times go. "Liberty" is a thing men are determined to have.

But truly, as I had to remark in the meanwhile, "the liberty of not being oppressed by your fellow man" is an indispensable, yet one of the most insignificant fractional parts of Human Liberty. No man oppresses thee, can bid thee fetch or carry, come or go, without reason shown. True; from all men thou art emancipated: but from Thyself and from the Devil—? No man, wiser, unwiser, can make thee come or go: but thy own futilities, bewilderments, thy false appetites for Money, Windsor Georges [6] and suchlike? No man oppresses thee O free and independent Franchiser: but does not this stupid Porterpot oppress thee? No Son of Adam can bid thee come or go; but this absurd Pot of Heavy-wet, this can and does! Thou art the thrall not of Cedric the Saxon, but of thy own brutal appetites and this scoured dish of liquor. And thou pratest of thy "liberty"? Thou entire blockhead!

Heavy-wet and gin: alas, these are not the only kinds of thraldom. Thou who walkest in a vain show, looking out with ornamental dilettante sniff and serene supremacy at all Life and all Death; and amblest jauntily; perking up thy poor talk into crotchets, thy poor conduct into fatuous somnambulisms; —and *art* as an "enchanted Ape" under God's sky, where thou mightest have been a man, had proper Schoolmasters and Conquerors, and Constables with cat-o'-nine tails, been vouchsafed thee; dost thou call that "liberty"? Or your unreposing Mammon-worshipper again, driven, as if by Galvanisms, by Devils, and Fixed-ideas, who rises early and sits late, chasing the impossible; straining every faculty to "fill himself with the east wind,"—how merciful were it, could you, by mild persuasion, or by the severest tyranny so-called, check him in his mad path, and turn him into a wiser one! All painful tyranny, in that case again, were but mild "surgery"; the pain of it cheap, as health and life, instead of galvanism and fixed-idea, are cheap at any price.

Sure enough, of all paths a man could strike into, there *is*, at any given moment, a *best path* for every man; a thing which, here and now, it were of all things *wisest* for him to do;—which could he be but led or driven to do, he were then doing "like a man," as we phrase it; all men and gods agreeing with him, the whole Universe virtually exclaiming Well-done to him! His success, in such case, were complete; his felicity a maximum. This path, to find this path and walk in it, is the one thing needful for him. Whatsoever forwards him in that, let it come to him even in the shape of blows and spurnings, is liberty: whatsoever hinders him, were it wardmotes, open-vestries pollbooths, tremendous cheers, rivers of heavy-wet, is slavery.

The notion that a man's liberty consists in giving his vote at election-hustings, and saying, "Behold, now I too have my twenty-thousandth part of a Talker in our National Palaver; will not all the gods be good to me?"—is one of the pleasantest! Nature nevertheless is kind at present; and puts it into the heads of many, almost of all. The liberty especially which has to purchase itself by social isolation, and each man standing separate from the other, having "no business with him" but a cash-account: this is such a liberty as the Earth seldom saw;—as the Earth will not long put up with, recommend it how you may. This liberty turns out, before it have long continued in action, with all men flinging up their caps round it, to be, for the Working Millions a liberty to die by want of food; for the Idle Thousands and Units, alas, a still more fatal liberty to live in want of work; to have no earnest duty to do in this God's-World any more. What becomes a man in such predicament? Earth's Laws are silent; and Heaven's speak in a voice which is not heard. No work, and the ineradicable need of work, give rise to new very wondrous life-philosophies, new very wondrous life-practices! Dilettantism, Pococurantism,[7] Beau-Brummelism,[8] with perhaps an occasional, half-mad, protesting burst of Byronism, establish themselves: at the end of a certain period,—if you go back to "the Dead Sea," there is, say our Moslem friends, a very strange "Sabbath-day" transacting itself there!—Brethren, we know but imperfectly yet, after ages of Constitutional Government, what Liberty and Slavery are.

Democracy, the chase of Liberty in that direction, shall go its full course; unrestrainable by him of Pferdefuss-Quacksalber, or any of *his* household. The Toiling Millions of Mankind, in most vital need and passionate instinctive desire of Guidance, shall cast away False-Guidance; and hope, for an hour, that No-Guidance will suffice them: but it can be for an hour only. The smallest item of human Slavery is the oppression of man by his Mock-Superiors; the palpablest, but I say at bottom the smallest. Let him shake-off such oppression, trample it indignantly under his feet; I blame him not, I pity and commend him. But oppression by your Mock-Superiors well shaken off, the grand problem yet remains to solve: That of finding government by your Real-Superiors! Alas, how shall we ever learn the solution of that, benighted, bewildered, sniffing, sneering, godforgetting unfortunates as we are? It is a work for centuries; to be taught us by tribulations, confusions, insurrections, obstructions; who knows if not by conflagration and despair! It is a lesson inclusive of all other lessons; the hardest of all lessons to learn.

One thing I do know: Those Apes, chattering on the branches by the Dead Sea, never got it learned; but chatter there to this day. To them no Moses need come a second time; a thousand Moseses would be but so many painted Phantasms, interesting Fellow-Apes of new strange aspect,— whom they would "invite to dinner," be glad to meet with in lion-soirées. To them the voice of Prophecy, of heavenly monition, is quite ended. They chatter there, all Heaven shut to them, to the end of the world. The unfortunates! Oh, what is dying of hunger, with honest tools in your hand, with a manful purpose in your heart, and much real labor lying round you done, in comparison? You honestly quit your tools; quit a most muddy confused coil of sore work, short rations, of sorrows, dispiritments and contradictions, having now honestly done with it all;—and await, not entirely in a distracted manner, what the Supreme Powers, and the Silences and the Eternities may have to say to you.

A second thing I know: This lesson will have to be learned, —under penalties! England will either learn it, or England also will cease to exist among Nations. England will either learn to reverence its Heroes, and discriminate them from its Sham-Heroes and Valets and gaslighted Histrios; and to prize them as the audible God's-voice, amid all inane jargons and temporary market-cries, and say to them with heart-loyalty, "Be ye King and Priest, and Gospel and Guidance for us": or else England will continue to worship new and ever-new forms of Quackhood,—and so, with what resiliences and reboundings matters little, go down to the Father of Quacks! Can I dread such things of England? Wretched, thick-eyed, grosshearted mortals, why will ye worship lies, and "Stuffed Clothes-suits created by the ninth-parts of men!" It is not your purses that suffer; your farm-rents, your commerces, your mill-revenues, loud as ye lament over these; no, it is not these alone, but a far deeper than these: it is your souls that lie dead, crushed down under despicable Nightmares, Atheisms, Brain-fumes; and are not souls at all, but mere succedanea for *salt* to keep your bodies and their appetites from putrefying! Your cotton-spinning and thrice-miraculous mechanism, what is this too, by itself, but a larger kind of Animalism? Spiders can spin, Beavers can build and show contrivance; the Ant lays-up accumulation of capital, and has, for aught I know, a Bank of Antland. If there is no soul in man higher than all that, did it reach to sailing on the cloud-rack and spinning sea-sand; then I say, man is but an animal, a more cunning kind of brute: he has no soul, but only a succedaneum for salt. Whereupon, seeing himself to be truly of the beasts that perish, he ought to admit it, I think;—and also straightway universally to kill himself; and so, in a manlike manner at least *end*, and wave these brute-worlds *his* dignified farewell!—

NOTES

1. A hero of the First Crusade, celebrated in Tasso's *Jerusalem Delivered.*
2. The son of Earl Leofric. He held out against William the Conqueror. He was the hero of Kingsley's novel, *Hereward the Wake.*
3. A reference to revolts which William suppressed.
4. By the splendor of God, a favorite oath of William.
5. Joseph Manton (1766–1835) was a gunsmith. His name suggests the sporting aristocracy.
6. Decorations granted by King George.
7. Pococurantism, from Pococurante, a character in Voltaire's

Candide, who, with wealth and command of all the arts, is yet incapable of enjoying himself. The name means "caring little."
8. George Bryan Brummell (1778–1840), a leader of London Society.

Self-Reliance
"Ne te quaesiveris extra." [1]

RALPH WALDO EMERSON

Ralph Waldo Emerson (1803–1882), like Thomas Carlyle, prepared for the ministry but turned instead to literature. He became famous as an essayist, poet and expositor of the intellectual movement known as transcendentalism. He is the author of Nature, Representative Men *and* English Traits, *which are still widely read today. "Self-reliance" is generally regarded as indispensable for a clear understanding of Emerson's matured philosophy of individualism.*

Man is his own star; and the soul that can
Render an honest and a perfect man
Commands all light, all influence, all fate;
Nothing to him falls early or too late.
Our acts our angels are, or good or ill,
Our fatal shadows that walk by us still.
  —EPILOGUE TO BEAUMONT AND
   FLETCHER'S HONEST MAN'S FORTUNE

Cast the bantling on the rocks,
Suckle him with the she-wolf's teat,
Wintered with the hawk and fox,
Power and speed be hands and feet.

I read the other day some verses written by an eminent painter [2] which were original and not conventional. The soul always hears an admonition in such lines, let the subject be what it may. The sentiment they instil is of more value than any thought they may contain. To believe your own thought, to believe that what is true for you in your private heart is true for all men,—that is genius. Speak your latent conviction, and it shall be the universal sense; for the inmost in due time becomes the outmost,—and our first thought is rendered back to us by the trumpets of the Last Judgment. Familiar as the voice of the mind is to each, the highest merit we ascribe to Moses, Plato, and Milton is that they set at naught books and traditions, and spoke not what men, but what they thought. A man should learn to detect and watch that gleam of light which flashes across his mind from within, more than the lustre of the firmament of bards and sages. Yet he dismisses without notice his thought, because it is his. In every work of genius we recognize our own rejected thoughts: they come back to us with a certain alienated majesty. Great works of art have no more affecting lesson for us than this. They teach us to abide by our spontaneous impression with good-humored inflexibility then most when the whole cry of voices is on the other side. Else, to-morrow a stranger will say with masterly good sense precisely what we have thought and felt all the time, and we shall be forced to take with shame our own opinion from another.

There is a time in every man's education when he arrives at the conviction that envy is ignorance; that imitation is suicide; that he must take himself for better for worse as his portion; that though the wide universe is full of good, no kernel of nourishing corn can come to him but through his toil bestowed on that plot of ground which is given to him to till. The power which resides in him is new in nature, and none but he knows what that is which he can do, nor does he know until he has tried. Not for nothing one face, one character, one fact, makes much impression on him, and another none. This sculpture in the memory is not without preëstablished harmony. The eye was placed where one ray should fall, that it might testify of that particular ray. We but half express ourselves, and are ashamed of that divine idea which each of us represents. It may be safely trusted as proportionate and of good issues, so it be faithfully imparted, but God will not have his work made manifest by cowards. A man is relieved and gay when he has put his heart into his work and done his best; but what he has said or done otherwise shall give him no peace. It is a deliverance which does not deliver. In the attempt his genius deserts him; no muse befriends; no invention, no hope.

Trust thyself: every heart vibrates to that iron string. Accept the place the divine providence has found for you, the society of your contemporaries, the connection of events. Great men have always done so, and confided themselves childlike to the genius of their age, betraying their perception that the absolutely trustworthy was seated at their heart, working through their hands, predominating in all their being. And we are now men, and must accept in the highest mind the same transcendent destiny; and not minors and invalids in a protected corner, not cowards fleeing before a revolution, but guides, redeemers, and benefactors, obeying the Almighty effort, and advancing on Chaos and the Dark.[3]

What pretty oracles nature yields us on this text, in the face and behaviour of children, babes, and even brutes! That divided and rebel mind, that distrust of a sentiment because our arithmetic has computed the strength and means opposed to our purpose, these have not. Their mind being whole, their eye is as yet unconquered, and when we look in their faces, we are disconcerted. Infancy conforms to nobody: all conform to it, so that one babe commonly makes four or five out of the adults who prattle and play to it. So God has armed youth and puberty and manhood no less with its own piquancy and charm, and made it enviable and gracious and its claims not to be put by, if it will stand by itself. Do not think the youth has no force, because he cannot speak to you and me. Hark! in the next room his voice is sufficiently clear and emphatic. It seems he knows how to speak to his contemporaries. Bashful or bold, then, he will know how to make us seniors very unnecessary.

The nonchalance of boys who are sure of a dinner, and would disdain as much as a lord to do or say aught to conciliate one, is the healthy attitude of human nature. A boy is in the parlour what the pit [4] is in the playhouse; independent, irresponsible, looking out from his corner on such people and facts as pass by, he tries and sentences them on their merits, in the swift, summary ways of boys, as good, bad, interesting, silly, eloquent, troublesome. He cumbers himself never about consequences, about interests: he gives an independent, genuine verdict. You must court him: he does not court you. But the man is, as it were, clapped into jail by his consciousness. As soon as he has once acted or spoken with éclat, he is a committed person, watched by the sympathy or the hatred of hundreds, whose affections must now enter into his account. There is no Lethe [5] for this. Ah, that he could pass again into his neutrality! Who can thus avoid all pledges, and having observed, observe again from the same unaffected, unbiased, unbribable, unaffrighted innocence, must always be formidable. He would utter opinions on all passing affairs, which being seen to be not private, but necessary, would sink like darts into the ear of men, and put them in fear.

These are the voices which we hear in solitude, but they grow faint and inaudible as we enter into the world. Society everywhere is in conspiracy against the manhood of every one of its members. Society is a joint-stock company, in which the members agree, for the better securing of his bread to each shareholder, to surrender the liberty and culture of the eater. The virtue in most request is conformity. Self-reliance is its aversion. It loves not realities and creators, but names and customs.

Whoso would be a man, must be a nonconformist. He who would gather immortal palms must not be hindred by the name of goodness, but must explore if it be goodness. Nothing is at last sacred but the integrity of your own mind. Absolve you to yourself, and you shall have the suffrage of the world. I remember an answer which when quite young I was prompted to make to a valued adviser, who was wont to importune me with the dear old doctrines of the church. On my saying, What have I to do with the sacredness of traditions, if I live wholly from within? my friend suggested,— "But these impulses may be from below, not from above." I replied, "They do not seem to me to be such; but if I am the

Devil's child, I will live then from the Devil." No law can
be sacred to me but that of my nature. Good and bad are but
names very readily transferable to that or this; the only right
is what is after my constitution, the only wrong what is against
it. A man is to carry himself in the presence of all opposition
as if everything were titular and ephemeral but he. I am
ashamed to think how easily we capitulate to badges and
names, to large societies and dead institutions. Every decent
and well-spoken individual affects and sways me more than
is right. I ought to go upright and vital, and speak the rude
truth in all ways. If malice and vanity wear the coat of phi-
lanthropy, shall that pass? If an angry bigot assumes this
bountiful cause of Abolition, and comes to me with his last
news from Barbadoes,[6] why should I not say to him, "Go love
thy infant; love thy wood-chopper; be good-natured and modest: have that grace; and never varnish your hard, uncharita-
ble ambition with this incredible tenderness for black folk a
thousand miles off. Thy love afar is spite at home." Rough
and graceless would be such greeting, but truth is handsomer
than the affectation of love. Your goodness must have some
edge to it,—else it is none. The doctrine of hatred must be
preached as the counteraction of the doctrine of love when
that pules and whines. I shun father and mother and wife
and brother, when my genius calls me.[7] I would write on the
lintels of the door-post, *Whim*.[8] I hope it is somewhat better
than whim at last, but we cannot spend the day in explanation. Expect me not to show cause why I seek or why I exclude
company. Then, again, do not tell me, as a good man did today, of my obligation to put all poor men in good situations.
Are they *my* poor? I tell thee, thou foolish philanthropist,
that I grudge the dollar, the dime, the cent I give to such
men as do not belong to me and to whom I do not belong.
There is a class of persons to whom by all spiritual affinity I
am bought and sold; for them I will go to prison, if need be;
but your miscellaneous popular charities; the education at college of fools; the building of meeting-houses to the vain end
to which many now stand; alms to sots; and the thousandfold
Relief Societies;—though I confess with shame I sometimes
succumb and give the dollar, it is a wicked dollar, which by
and by I shall have the manhood to withhold.

Virtues are, in the popular estimate, rather the exception than the rule. There is the man *and* his virtues. Men do what is called a good action, as some piece of courage or charity, much as they would pay a fine in expiation of daily non-appearance on parade. Their works are done as an apology or extenuation of their living in the world,—as invalids and the insane pay a high board. Their virtues are penances. I do not wish to expiate, but to live. My life is for itself and not for a spectacle. I much prefer that it should be of a lower strain, so it be genuine and equal, than that it should be glittering and unsteady. I wish it to be sound and sweet, and not to need diet and bleeding. I ask primary evidence that you are a man, and refuse this appeal from the man to his actions. I know that for myself it makes no difference whether I do or forbear those actions which are reckoned excellent. I cannot consent to pay for a privilege where I have intrinsic right. Few and mean as my gifts may be, I actually am, and do not need for my own assurance or the assurance of my fellows any secondary testimony.

What I must do is all that concerns me, not what the people think. This rule, equally arduous in actual and in intellectual life, may serve for the whole distinction between greatness and meanness. It is the harder, because you will always find those who think they know what is your duty better than you know it. It is easy in the world to live after the world's opinion; it is easy in solitude to live after our own; but the great man is he who in the midst of the crowd keeps with perfect sweetness the independence of solitude.

The objection to conforming to usages that have become dead to you is, that it scatters your force. It loses your time and blurs the impression of your character. If you maintain a dead church, contribute to a dead Bible-society, vote with a great party either for the government or against it, spread your table like base housekeepers,—under all these screens I have difficulty to detect the precise man you are. And, of course, so much force is withdrawn from all your proper life. But do your work, and I shall know you. Do your work, and you shall reinforce yourself. A man must consider what a blind man's-bluff is this game of conformity. If I know your sect, I anticipate your argument. I hear a preacher announce for his text and topic the expediency of one of the institutions of his church. Do I not know beforehand that not possibly can he say a new and spontaneous word? Do I not know that, with all this ostentation of examining the grounds of the institution, he will do no such thing? Do I not know that he is pledged to himself not to look but at one side,—the permitted side, not as a man, but as a parish minister? He is a retained attorney, and these airs of the bench are the emptiest affection. Well, most men have bound their eyes with one or another handkerchief, and attached themselves to some one of these communities of opinion. This conformity makes them not false in a few particulars, authors of a few lies, but false in all particulars. Their every truth is not quite true. Their two is not the real two, their four not the real four; so that every word they say chagrins us, and we know not where to begin to set them right. Meantime nature is not slow to equip us in the prison-uniform of the party to which we adhere. We come to wear one cut of face and figure, and acquire by degrees the gentlest asinine expression. There is a mortifying experience in particular, which does not fail to wreak itself also in the general history; I mean "the foolish face of praise," [9] the forced smile which we put on in company where we do not feel at ease in answer to conversation which does not interest us. The muscles, not spontaneously moved, but moved by a low usurping wilfulness, grow tight about the outline of the face, with the most disagreeable sensation.

For nonconformity the world whips you with its displeasure. And therefore a man must know how to estimate a sour face. The bystanders look askance on him in the public street or in the friend's parlour. If this aversion had its origin in contempt and resistance like his own, he might well go home with a sad countenance; but the sour faces of the multitude, like their sweet faces, have no deep cause, but are put on and off as the wind blows and a newspaper directs. Yet is the discontent of the multitude more formidable than that of the senate and the college. It is easy enough for a firm man who knows the world to brook the rage of the cultivated classes. Their rage is decorous and prudent, for they are timid as being very vulnerable themselves. But when to their feminine rage the indignation of the people is added, when the ignorant and the poor are aroused, when the unintelligent brute force that lies at the bottom of society is made to growl and mow,[10] it needs the habit of magnanimity and religion to treat it godlike as a trifle of no concernment.

The other terror that scares us from self-trust is our consistency; a reverence for our past act or word, because the eyes of others have no other data for computing our orbit than our past acts, and we are loth to disappoint them.

But why should you keep your head over your shoulder? Why drag about this corpse of your memory, lest you contradict somewhat you have stated in this or that public place? Suppose you should contradict yourself; what then? It seems to be a rule of wisdom never to rely on your memory alone, scarcely even in acts of pure memory, but to bring the past for judgment into the thousand-eyed present, and live ever in a new day. In your metaphysics you have denied personality to the Deity: yet when the devout motions of the soul come, yield to them heart and life, though they should clothe God with shape and color. Leave your theory, as Joseph his coat in the hand of the harlot,[11] and flee.

A foolish consistency is the hobgoblin of little minds, adored by little statesmen and philosophers and divines. With consistency a great soul has simply nothing to do. He may as well concern himself with his shadow on the wall. Speak what you think now in hard words, and to-morrow speak what to-morrow thinks in hard words again, though it contradict every thing you said to-day.—"Ah, so you shall be sure to be misunderstood."—Is it so bad, then, to be misunderstood? Pythagoras was misunderstood, and Socrates, and Jesus, and Luther, and Corpernicus, and Galileo,[12] and Newton, and every pure and wise spirit that ever took flesh. To be great is to be misunderstood.

I suppose no man can violate his nature. All the sallies of his will are rounded in by the law of his being, as the inequalities of Andes and Himmaleh are insignificant in the curve of the sphere. Nor does it matter how you gauge and try him. A character is like an acrostic or Alexandrian stanza;[13]—read it forward, backward, or across, it still spells the same thing. In this pleasing, contrite wood-life which God allows me, let me record day by day my honest thought without prospect or retrospect, and, I cannot doubt, it will be found symmetrical, though I mean it not, and see it not. My book should smell of pines and resound with the hum of insects. The swallow over my window should interweave that thread or straw he carries in his bill into my web also. We pass for what we are. Character teaches above our wills. Men imagine that they communicate their virtue or vice only by overt actions, and do not see that virtue or vice emit a breath every moment.

There will be an agreement in whatever variety of actions, so they be each honest and natural in their hour. For of one will, the actions will be harmonious, however unlike they seem. These varieties are lost sight of at a little distance, at a little height of thought. One tendency unites them all. The voyage of the best ship is a zigzag line of a hundred tacks. See the line from a sufficient distance, and it straightens itself to the average tendency. Your genuine action will explain itself, and will explain your other genuine actions. Your conformity explains nothing. Act singly, and what you have already done singly will justify you now. Greatness appeals to the future. If I can be firm enough to-day to do right, and scorn eyes, I must have done so much right before as to defend me now. Be it how it will, do right now. Always scorn appearances, and you always may. The force of character is cumulative. All the foregone days of virtue work their health into this. What makes the majesty of the heroes of the senate and the field, which so fills the imagination? The consciousness of a train of great days and victories behind. They shed a united light on the advancing actor. He is attended as by a visible escort of angels. That is it which throws thunder into Chatham's [14] voice, and dignity into Washington's port, and America into Adams's [15] eye. Honor is venerable to us because it is no ephemera. It is always ancient virtue. We worship it to-day because it is not of to-day. We love it and pay it homage, because it is not a trap for our love and homage, but is self-dependent, self-derived, and therefore of an old immaculate pedigree, even if shown in a young person.

I hope in these days we have heard the last of conformity

and consistency. Let the words be gazetted [16] and ridiculous henceforward. Instead of the gong for dinner, let us hear a whistle from the Spartan fife.[17] Let us never bow and apologize more. A great man is coming to eat at my house. I do not wish to please him; I wish that he should wish to please me. I will stand here for humanity, and though I would make it kind, I would make it true. Let us affront and reprimand the smooth mediocrity and squalid contentment of the times, and hurl in the face of custom, and trade, and office, the fact which is the upshot of all history, that there is a great responsible Thinker and Actor working wherever a man works; that a true man belongs to no other time or place, but is the centre of things. Where he is, there is nature. He measures you, and all men, and all events. Ordinarily, every body in society reminds us of somewhat else, or of some other person. Character, reality, reminds you of nothing else; it takes place of the whole creation. The man must be so much, that he must make all circumstances indifferent. Every true man is a cause, a country, and an age; requires infinite spaces and numbers and time fully to accomplish his design;—and posterity seem to follow his steps as a train of clients. A man Caesar is born, and for ages after we have a Roman Empire. Christ is born, and millions of minds so grow and cleave to his genius that he is confounded with virtue and the possible of man. An institution is the lengthened shadow of one man; as, Monachism, of the Hermit Antony; [18] the Reformation, of Luther; Quakerism, of Fox; [19] Methodism, of Wesley; Abolition, of Clarkson.[20] Scipio, Milton called "the height of Rome"; [21] and all history resolves itself very easily into the biography of a few stout and earnest persons.

Let a man then know his worth, and keep things under his feet. Let him not peep or steal, or skulk up and down with the air of a charity-boy, a bastard, or an interloper, in the world which exists for him. But the man in the street, finding no worth in himself which corresponds to the force which built a tower or sculptured a marble god, feels poor when he looks on these. To him a palace, a statue, or a costly book have an alien and forbidding air, much like a gay equipage, and seem to say like that, "Who are you, Sir?" Yet they all are his, suitors for his notice, petitioners to his faculties that they will come out and take possession. The picture waits for my verdict: it is not to command me, but I am to settle its claims to praise. That popular fable [22] of the sot who was picked up dead drunk in the street, carried to the duke's house, washed and dressed and laid in the duke's bed, and, on his waking, treated with all obsequious ceremony like the duke, and assured that he had been insane, owes its popularity to the fact, that it symbolizes so well the state of man, who is in the world a sort of sot, but now and then wakes up, exercises his reason and finds himself a true prince.

Our reading is mendicant and sycophantic. In history, our imagination plays us false. Kingdom and lordship, power and estate, are a gaudier vocabulary than private John and Edward in a small house and common day's work; but the things of life are the same to both; the sum total of both is the same. Why all this deference to Alfred,[23] and Scanderbeg,[24] and Gustavus? [25] Suppose they were virtuous; did they wear out virtue? As great a stake depends on your private act to-day, as followed their public and renowned steps. When private men shall act with original views, the lustre will be transferred from the actions of kings to those of gentlemen.

The world has been instructed by its kings, who have so magnetized the eyes of nations. It has been taught by this colossal symbol the mutual reverence that is due from man to man. The joyful loyalty with which men have everywhere suffered the king, the noble, or the great proprietor to walk among them by a law of his own, make his own scale of men and things, and reverse theirs, pay for benefits not with money but with honor, and represent the law in his person, was the hieroglyphic by which they obscurely signified their consciousness of their own right and comeliness, the right of every man.

The magnetism which all original action exerts is explained when we inquire the reason of self-trust. Who is the Trustee? What is the aboriginal Self, on which a universal reliance may be grounded? What is the nature and power of that science-baffling star, without parallax,[26] without calculable elements, which shoots a ray of beauty even into trivial and impure actions, if the least mark of independence appear? The inquiry leads us to that source, at once the essence of genius, of virtue, and of life, which we call Spontaneity or Instinct. We denote this primary wisdom as Intuition, whilst all later teachings are tuitions. In that deep force, the last fact behind which analysis cannot go, all things find their common origin. For the sense of being which in calm hours rises, we know not how, in the soul, is not diverse from things, from space, from light, from time, from man, but one with them, and proceeds obviously from the same source whence their life and being also proceed. We first share the life by which things exist, and afterwards see them as appearances in nature, and forget that we have shared their cause. Here is the fountain of action and of thought. Here are the lungs of that inspiration which giveth man wisdom, and which cannot be denied without impiety and atheism. We lie in the lap of immense intelligence, which makes us receivers of its truth and organs of its activity. When we discern justice, when we discern truth, we do nothing of ourselves, but allow a passage to its beams. If we ask whence this comes, if we seek to pry into the soul that causes, all philosophy is at fault. Its presence or its absence is all we can affirm. Every man discriminates between the voluntary acts of his mind, and his involuntary perceptions, and knows that to his involuntary perceptions a perfect faith is due. He may err in the expression of them, but he knows that these things are so, like day and night, not to be disputed. My wilful actions and acquisitions are but roving;—the idlest reverie, the faintest native emotion, command my curiosity and respect. Thoughtless people contradict as readily the statement of perceptions as of opinions, or rather much more readily; for they do not distinguish between perception and notion. They fancy that I choose to see this or that thing. But perception is not whimsical, but fatal. If I see a trait, my children will see it after me, and in course of time, all mankind,— although it may chance that no one has seen it before me. For my perception of it is as much a fact as the sun.

The relations of the soul to the divine spirit are so pure, that it is profane to seek to interpose helps. It must be that when God speaketh he should communicate, not one thing, but all things; should fill the world with his voice; should scatter forth light, nature, time, souls, from the centre of the present thought; and new date and new create the whole. Whenever a mind is simple, and receives a divine wisdom, old things pass away,—means, teachers, texts, temples fall; it lives now, and absorbs past and future into the present hour. All things are made sacred by relation to it,—one as much as another. All things are dissolved to their centre by their cause, and, in the universal miracle, petty and particular miracles disappear. If, therefore, a man claims to know and speak of God, and carries you backward to the phraseology of some old mouldered nation in another country, in another world, believe him not. Is the acorn better than the oak which is its fulness and completion? Is the parent better than the child into whom he has cast his ripened being? Whence, then, this worship of the past? The centuries are conspirators against the sanity and authority of the soul. Time and space are but physiological colors which the eye makes, but the soul is light; where it is, is day; where it was, is night; and history is an impertinence and an injury, if it be anything more than a cheerful apologue or parable of my being and becoming.

Man is timid and apologetic; he is no longer upright; he dares not say "I think," "I am," but quotes some saint or sage. He is ashamed before the blade of grass or the blowing rose. These roses under my window make no reference to former roses or to better ones; they are for what they are; they exist with God to-day. There is no time to them. There is simply the rose; it is perfect in every moment of its existence. Before a leaf-bud has burst, its whole life acts; in the full-blown flower there is no more; in the leafless root there is no less. Its nature is satisfied, and it satisfies nature, in all moments alike. But man postpones or remembers; he does not live in the present, but with reverted eye laments the past, or, heedless of the riches that surround him, stands on tiptoe to foresee the future. He cannot be happy and strong until he too lives with nature in the present, above time.

This should be plain enough. Yet see what strong intellects dare not yet hear God himself, unless he speaks the phraseology of I know not what David, or Jeremiah, or Paul. We shall not always set so great a price on a few texts, on a few lives. We are like children who repeat by rote the sentences of grandames and tutors, and, as they grow older, of the men of talents and character they chance to see,—painfully recollecting the exact words they spoke; afterwards, when they come into the point of view which those had who uttered these sayings, they understand them, and are willing to let the words go; for, at any time, they can use words as good when occasion comes. If we live truly, we shall see truly. It is as easy for the strong man to be strong, as it is for the weak to be weak. When we have new perception, we shall gladly disburden the memory of its hoarded treasures as old rubbish. When a man lives with God, his voice shall be as sweet as the murmur of the brook and the rustle of the corn.

And now at last the highest truth on this subject remains unsaid; probably cannot be said; for all that we say is the far-off remembering of the intuition. That thought, by what I can now nearest approach to say it, is this. When good is near you, when you have life in yourself, it is not by any known or accustomed way; you shall not discern the foot-prints of any other; you shall not see the face of man; you shall not hear any name;—the way, the thought, the good, shall be wholly strange and new. It shall exclude example and experience. You take the way from man, not to man. All persons that ever existed are its forgotten ministers. Fear and hope are alike beneath it. There is somewhat low even in hope. In the hour of vision, there is nothing that can be called gratitude, nor properly joy. The soul raised over passion beholds identity and eternal causation, perceives the self-existence of Truth and Right, and calms itself with knowing that all things go well. Vast spaces of nature, the Atlantic Ocean, the South Sea,—long intervals of times, years, centuries,—are of no account. This which I think and feel underlay every former state of life and circumstances, as it does underlie my present, and what is called life, and what is called death.

Life only avails, not the having lived. Power ceases in the instant of repose; it resides in the moment of transition from a past to a new state, in the shooting of the gulf, in the darting to an aim. This one fact the world hates, that the soul *be-*

comes; for that forever degrades the past, turns all riches to poverty, all reputation to a shame, confounds the saint with the rogue, shoves Jesus and Judas equally aside. Why, then, do we prate of self-reliance? Inasmuch as the soul is present, there will be power not confident but agent. To talk of reliance is a poor external way of speaking. Speak rather of that which relies, because it works and is. Who has more obedience than I masters me, though he should not raise his finger. Round him I must revolve by the gravitation of spirits. We fancy it rhetoric, when we speak of eminent virtue. We do not yet see that virtue is Height, and that a man or a company of men, plastic and permeable to principles, by the law of nature must overpower and ride all cities, nations, kings, rich men, poets, who are not.

This is the ultimate fact which we so quickly reach on this, as on every topic, the resolution of all into the ever-blessed ONE. Self-existence is the attribute of the Supreme Cause, and it constitutes the measure of good by the degree in which it enters into all lower forms. All things real are so by so much virtue as they contain. Commerce, husbandry, hunting, whaling, war, eloquence, personal weight, are somewhat and engage my respect as examples of its presence and impure action. I see the same law working in nature for conservation and growth. Power is in nature the essential measure of right. Nature suffers nothing to remain in her kingdoms which cannot help itself. The genesis and maturation of a planet, its poise and orbit, the bended tree recovering itself from the strong wind, the vital resources of every animal and vegetable, are demonstrations of the self-sufficing, and therefore self-relying soul.

Thus all concentrates: let us not rove; let us sit at home with the cause. Let us stun and astonish the intruding rabble of men and books and institutions, by a simple declaration of the divine fact. Bid the invaders take the shoes from off their feet, for God is here within.[27] Let our simplicity judge them, and our docility to our own law demonstrate the poverty of nature and fortune beside our native riches.

But now we are a mob. Man does not stand in awe of man, nor is his genius admonished to stay at home, to put itself in communication with the internal ocean, but it goes abroad to beg a cup of water of the urns of other men. We must go alone. I like the silent church before the service begins, better than any preaching. How far off, how cool, how chaste the persons look, begirt each one with a precinct or sanctuary! So let us always sit. Why should we assume the faults of our friends, or wife, or father, or child, because they sit around our hearth, or are said to have the same blood? All men have my blood, and I all men's. Not for that will I adopt their petulance or folly, even to the extent of being ashamed of it. But your isolation must not be mechanical, but spiritual, that is, must be elevation. At times the whole world seems to be in conspiracy to importune you with emphatic trifles. Friend, client, child, sickness, fear, want, charity, all knock at once at they closet door, and say,—"Come out unto us." But keep thy state; come not into their confusion. The power men possess to annoy me, I give them by a weak curiosity. No man can come near me but through my act. "What we love that we have, but by desire we bereave ourselves of the love."

If we cannot at once rise to the sanctities of obedience and faith, let us at least resist our temptations; let us enter into the state of war, and wake Thor [28] and Woden,[29] courage and constancy, in our Saxon breasts. This is to be done in our smooth times by speaking the truth. Check this lying hospitality and lying affection. Live no longer to the expectation of these deceived and deceiving people with whom we converse. Say to them, "O father, O mother, O wife, O brother, O friend, I have lived with you after appearances hitherto. Henceforward I am the truth's. Be it known unto you that henceforward I obey no law less than the eternal law. I will have no covenants but proximities. I shall endeavor to nourish my parents to support my family, to be the chaste husband of one wife,—but these relations I must fill after a new and unprecedented way. I appeal from your customs. I must be myself. I cannot break myself any longer for you, or you. If you can love me for what I am, we shall be the happier. If you cannot, I will still seek to deserve that you should. I will not hide my tastes or aversions. I will so trust that what is deep is holy, that I will do strongly before the sun and moon whatever inly rejoices me, and the heart appoints. If you are noble, I will love you; if you are not, I will not hurt you and myself by hypocritical attentions. If you are true, but not in the same truth with me, cleave to your companions; I will seek my own. I do this not selfishly but humbly and truly. It is alike your interest, and mine, and all men's, however long we have dwelt in lies, to live in truth. Does this sound harsh to-day? You will soon love what is dictated by your nature as well as mine, and if we follow the truth, it will bring us out safe at last."—But so you may give these friends pain. Yes, but I cannot sell my liberty and my power, to save your sensibility. Besides, all persons have their moments of reason, when they look out into the region of absolute truth; then will they justify me, and do the same thing.

The populace think that your rejection of popular standards is a rejection of all standard, and mere antinomianism; [30] and the bold sensualist will use the name of philosophy to gild his crimes. But the law of consciousness abides. There are two confessionals, in one or the other of which we must be shriven. You may fulfil your round of duties by clearing yourself in the *direct*, or in the *reflex* way. Consider whether you have satisfied your relations to father, mother, cousin, neighbour, town, cat and dog; whether any of these can upbraid you. But I may also neglect this reflex standard and absolve me to myself. I have my own stern claims and perfect circle. It denies the name of duty to many offices that are called duties. But if I can discharge its debts, it enables me to dispense with the popular code. If any one imagines that this law is lax, let him keep its commandment one day.

And truly it demands something godlike in him who has cast off the common motives of humanity, and has ventured to trust himself for a taskmaster. High be his heart, faithful his will, clear his sight, that he may in good earnest be doctrine, society, law, to himself, that a simple purpose may be to him as strong as iron necessity is to others!

If any man consider the present aspects of what is called by distinction *society*, he will see the need of these ethics. The sinew and heart of man seem to be drawn out, and we are become timorous, desponding whimperers. We are afraid of truth, afraid of fortune, afraid of death, and afraid of each other. Our age yields no great and perfect persons. We want men and women who shall renovate life and our social state, but we see that most natures are insolvent, cannot satisfy their own wants, have an ambition out of all proportion to their practical force and do lean and beg day and night continually. Our housekeeping is mendicant, our arts, our occupations, our marriages, our religion, we have not chosen, but society has chosen for us. We are parlour soldiers. We shun the rugged battle of fate, where strength is born.

If our young men miscarry in their first enterprises, they lose all heart. If the young merchant fails, men say he is *ruined*. If the finest genius studies at one of our colleges, and is not installed in an office within one year afterwards in the cities or suburbs of Boston or New York, it seems to his friends and to himself that he is right in being disheartened, and in complaining the rest of his life. A sturdy lad from New Hampshire or Vermont, who in turn tries all the professions, who *teams it, farms it, peddles*, keeps a school, preaches, edits a newspaper, goes to Congress, buys a township, and so forth, in successive years, and always, like a cat, falls on his feet, is worth a hundred of these city dolls. He walks abreast with his days, and feels no shame in not "studying a profession," for he does not postpone his life, but lives already. He has not one chance, but a hundred chances. Let a Stoic [31] open the resources of man, and tell men they are not leaning willows, but can and must detach themselves; that with the exercise of self-trust, new powers shall appear; that a man is the word made flesh,[32] born to shed healing to the nations, that he should be ashamed of our compassion, and that the moment he acts from himself, tossing the laws, the books, idolatries, and customs out of the window, we pity him no more, but thank and revere him,—and that teacher shall restore the life of man to splendor, and make his name dear to all history.

It is easy to see that a greater self-reliance must work a revolution in all the offices and relations of men; in their religion; in their education; in their pursuits; their modes of living; their association; in their property; in their speculative views.

1. In what prayers do men allow themselves! That which they call a holy office is not so much as brave and manly. Prayer looks abroad and asks for some foreign addition to come through some foreign virtue, and loses itself in endless mazes of natural and supernatural, and mediatorial and miraculous. Prayer that craves a particular commodity,—anything less than all good,—is vicious. Prayer is the contemplation of the facts of life from the highest point of view. It is the soliloquy of a beholding and jubilant soul. It is the spirit of God pronouncing his works good.[33] But prayer as a means to effect a private end is meanness and theft. It supposes dualism and not unity in nature and consciousness. As soon as the man is at one with God, he will not beg. He will then see prayer in all action. The prayer of the farmer kneeling in his field to weed it, the prayer of the rower kneeling with the stroke of his oar, are true prayers heard throughout nature, though for cheap ends. Caratach, in Fletcher's Bonduca,[34] when admonished to inquire the mind of the god Audate, replies,—

> His hidden meaning lies in our endeavours;
> Our valors are our best gods.

Another sort of false prayers are our regrets. Discontent is the want of self-reliance: it is infirmity of will. Regret calamities, if you can thereby help the sufferer; if not, attend your own work, and already the evil begins to be repaired. Our sympathy is just as base. We come to them who weep foolishly, and sit down and cry for company, instead of imparting to them truth and health in rough electric shocks, putting them once more in communication with their own reason. The secret of fortune is joy in our hands. Welcome evermore to gods and men is the self-helping man. For him all doors are flung wide: him all tongues greet, all honors crown, all eyes follow with desire. Our love goes out to him and embraces him, because he did not need it. We solicitously and apologetically caress and celebrate him, because he held on his way and scorned our disapprobation. The gods love him because men hated him. "To the persevering mortal," said Zoroaster,[35] "the blessed Immortals are swift."

As men's prayers are a disease of the will, so are their creeds a disease of the intellect. They say with those foolish Israelites, "Let not God speak to us, lest we die. Speak thou, speak any man with us, and we will obey." [36] Everywhere I am hindered of meeting God in my brother, because he has shut his own temple doors, and recites fables merely of his brother's, or his brother's brother's God. Every new mind is a new classification. [37] If it prove a mind of uncommon activity and power, a Locke, a Lavoisier, a Hutton, a Bentham, a Fourier, it imposes its classification on other men, and lo! a new system. In proportion to the depth of the thought, and so to the number of the objects it touches and brings within reach of the pupil, is his complacency. But chiefly is this apparent in creeds and churches, which are also classifications of some powerful mind acting on the elemental thought of duty, and man's relation to the Highest. Such is Calvinism, Quakerism, Swedenborgism. The pupil takes the same delight in subordinating every thing to the new terminology, as a girl who has just learned botany in seeing a new earth and new seasons thereby. It will happen for a time, that the pupil will find his intellectual power has grown by the study of his master's mind. But in all unbalanced minds, the classification is idolized, passes for the end, and not for a speedily exhaustible means, so that the walls of the system blend to their eye in the remote horizon with the walls of the universe; the luminaries of heaven seem to them hung on the arch their master built. They cannot imagine how you aliens have any right to see,—how you can see; "It must be somehow that you stole the light from us." They do not yet perceive that light, unsystematic, indomitable, will break into any cabin, even into theirs. Let them chirp awhile and call it their own. If they are honest and do well, presently their neat new pinfold will be too strait and low, will crack, will lean, will rot and vanish, and the immortal light, all young, and joyful, million-orbed, million-colored, will beam over the universe as on the first morning.

2. It is for want of self-culture that the superstition of Travelling, whose idols are Italy, England, Egypt, retains its fascination for all educated Americans. They who made Eng-

land, Italy, or Greece venerable in the imagination did so by sticking fast where they were, like an axis of the earth. In manly hours, we feel that duty is our place. The soul is no traveller; the wise man stays at home, and when his necessities, his duties, on any occasion call him from his house, or into foreign lands, he is at home still, and shall make men sensible by the expression of his countenance, that he goes the missionary of wisdom and virtue, and visits cities and men like a sovereign, and not like an interloper or a valet.

I have no churlish objection to the circumnavigation of the globe, for the purposes of art, of study, and benevolence, so that the man is first domesticated, or does not go abroad with the hope of finding somewhat greater than he knows. He who travels to be amused, or to get somewhat which he does not carry, travels away from himself, and grows old even in youth among old things. In Thebes, in Palmyra, his will and mind have become old and dilapidated as they. He carries ruins to ruins.

Travelling is a fool's paradise. Our first journeys discover to us the indifference of places. At home I dream that at Naples, at Rome, I can be intoxicated with beauty, and lose my sadness. I pack my trunk, embrace my friends, embark on the sea and at last wake up in Naples, and there beside me is the stern fact, the sad self, unrelenting, identical, that I fled from. I seek the Vatican, and the palaces. I affect to be intoxicated with sights and suggestions, but I am not intoxicated. My giant goes with me wherever I go.

3. But the rage of travelling is a symptom of a deeper unsoundness affecting the whole intellectual action. The intellect is vagabond, and our system of education fosters restlessness. Our minds travel when our bodies are forced to stay at home. We imitate; and what is imitation but the travelling of the mind? Our houses are built with foreign taste; our shelves are garnished with foreign ornaments; our opinions, our tastes, our faculties, lean, and follow the Past and the Distant. The soul created the arts wherever they have flourished. It was in his own mind that the artist sought his model. It was an application of his own thought to the thing to be done and the conditions to be observed. And why need we copy the

Doric or the Gothic model? Beauty, convenience, grandeur of thought, and quaint expression are as near to us as to any, and if the American artist will study with hope and love the precise thing to be done by him, considering the climate, the soil, the length of the day, the wants of the people, the habit and form of the government, he will create a house in which all these will find themselves fitted, and taste and sentiment will be satisfied also.

Insist on yourself; never imitate. Your own gift you can present every moment with the cumulative force of a whole life's cultivation; but of the adopted talent of another, you have only an extemporaneous, half possession. That which each can do best, none but his Maker can teach him. No man yet knows what it is, nor can, till that person has exhibited it. Where is the master who could have taught Shakspeare? Where is the master who could have instructed Franklin, or Washington, or Bacon, or Newton? Every great man is unique. The Scipionism of Scipio is precisely that part he could not borrow.[38] Shakspeare will never be made by the study of Shakspeare. Do that which is assigned you, and you cannot hope too much or dare too much. There is at this moment for you an utterance brave and grand as that of the colossal chisel of Phidias,[39] or trowel of the Egyptians, or the pen of Moses, or Dante, but different from all these. Not possibly will the soul, all rich, all eloquent, with thousand-cloven tongue, deign to repeat itself but if you can hear what these patriarchs say, surely you can reply to them in the same pitch of voice; for the ear and the tongue are two organs of one nature. Abide in the simple and noble regions of thy life, obey thy heart, and thou shall reproduce the Foreworld again.

4. As our Religion, our Education, our Art look abroad, so does our spirit of society. All men plume themselves on the improvement of society, and no man improves.

Society never advances. It recedes as fast on one side as it gains on the other. It undergoes continual changes; it is barbarous, it is civilized, it is christianized, it is rich, it is scientific; but this change is not amelioration. For every thing that is given, something is taken. Society acquires new arts, and loses old instincts. What a contrast between the well-clad, reading, writing, thinking American, with a watch, a pencil, and a bill of exchange in his pocket and the naked New Zealander, whose property is a club, a spear, a mat, and an undivided twentieth of a shed to sleep under! But compare the health of the two men, and you shall see that the white man has lost his aboriginal strength. If the traveller tell us truly, strike the savage with a broad-axe and in a day or two the flesh shall unite and heal as if you struck the blow into soft pitch, and the same blow shall send the white to his grave.

The civilized man has built a coach, but has lost the use of his feet. He is supported on crutches, but lacks so much support of muscle. He has a fine Geneva watch, but he fails of the skill to tell the hour by the sun. A Greenwich nautical almanac he has, and so being sure of the information when he wants it, the man in the street does not know a star in the sky. The solstice he does not observe; the equinox he knows as little; and the whole bright calendar of the year is without a dial in his mind. His note-books impair his memory; his libraries overload his wit; the insurance-office increases the number of accidents; and it may be a question whether machinery does not encumber; whether we have not lost by refinement some energy, by a Christianity, entrenched in establishments and forms, some vigor of wild virtue. For every Stoic was a Stoic; but in Christendom where is the Christian?

There is no more deviation in the moral standard than in the standard of height or bulk. No greater men are now than ever were. A singular equality may be observed between the great men of the first and of the last ages; nor can all the science, art, religion, and philosophy of the nineteenth century avail to educate greater men than Plutarch's [40] heroes, three or four and twenty centuries ago. Not in time is the race progressive. Phocion, Socrates, Anaxagoras, Diogenes, are great men, but they leave no class. He who is really of their class will not be called by their name, but will be his own man, and in his turn the founder of a sect. The arts and inventions of each period are only its costume, and do not invigorate men. The harm of the improved machinery may compensate its good. Hudson and Behring accomplished so much in their fishing-boats, as to astonish Parry and Franklin,[41] whose equipment exhausted the resources of science and art. Galileo, with an opera-glass,[42] discovered a more splendid series of celestial phenomena than any one since. Columbus found the New World in an undecked boat. It is curious to see the periodical disuse and perishing of means and machinery, which were introduced with loud laudation a few years or centuries before. The great genius returns to essential man. We reckoned the improvements of the art of war among the triumphs of science, and yet Napoleon conquered Europe by the bivouac, which consisted of falling back on naked valor, and disencumbering it of all aids. The Emperor held it impossible to make a perfect army, says Las Casas,[43] "without abolishing our arms, magazines, commissaries, and carriages, until, in imitation of the Roman custom, the soldier should receive his supply of corn, grind it in his hand-mill, and bake his bread himself."

Society is a wave. The wave moves onward, but the water of which it is composed does not. The same particle does not rise from the valley to the ridge. Its unity is only phenomenal. The persons who make up a nation to-day, next year die, and their experience dies with them.

And so the reliance on Property, including the reliance on governments which protect it, is the want of self-reliance. Men have looked away from themselves and at things so long, that they have come to esteem the religious, learned, and civil institutions as guards of property, and they deprecate assaults on these, because they feel them to be assaults on property. They measure their esteem of each other by what each has, and not by what each is. But a cultivated man becomes ashamed of his property, out of new respect for his nature. Especially he hates what he has, if he sees that it is accidental, —came to him by inheritance, or gift, or crime; then he feels that it is not having, it does not belong to him, has no root in him, and merely lies there, because no revolution or no robber takes it away. But that which a man is, does always by necessity acquire, and what the man acquires is living property, which does not wait the beck of rulers, or mobs, or revolutions, or fire, or storm, or bankruptcies, but perpetually renews itself wherever the man breathes. "Thy lot or portion of life," said the Caliph Ali,[44] "is seeking after thee; therefore be at rest from seeking after it." Our dependence on these foreign goods leads us to our slavish respect for numbers. The political parties meet in numerous conventions; the greater the concourse, and with each new uproar of announcement, The delegation from Essex! The Democrats from New Hampshire! The Whigs of Maine! the young patriot feels himself stronger than before by a new thousand of eyes and arms. In like manner the reformers summon conventions, and vote and resolve in multitude. Not so, O friends! will the God deign to enter and inhabit you, but by a method precisely the reverse. It is only as a man puts off all foreign support, and stands alone, that I see him to be strong and to prevail. He is weaker by every recruit to his banner. Is not a man better than a town? Ask nothing of men, and, in the endless mutation, thou only firm column must presently appear the upholder of all that surrounds thee. He who knows that power is inborn, that he is weak because he has looked for good out of him and elsewhere, and so perceiving, throws himself unhesitatingly on his thought, instantly rights himself, stands in the erect position, commands his limbs, works miracles; just as a man who stands on his feet is stronger than a man who stands on his head.

So use all that is called Fortune. Most men gamble with her, and gain all, and lose all, as her wheel rolls.[45] But do thou save as unlawful these winnings, and deal with Cause and Effect, the chancellors of God. In the Will work and acquire, and thou hast chained the wheel of Chance, and shalt sit hereafter out of fear from her rotations. A political victory, a rise of rents, the recovery of your sick, or the return of your absent friend, or some other favorable event, raises your spirits, and you think good days are preparing for you. Do not believe it. Nothing can bring you peace but yourself. Nothing can bring you peace but the triumph of principles.

NOTES

1. "Do not seek [answers] outside yourself." The first edition of "Self-Reliance" bore all three epigraphs as printed here. Emer-

son composed the quatrain himself, and dropped it from the second edition (1847). It was restored by later editors of the essay and also appears in the *Poems* as "Power."

2. The painter-poet may be the American Washington Allston (1779–1843), or the English William Blake (1757–1827), according to E. W. Emerson (Centenary Edition, Vol. II, p. 390).

3. *Cf.* Milton, *Paradise Lost,* Book I, 1. 543.

4. In old theaters, the cheaper seats behind the orchestra, below the level of the stage.

5. In Greek myth, a river of forgetfulness in the nether world.

6. British legislation abolished slavery in the West Indies, including Barbadoes, in 1833.

7. *Cf.* Matthew x: 34–37.

8. *Cf.* Exodus xii: 17. In Hebrew and other Eastern cultures, a mark on the lintel or doorframe characterized the resident. Emerson's "Whim" signifies individualism, not capriciousness.

9. *Cf.* Alexander Pope, "Epistle to Dr. Arbuthnot," 1. 212.

10. To mock or grimace.

11. *Cf.* Joseph and Potiphar's wife, Genesis xxxix: 12.

12. Pythagoras, Greek thinker of the fifth century B.C., aroused controversy by his revolutionary ideas and mathematical discoveries; Copernicus (1473–1543) risked charges of impiety in promulgating the theory of the solar system now accepted; Galileo (1564–1642) was tried by the Inquisition and condemned to retirement for supporting the theories of Copernicus. The remainder of these names suggest familiar controversies.

13. An Alexandrian stanza is a palindrome, or an arrangement of words which read the same backward as forward.

14. The Earl of Chatham, William Pitt (1708–1778), greatest English orator of his day; he supported the American colonists in Parliament.

15. By 1841 there had been three Adamses to whom this reference might apply: Samuel, a leader of the Revolution; John, who became the second president; and John Quincy, the sixth president.

16. *I.e.,* "dismissed." The British official "gazettes" announced dismissals, bankruptcies, and the like, as well as honors.

17. The strict discipline of the Spartans extended to musical instruments.

18. The hermitages of St. Anthony (ca. 250–350) were the beginnings of Christian monasticism.

19. George Fox (1624–1691) founded the Society of Friends in England (1647).

20. Thomas Clarkson (1760–1846) was the pioneer of the British antislavery movement.

21. *Cf.* John Milton, *Paradise Lost,* Book IX, 1. 510. Scipio Afri-

canus "the Elder" (237–183 B.C.), conqueror of Hannibal, was the greatest Roman general before Julius Caesar.

22. *Cf.* the same story in Shakespeare's "Induction," *The Taming of the Shrew* (Centenary Edition, Vol. II, p. 392).

23. Alfred (849–899), called "the Great" among Saxon kings of Britain.

24. Scanderbeg (Turkish title, "Iskander Bey") was George Castriota (1403?–1468), national hero of the Albanians, whom he led against the Turks.

25. Sweden's King Gustavus I (Gustavus Vasa, 1496–1560) defeated the Danes, and proclaimed Christianity; Gustavus II (Gustavus Adolphus, 1594–1632) freed Swedish territories occupied by Denmark, Russia, and Poland.

26. *I.e.,* "incalculable."

27. *Cf.* Joshua v: 15; Exodus iii: 5.

28. In Norse myth, "the Thunderer," god of war.

29. Anglo-Saxon form of the name of Odin—in Teutonic myth the god of war but also the patron of the slain.

30. The doctrine of salvation by faith alone, without reference to breaches of the moral law.

31. The original Stoics, led by Zeno of Athens after 300 B.C., taught passionless self-reliance and submission to natural law.

32. *Cf.* John i: 14.

33. *Cf.* Genesis i: 25.

34. The Elizabethan playwright John Fletcher wrote *Bonduca* (1618) perhaps in collaboration with Francis Beaumont.

35. Reputed founder (sixth century B.C.?) of ancient Persian religion, recorded in the Avesta, here quoted.

36. *Cf.* the words of the Israelites to Moses concerning the Ten Commandments: Exodus xx: 19.

37. Each of the following was a pioneer of the "systematic" science: John Locke (1632–1704) developed a theory of knowledge; Antoine Laurent Lavoisier (1743–1794) pioneered in chemistry and James Hutton (1726–1797) in geology; Jeremy Bentham (1748–1832) formulated utilitarian concepts of law and government; François Marie Charles Fourier (1772–1837) originated plans for the co-operative organization of society.

38. The essay "Self-Reliance" originated as a development of the preceding portion of this paragraph, which formed an entry in Emerson's journal for 1832 (*cf.* Centenary Edition, Vol. II, p. 395).

39. The greatest of ancient Greek sculptors (*fl.* fifth century B.C.).

40. Graeco-Roman biographer (46?–120?), whose *Lives* became a source book for Renaissance literature, especially the Elizabethan.

41. The earlier explorers, Henry Hudson (died 1611) and Vitus Bering (Behring) (1680–1741), left their names on the map

of North America; Sir William E. Parry (1790–1855) and Sir John Franklin (1786–1847) were English Arctic explorers famous in Emerson's day.

42. The "opera-glass" of Galileo (1564–1642), Italian astronomer, was the first modern refracting telescope.

43. Properly Las Cases (Comte Emmanuel Augustin Dieudonné de, 1766–1842), Napoleon's secretary during his exile on St. Helena, who compiled from the Emperor's conversations the *Mémorial de Sainte Hélène* (1818, revised 1823) which Emerson here paraphrases.

44. Ali ibn-abu-Talib (600?–661), the fourth Moslem Caliph and son-in-law of the Prophet; his reputed sayings, surviving as proverbs, had appeared in English translation (1832).

45. The ancients sometimes pictured Fortuna as dispensing her gifts at the whim of a wheel of chance.

Civil Disobedience

HENRY DAVID THOREAU

A close friend and disciple of Ralph Waldo Emerson, Henry David Thoreau (1817–1862) became an outstanding American philosopher, essayist, poet and exponent of self-reliance. His works include such important documents as Walden *and the* Journals. *During the student uprising at Berkeley in the fall of 1964, students in the Free Speech Movement frequently invoked the ideas which Thoreau expressed in his essay on "Civil Disobedience."* [1]

I heartily accept the motto,—"That government is best which governs least;" [2] and I should like to see it acted up to more rapidly and systematically. Carried out, it finally amounts to this, which also I believe,—"That government is best which governs not at all;" and when men are prepared for it, that will be the kind of government which they will have. Government is at best but an expedient; but most governments are usually, and all governments are sometimes, inexpedient. The objections which have been brought against a standing army, and they are many and weighty, and deserve to prevail, may also at last be brought against a standing government. The standing army is only an arm of the standing government. The government itself, which is only the mode which the people have chosen to execute their will, is equally liable to be abused and perverted before the people can act through it. Witness the present Mexican war, the work of comparatively a few individuals [3] using the standing government as their tool; for, in the outset, the people would not have consented to this measure.

This American government,—what is it but a tradition, though a recent one, endeavoring to transmit itself unimpaired to posterity, but each instant losing some of its integrity? It has not the vitality and force of a single living man; for a single man can bend it to his will. It is a sort of wooden gun to the people themselves. But it is not the less necessary for this; for the people must have some complicated machinery or other, and hear its din, to satisfy that idea of government which they have. Governments show thus how successfully men can be imposed on, even impose on themselves, for their own advantage. It is excellent, we must all allow. Yet this government never of itself furthered any enterprise, but by the alacrity with which it got out of its way. *It* does not keep the country free. *It* does not settle the West. *It* does not educate. The character inherent in the American people has done all that has been accomplished; and it would have done somewhat more, if the government had not sometimes got in its way. For government is an expedient by which men would fain succeed in letting one another alone; and, as has been said, when it is most expedient, the governed are most let alone by it. Trade and commerce, if they were not made of India-rubber, would never manage to bounce over the obstacles which legislators are continually putting in their way; and, if one were to judge these men wholly by the effects of their actions and not partly by their intentions, they would deserve to be classed and punished with those mischievous persons who put obstructions on the railroads.

But, to speak practically and as a citizen, unlike those who call themselves no-government men, I ask for, not at once no government, but *at once* a better government. Let every man make known what kind of government would command his respect, and that will be one step toward obtaining it.

After all, the practical reason why, when the power is once in the hands of the people, a majority are permitted, and for a long period continue, to rule is not because they are most likely to be in the right, nor because this seems fairest to the minority, but because they are physically the strongest. But a government in which the majority rule in all cases cannot be based on justice, even as far as men understand it. Can there not be a government in which majorities do not virtually decide right and wrong, but conscience? [4]—in which majorities decide only those questions to which the rule of expediency is applicable? Must the citizen ever for a moment, or in the least degree, resign his conscience to the legislator? Why has every man a conscience, then? I think that we should be men first, and subjects afterward. It is not desirable to cultivate a respect for the law, so much as for the right. The only obligation which I have a right to assume is to do at any time what I think right. It is truly enough said that a corporation has no conscience; but a corporation of conscientious men is a corporation *with* a conscience. Law never made men a whit more just; and, by means of their respect for it, even the well-disposed are daily made the agents of injustice. A common and natural result of an undue respect for law is, that you may see a file of soldiers, colonel, captain, corporal, privates, powder-monkeys, and all, marching in admirable order over hill and dale to the wars, against their wills, ay, against their common sense and consciences, which makes it very steep marching indeed, and produces a palpitation of the heart. They have no doubt that it is a damnable business in which they are concerned; they are all peaceably inclined. Now, what are they? Men at all? or small movable forts and magazines, at the service of some unscrupulous man in power? Visit the Navy-Yard, and behold a marine, such a man as an American government can make, or such as it can make a man with its black arts,—a mere shadow and reminiscence of humanity, a man laid out alive and standing, and already, as one may say, buried under arms with funeral accompaniments, though it may be,—

Not a drum was heard, not a funeral note,
    As his corse to the rampart we hurried;
Not a soldier discharged his farewell shot
    O'er the grave where our hero we buried.[5]

The mass of men serve the state thus, not as men mainly, but as machines, with their bodies. They are the standing army, and the militia, jailers, constables, *posse comitatus*,[6] etc. In most cases there is no free exercise whatever of the judgment or of the moral sense; but they put themselves on a level with wood and earth and stones; and wooden men can perhaps be manufactured that will serve the purpose as well. Such command no more respect than men of straw or a lump of dirt. They have the same sort of worth only as horses and dogs. Yet such as these even are commonly esteemed good citizens. Others—as most legislators, politicians, lawyers, ministers, and office-holders—serve the state chiefly with their heads; and, as they rarely make any moral distinctions, they are as likely to serve the devil, without *intending* it, as God. A very few,—as heroes, patriots, martyrs, reformers in the great sense and *men*—serve the state with their consciences also, and so necessarily resist it for the most part; and they are commonly treated as enemies by it. A wise man will only be useful as a man, and will not submit to be "clay," and "stop a hole to keep the wind away," [7] but leave that office to his dust at least: —

I am too high-born to be propertied,
To be a secondary at control,
Or useful serving-man and instrument
To any sovereign state throughout the world.[8]

He who gives himself entirely to his fellow-men appears to them useless and selfish; but he who gives himself partially to them is pronounced a benefactor and philanthropist.

How does it become a man to behave toward this American government to-day? I answer, that he cannot without disgrace be associated with it.[9] I cannot for an instant recognize that political organization as *my* government which is the *slave's* government also.

All men recognize the right of revolution; that is, the right to refuse allegiance to, and to resist, the government, when its tyranny or its inefficiency are great and unendurable. But almost all say that such is not the case now. But such was the case, they think, in the Revolution of '75. If one were to tell me that this was a bad government because it taxed certain foreign commodities brought to its ports, it is most probable that I should not make an ado about it, for I can do without them. All machines have their friction; and possibly this does enough good to counterbalance the evil. At any rate, it is a great evil to make a stir about it. But when the friction comes to have its machine, and oppression and robbery are organized, I say, let us not have such a machine any longer. In other words, when a sixth of the population of a nation which has undertaken to be the refuge of liberty are slaves, and a whole country [10] is unjustly overrun and conquered by a foreign army, and subjected to military law, I think that it is not too soon for honest men to rebel and revolutionize. What makes this duty the more urgent is the fact that the country so overrun is not our own, but ours is the invading army.

Paley,[11] a common authority with many on moral questions, in his chapter on the "Duty of Submission to Civil Government," resolves all civil obligation into expediency; and he proceeds to say "that so long as the interest of the whole society requires it, that is, so long as the established government cannot be resisted or changed without public inconveniency, it is the will of God . . . that the established government be obeyed,—and no longer. This principle being admitted, the justice of every particular case of resistance is reduced to a computation of the quantity of the danger and grievance on the one side, and of the probability and expense of redressing it on the other." Of this, he says, every man shall judge for himself. But Paley appears never to have contemplated those cases to which the rule of expediency does not apply, in which a people, as well as an individual, must do justice, cost what it may. If I have unjustly wrested a plank from a drowning man, I must restore it to him though I drown myself. This, according to Paley, would be inconvenient. But he that would save his life, in such a case, shall lose it.[12] This people must cease to hold slaves, and to make war on Mexico, though it cost them their existence as a people.

In their practice, nations agree with Paley; but does any one think that Massachusetts does exactly what is right at the present crisis?

A drab of state, a cloth-o'-silver slut,
To have her train borne up, and her soul trail in the dirt.

Practically speaking, the opponents to a reform in Massachusetts are not a hundred thousand politicians at the South, but a hundred thousand merchants and farmers here, who are more interested in commerce and agriculture than they are in humanity, and are not prepared to do justice to the slave and to Mexico, *cost what it may*. I quarrel not with far-off foes, but with those who, near at home, coöperate with, and do the bidding of, those far away, and without whom the latter would be harmless. We are accustomed to say, that the mass of men are unprepared; but improvement is slow, because the few are not materially wiser or better than the many. It is not so important that many should be as good as you, as that there be some absolute goodness somewhere; for that will leaven the whole lump.[13] There are thousands who are *in opinion* opposed to slavery and to the war, who yet in effect do nothing to put an end to them; who, esteeming themselves children of Washington and Franklin, sit down with their hands in their pockets, and say that they know not what to do, and do nothing; who even postpone the question of freedom to the question of free trade, and quietly read the prices-current along with the latest advices from Mexico, after dinner, and, it may be, fall asleep over them both. What is the price-current of an honest man and patriot today? They hesitate, and they regret, and sometimes they petition; but they do nothing in earnest and with effect. They will wait, well disposed, for others to remedy the evil, that they may no longer have it to regret. At most, they give only a cheap vote, and a feeble countenance and God-speed, to the right, as it goes by them. There are nine hundred and ninety-nine patrons of virtue to one virtuous man. But it is easier to deal with the real possessor of a thing than with the temporary guardian of it.

All voting is a sort of gaming, like checkers or backgammon, with a slight moral tinge to it, a playing with right and wrong, with moral questions; and betting naturally accompanies it. The character of the voters is not staked. I cast my vote, perchance, as I think right; but I am not vitally concerned that that right should prevail. I am willing to leave it to the majority. Its obligation, therefore, never exceeds that of expediency. Even voting *for the right* is *doing* nothing for it. It is only expressing to men feebly your desire that it should prevail. A wise man will not leave the right to the mercy of chance, nor wish it to prevail through the power of the majority. There is but little virtue in the action of masses of men. When the majority shall at length vote for the abolition of slavery, it will be because they are indifferent to slavery, or because there is but little slavery left to be abolished by their vote. *They* will then be the only slaves. Only *his* vote can hasten the abolition of slavery who asserts his own freedom by his vote.

I hear of a convention to be held at Baltimore,[14] or elsewhere, for the selection of a candidate for the Presidency, made up chiefly of editors, and men who are politicians by profession; but I think, what is it to any independent, intelligent, and respectable man what decision they may come to? Shall we not have the advantage of his wisdom and honesty, nevertheless? Can we not count upon some independent votes? Are there not many individuals in the country who do not attend conventions? But no: I find that the respectable man, so called, has immediately drifted from his position, and despairs of his country, when his country has more reason to despair of him. He forthwith adopts one of the candidates thus selected as the only *available* one, thus proving that he is himself *available* for any purposes of the demagogue. His vote is of no more worth than that of any unprincipled foreigner or hireling native, who may have been bought. O for a man who is a *man*, and, as my neighbor says, has a bone in

his back which you cannot pass your hand through! Our statistics are at fault: the population has been returned too
large. How many *men* are there to a square thousand miles in
this country? Hardly one. Does not America offer any induce-
ment for men to settle here? The American has dwindled into
an Odd Fellow,[15]—one who may be known by the development
of his organ of gregariousness, and a manifest lack of intellect
and cheerful self-reliance; whose first and chief concern, on
coming into the world, is to see that the almshouses are in
good repair; and, before yet he has lawfully donned the
virile garb,[16] to collect a fund for the support of the widows
and orphans that may be; who, in short, ventures to live
only by the aid of the Mutual Insurance company, which
has promised to bury him decently.

It is not a man's duty, as a matter of course, to devote himself to the eradication of any, even the most enormous, wrong;
he may still properly have other concerns to engage him; but
it is his duty, at least, to wash his hands of it, and, if he gives
it no thought longer, not to give it practically his support.
If I devote myself to other pursuits and contemplations, I must
first see, at least, that I do not pursue them sitting upon another man's shoulders. I must get off him first, that he may
pursue his contemplations too. See what gross inconsistency
is tolerated. I have heard some of my townsmen say, "I should
like to have them order me out to help put down an insurrec-
tion of the slaves, or to march to Mexico;—see if I would go;"
and yet these very men have each, directly by their allegiance,
and so indirectly, at least, by their money, furnished a substitute. The soldier is applauded who refuses to serve in an
unjust war by those who do not refuse to sustain the unjust
government which makes the war; is applauded by those
whose own act and authority he disregards and sets at naught;
as if the state were penitent to that degree that it hired one
to scourge it while it sinned, but not to that degree that it
left off sinning for a moment. Thus, under the name of Order
and Civil Government, we are all made at last to pay homage
to and support our own meanness. After the first blush of sin
comes its indifference; and from immoral it becomes, as it
were, *un*moral, and not quite unnecessary to that life which
we have made.

The broadest and most prevalent error requires the most disinterested virtue to sustain it. The slight reproach to which the virtue of patriotism is commonly liable, the noble are most likely to incur. Those who, while they disapprove of the character and measures of a government, yield to it their allegiance and support are undoubtedly its most conscientious supporters, and so frequently the most serious obstacles to reform. Some are petitioning the State to dissolve the Union, to disregard the requisitions of the President. Why do they not dissolve it themselves,—the union between themselves and the State,—and refuse to pay their quota into its treasury? Do not they stand in the same relation to the State that the State does to the Union? And have not the same reasons prevented the State from resisting the Union which have prevented them from resisting the State?

How can a man be satisfied to entertain an opinion merely, and enjoy *it*? Is there any enjoyment in it, if his opinion is that he is aggrieved? If you are cheated out of a single dollar by your neighbor, you do not rest satisfied with knowing that you are cheated, or with saying that you are cheated, or even with petitioning him to pay you your due; but you take effectual steps at once to obtain the full amount, and see that you are never cheated again. Action from principle, the perception and the performance of right, changes things and relations; it is essentially revolutionary, and does not consist wholly with anything which was. It not only divides States and churches, it divides families; ay, it divides the *individual*, separating the diabolical in him from the divine.

Unjust laws exist: shall we be content to obey them, or shall we endeavor to amend them, and obey them until we have succeeded, or shall we transgress them at once? Men generally, under such a government as this, think that they ought to wait until they have persuaded the majority to alter them. They think that, if they should resist, the remedy would be worse than the evil. But it is the fault of the government itself that the remedy *is* worse than the evil. *It* makes it worse. Why is it not more apt to anticipate and provide for reform? Why does it not cherish its wise minority? Why does it cry and resist before it is hurt? Why does it not encourage its citizens to be on the alert to point out its faults, and *do* better than it would have them? Why does it always crucify Christ, and excommunicate Copernicus and Luther,[17] and pronounce Washington and Franklin rebels?

One would think, that a deliberate and practical denial of its authority was the only offense never contemplated by government; else, why has it not assigned its definite, its suitable and proportionate penalty? If a man who has no property refuses but once to earn nine shillings for the State, he is put in prison for a period unlimited by any law that I know, and determined only by the discretion of those who place him there; but if he should steal ninety times nine shillings from the State, he is soon permitted to go at large again.

If the injustice is part of the necessary friction of the machine of government, let it go, let it go: perchance it will wear smooth,—certainly the machine will wear out. If the injustice has a spring, or a pulley, or a rope, or a crank, exclusively for itself, then perhaps you may consider whether the remedy will not be worse than the evil; but if it is of such a nature that it requires you to be the agent of injustice to another, then, I say, break the law. Let your life be a counter friction to stop the machine. What I have to do is to see, at any rate, that I do not lend myself to the wrong which I condemn.

As for adopting the ways which the State has provided for remedying the evil, I know not of such ways. They take too much time, and a man's life will be gone. I have other affairs to attend to. I came into this world, not chiefly to make this a good place to live in, but to live in it, be it good or bad. A man has not everything to do, but something; and because he cannot do *everything*, it is not necessary that he should do *something* wrong. It is not my business to be petitioning the Governor or the Legislature any more than it is theirs to petition me; and if they should not hear my petition, what should I do then? But in this case the State has provided no way: its very Constitution is the evil. This may seem to be harsh and stubborn and unconciliatory; but it is to treat with the utmost kindness and consideration the only spirit that can appreciate or deserves it. So is all change for the better, like birth and death, which convulse the body.

I do not hesitate to say, that those who call themselves Abolitionists should at once effectually withdraw their support, both in person and property, from the government of Massachusetts, and not wait till they constitute a majority of one, before they suffer the right to prevail through them. I think that it is enough if they have God on their side, without waiting for that other one.[18] Moreover, any man more right than his neighbors constitutes a majority of one already.

I meet this American government, or its representative, the State government, directly, and face to face, once a year—no more—in the person of its tax-gatherer; this is the only mode in which a man situated as I am necessarily meets it; and it then says distinctly, Recognize me; and the simplest, the most effectual, and, in the present posture of affairs, the indispensablest mode of treating with it on this head, of expressing your little satisfaction with and love for it, is to deny it then. My civil neighbor, the tax-gatherer, is the very man I have to deal with,—for it is, after all, with men and not with parchment that I quarrel,—and he has voluntarily chosen to be an agent of the government. How shall he ever know well what he is and does as an officer of the government, or as a man, until he is obliged to consider whether he shall treat me, his neighbor, for whom he has respect, as a neighbor and well-disposed man, or as a maniac and disturber of the peace, and see if he can get over this obstruction to his neighborliness without a ruder and more impetuous thought or speech corresponding with his action. I know this well, that if one thousand, if one hundred, if ten men whom I could name,—if ten *honest* men only,—ay, if *one* HONEST man, in this State of Massachusetts *ceasing to hold slaves,* were actually to withdraw from this copartnership, and be locked up in the county jail therefor, it would be the abolition of slavery in America.[19] For it matters not how small the beginning may seem to be: what is once well done is done forever. But we love better to talk about it: that we say is our mission. Reform keeps many scores of newspapers in its service, but not one man. If my esteemed neighbor, the State's ambassador,[20] who will devote his days to the settlement of the question of human rights in the Council Chamber, instead of being threatened with the prisons of Carolina, were to sit down the prisoner of Massachusetts, that State which is so anxious to foist the sin of slavery upon her sister,—though at present she can discover only an act of inhospitality to be the ground of a quarrel with her,—the Legislature would not wholly waive the subject the following winter.

Under a government which imprisons any unjustly, the true place for a just man is also a prison. The proper place to-day, the only place which Massachusetts has provided for her freer and less desponding spirits, is in her prisons, to be put out and locked out of the State by her own act, as they have already put themselves out by their principles. It is there that the fugitive slave, and the Mexican prisoner on parole, and the Indian come to plead the wrongs of his race should find them; on that separate, but more free and honorable ground, where the State places those who are not *with* her, but *against* her,—the only house in a slave State in which a free man can abide with honor. If any think that their influence would be lost there, and their voices no longer afflict the ear of the State, that they would not be an enemy within its walls, they do not know by how much truth is stronger than error, nor how much more eloquently and effectively he can combat injustice who has experienced a little in his own person. Cast your whole vote, not a strip of paper merely, but your whole influence. A minority is powerless while it conforms to the majority; it is not even a minority then; but it is irresistible when it clogs by its whole weight. If the alternative is to keep all just men in prison, or give up war and slavery, the State will not hesitate which to choose. If a thousand men were not to pay their tax-bills this year, that would not be a violent and bloody measure, as it would be to pay them, and enable the State to commit violence and shed innocent blood. This is, in fact, the definition of a peaceable revolution, if any such is possible. If the tax-gatherer, or any other public officer, asks me, as one has done, "But what shall I do?" my answer is, "If you really wish to do anything, resign your office." When the subject has refused allegiance, and the officer has resigned his office, then the revolution is accomplished. But even suppose blood should flow.

Is there not a sort of blood shed when the conscience is wounded? Through this wound a man's real manhood and immortality flow out, and he bleeds to an everlasting death. I see this blood flowing now.

I have contemplated the imprisonment of the offender, rather than the seizure of his goods,—though both will serve the same purpose,—because they who assert the purest right, and consequently are most dangerous to a corrupt State, commonly have not spent much time in accumulating property. To such the State renders comparatively small service, and a slight tax is wont to appear exorbitant, particularly if they are obliged to earn it by special labor [21] with their hands. If there were one who lived wholly without the use of money, the State itself would hesitate to demand it of him. But the rich man—not to make any invidious comparison—is always sold to the institution which makes him rich. Absolutely speaking, the more money, the less virtue; for money comes between a man and his objects, and obtains them for him and it was certainly no great virtue to obtain it. It puts to rest many questions which he would otherwise be taxed to answer; while the only new question which it puts is the hard but superfluous one, how to spend it. Thus his moral ground is taken from under his feet. The opportunities of living are diminished in proportion as what are called the "means" are increased. The best thing a man can do for his culture when he is rich is to endeavor to carry out those schemes which he entertained when he was poor. Christ answered the Herodians according to their condition. "Show me the tribute-money," said he;—and took one penny out of his pocket;—if you use money which has the image of Caesar on it and which he has made current and valuable, that is, *if you are men of the State*, and gladly enjoy the advantages of Caesar's government, then pay him back some of his own when he demands it. "Render therefore to Caesar that which is Caesar's, and to God those things which are God's," [22]—leaving them no wiser than before as to which was which; for they did not wish to know.

When I converse with the freest of my neighbors, I perceive that, whatever they may say about the magnitude and seriousness of the question, and their regard for the public tranquillity, the long and the short of the matter is, that they cannot spare the protection of the existing government, and they dread the consequences to their property and families of disobedience to it. For my own part, I should not like to think that I ever rely on the protection of the State. But, if I deny the authority of the State when it presents its tax-bill, it will soon take and waste all my property, and so harass me and my children without end. This is hard. This makes it impossible for a man to live honestly, and at the same time comfortably, in outward respects. It will not be worth the while to accumulate property; that would be sure to go again. You must hire or squat somewhere, and raise but a small crop, and eat that soon. You must live within yourself, and depend upon yourself always tucked up and ready for a start, and not have many affairs. A man may grow rich in Turkey even, if he will be in all respects a good subject of the Turkish government. Confucius [23] said: "If a state is governed by the principles of reason, poverty and misery are subjects of shame; if a state is not governed by the principles of reason, riches and honors are the subjects of shame." No: until I want the protection of Massachusetts to be extended to me in some distant Southern port, where my liberty is endangered, or until I am bent solely on building up an estate at home by peaceful enterprise, I can afford to refuse allegiance to Massachusetts, and her right to my property and life. It costs me less in every sense to incur the penalty of disobedience to the State than it would to obey. I should feel as if I were worth less in that case.

Some years ago, the State met me in behalf of the Church, and commanded me to pay a certain sum toward the support of a clergyman whose preaching my father attended, but never I myself. "Pay," it said, "or be locked up in the jail." [24] I declined to pay. But, unfortunately, another man saw fit to pay it. I did not see why the schoolmaster should be taxed to support the priest, and not the priest the schoolmaster; for I was not the State's schoolmaster, but I supported myself by voluntary subscription. I did not see why the lyceum should not present its tax-bill, and have the State to back its demand, as well as the Church. However, at the request of the select-men, I condescended to make some such statement as this in writing:—"Know all men by these presents, that I, Henry Thoreau, do not wish to be regarded as a member of any incorporated society which I have not joined." This I gave to the town clerk; and he has it. The State, having thus learned that I did not wish to be regarded as a member of that church, has never made a like demand on me since; though it said that it must adhere to its original presumption that time. If I had known how to name them, I should then have signed off in detail from all the societies which I never signed on to; but I did not know where to find a complete list.

I have paid no poll-tax for six years. I was put into a jail once on this account, for one night; [25] and, as I stood consider-ing the walls of solid stone, two or three feet thick, the door of wood and iron, a foot thick, and the iron grating which strained the light, I could not help being struck with the fool-ishness of that institution which treated me as if I were mere flesh and blood and bones, to be locked up. I wondered that it should have concluded at length that this was the best use it could put me to, and had never thought to avail itself of my services in some way. I saw that, if there was a wall of stone between me and my townsmen, there was a still more difficult one to climb or break through before they could get to be as free as I was. I did not for a moment feel confined, and the walls seemed a great waste of stone and mortar. I felt as if I alone of all my townsmen had paid my tax. They plainly did not know how to treat me, but behaved like per-sons who are underbred. In every threat and in every compli-ment there was a blunder; for they thought that my chief desire was to stand the other side of that stone wall. I could not but smile to see how industriously they locked the door on my meditations, which followed them out again without let or hindrance, and *they* were really all that was dangerous. As they could not reach me, they had resolved to punish my body; just as boys, if they cannot come at some person against whom they have a spite, will abuse his dog. I saw that the State was half-witted, that it was timid as a lone woman with her silver spoons, and that it did not know its friends from its foes, and I lost all my remaining respect for it, and pitied it.

Thus the State never intentionally confronts a man's sense, intellectual or moral, but only his body, his senses. It is not armed with superior wit or honesty, but with superior physical strength. I was not born to be forced. I will breathe after my own fashion. Let us see who is the strongest. What force has a multitude? They only can force me who obey a higher law than I. They force me to become like themselves. I do not hear of *men* being *forced* to live this way or that by masses of men. What sort of life were that to live? When I meet a government which says to me, "Your money or your life," why should I be in haste to give it my money? It may be in a great strait, and not know what to do: I cannot help that. It must help itself; do as I do. It is not worth the while to snivel about it. I am not responsible for the successful working of the machinery of society. I am not the son of the engineer. I perceive that, when an acorn and a chestnut fall side by side, the one does not remain inert to make way for the other, but both obey their own laws, and spring and grow and flourish as best they can, till one, perchance, overshadows and destroys the other. If a plant cannot live according to its nature, it dies; and so a man.

The night in prison was novel and interesting enough. The prisoners in their shirt-sleeves were enjoying a chat and the evening air in the doorway, when I entered. But the jailer said, "Come, boys, it is time to lock up;" and so they dispersed, and I heard the sound of their steps returning into the hollow apartments. My room-mate was introduced to me by the jailer as "a first-rate fellow and a clever [26] man." When the door was locked, he showed me where to hang my hat, and how he managed matters there. The rooms were whitewashed once a month; and this one, at least, was the whitest, most simply furnished, and probably the neatest apartment in the town. He naturally wanted to know where I came from, and what brought me there; and, when I had told him, I asked him in my turn how he came there, presuming him to be an honest man, of course; and, as the world goes, I believe he was. "Why," said he, "they accuse me of burning a barn; but I never did it." As near as I could discover, he had probably gone to bed in a barn when drunk, and smoked his pipe there;

and so a barn was burnt. He had the reputation of being a clever man, had been there some three months waiting for his trial to come on, and would have to wait as much longer; but he was quite domesticated and contented, since he got his board for nothing, and thought that he was well treated.

He occupied one window, and I the other; and I saw that if one stayed there long, his principal business would be to look out the window. I had soon read all the tracts that were left there, and examined where former prisoners had broken out, and where a grate had been sawed off, and heard the history of the various occupants of that room; for I found that even here there was a history and a gossip which never circulated beyond the walls of the jail. Probably this is the only house in the town where verses are composed, which are afterward printed in circular form, but not published. I was shown quite a long list of verses which were composed by some young men who had been detected in an attempt to escape, who avenged themselves by singing them.

I pumped my fellow-prisoner as dry as I could, for fear I should never see him again; but at length he showed me which was my bed, and left me to blow out the lamp.

It was like traveling into a far country, such as I had never expected to behold, to lie there for one night. It seemed to me that I never had heard the town clock strike before, nor the evening sounds of the village; for we slept with the windows open, which were inside the grating. It was to see my native village in the light of the Middle Ages, and our Concord was turned into a Rhine stream, and visions of knights and castles passed before me. They were the voices of old burghers that I heard in the streets. I was an involuntary spectator and auditor of whatever was done and said in the kitchen of the adjacent village-inn,—a wholly new and rare experience to me. It was a closer view of my native town. I was fairly inside of it. I never had seen its institutions before. This is one of the peculiar institutions; for it is a shire town. I began to comprehend what its inhabitants were about.

In the morning, our breakfasts were put through the hole in the door, in small oblong-square tin pans, made to fit, and holding a pint of chocolate, with brown bread, and an iron spoon. When they called for the vessels again, I was green enough to return what bread I had left; but my comrade seized it, and said that I should lay that up for lunch or dinner. Soon after he was let out to work at haying in a neighboring field, whither he went every day, and would not be back till noon; so he bade me good-day, saying that he doubted if he should see me again.

When I came out of prison,—for some one interfered, and paid that tax,[27]—I did not perceive that great changes had taken place on the common, such as he observed who went in a youth and emerged a tottering and gray-headed man; and yet a change had to my eyes come over the scene,—the town, the State, and country,—greater than any that mere time could effect. I saw yet more distinctly the State in which I lived. I saw to what extent the people among whom I lived could be trusted as good neighbors and friends; that their friendship was for summer weather only; that they did not greatly propose to do right; that they were a distinct race from me by their prejudices and superstitions, as the Chinamen and Malays are; that in their sacrifices to humanity they ran no risks, not even to their property; that after all they were not so noble but they treated the thief as he had treated them, and hoped, by a certain outward observance and a few prayers, and by walking in a particular straight though useless path from time to time, to save their souls. This may be to judge my neighbors harshly; for I believe that many of them are not aware that they have such an institution as the jail in their village.

It was formerly the custom of our village, when a poor debtor came out of jail, for his acquaintances to salute him, looking through their fingers, which were crossed to represent the greating of a jail window, "How do ye do?" My neighbors did not thus salute me, but first looked at me, and then at one another, as if I had returned from a long journey. I was put into jail as I was going to the shoemaker's to get a shoe which was mended. When I was let out the next morning, I proceeded to finish my errand, and having put on my mended shoe, joined a huckleberry party, who were impatient to put themselves under my conduct; and in half an hour,—for the horse was soon tackled,—was in the midst of a huckleberry field, on one of our highest hills, two miles off, and then the State was nowhere to be seen.

This is the whole history of "My Prisons." [28]

I have never declined paying the highway tax, because I am as desirous of being a good neighbor as I am of being a bad subject; and as for supporting schools, I am doing my part to educate my fellow-countrymen now. It is for no particular item in the tax-bill that I refuse to pay it. I simply wish to refuse allegiance to the State, to withdraw and stand aloof from it effectually. I do not care to trace the course of my dollar, if I could, till it buys a man or a musket to shoot one with,—the dollar is innocent,—but I am concerned to trace the effects of my allegiance. In fact, I quietly declare war with the State, after my fashion, though I will still make what use and get what advantage of her I can, as is usual in such cases.

If others pay the tax which is demanded of me, from a sympathy with the State, they do but what they have already done in their own case, or rather they abet injustice to greater extent than the State requires. If they pay the tax from a mistaken interest in the individual taxed, to save his property, or prevent his going to jail, it is because they have not considered wisely how far they let their private feelings interfere with the public good.

This, then, is my position at present. But one cannot be too much on his guard in such a case, lest his action be biased by obstinacy or an undue regard for the opinions of men. Let him see that he does only what belongs to himself and to the hour.

I think sometimes, Why, this people mean well, they are only ignorant; they would do better if they knew how: why give your neighbors this pain to treat you as they are not inclined to? But I think again, This is no reason why I should do as they do, or permit others to suffer much greater pain of a different kind. Again, I sometimes say to myself, When many millions of men, without heat, without ill will, without personal feeling of any kind, demand of you a few shillings only, without the possibility, such is their constitution, of retracting or altering their present demand, and without the possibility, on your side, of appeal to any other millions, why expose yourself to this overwhelming brute force? You do not resist cold and hunger, the winds and the waves, thus obstinately; you quietly submit to a thousand similar necessities. You do not put your head into the fire. But just in proportion as I regard this as not wholly brute force, but partly a human force, and consider that I have relations to those millions as to so many millions of men, and not of mere brute or inanimate things, I see that appeal is possible, first and instantaneously, from them to the Maker of them, and, secondly, from them to themselves. But if I put my head deliberately into the fire, there is no appeal to fire or to the Maker of fire, and I have only myself to blame. If I could convince myself that I have any right to be satisfied with men as they are, and to treat them accordingly, and not according, in some respects, to my requisitions and expectations of what they and I ought to be, then, like a good Mussulman and fatalist, I should endeavor to be satisfied with things as they are, and say it is the will of God. And, above all, there is this difference between resisting this and a purely brute or natural force, that I can resist this with some effect; but I cannot expect, like Orpheus,[29] to change the nature of the rocks and trees and beasts.

I do not wish to quarrel with any man or nation. I do not wish to split hairs, to make fine distinctions, or set myself up as better than my neighbors. I seek rather, I may say, even an excuse for conforming to the laws of the land. I am but too ready to conform to them. Indeed, I have reason to suspect myself on this head; and each year, as the tax-gatherer comes round, I find myself disposed to review the acts and position of the general and State governments, and the spirit of the people, to discover a pretext for conformity.

> We must affect our country as our parents,
> And if at any time we alienate
> Our love or industry from doing it honor,
> We must respect effects and teach the soul

Matter of conscience and religion,
And not desire of rule or benefit.

I believe that the State will soon be able to take all my work of this sort out of my hands, and then I shall be no better a patriot than my fellow-countrymen. Seen from a lower point of view, the Constitution, with all its faults, is very good; the law and the courts are very respectable; even this State and this American government are, in many respects, very admirable, and rare things, to be thankful for, such as a great many have described them; but seen from a point of view a little higher, they are what I have described them; seen from a higher still, and the highest, who shall say what they are, or that they are worth looking at or thinking of at all?

However, the government does not concern me much, and I shall bestow the fewest possible thoughts on it. It is not many moments that I live under a government, even in this world. If a man is thought-free, fancy-free, imagination-free, that which *is not* never for a long time appearing *to be* to him, unwise rulers or reformers cannot fatally interrupt him.

I know that most men think differently from myself; but those whose lives are by profession devoted to the study of these or kindred subjects content me as little as any. Statesmen and legislators, standing so completely within the institution, never distinctly and nakedly behold it. They speak of moving society, but have no resting-place without it. They may be men of a certain experience and discrimination, and have no doubt invented ingenious and even useful systems, for which we sincerely thank them; but all their wit and usefulness lie within certain not very wide limits. They are wont to forget that the world is not governed by policy and expediency. Webster [30] never goes behind government, and so cannot speak with authority about it. His words are wisdom to those legislators who contemplate no essential reform in the existing government; but for thinkers, and those who legislate for all time, he never once glances at the subject. I know of those whose serene and wise speculations on this theme would soon reveal the limits of his mind's range and hospitality. Yet, compared with the cheap professions of most reformers, and the still cheaper wisdom and eloquence of politicians in general, his are almost the only sensible and valuable words, and we thank Heaven for him. Comparatively, he is always strong, original, and, above all, practical. Still, his quality is not wisdom, but prudence. The lawyer's truth is not Truth, but consistency or a consistent expediency. Truth is always in harmony with herself, and is not concerned chiefly to reveal the justice that may consist with wrong-doing. He well deserves to be called, as he has been called, the Defender of the Constitution. There are really no blows to be given by him but defensive ones. He is not a leader, but a follower. His leaders are the men of '87.[31] "I have never made an effort," he says, "and never propose to make an effort; I have never countenanced an effort, and never mean to countenance an effort, to disturb the arrangement as originally made, by which the various States came into the Union." Still thinking of the sanction which the Constitution gives to slavery, he says, "Because it was a part of the original compact,—let it stand." Notwithstanding his special acuteness and ability, he is unable to take a fact out of its merely political relations, and behold it as it lies absolutely to be disposed of by the intellect,— what, for instance, it behooves a man to do here in America to-day with regard to slavery,—but ventures, or is driven, to make some such desperate answer as the following, while professing to speak absolutely, and as a private man,—from which what new and singular code of social duties might be inferred? "The manner," says he, "in which the governments of those States where slavery exists are to regulate it is for their own consideration, under their responsibility to their constituents, to the general laws of propriety, humanity, and justice, and to God. Associations formed elsewhere, springing from a feeling of humanity, or any other cause, have nothing whatever to do with it. They have never received any encouragement from me, and they never will."

They who know of no purer sources of truth, who have traced up its stream no higher, stand, and wisely stand, by the Bible and the Constitution, and drink at it there with reverence and humility; but they who behold where it comes trickling into this lake or that pool, gird up their loins once more, and continue their pilgrimage toward its fountain-head.

No man with a genius for legislation has appeared in America. They are rare in the history of the world. There are orators, politicians, and eloquent men, by the thousand; but the speaker has not yet opened his mouth to speak who is capable of settling the much-vexed questions of the day. We love eloquence for its own sake, and not for any truth which it may utter, or any heroism it may inspire. Our legislators have not yet learned the comparative value of free trade and of freedom, of union, and of rectitude, to a nation. They have no genius or talent for comparatively humble questions of taxation and finance, commerce and manufactures and agriculture. If we were left solely to the wordy wit of legislators in Congress for our guidance, uncorrected by the seasonable experience and the effectual complaints of the people, America would not long retain her rank among the nations. For eighteen hundred years, though perchance I have no right to say it, the New Testament has been written; yet where is the legislator who has wisdom and practical talent enough to avail himself of the light which it sheds on the science of legislation?

The authority of government, even such as I am willing to submit to,—for I will cheerfully obey those who know and can do better than I, and in many things even those who neither know nor can do so well,—is still an impure one: to be strictly just, it must have the sanction and consent of the governed. It can have no pure light over my person and property but what I concede to it. The progress from an absolute to a limited monarchy, from a limited monarchy to a democracy, is a progress toward a true respect for the individual. Even the Chinese philosopher was wise enough to regard the individual as the basis of the empire. Is a democracy, such as we know it, the last improvement possible in government? Is it not possible to take a step further towards recognizing and organizing the rights of man? There will never be a really free and enlightened State until the State comes to recognize the individual as a higher and independent power, from which all its own power and authority are derived, and treats him accordingly. I please myself with imagining a State at last which can afford to be just to all men, and to treat the individual with respect as a neighbor; which even would not think it inconsistent with its own repose if a few were to live aloof from it, not meddling with it, nor embraced by it, who fulfilled all the duties of neighbors and fellow-men. A State which bore this kind of fruit, and suffered it to drop off as fast as it ripened, would prepare the way for a still more perfect and glorious State, which also I have imagined, but not yet anywhere seen.

NOTES

1. "Civil Disobedience" was neglected for more than half a century, although it formulates democratic ideas inherent in *Walden*. Thoreau believed, and demonstrated by example, that if government, responding to expediency or majority pressures, infringes upon the fundamental freedom of thought or choice of moral alternatives of the individual or the minority, the remedy is nonviolent, or pacific, resistance. Recently these ideas have had increasing attention wherever rising population and industrial pressures endanger the preservation of democratic individualism. More strikingly, through its acknowledged influence on Mahatma Gandhi, the essay became associated with a movement of incalculable significance for Asia and the world. This essay first appeared in the anthology *Aesthetic Essays* (1849), edited by Elizabeth Palmer Peabody, transcendentalist bookseller in Boston. There it was entitled "Resistance to Civil Government." Under its present title it appeared in the posthumous collections *A Yankee in Canada* (1866) and *Miscellanies* (1893).
2. These words echo Paine and Jefferson; the belief that government was a social contract sanctioned only by necessity was an active influence during the Revolution and the Constitutional Convention.
3. The war was regarded by northern reformers as resulting primarily from the selfish interest of southern politicians and northern cotton merchants in extending slave territory.
4. Recalling a principal controversy of the Constitutional Convention, where the conservative minority, represented by Hamilton and Adams, were overcome by the Jeffersonians, who favored majority rule.
5. Charles Wolfe (1791–1823), Irish clergyman who died at thirty-two, won several decades of remembrance by his "Burial of Sir John Moore at Corunna" (1817), of which this is the opening.
6. Legal Latin, meaning "having the authority of the county"; *cf.* the sheriff's "posse."

7. *Cf.* Shakespeare, *Hamlet,* Act V, Scene 1, 11. 236–237.
8. *Cf.* Shakespeare, *King John,* Act V, Scene 2, 11. 79–82.
9. Many accused Polk's administration (1845–1849) of strengthening slavery through fugitive-slave laws and the Mexican War.
10. Mexico.
11. William Paley (1743–1805), British thinker, whose utilitarianism motivates this quotation from his *Principles of Moral and Political Philosophy,* (1785).
12. *Cf.* Luke ix: 24.
13. *Cf.* I Corinthians v: 6.
14. The Democratic convention at Baltimore, in May, 1848, fulfilled Thoreau's prediction of expediency in its platform, and in its man, Lewis Cass, "a northern man with southern principles."
15. The Independent Order of Odd Fellows, one of numerous secret fraternal societies then being developed for social diversion and mutual insurance.
16. *Cf.* the *toga virilis,* which the Roman boy was permitted to wear on attaining the age of fourteen.
17. Copernicus was on his deathbed (1543) when his description of the solar system was published, later to come under the ban of the Church; but Luther, the founder of the German Reformation, was officially excommunicated in 1521, twenty-five years before his death.
18. *Cf.* the proverb "One on God's side is a majority."
19. An example of the operation of passive resistance, the doctrine for which Gandhi acknowledged indebtedness to Thoreau.
20. Samuel Hoar (1778–1856), distinguished Concord lawyer and congressman, was officially delegated to South Carolina to test certain laws denying the ports to Negro seamen on Massachusetts ships, under penalty of arrest and possible enslavement. Hoar was forcibly expelled from South Carolina by action of the legislature.
21. Referring to his stand against the Massachusetts church tax and poll tax, assessed against all males.
22. *Cf.* Matthew xxii: 16–21.
23. Confucius (551?–479? B.C.) was primarily a utilitarian and social philosopher; his formulation of Chinese "wisdom," preserved in the *Analects,* was familiar in translation to the transcendentalists.
24. Thoreau's resistance to compulsory church taxes occurred in 1838, and he was not jailed. The failure to comply with the poll tax probably began in 1840 (see the next paragraph).
25. Bronson Alcott had resisted the tax and been jailed for one night in 1843. The fundamental reason for resistance, for both men, was repugnance at supporting a state that recognized slavery, as Massachusetts still did in legal fact. H. S. Canby in

his *Thoreau* (p. 473) dates Thoreau's experience in jail as July 23 or 24, 1846.

26. American dialect for "honest," "kind."
27. It is legendary but unlikely that Emerson paid the tax. Family reminiscence ascribed the deed to his Aunt Maria.
28. English translation of the title *Le mie prigioni* (1832), a record of his years of hard labor in Austrian prisons by Silvio Pellico (1789–1854), Italian poet, playwright, and patriot.
29. Orpheus, a mythical Greek poet-musician, caused "rocks and trees and beasts" to follow the music of his lute.
30. Daniel Webster's respect for authority won him the title (mentioned later in this paragraph) "Defender of the Constitution"; he was therefore willing to compromise about slavery while it was "constitutional," thus losing many northern supporters.
31. *I.e.*, the framers of the Constitution, which was sent to the states for ratification in 1787.

The Conservative View of Man and Society

CLINTON ROSSITER

Clinton Rossiter was born in Philadelphia, graduated from Cornell, and received his doctorate in political science at Princeton. In 1946 he joined the Department of Government at Cornell. His study of American colonial history, Seedtime of the Republic, *won both the Bancroft and the Woodrow Wilson awards for American history, and his later books, among them* Conservatism in American History, The First American Revolution *and* The American Presidency, *have further established his reputation. Rossiter has received wide notice for his calm, reasoned expositions of the intelligent conservative's point of view on contemporary social and political issues.*

THE Conservative engages reluctantly in political speculation. Distaste, not affection, for a way of life persuades a man to think deeply and persistently about government. The Conservative's best of all possible worlds is already here, and he refuses to contemplate Utopia, much less draw up plans for it. Indeed, so foreign to his usual needs and tastes is the art of political theory that he will not even vindicate his own way of life unless it is openly and dangerously attacked. He then turns to strengthen those parts of his defense under heaviest assault. As a result, Conservatism appears at first glance to be a sort of gingerbread castle. Too many men from too many generations, most of whom went to their labors under the guns of reform, have taken part in its building.

A closer inspection reveals that the castle is sound and well proportioned; beneath the gingerbread there are iron and stone. The many builders from the many generations have shared a common faith and common purpose. The political tradition they have created and are still creating exhibits a high degree of unity and internal consistency. Out of the vast literature of Conservatism—a mass of principles, prejudices, intuitions, dogmas, assumptions, theories, and moral explosions—one may extract a harmonious system of political principles.

The Conservative holds definite opinions about man's nature, his capacity for self-government, his relations with other men, the kind of life he should lead, and the rights he may properly claim. On these opinions rests the whole Conservative tradition.

Man, says the Conservative, is a composite of good and evil, a blend of ennobling excellences and degrading imperfections. He is not perfect; he is not perfectible. If educated properly, placed in a favorable environment, and held in restraint by tradition and authority, he may display innate qualities of rationality, sociability, industry, decency, and love of liberty. Never, no matter how he is educated or situated or restrained, will he throw off completely his other innate qualities of irrationality, selfishness, laziness, depravity, and corruptibility. Man's nature is essentially immutable, and the immutable strain is one of deep-seated wickedness. Although some Conservatives find support for their skeptical view of man in recent experiments in psychology, most continue to rely on religious teaching and the study of history. Those who are Christians, and most Conservatives are, prefer to call the motivation for iniquitous and irrational behavior by its proper name: Original Sin.

The Conservative is often accused of putting too much stress on man's wickedness and irrationality and of overlooking his many good qualities, especially his capacity for reason. The Conservative's answer is candid enough. He is well aware of man's potentialities, but he must counter the optimism of the liberal and radical with certain cheerless reminders that are no less true for telling only half the truth: that evil exists independently of social or economic maladjustments; that we must search for the source of our discontents in defective human nature rather than in a defective social order; and that man, far from being malleable, is subject to cultural alteration only slowly and to a limited degree. The Conservative therefore considers it his stern duty to call attention, as did John Adams, to "the general frailty and depravity of human nature."

This view of human nature is saved from churlish cynicism by two splendid beliefs. First, man is touched with eternity. He has a precious soul; he is a religious entity. His urges toward sin are matched, and with God's grace are overmatched if never finally beaten down, by his aspiration for good. For this reason, the Conservative asserts, man is an object of reverence, and a recognition of man's heaven-ordained shortcomings serves only to deepen this reverence. Second, to quote from Burke, the father of all Conservatives, "The nature of man is intricate." The confession of an eminent psychologist, Gardner Murphy, "Not much, I believe, is known about man," is applauded by the Conservative, who then adds: "Not much, I believe, will ever be known about him." Man is a mysterious and complex being, and no amount of psychological research will ever solve the mystery or unravel the complexity.

No truth about human nature and capabilities is more important than this: man can govern himself, but there is no certainty that he will; free government is possible but far from inevitable. Man will need all the help he can get from education, religion, tradition, and institutions if he is to enjoy even a limited success in his experiments in self-government. He must be counseled, encouraged, informed, and checked. Above all, he must realize that the collective wisdom of the community, itself the union of countless partial and imperfect wisdoms like his own, is alone equal to the mightiest of social tasks. A clear recognition of man's conditional capacity for ruling himself and others is the first requisite of constitution-making.

Conservatism holds out obstinately against two popular beliefs about human relations in modern society: individualism and equality. . . . Let us hear what he has to say about the explosive question of equality.

Each man is equal to every other man in only one meaningful sense: he is a man, a physical and spiritual entity, and is thus entitled by God and nature to be treated as end rather than means. From the basic fact of moral equality come several secondary equalities that the modern Conservative recognizes, more eloquently in public than in private: equality of opportunity, the right of each individual to exploit his own talents up to their natural limits; equality before the law, the right to justice on the same terms as other men; and political equality, which takes the form of universal suffrage. Beyond this the Conservative is unwilling to go. Recognizing the infinite variety among men in talent, taste, appearance, intelligence, and virtue, he is candid enough to assert that this variety extends vertically as well as horizontally. Men are grossly unequal—and, what is more, can never be made equal —in all qualities of mind, body, and spirit.

The good society rests solidly on this great truth. The social order is organized in such a way as to take advantage of ineradicable natural distinctions among men. It exhibits a class structure in which there are several quite distinct levels; most men find their level early and stay in it without rancor, and equality of opportunity keeps the way at least partially open to ascent and decline. At the same time, the social order aims to temper those distinctions that are not natural. It recognizes the inevitability and indeed the necessity of orders and classes, but it insists that all privileges, ranks, and other visible signs of inequality be as natural and functional as possible. The Conservative, of course—and this point is of decisive importance—is much more inclined than other men to consider artificial distinctions as natural. Equity rather than equality is the mark of his society; the reconciliation rather than the abolition of classes is his constant aim. When he is forced to choose between liberty and equality, he throws his support unhesitatingly to liberty. Indeed, the preference for liberty over equality lies at the root of the Conservative tradition.

While Conservatism has retreated some distance from Burke and Adams under the pressures of modern democracy, it has refused to yield one salient: the belief in a ruling and serving aristocracy. "If there is any one point," Gertrude Himmelfarb writes, "any single empirical test, by which conservatism can be distinguished from liberalism, it is a respect for aristocracy and aristocratic institutions. Every tenet of liberalism repudiates the idea of a fixed aristocracy; every tenet of conservatism affirms it." If it is no longer good form to use the word *aristocracy* in political debate, nor good sense to expect that an aristocracy can be "fixed" to the extent that it was one hundred and fifty years ago, the Conservative is still moved powerfully by the urge to seek out the best men and place them in positions of authority. He continues to assert the beneficence of an aristocracy of talent and virtue, one that is trained for special service and thus entitled to special consideration. He continues to believe that it takes more than one generation to make a genuine aristocrat.

The world being what it is today, the Conservative spends a good deal of his time in the pulpit exhorting his fellow men to live godly, righteous, and sober lives. He does not do this gladly, for he is not by nature a Puritan, but the times seem to have made him our leading "moral athlete."

Man, the Conservative asserts, is stamped with sin and carnality, but he is also blessed with higher aspirations. If human nature in general can never be much improved, each individual may nevertheless bring his own savage and selfish impulses under control. It is his duty to himself, his fellows, and God to do just this—to shun vice, cultivate virtue, and submit to the guidance of what Lincoln called "the better angels of our nature." Only thus, through the moral striving of many men, can free government be secured and society be made stable.

What virtues must the individual cultivate? The Conservative of the tower, the Conservative of the field, the Conservative of the market place, and the Conservative of the assembly each give a somewhat different answer to this question, yet all agree to this catalogue of primary virtues: wisdom, justice, temperance, and courage; industry, frugality, piety, and honesty; contentment, obedience, compassion, and good manners. The good man is peaceful but not resigned and is conservative through habit and choice rather than sloth and cowardice. He assumes that duty comes before pleasure, self-sacrifice before self-indulgence. Believing that the test of life is accomplishment rather than enjoyment, he takes pride in doing a good job in the station to which he has been called. He is alert to the identity and malignity of the vices he must shun: ignorance, injustice, intemperance, and cowardice; laziness, luxury, selfishness, and dishonesty; envy, disobedience, violence, and bad manners. And he is aware, too, of the larger implications of his own life of virtue: self-government is for moral men; those who would be free must be virtuous.

Education starts a man on the road that leads through virtue to freedom. Only through education—in family, church, and school—can children be shaped into civilized men. Only through education can man's vices, which are tough, be brought under control and his virtues, which are frail, be nourished into robust health. The instruments of education should teach a man to think, survive, ply a trade, and enjoy his leisure. Their great mission, however, is to act as a conserving, civilizing force: to convey to each man his share of the inherited wisdom of the race, to train him to lead a moral, self-disciplined life, and to foster a love of order and respect for authority.

The Conservative's understanding of the mission of education explains his profound mistrust of modern theories, most of which, he feels, are grounded in a clear misreading of the nature and needs of children. The school has always been a conservative force in society, and the Conservative means to keep it that way. He admits that there is a stage in the education of some individuals—those who are to go on to leadership —when self-development and self-expression should get prime consideration. First things must come first, however, and before this stage is reached, the individual must be taught his community's values and be integrated into its structure.

The Conservative's best thoughts are directed to society and the social process. The key points of his social theory appear to be these:

Society is a living organism with roots deep in the past. The true community, the Conservatives like to say, is a tree, not a machine. It rose to its present strength and glory through centuries of growth, and men must forbear to think of it as a mechanical contrivance that can be dismantled and reassembled in one generation. Prescription, not fiat, is the chief creative force in the social process.

Society is cellular. It is not an agglomeration of lonely individuals, but a grand, complex union of functional groups. Man is a social animal whose best interests are served by co-operating with other men. Indeed, he has no real meaning except as contributing member of one or more of these intrinsic groups: family, church, local community, and, at certain stages of historical development, occupational association. The group is important not only because it gives life, work, comfort, and spiritual support to the individual, but because it joins with thousands of other groups to form the one really stubborn roadblock against the march of the all-powerful state. The Conservative is careful not to ride the cellular analogy too hard, for he is aware that it can lead to a social theory in which man loses all dignity and personality.

In addition to the intrinsic groups, a healthy society will display a balanced combination of "institutions": constitution, common law, monarchy or presidency, legislature, courts, civil service, armed services and subdivisions, colleges, schools, forms of property, corporations, co-operatives, trade unions, guilds, fraternal orders, and dozens of other instrumentalities and understandings that mold the lives of men. Such symbols of national unity and continuity as anthems, flags, rituals, battlefields, monuments, and pantheons of heroes are equally dear to the Conservative heart. All men are stanch defenders of the institutions that meet their practical and spiritual needs, but the Conservative places special trust in them. "Individuals may form communities," Disraeli warned, "but it is institutions alone that can create a nation."

Society is a unity. In the healthy community all these groups and institutions fit together into a harmonious unity, and attempts to reshape one part of society must inevitably disturb other parts. The Conservative, though something of a pluralist, never loses sight of the ultimate unity into which all groups and institutions must merge. He sees the social structure not as a series of neat strata laid one on top of another, but, in Coleridge's phrase, as "an indissoluble blending and interfusion of persons from top to bottom."

Society cannot be static. Change is the rule of life, for societies as for men. A community cannot stand still; it must develop or decline. "Society must alter," Russell Kirk acknowledges in *The Conservative Mind,* "for slow change is the means of its conservation, like the human body's perpetual renewal." In recognizing this great truth, the Conservative shows himself to be neither a reactionary nor stand-patter. Yet he is just as emphatically not a liberal or radical, and he therefore sets severe conditions upon social change, especially if it is to be worked by active reform. Change, he insists, must never be taken for its own sake; must have preservation, if possible even restoration, as its central object; be severely limited in scope and purpose; be a response to an undoubted social need—for example, the renovation or elimination of an institution that is plainly obsolete; be worked out by slow and careful stages; represent progress, "a change for the better"; be brought off under Conservative auspices, or with Conservatives intervening at the decisive moment; and finally, in Disraeli's words, "be carried out in deference to the manners, the customs, the laws, the traditions of the people." The essence of Conservatism is the feeling for the possibilities and limits of natural, organic change. In the eloquent phrases of R. J. White, of Cambridge:

To discover the order which inheres in things rather than to impose an order upon them; to strengthen and perpetuate that order rather than to dispose things anew according to some formula which may be nothing more than a fashion; to legislate along the grain of human nature rather than against it; to pursue limited objectives with a watchful eye; to amend here, to prune there; in short to preserve the method of nature in the conduct of the state . . . this is Conservatism.

Society must be stable. Although men can never hope to see their community completely stable, they can create an endurable condition of peace and order. To achieve this end, they must work unceasingly for a society that has this ideal appearance:

Common agreement on fundamentals exists among men of all ranks and stations. Loyalty, good will, fraternal sympathy, and a feeling for compromise pervade the political and social scene.

Institutions and groups are in functional adjustment. Political, economic, social, and cultural power is widely diffused among persons, groups, and other instruments; these are held by law, custom, and constitution in a state of operating equilibrium. For every show of power there is corresponding responsibility. A minimum of friction and maximum of accommodation exist between government and group, government and individual, group and individual.

The authority of each group, and especially of the government, is legitimate. The laws honor the traditions of the nation, are adjusted to the capacities of the citizenry, meet the requirements of abstract justice, and satisfy the needs of society. Men obey the laws cheerfully and readily, and they know why they obey them. They know, too, the difference between authority and authoritarianism.

Men are secure; they have a sense of being, belonging, and creating. Their labors are rewarded, their sorrows comforted, their needs satisfied. They have the deep feeling of serenity that arises not merely from material well-being, but from confidence in the future, from daily contact with decent and trustworthy men, and from participation in an even-handed system of justice. Predictability, morality, and equity are important ingredients of their security. Most important, however, is ordered liberty, which makes it possible for men to pursue their talents and tastes within a sheltering order.

Change and reform are sure-footed, discriminating, and respectful of the past. "Men breathe freely," as F. E. Dessauer puts it, "because change is limited. . . . The changes which are taking place do not frighten the affected." The currents of change are channeled into the stream of progress by institutions and values that have stood the tests of time and service.

Unity, balance, authority, security, continuity—these are the key elements of social stability. In longing for a society in which peace and order reign, the Conservative comes closest to the utopianism that he ridicules in others.

Freedom of Dissent

LEARNED HAND

Learned Hand (1872–1961) was born in Albany, New York, and received his undergraduate and law degrees at Harvard. After his admission to the New York Bar in 1897, he practiced law until 1909, when he was appointed Federal District Judge of the Southern District of New York. He held this post until 1924, when he was made Judge of the United States District Court, Second Circuit, a position he maintained for twenty-seven years, until his retirement in 1951. He is accounted one of the most distinguished men in American judicial history.

W HAT do we mean by "principles of civil liberties and human rights"? We cannot go far in that inquiry until we have achieved some notion of what we mean by Liberty; and that has always proved a hard concept to define. The natural, though naïve, opinion is that it means no more than that each individual shall be allowed to pursue his own desires without let or hindrance; and that, although it is true that this is practically impossible, still it does remain the goal, approach to which measures our success. Why, then, is not a beehive or an anthill a perfect example of a free society? Surely you have been a curious and amused watcher beside one of these.

In and out of their crowded pueblo the denizens pass in great number, each bent upon his own urgent mission, quite oblivious of all the rest except as he must bend his path to avoid them. It is a scene of strenuous, purposeful endeavor in which each appears to be, and no doubt in fact is, accomplishing his own purpose; and yet he is at the same time accomplishing the purpose of the group as a whole. As I have gazed at it, the sentence from the Collect of the Episcopal prayer-book has come to me: "Whose service is perfect freedom."

Why is it, then, that we so positively rebel against the hive and the hill as a specimen of a free society? Why is it that such prototypes of totalitarianisms arouse our deepest hostility? Unhappily it is not because they cannot be realized, or at least because they cannot be approached, for a substantial period. Who can be sure that such appalling forecasts as Aldous Huxley's *Brave New World* or Orwell's *1984* are not prophetic? Indeed, there have often been near approaches to such an order.

Germany at the end of 1940 was probably not far removed from one, and who of us knows that there are not countless persons today living within the boundaries of Russia and perhaps of China who are not willing partners, accepting as their personal aspirations the official definitions of the good, the true and the beautiful? Indeed, there have been, and still are, in our own United States large and powerful groups who, if we are to judge their purposes by their conduct, see treason in all dissidence and would welcome an era in which all of us should think, feel and live in consonance with duly prescribed patterns.

Human nature is malleable, especially if you can indoctrinate the disciple with indefectible principles before anyone else reaches him. (I fancy that the Janissaries were as fervent Mohammedans as the authentic Turks.) Indeed, we hear from those who are entitled to an opinion that at times the abject confessions made in Russia by victims who know that they are already marked for slaughter are not wrung from them by torture or threats against their families. Rather, they come from partisans, so obsessed with the faith that when they are told that the occasion calls for scapegoats and that they have been selected, recognize and assent to the propriety of the demand and cooperate in its satisfaction. It is as though when the right time comes, the drones agreed to their extinction in the interest of the hive.

Nor need we be surprised that men so often embrace almost any doctrines, if they are proclaimed with a voice of absolute assurance. In a universe that we do not understand, but with which we must in one way or another somehow manage to deal, and aware of the conflicting desires that clamorously beset us, between which we must choose and which we must therefore manage to weigh, we turn in our bewilderment to those who tell us that they have found a path out of the thickets and possess the scales by which to appraise our needs.

Over and over again such prophets succeed in converting us to unquestioning acceptance; there is scarcely a monstrous belief that has not had its day and its passionate adherents, so eager are we for safe footholds in our dubious course. How certain is any one of us that he, too, might not be content to follow any fantastic creed, if he was satisfied that nothing would ever wake him from the dream? And, indeed, if there were nothing to wake him, how should he distinguish its articles from the authentic dictates of verity?

Remember, too, that it is by no means clear that we are happier in the faith we do profess than we should be under the spell of an orthodoxy that was safe against all heresy. Cruel and savage as orthodoxies have always proved to be, the faithful seem able to convince themselves that the heretics, as they continue to crop up, get nothing worse than their due, and to rest with an easy conscience.

In any event, my thesis is that the best answer to such systems is not so much in their immoral quality—immoral though they be—as in the fact that they are inherently unstable, because they are at war with our only trustworthy way of living in accord with the facts. For I submit that it is only by trial and error, by insistent scrutiny and by readiness to re-examine presently accredited conclusions that we have risen, so far as in fact we have risen, from our brutish ancestors, and I believe that in our loyalty to these habits lies our only chance, not merely of progress, but even of survival.

They were not indeed a part of our aboriginal endowment: Man, as he emerged, was not prodigally equipped to master the infinite diversity of his environment. Obviously, enough of us did manage to get through; but it has been a statistical survival, for the individual's native powers of adjustment are by no means enough for his personal safety any more than are those of other creatures. The precipitate of our experience is far from absolute verity, and our exasperated resentment at all dissent is a sure index of our doubts. Take, for instance, our constant recourse to the word, "subversive," as a touchstone of impermissible deviation from accepted canons.

All discussions, all debate, all dissidence tends to question and in consequence to upset existing convictions: that is precisely its purpose and its justification. He is, indeed, a "subversive" who disputes those precepts that I most treasure and seeks to persuade me to substitute his own. He may have no shadow of desire to resort to anything but persuasion; he may be of those to whom any forcible sanction of conformity is anathema; yet it remains true that he is trying to bring about my apostasy, and I hate him just in proportion as I fear his success.

Contrast this protective resentment with the assumption that lies at the base of our whole system that the best chance for truth to emerge is a fair field for all ideas. Nothing, I submit, more completely betrays our latent disloyalty to this premise to all that we pretend to believe than the increasingly common resort to this and other question-begging words. Their imprecision comforts us by enabling us to suppress arguments that disturb our complacency and yet to continue to congratulate ourselves on keeping the faith as we have received it from the Founding Fathers.

Heretics have been hateful from the beginning of recorded time; they have been ostracized, exiled, tortured, maimed and butchered; but it has generally proved impossible to smother them, and when it has not, the society that has succeeded has always declined. Facades of authority, however imposing, do not survive after it has appeared that they rest upon the sands of human conjecture and compromise.

And so, if I am to say what are "the principles of civil liberties and human rights," I answer that they lie in habits, customs—conventions, if you will—that tolerate dissent and can live without irrefragable certainties; that are already to overhaul existing assumptions; that recognize that we never see save through a glass, darkly, and that at long last we shall succeed only so far as we continue to undertake "the intolerable labor of thought"—that most distasteful of all our activities.

If such a habit and such a temper pervade a society, it will not need institutions to protect its "civil liberties and human rights"; so far as they do not, I venture to doubt how far anything else can protect them: whether it be Bills of Rights, or courts that must in the name of interpretation read their meaning into them.

This may seem to you a bleak and cheerless conclusion, too alien to our nature to be practical. "We must live from day to day"—you will say—"to live is to act, and to act is to choose and decide. How can we carry on at all without some principles, some patterns to meet the conflicts in which each day involves us?" Indeed, we cannot, nor am I suggesting that we should try; but I *am* suggesting that it makes a vital difference—*the* vital difference—whether we deem our principles and our patterns to be eternal verities, rather than the best postulates so far attainable.

Was it not Holmes who said: "The highest courage is to stake everything on a premise that you know tomorrow's evidence may disprove"? "Ah"—you will reply—"there's the rub. That may be the highest courage, but how many have it? You are hopelessly wrong if you assume the general prevalence of such a virtue; ordinary men must be given more than conjectures if they are to face grave dangers."

But do you really believe that? Do you not see about you every day and everywhere the precise opposite? Not alone on the battlefield but in the forest, the desert and the plain; in the mountains, at sea, on the playing field, even in the laboratory and the factory—yes (do not laugh), at the card table and the racetrack—men are forever putting it "upon the touch to win or lose it all." Without some smack of uncertainty and danger, to most of us the world would be a tepid, pallid show.

Surely, like me, you have all felt something of this when you have looked on those pathetic attempts to depict in paint or stone the delights of Paradise. I own that the torments of hell never fail to horrify me; not even the glee of the demons in charge is an adequate relief, though the artist has generally been successful in giving a veracious impression of the gusto with which they discharge their duties.

But when I turn to the Congregation of the Blessed, I cannot avoid a sense of anti-climax; strive as I may, the social atmosphere seems a bit forced; and I recall those very irreverent verses of Lowes Dickinson:

> Burning at first no doubt would be worse,
> But time the impression would soften,
> While those who are bored with praising the Lord,
> Would be more bored with praising him often.

By some happy fortuity man is a projector, a designer, a builder, a craftsman; it is among his most dependable joys to impose upon the flux that passes before him some mark of himself, aware though he always must be of the odds against him. His reward is not so much in the work as in its making; not so much in the prize as in the race. We may win when we lose, if we have done what we can; for by so doing we have made real at least some part of that finished product in whose fabrication we are most concerned—ourselves.

And if at the end some friendly critic shall pass by and say, "My friend, how good a job do you really think you have made of it all?" we can answer, "I know as well as you that it is not of high quality, but I did put into it whatever I had, and that was the game I started out to play."

It is still in the lap of the gods whether a society can succeed, based on "civil liberties and human rights," conceived as I have tried to describe them; but of one thing at least we may be sure: the alternatives that have so far appeared have been immeasurably worse, and so, whatever the outcome, I submit to you that we must press along. Borrowing from Epictetus, let us say to ourselves: "Since we are men we will play the part of a Man," and how can I better end than by recalling to you the concluding passage of "Prometheus Unbound"?

> To suffer woes which Hope thinks infinite;
> To forgive wrongs darker than death or night;
> To defy Power, which seems omnipotent
> To love, and bear; to hope till Hope creates
> From its own wreck the thing it contemplates;
> Neither to change, nor falter, nor repent;
> This, like thy glory, Titan, is to be
> Good, great and joyous, beautiful and free;
> This is alone Life, Joy, Empire and Victory.

Part Three: THE TRADITION OF LIBERTY AND RESPONSIBILITY

QUESTIONS FOR STUDY AND RESEARCH

1. Gray states that "the conflict between individual freedom and socio-political authority which [Socrates] dramatizes expresses [the students'] own central dilemma." Support or refute Plato's argument in *The Crito*. Is his argument applicable to the student-administration relationship in a modern college or university? Does the nature of the "multiversity" tend to weaken this application of Plato's argument?
2. Aristotle affirms that happiness is virtuous and wise activity on the part of both the citizen and the state. Examine the activities of the FSM and the faculty-administration at Berkeley to determine which activities were virtuous or wise, which were not. Were the FSM students "high-spirited and intelligent" *both*? Support your answers with reference to specific activities.
3. Compare Aristotle's comments on education of youth with Newman's, and with Whitehead's ideas on education. Do you believe that some of the activities of the "multiversity" are in Aristotle's meaning of the word "vulgar"?
4. According to Aristotle, what type of leader "ought we to follow and obey"? How do the FSM leaders (Savio, for example) measure up to this definition? Do you agree with Aristotle's principle that "he who violates the law can never recover by

any success, however great, what he has already lost in departing from virtue"? Compare Emerson and Thoreau's views on
this last point.

5. What condition, according to Kant, is a prerequisite for "enlightenment"? Compare Kant's essay with Becker's in this regard. Cite an example on your campus in which the application
of this condition has resulted in enlightenment.

6. What is Kant's distinction between the public and the private
use of freedom? Does Thoreau agree with this distinction?
Emerson? Did the FSM's actions violate this distinction?
Which of their activities were, in Kant's sense, "public," and
which were "private"?

7. Apply Burke's discussion of "the real rights of man" to the
rights demanded by the FSM. Do you agree or disagree with
Burke's contention that "the share of power, authority, and
direction which each individual ought to have in the management of the state [or university], . . . I must deny to be
amongst the direct original rights of man in civil society?"

8. Burke writes (in "Conservative Reform") that "our patience
will achieve more than our force." An FSM leader has been
quoted as saying: "The sit-in did not obstruct, but rather
caused, the first rational discussion of the problem on campus."
Discuss these opposing views by reference to Berkeley.

9. What is Mill's "very simple principle" as to the compulsions
and controls which society is entitled to enforce in its dealings
with the individual? Does Mill's principle justify Chancellor
Strong's disciplinary measures against the FSM for its having
"materially impaired" the "purpose and work of the university"?

10. Compare Carlyle in "Democracy" and Burke in "True Liberty."
Which of the FSM activities would either or both disapprove of?

11. Define "civil disobedience" according to Thoreau's essay.
When is it justified? When is it unjustified? Consider Raskin's,
Glazer's, Hook's and May's remarks on these points.

12. Henry F. May writes, "In the person of Savio, the movement
speaks with a voice that has been heard in America since
the beginning, the voice of an exalted, quasi-religious romantic
anarchism." Elaborate on this observation by reference to
statements made by FSM leaders and to Emerson and Thoreau's views. Comment on May's observation that "actually the
intensely individualistic discipline of Thoreau contrasts sharply
with the FSM's dependence on crowd emotion."

13. The metaphor of "machines" and "machinery" appears in Kant,
Emerson and Thoreau. Examine how this metaphor is employed by these three authors and by some of the student
spokesmen who are quoted in several of the essays. Before

you examine the use of these terms in their various contexts, consult the *Oxford English Dictionary* and study the evolution of the words *machine* and *machinery*.

14. Consider Rossiter's view that man is "a composite of good and evil." How does Ward's description of the motives in the Syracuse demonstration apply to this "conservative view of man"? Do Rossiter and Carlyle agree on the need for an "aristocracy"? Support or argue against this position.

15. What is Learned Hand's definition of the "subversive"? Why does he believe that we must "tolerate dissent"? Does the outcome of the Berkeley rebellion justify his belief in this need to tolerate dissent?

16. Which of the authors in this section would have approved of the FSM? Which would have disapproved? Support your position by specific references to the arguments in the appropriate texts.

READINGS FOR FURTHER STUDY AND RESEARCH

Arendt, Hannah. *The Origins of Totalitarianism,* 1951.

Aristotle, *The Politics.*

Bacon, Sir Francis. *The Advancement of Learning* (esp. Book I), 1605.

Becker, Carl Lotus. *Freedom and Responsibility in the American Way of Life,* 1945.

Bell, Daniel. *The End of Ideology,* 1960.

Biddle, Francis. *The Fear of Freedom,* 1951.

The Bill of Rights.

Brinton, Crane. *The Anatomy of Revolution,* 1938.

Bury, J. B. *A History of Freedom of Thought,* 1952.

Cardozo, Benjamin. *The Nature of the Judicial Process,* 1921.

Carr, E. H. *The New Society,* 1951.

Cassirer, Ernst. "The Technique of the Modern Political Myths," *The Myth of the State,* 1946.

Chafee, Zechariah, Jr. *Free Speech in the United States,* 1948.

Counts, George S. "Education in a Democracy," *Vital Speeches* (February 15, 1949).

The Declaration of Independence.

Defoe, Daniel. *The Shortest Way with Dissenters,* 1702.

Emerson, Ralph Waldo. *The American Scholar,* 1837.

Emerson, Thomas Irwin, and Haber, David. *Political and Civil Rights in the United States,* 1952.

Fitch, Robert E. "Extremism in the Defense of . . . ," *The Christian Century* (January 6, 1965).

Frankel, Charles. "The Morality of Civil Disobedience," *The Love of Anxiety and Other Essays*, 1965.

Freedman, Morris. "The Dangers of Nonconformism," *The American Scholar* (Winter, 1958–59).

Freedom and Education, edited by Helen Huus, 1965.

Fromm, Erich. *The Dogma of Christ, and Other Essays on Religion, Psychology, and Culture*, 1955.

————. "The Illusion of Individuality," *Escape from Freedom*, 1941.

Hand, Learned. "Liberty," *Yale Alumni Magazine* (June 6, 1941).

————. "Sources of Tolerance," *University of Pennsylvania Law Review*, Vol. 79.

Hare, R. M. *Freedom and Reason*, 1965.

Hobbes, Thomas. *Leviathan* (esp. Chapters XVII–XXII), 1651.

Hocutt, John E. *Supervision and Control of Student Publications*, 1961.

Hofstadter, Richard. *The Age of Reform; From Bryan to F. D. R.*, 1955.

Hook, Sidney, *Heresy, Yes—Conspiracy, No!*, 1953.

————. "Intelligence, Conscience and the Right to Revolution," *The Paradoxes of Freedom*, 1961.

Huxley, Aldous L. "Words and Behaviour," *The Olive Tree*, 1937.

Innocence and Power: Individualism in Twentieth-Century America, edited by Gordon Mills, 1965.

Kerr, Clark. "The University: Civil Rights and Civic Responsibilities," *University Bulletin* (May 18, 1964).

Krutch, Joseph Wood. "If You Don't Mind My Saying So," *The American Scholar* (Summer, 1960).

Lasch, Christopher. *The New Radicalism in America 1889–1963*, 1965.

Lecky, W. E. H. *Democracy and Liberty*, 1896.

Lippman, Walter. *Essays in the Public Philosophy*, 1955.

————. *The Good Society*, 1937.

————. *The Method of Freedom*, 1934.

————. "On the Importance of Being Free," *Encounter* (August, 1965).

Lipset, Seymour Martin. "Opinion Formation in a Crisis Situation," *Public Opinion Quarterly* (Spring, 1953).

Lipset, Seymour Martin, and Bendix, R. *Political Man*, 1960.

Locke, John. *Concerning Civil Government* (Second Essay), 1690.

Lowell, James Russell. *Democracy*, 1884.

Mannheim, Karl. *Ideology and Utopia*, 1936.

Marcel, Gabriel. *Man Against Mass Society*, 1952.

Mill, John Stuart. *On Liberty*, 1859.

————. *Representative Government*, 1861.

Miller, Helen Hill. *The Case for Liberty*, 1965.

Mills, C. Wright. *The Power Elite*, 1956.

Milton, John. *Areopagitica,* 1645.

———. *Tractate on Education,* 1644.

Montaigne. *On the Institution and Education of Children,* 1588.

Monypenny, Phillip. "Toward a Standard for Student Academic Freedom," *Law and Contemporary Problems* (Summer, 1963).

Negley, Glenn. *Political Authority and Moral Judgment,* 1965.

Niebuhr, Reinhold. "Liberalism: Illusions and Realities," *The New Republic* (July 4, 1955).

———. *The Search for America,* 1959.

Orwell, George. "Politics and the English Language," *Shooting an Elephant and Other Essays,* 1945.

Perry, Ralph Barton. *Realms of Value,* 1954.

Plato. *The Apology.*

———. *The Crito.*

———. *The Republic,* Books IV and V.

Riesman, David, and Glazer, Nathan. *Faces in the Crowd,* 1965.

Riesman, David, et al. *Individualism Reconsidered,* 1954.

———. *The Lonely Crowd,* 1950.

Roche, John P. "American Liberty: An Examination of the 'Tradition' of Freedom," *Aspects of Liberty,* 1958.

Rossiter, Clinton. *Conservatism in America,* 1955.

Rousseau, Jean Jacques. *A Discourse upon the Origin and the Foundations of the Inequality Among Mankind,* 1754.

———. *The Social Contract,* 1762.

Sabine, George. *A History of Political Theory,* 1937.

Schlesinger, Arthur M. "Walter Lippmann: The Intellectual v. Politics," *Walter Lippmann and His Times,* 1959.

Sears, Laurence. "Liberals and Conservatives," *The Antioch Review* (Fall, 1953).

Selvin, Hanan C., and Hagstrom, Warren O. "Determinants of Support for Civil Liberties," *British Journal of Sociology,* Vol. II, 1960.

Shelley, Percy Bysshe. *An Address to the Irish People,* 1812.

Spinoza, Baruch. "Of the Foundations of a State: Of the Natural and Civil Rights of Individuals: And of the Rights of the Sovereign Power," *Tractatus theologico-politicus,* 1670.

Sullivan, Richard E. "The End of the 'Long Run,'" *The Centennial Review of Arts and Sciences* (Summer, 1960).

Tocqueville, A. de. *Democracy in America,* 1835–1839.

Viereck, Peter. *Conservatism Revisited,* 1949.

Weiner, Norbert. *The Human Use of Human Beings,* 1954.

White, E. B. "Freedom," *One Man's Meat,* 1938.